A NEW GLOBAL AGENDA

PRIORITIES, PRACTICES, AND PATHWAYS

OF THE INTERNATIONAL COMMUNITY

EDITED BY

DIANA AYTON-SHENKER

THE NEW SCHOOL

FOREWORD BY ANDREW ZOLLI

ROWMAN &
LITTLEFIELD

LANHAM • BOULDER • NEW YORK • LONDON

Executive Editor: Traci Crowell
Assistant Editor: Mary Malley
Senior Marketing Manager: Amy Whitaker
Cover Image: William T. Ayton
Cover Designer: Sally Rinehart

Credits and acknowledgments for material borrowed from other sources, and reproduced with
permission, appear on the appropriate page within the text.

Published by Rowman & Littlefield
An imprint of The Rowman & Littlefield Publishing Group, Inc.
4501 Forbes Boulevard, Suite 200, Lanham, Maryland 20706
www.rowman.com

Unit A, Whitacre Mews, 26-34 Stannary Street, London SE11 4AB, United Kingdom

British Library Cataloguing in Publication Information Available

Library of Congress Cataloging-in-Publication Data
Names: Ayton-Shenker, Diana, editor.
Title: A new global agenda : priorities, practices, and pathways of the international
    community / edited by Diana Ayton-Shenker.
Description: Lanham : Rowman & Littlefield, [2018] | Includes bibliographical
    references and index. |
Identifiers: LCCN 2017050524 (print) | LCCN 2017061749 (ebook) | ISBN 9781538106037
    (electronic) | ISBN 9781538106013 (cloth : alk. paper) | ISBN 9781538106020
    (pbk : alk. paper)
Subjects: LCSH: Social justice. | Human rights. | Responsibility. | International relations.
Classification: LCC HM671 (ebook) | LCC HM671 .N44 2018 (print) | DDC 303.3/72—dc23
LC record available at https://lccn.loc.gov/2017050524

♾™ The paper used in this publication meets the minimum requirements of American National
Standard for Information Sciences—Permanence of Paper for Printed Library Materials, ANSI/
NISO Z39.48-1992.

Printed in the United States of America

Dedication

To Naomi for illuminating priorities, practices, and pathways

Contents

Foreword

On Fear and the Future

Andrew Zolli

Forewords are an odd literary convention. Part encomium, part *amuse-bouche*, they are intended to establish a book's thematic relevance, impart the urgency of its agenda, and tantalize the reader with what's to come.

Yet circumstances have made any such foreword to *this* book unnecessary. After all, who could possibly argue with the need for a new global agenda, when every day we witness the international order being doused with gasoline by a posse of arsonists who would rather reign over its ashes?

Those arsonists' fuel is fear: fear of the loss of jobs, of "sovereignty," of position, of privilege, and, above all, fear of the other, and the fear of the future.

Fear is always combustible. Concentrated, it becomes explosive. Strategically placed, it can be used to detonate institutions, norms, and trust—the three pillars that underwrite cooperation at every scale. It's little wonder that the arsonists are stockpiling it.

There can be no new global agenda without the retrenchment of fear. So it seems apt that in addition to the many worthy developmental, economic, and technical recommendations contained in this volume, I might add a brief, impractical word or two about fear and the future.

We live at a moment of undeniable peril. In our profligate abundance, we are surpassing the boundaries of the systems that make life on Earth possible. This calamity is mirrored in the breakdown of economic and social systems, which no longer serve the majority of their purported beneficiaries. Some communities face inescapable acute and chronic stressors, passed from generation to generation. Dwindling numbers of their wealthier neighbors wall themselves off, in a fiction of apparent separation. But fear is a gas. There is no wall high enough to keep it out.

All of this drives the great trend of the present age, which we might call the Great Repudiation. It is manifested as indifference, self-segregation, zero-sum thinking, future-blindness, and narcissism—a turning away from that which is held in common. Some tune out in disgust or despair. Others fall into the inebriation of consumption. Yet more abandon the civic square for the solipsistic fields of social media, where everything is true and nothing is.

Yet all is not lost. Restoration is possible. What's needed are experiences, policies, and new agendas that cultivate greater compassion, and with it structural renewal, self-desegregation, postmaterialism, non-zero-sum thinking, future-orientation, and the revitalization of the public square.

Happily, our cultivation of compassion, the reduction of fear, and our ability to think about the future emerge from a common set of behaviors, each a consequence of the other.

There is an ancient and persistent quirk of human cognition, in which we naturally discount the future and overemphasize the present. Everyone suffers from this, but social psychologists find that those experiencing chronic stress, anxiety, and fear have an even *more* exaggerated present-tense bias. This often dissuades them from making necessary investments in the future and ties them to the often impoverished circumstances of today.

But researchers, including David DeSteno at Northeastern University, have found the reverse can also be true: that by cultivating our compassion for others, through many means, we can improve our ability to think about the future, even as we expand our ideas of who we wish to see coinhabit that future with us.

This is a foundational truth that all of the world's great spiritual traditions have understood: that, with care and concentration, we can slip the bonds of parochial egotism and come to experience our own sacredness, the sacredness of others, and our interconnectedness within a larger whole. Over time, this understanding compels us to expand our moral community to include ever-widening circles of humanity—and, ultimately, all of life itself—in an embrace of solidarity, generosity, and love.

Yet this is not an argument for pieties but one for policies. We need practical mechanisms that bring us into real engagement with each other, and with the future itself.

Research by psychologist Hal Hershfield at UCLA offers a tantalizing glimpse of one way we might do that. In experiments, Hershfield showed college students images of their own faces digitally altered to appear forty years older. By encountering their future selves, they instantly become better savers, deferring present-tense pleasures for future ones. Imagine if we could prime such future-thinking around climate change, or protecting the world's endangered species, or toward any of the other countless strands in the giant hairball of entangled global concerns that predominate today?

Results like Hershfield's show what happens when you make the future salient for people. Their thinking changes. Likewise, we need to show people a future of fulfillment and creative possibility, one they have a place within. We also need to acknowledge the validity of mourning the loss of a past which is not so much great because it was better, but because it was ours.

In the face of fear, optimism, compassion, and vision are not just moral choices but also moral weapons. Our new global agenda should be armed to the teeth with them. And all our efforts—like the in this exemplary book—should be guided by them. Congratulations to Diana Ayton-Shenker and all of the contributors for bringing forth such a vital project.
In gratitude,

Andrew Zolli
Saint Paul, MN

Acknowledgments

A New Global Agenda would not have been made possible without the invaluable support, participation, and inspiration of many people to whom I owe a debt of gratitude and appreciation. It is my privilege and pleasure to acknowledge and thank everyone who helped me nurture this idea and navigate the road from its inception to its publication.

I acknowledge and thank the team at Rowman & Littlefield, for publishing *A New Global Agenda*. It was a pleasure to reconnect with Rowman & Littlefield, and to work with Traci Crowell and Mary Malley. Traci's wonderful energy and guidance were especially helpful and appreciated.

I acknowledge and thank The New School for appointing me to serve as Global Catalyst Senior Fellow. This fellowship was singularly instrumental in allowing me the time, intellectual freedom, and vital support to complete this book. I am most appreciative of the encouragement, collaboration, and thought partnership of New School colleagues, in particular: Mary Watson, Michele Kahane, Alex Aleinikoff, Michael Cohen, Lena Simet, and Tim Marshall. Special thanks to Mike for gently pushing me to stretch beyond my comfort zone with this project.

I acknowledge and thank all the New Global Agenda Research Fellows, whose dedication and enthusiasm brought fresh energy and valuable new perspectives: Rehab Abdelwahab (Yale), Caroline Azem (Cornell), Nina Bechman (Columbia), Dina Chotrani (Princeton), Miguelangel Des Armas (University of Pennsylvania), Cem Gultaken (Columbia), Sarah Jacobs (University of Pennsylvania), Jazz Munitz (Cornell), Lindsey Powell (University of Pennsylvania), Namrata Ramakrishna (Dartmouth), Andrea Sedlacek (Dartmouth), and Chris Yoon (Brown).

I acknowledge and thank Peter Deitrich for his invaluable work as senior assistant editor and project coordinator. I am most grateful to Pete for his commitment and collaboration in editing *A New Global Agenda*. He meticulously checked every comma, proofread, copyedited the entire manuscript, and read every word that went into the book, except this one: thanks.

I acknowledge and thank all the contributing authors who brought their formidable expertise, insight, and thought leadership to *A New Global Agenda*. Without exception, I learned from each and every one of them. I am deeply honored and humbled to have had the opportunity to collaborate with such stellar colleagues, whose work I admire and applaud.

In addition to the contributing authors, I thank and acknowledge my extended braintrust of valued thought partners whom I also admire, and whose input, counsel, connection, and early conversations shed light on *A New Global Agenda*, in particular: Alice Albright, Johann Berlin, Bob Costanza, Mallika Dutt, Sakiko Fukuda-Parr, Lara Galinsky, Mark Goldberg, Shareen Hertel, Joel Oestreich, Robert Ransick, Kate Raworth, Zainab Salbi, Scott Sherman, Olinga Ta'eed, Uma Viswanathan, and Andrew Zolli.

I acknowledge and thank the UNA-USA and the UN Foundation for their important work. I am grateful to have worked with UNA-USA as editor of several editions of the former annual publication series *A Global Agenda: Issues before the U.N.*, which was a formative experience and precursor leading up to *A New Global Agenda*.

I acknowledge and thank my friends and family who provide my greatest inspiration, and who infuse my work and life with joy and meaning. I thank my friend Naomi for sharing her tremendous intellect, insight, support, and companionship. I thank my parents, Arden and Lois Shenker, for instilling in me the value of *Tikkun Olam* through their words, actions, and love. I thank my children, Sarah, Elizabeth, and James, for being who they are in our family and in our world. I thank my love, Bill, for bringing beauty to this book, and to my life every day.

Diana Ayton-Shenker
August 2017

Challenges of a New Global Agenda
A Call to Action
Diana Ayton-Shenker

Another world is not only possible, she is on her way.
On a quiet day, I can hear her breathing.
—Arundhati Roy

All around us, we are being called on to redefine our roles and reclaim responsibility in shaping the world we inhabit. We hear this call to action from inner voices of conscience, external demands to step up, the expectant looks of children, the silent cries of our degraded environment and depleted natural resources. The time to answer this call is now. Ready or not, *we are the ones we've been waiting for.*[1]

Former United Nations (UN) Secretary-General Ban Ki-moon reinforces this urgency in reminding us, "There can be no Plan B, because there is no planet B." *A New Global Agenda* prompts us to ask: What is Plan A? How do we make sense of our fragile world and our tenuous place in it? What are the priorities, practices, and pathways before us today?

In 2016, the international community embraced historic global agendas as priority frameworks for action on three topics: sustainable development, climate change, and urbanization. These three agreements, the 2030 Agenda for Sustainable Development (the Sustainable Development Goals, or SDGs),[2] the Paris Accord on Climate Change,[3] and the New Urban Agenda (Habitat III),[4] mark unprecedented efforts in global agenda setting, both in terms of collaborative process and comprehensive scope. The extent to which these agendas succeed depends largely on what we do with them; how we will synchronize, animate, activate, and integrate them. While their outcomes are yet to be determined, their potential to inspire and mobilize action offers hope to us all.

Their achievement should have heralded 2016 as the watershed year of international cooperation and the triumph of globalization. It did not. Coinciding with these accomplishments, 2016 ushered in a spate of political upsets and civil erosion reflecting a groundswell of populism, nationalism, and anti-globalization. In addition to dramatic political events (e.g., the US election of Donald Trump; Britain's vote to leave the European Union—"Brexit"), global shifts sent shockwaves that continue to reverberate from massive humanitarian crises; increasing inequality within and between countries; entrenched poverty; climate instability and natural resource depletion; looming public health threats; surging violent extremism; and resurgent racism, Islamophobia, and

1

anti-Semitism. Compounding these alarming trends are threats that undermine our ability to confront them. Public scrutiny, accountability, and the capacity to make informed choices are eroded by political and social tactics that target free press, affront media freedom, limit access to digital information, and dismiss the value and even the validity of truth, data, and science itself. And all these developments have transpired at a dizzying pace, coinciding with breakthrough technological innovations and advances poised to disrupt most systems of human experience.

The acceleration of change and its inherent volatility, as Andrew Zolli suggests, may have "become the new normal." The volatility of our time has generated uncertainty, insecurity, and a sense of disorientation. It may also fast-track us into action. The international community recognizes that today's global challenges threaten human security, stability, and sustainability. This fuels fear-based resistance, sparks reactionary politics, and triggers the lowest common denominator of base survival instincts. We need a reorientation to face fears and counter them with the hope of action, clarity, and determination. We need a shift from being reactive to proactive, from resistance to insistence on a finer future, one in which we not only survive but thrive. Zolli advises, "If we cannot control the volatile tides of change, we can learn to build better boats." And we'll need better navigational tools to illuminate and guide our way.

That's where *A New Global Agenda* comes in, offering insight and foresight to steer us through the uncharted and choppy waters rising around us. While many chapters make recommendations, propose solutions, or outline potential next steps to take, they raise more questions than answers. Ultimately, the vision of this book is to invite and frame an emerging dialogue on how we connect the dots, provoke further engagement, pilot new initiatives, and forge potential partnerships for action.

This book is the companion to gnawing questions I can neither fully answer nor ignore. They keep me up at night and get me up in the morning. How does our place in the world and our brief time here honor the legacy of our parents, realize the potential of our vision, and safeguard the future for our children? How do we make sense of and make headway on seemingly intractable challenges threatening human life and the planet that sustains us? How do we anticipate emerging issues and opportunities stemming from technology, innovation, and the unintended consequences of our action, inaction, interaction, and ingenuity? How do we shape a new global agenda, and what role does this play in our lives and spheres of influence? How do we embody and emulate this agenda, both as members of the international community and as individuals, serving as central nodes in our own networks, communities, families? And how might we, both in the process and in the outcome, evolve to become more human and humane? Doing so will require a deeper understanding and practice of resilience, curiosity, humility, compassion, and courage. Our capacity to cultivate these traits will help us make and see our way forward.

In order to "be the change you want to see in the world," we must first *see* the change we want to be. To help us see the changes we want to be in the world, *A New Global Agenda* explores the most compelling issues of our time as a call to action. The change I see calls on each and all of us to be more human and become more humane in pursuit of a world that is just, safe, sustainable, regenerative, vibrant, vital. Our humanity, if not our survival, may depend on it.

One of the challenges in approaching *A New Global Agenda* stems from my experience editing its precursor, *A Global Agenda: Issues before the General Assembly of the U.N.*[5] When I last edited the former annual publication series with the United Nations Association of the United States of America, fifteen years ago, I recall thinking what we really need is a *human* agenda to extend the work of the UN to a broader international community of global citizens worldwide. Today, we recognize that the international community is not only composed of the UN and international diplomats but also includes, and is influenced by, the private sector, business, government, academia, philanthropy, advocacy, media, public intellectuals, civil society, and, yes, global citizens everywhere. Setting *A New Global Agenda* in this context of cross-sectoral perspectives and multistakeholder partnerships asserts that we are all in this together. The work of safeguarding and improving our world is not a task to be abdicated to others; the responsibility lies in many hands, beginning with our own.

Three major shifts distinguish *A New Global Agenda* from the old series, as suggested by this book's title and subtitle. First, this book attempts to set a *new* agenda, highlighting the most compelling challenges of our time, determined less by the operational structure of the UN, and more by the emerging needs of the *Anthropocene.*[6] Second, the book shifts from "Issues" to *priorities, practices, and pathways.* This shift seeks to animate and activate the agenda from a list of "what" needs to be addressed, to a framework for "how" progress can be made to achieve the better world we see and seek. The book attempts to elucidate strategies rather than impose solutions, illuminating possible ways forward. Third, *A New Global Agenda* extends beyond an exclusive focus on the UN to include a broader spectrum of the *international community.* In taking a more inclusive approach, the book engages thought leaders as contributing authors representing diverse perspectives, personalities, professional backgrounds, and fields of expertise.

Another challenge stemmed from inviting collaborative innovation in the process of editing and writing the book. This collaboration became invaluable to developing *A New Global Agenda.* In discussing the book with a contributing author early on in the project, my colleague gently pushed me to host a convening of all available contributing authors, together with research fellows, to identify and share some common questions, themes, and thinking before we even began writing. The idea was to create a collaborative experience for authors and researchers from the outset, to allow and facilitate dialogue and engagement, as a kind of cross-pollinating, collective intellectual experiment.

It was messy, imperfect, invigorating, inspiring. Participants revealed different and differing opinions and orientations; they raised hard and uncomfortable questions; personalities clicked and clashed; new collaborations were born; and old assumptions were confronted. We wrestled with the term "agenda" itself, struggling with the inherent rigidity of an agenda as a fixed list or schedule, as well as with the implicit arrogance of presuming a few dozen people are entitled to interpret the priorities for all. "Who are we," asked one of the contributors, "to set the global agenda for the world?" We gravitated toward the audacity of *agenda* as a launchpad and platform to invite ongoing, iterative, and interactive engagement.

Challenges also arose around the book's content and structure. Initially, the proposed Table of Contents was really just a new agenda of old topics. Our team of young research fellows quickly brought to light the gaps between residual twentieth-century priorities and rising concerns of the emerging generation. Their input, together with an intergenerational brain trust of colleagues, reshaped *A New Global Agenda* to include the contents that follow. The book takes an anthropocentric approach to where we are and where we are headed in our world. This is a book by, for, and about humans, regarding humankind and the human experience as its central element; it is not a global agenda for Earth, rather for its human inhabitants. In addition to what goes into a compilation such as this, inevitably there are missing pieces from my wish list of what I'd hoped to include. My hope now is that any omissions create openings for further thought leadership.

The structural design itself creates the challenge of how to present inherently interconnected, interdependent topics within the linear constraints of a book format. While acknowledging that many, if not all, of the chapters could be reshuffled to emphasize different aspects of the issues explored, *A New Global Agenda* is organized around three main parts: People, Society, and Planet. *Part I: People* looks at how to promote human rights and pursue justice; how to protect vulnerable people, including refugees and other forced migrants, and women survivors of conflict and violence; and how to safeguard essential freedoms, including global press freedom and digital information access. *Part II: Society* looks at how to improve human systems and structures through regenerative development, health and wellness, and collaborative leadership. *Part III: Planet* looks at how to assure planetary resilience and stability, examining climate change, biodiversity, and urbanization; and how to bring peace and security, through peacekeeping and by containing threats posed by nuclear weapons, terrorism, and new geopolitical dynamics.

In its efforts to articulate a framework and catalyze regenerative solutions for People, Society, and Planet, *A New Global Agenda* plays perhaps a limited yet pivotal role in guiding us to turn aspirational vision into actual reality. In this way, the audacity of agenda is made more meaningful as an imperative for our time to start where we are and acknowledge that it is incumbent on each of us to do what we can. The work to become more human and humane has already begun. We are not required to be the ones to complete this process, nor can we finish the job alone; rather, we commit to its ongoing progress and practice in pursuit of a more perfect union between our values and actions, a more perfect world for humanity.

Notes

[1] The poet June Jordan first wrote these words in "Poem for South African Women," (*Passion*, 1980). The phrase has also been made famous as the title of a book by Alice Walker, quoted in a speech by President Barack Obama, sung by Sweet Honey in the Rock, and is often attributed to Hopi Elders as well.

[2] The SDGs came into effect on January 1, 2016 (*Transforming Our World: The 2030 Agenda for Sustainable Development*, UNGA A/Res/70/1; https://sustainabledevelopment.un.org/content/documents/21252030%20Agenda%20for%20Sustainable%20Development%20web.pdf).

[3] The Paris Accords were agreed in April 2016, https://unfccc.int/files/meetings/paris_nov_2015/application/pdf/paris_agreement_english_.pdf.

[4] Habitat III was agreed in July 2016, http://habitat3.org/the-new-urban-agenda/.

[5] Diana Ayton-Shenker, ed., *A Global Agenda 2002–03: Issues before the 57th General Assembly of the United Nations*, a publication of the UNA-USA (Lanham, MD: Rowman & Littlefield, 2001); Diana Ayton-Shenker and John Tessitore, eds., *A Global Agenda 2001–02: Issues before the 56th General Assembly of the United Nations*, a publication of the UNA-USA (Lanham, MD: Rowman & Littlefield, 2001); hailed by former UN Secretary-General Ban Ki-moon as "essential reading" and "an invaluable reference," and by former UN Secretary-General Kofi Annan as "the bible" of the international community.

[6] "Anthropocene" refers to the current geological age, viewed as the period during which human activity has been the dominant influence on climate and the environment.

PART I

PEOPLE

CHAPTER 1

We Do Matter
A Renewed Global Agenda for Protecting Human Rights
Alex Neve

The world knows what is happening to us. But the world
does nothing. We're left to ask, do we not matter?[1]

—*Alfadil Khalifa Mohamed*

In South Sudan and Yemen, staggering human rights and humanitarian catastrophes have unfolded over several years now, seeming to attract little more than a batted eyelid of international attention from time to time. Armed conflict in both countries has fueled and exacerbated famine.[2] Arms flow to all sides of both conflicts unabated.[3] Abuses against civilians are the hallmark of the fighting. South Sudan is now the source of the world's fastest-growing refugee crisis, with between one thousand and two thousand refugees arriving daily in neighboring Uganda.[4] Yemen faces a cholera epidemic, which grows by five thousand new cases daily.[5]

Prisoners of conscience languish and suffer in prison cells worldwide. Chinese indifference as the 2010 Nobel Peace Prize Laureate Liu Xiaobo, jailed (for the fourth time) since 2009, died—still a prisoner—from late-stage liver cancer, was cruel and callous in the extreme.[6] In an unprecedented move, both the Chair and the Director of Amnesty International's national section in Turkey are behind bars, facing spurious and unfounded allegations of supporting a terrorist organization.[7]

Frontline human rights defenders find it more perilous than ever to stand up for human rights in their communities.[8] The Mediterranean Sea and Mexican rainforests continue to become places of ever-greater danger for refugees and migrants braving journeys fueled by equal parts hope and desperation.[9] Around the world—from the United States to the Philippines and dozens of countries in between—the politics of fear, suspicion, and hate wins elections by unabashedly vilifying and targeting marginalized communities.[10]

And in Canada, great expectations that a long overdue national inquiry into the staggering levels of violence against indigenous women and girls in the country would finally lead to progress in addressing one of the country's most serious and neglected human rights problems now hang in the balance as the inquiry is increasingly hampered by internal problems, to the considerable disappointment of families and survivors.[11]

We could, of course, now seek to balance that gloomy opening with a companion recitation of more optimistic developments around the world, which do most assuredly abound. But that would not capture the mood. For there is no question that when it comes to the fundamental aspirations we all share—of equality, justice, safety, and well-being—these are trying and deeply difficult times.

Not a surprise then that many women, men, and young people around the world roundly condemn the failure of governments to live up to the grand vision and promise of the Universal Declaration of Human Rights, crafted in the raw and determined aftermath of the Second World War and further detailed through the many covenants, conventions, treaties, and principles that have followed over the seven decades since. More troubling, however, many question whether that vision and promise misses the mark entirely and will forever be hostage to politics, economics, prejudice, and apathy. They stand poised to give up on human rights.[12]

As the Universal Declaration of Human Rights approaches its seventieth anniversary in December 2018, there could be no more critical time to consider a renewed global agenda for human rights protection. Among other imperatives, that agenda must focus on ending atrocities, protecting people on the move, upholding the equality rights of women and girls, defending the defenders, and enforcing the promises.

Ending Atrocities

In many respects, one of the most disgraceful failures of the international human rights project over these past seventy years has been what can only be described as both an inability and unwillingness to end mass atrocities, so that there would be no repetition of the horrors of the Holocaust that had provided much of the impetus for developing the United Nations (UN) human rights system in the first place. Very sadly, that global human rights commitment of "never again" has instead, over the decades, very clearly been "again and again."

Be it carnage against civilians in armed conflict, deliberate campaigns of killings and enforced disappearances, or intransigent and systematic oppression, the list of perpetrators is a chilling indictment of the very worst of inhumanity: Cambodia, Rwanda, Sudan, Bosnia, Democratic Republic of Congo, East Timor, Liberia, Burundi, Syria, Haiti, Darfur, Sri Lanka, northern Iraq, South Africa, Yemen, South Sudan, Argentina, Tibet, Guatemala, Kosovo, Libya, Sierra Leone, Biafra, Bangladesh, North Korea, Afghanistan, Somalia, and the Israeli-Occupied Territories. Even more troubling, this list is far from complete. To even begin such a list is fraught, for in truth, it would likely fill an entire page.

What does that tell us? That mass human rights violations are unavoidable and it is beyond us as a collective global community to do anything about it? That most certainly would not be the response from the millions, even hundreds of millions, of women, men, and young people whose lives and rights are on the line. It is also not reflected in the deep anguish and sympathy felt by most people when a human rights or humanitarian crisis becomes known. Most people absolutely and understandably feel helpless or overwhelmed, but few would blithely go so far as to conclude that it is simply the inevitable state of affairs and we should refrain from preventing and responding to atrocities.

So what needs to change? The building blocks of a global agenda for atrocities prevention have been coming together over the years. What is needed now is political will to move forward. Three key components are international justice, arms control, and UN Security Council reform. While each face significant geopolitical hurdles, the urgency and need is undeniable.

International Justice

For decades, one of the most notable shortcomings in international human rights protection was the glaring absurdity that the world's worst criminals were the ones most likely to escape justice and accountability for their misdeeds. Someone who beat up one person in a back-alley brawl was more likely to face justice than a police commander who oversaw the systematic torture of thousands; someone who murdered one person was more likely to go to jail than a military leader who orchestrated the mass killing of hundreds of thousands of people.

All of that was supposed to change with the historic breakthrough of agreeing to the Rome Statute in 1998, which subsequently led to the establishment of the International Criminal Court in 2002. Nearly twenty years since the heady summer of 1998, 124 countries—close to two-thirds of the world's nation-states—are now parties to the Rome Statute.[13] That is a remarkable level of support for a concept—international justice—that governments did not even want to discuss for decades, and that gives hope. However, three of the permanent members who wield such power within the UN Security Council—China, Russia, and the United States—have not signed on and have made it clear they have no intention to do so.[14] And in more recent years, there has been growing pushback from African governments—including several who have been party to the Rome Statute for many years[15]—who allege that the Court has disproportionately targeted them in the first round of charges and trials.[16]

All of the consternation, pushback, and criticism is perhaps the strongest indication there could be as to how much this matters. Moving ahead, a revitalized campaign to support the International Criminal Court and universalize the dream of international justice must be at the heart of an atrocities prevention agenda.

Arms Control

Human rights and humanitarian groups have long known that one of the most obvious obstacles to preventing atrocities has been the unregulated and unbridled global arms trade. The ease with which weapons move across international borders and into the hands of governments and armed groups ready to commit terrible human rights violations is stunning. In the world of international trade, fewer rules applied to ammunition, shells, guns, tanks, and fighter jets than to a long list of much more innocuous commodities.

The need for established rules and oversight of the global arms trade is all the more pressing given the inability of states to come together when a particular conflict arises and put restrictions in place at that time. For instance, there is no comprehensive UN Security Council–imposed global arms embargo in place at this time with respect to a number of the world's most notable hotspots, including both Syria and South Sudan.[17]

After years of research, advocacy, and campaigning by civil society groups, states did at long last agree and adopt an Arms Trade Treaty (ATT) in April 2013, bringing human rights rules to this deadly global commerce. Over four years later, a respectable ninety-one countries are on board.[18] Once again, the same three of the Permanent Five (P5)—China, Russia, and the United States—are staying out. There is without question still far to go in ensuring that the ATT will become the effective bulwark against atrocities that it can and must be. But given that only ten years ago most observers felt that the idea of a global ATT was an unattainable illusion, progress to date has been encouraging.

UN Security Council Reform

It is impossible to consider preventing and responding to mass atrocities without turning attention to the Security Council, the one body with the global clout to pursue international justice,[19] stop the flow of arms, impose sanctions, and send in peacekeepers. Yet the Security Council has far more frequently failed to act than it has taken the steps needed. Much of the problem lies in the powers of the famous P5 members of the Security Council—China, France, Russia, the United Kingdom, and the United States—whose membership never expires and who have the power to veto any decision with which they disagree. A recent and notorious abuse of these powers has been the recent determination of Russia, supported by China, to veto many Security Council resolutions addressing the crisis in Syria.[20]

There have, of course, been many ambitious proposals for reform of the Security Council, including adding more permanent members. None have had much lift-off and all face the bottom-line challenge that the five existing permanent members have the power to block any reform they oppose. A less ambitious but tremendously important proposition that has gathered increasing support in recent years is for a Code of Conduct to be adopted which would constrain all members of the Security Council—permanent and non-permanent alike—from voting against resolutions dealing with war crimes,

crimes against humanity, and genocide.[21] The initiative has strong support from many countries, including one of the permanent members, France, and has now been endorsed by 110 states.[22] This pressure for principled Security Council action when faced with mass atrocity situations is sure to continue to build.

Protecting People on the Move

At a time when situations of widespread human rights violations are so glaringly commonplace, and meaningful and effective efforts to address those concerns are dismal at best and nonexistent at worst, it is not at all a surprise that the world faces levels of forced displacement not experienced since the Second World War. The United Nations High Commissioner for Refugees estimates that 65 million people have been forced to flee their homes worldwide, with approximately 22.5 million refugees and 42.5 million internally displaced persons.[23]

There is therefore much talk of a global refugee crisis. The situation for Syrian refugees, in particular, with more than five million women, men, and children now sheltering in a handful of neighboring countries, particularly Turkey, Lebanon, and Jordan, is certainly at the fore; but other crises such as the mass exodus of South Sudanese refugees to Uganda, Ethiopia, Kenya, and Sudan are also of grave concern. Meanwhile, governments, the media, and the general public continue to conflate refugees and migrants. That is particularly the case with the many thousands of people fleeing the so-called Northern Triangle of Central American states—Honduras, Guatemala, and El Salvador—through Mexico in an attempt to reach the United States. They are treated abysmally by all governments along the way and their plight is often dismissed as being that of migrants, not refugees. That mischaracterization ignores that substantial numbers of those fleeing the Central American countries do absolutely satisfy the UN refugee definition.[24] It also seems to intimate that the rights of migrants are of little concern.[25]

The numbers do certainly give a sense of crisis. About 1 out of every 112 people in the world is now forcibly displaced from her or his home, which is the equivalent of a country with a population the size of the United Kingdom.

But the crisis much more urgently lies in the measures being taken by governments in response, with much more focus and resources on restrictions and barriers than on protection and assistance. As such, desperate individuals and families increasingly take terrifying risks on the high seas, over mountain passes, across scorching deserts, and through dense rainforests, hoping to reach safety. Thousands are paying with their lives.

There are many explanations for this crisis. One clear problem is that the global refugee system, intended to be grounded in international cooperation,[26] is at its heart entirely unilateral. Frontline states that are the ones to receive an influx of refugees are the ones expected to shoulder that responsibility, with an unpredictable degree of (generally, woefully inadequate) charitable assistance from the international community. States further afield with the resources to do so are able to expend huge sums through border control, ocean patrols, and other measures, keeping refugees away.

There had been hope that governments would make headway in agreeing a more cooperative approach to refugee protection, including a binding framework for more equitable responsibility-sharing, at a major UN summit in September 2016. That did not materialize at that time, but a two-year process of further negotiations towards that goal is now underway, slated to come back to the UN General Assembly in September 2018. Expectations are not high, as most states continue to exhibit narrow self-interest over principled humanitarianism when it comes to making commitments to protect refugees. Nonetheless, this window of time offers the best chance in decades to push states to bind themselves to a cooperative model of international refugee protection. A parallel World Refugee Council, chaired by Canada's former Minister of Foreign Affairs Lloyd Axworthy, is actively working to explore new models; efforts of that nature need strong support at this critical time.[27]

Upholding the Equality of Women and Girls

By sheer numbers, there is no denying that the deep inequality faced by women and girls is the most severe human rights challenge the world faces, and faces everywhere. Despite commitments to gender equality and safeguards for upholding women's human rights being long enshrined in numerous treaties, including one dealing specifically with discrimination against women,[28] violence, inequality, and marginalization continue to be the human rights reality for women and girls the world over. And while the scale and nature of the abuses differs considerably, there is no denying that this is indeed of concern everywhere, be it the Global North or Global South; within all religious, cultural, and political traditions; and in countries considered to be wealthy and those facing high levels of extreme poverty.

It is beyond debate that upholding the rights of women and girls matters for two fundamentally important reasons. First and most pressing is the fact that the rights violations are serious, widespread, and indefensible and simply must be stopped. That the equality, dignity, and well-being of billions of women and girls around the world is so readily daily disregarded, and with such entrenched impunity, is a disgrace.

Second, it is well established that systematic discrimination against women and girls has far broader human rights, social, and economic impact as well. Respecting women's human rights is beneficial across society, be it through more effective protection for other marginalized groups, increased prosperity and well-being, and/or stronger commitments to peace and security.

Global determination to promote gender equality and women's human rights continues to grow. In July 2010, the United Nations General Assembly created UN Women, the United Nations Entity for Gender Equality and the Empowerment of Women, a significant step within the UN system.[29] The UN's important Sustainable Development Goals (SDGs), or 2030 Agenda, adopted in September 2015, include a specific goal focused on gender equality,[30] which many states are prioritizing and mainstreaming in how they implement the SDGs.[31]

Determination may be on the upswing, but there is still very far to go when it comes to changes and actions that make a real difference. Some states are at long last giving women's equality the priority attention it requires, domestically and internationally. Canada, for example, recently adopted the world's first specifically described Feminist International Assistance Policy.[32] Some struggles, such as the effort to promote the right of girls to education championed by Nobel Peace Prize Laureate Malala Yousafzai, are attracting greater support.[33] Such advances are, sadly, still the exception and not the rule. A renewed global human rights agenda must have efforts to protect the rights of women and girls at its very heart.

Defending the Defenders

Marking International Human Rights Day on December 10, 1998, also the fiftieth anniversary of the Universal Declaration of Human Rights, states adopted a new UN Human Rights Defenders Declaration.[34] In many respects, it was meant to be a moment of celebration, acknowledging the strength and vibrancy of activists within the burgeoning human rights movement around the world and reminding governments of the importance of respecting and supporting their work to uphold internally protected human rights.

Unfortunately, almost two decades since the Declaration was adopted, regard for the work of human rights defenders around the world has not at all consolidated and improved; it has deteriorated precipitously. A vocation and calling that should be among the most cherished in any society has now, to the contrary, become among the most perilous and vilified.[35] The measures may differ—legal harassment, public demonization, threats, physical attacks, and killings—but the message is the same: standing up for human rights carries a price.

It is a deeply troubling trend on two levels. Clearly, it is terribly worrying that a growing number of people, of all ages, face growing risks of human rights violations simply because they care about human rights. And there are some who are at even greater risk than others, including those defending the rights of the lesbian, gay, bisexual, transgender, and intersex community, defenders upholding the sexual and reproductive health rights of women and girls, and activists speaking up about human rights in the context of land and environmental struggles often related to the operations of extractives companies.[36] More widely, of course, greater danger for those who seek to defend human rights reflects growing contempt for the rights they strive to defend. That jeopardizes all of us.

No global human right agenda can or will succeed without a legion of young people, women, and men actively and passionately defending those rights, by mobilizing, educating, researching, advocating, and agitating. It is time for states to turn the spotlight on celebrating the courage and accomplishments of human rights defenders, while roundly condemning any efforts to silence their voices.

Enforcing the Promises

For years, the international community has focused the bulk of its human rights efforts on elaborating the fine promises laid out in a never-ending array of legal instruments and spending considerable time talking about and even lamenting the unrelenting transgressions of those instruments. And there has been much progress on both fronts. Despite the advances, however, the important final goal of enforcing the promises and turning the talk into action remains elusive at best.

Status Quo

Legally binding covenants, conventions, and treaties covering a wide range of human rights issues have most certainly been agreed. Those include overarching covenants dealing separately with civil and political rights on the one hand, and economic, social, and cultural (ESC) rights on the other. Conventions and declarations have been finalized focusing on groups particularly vulnerable to violations, including women and girls, refugees, children, migrant workers, and indigenous peoples. Another group of treaties deal with the abuses themselves, such as torture, enforced disappearances, and racial discrimination.

At the same time, there has been considerable evolution in the bodies and fora within which states come together to debate and take decision about human rights concerns. In the early days, that was largely limited to the UN Commission on Human Rights, established in 1946 and dissolved sixty years later in 2006. While change came slowly, over those six decades, the Commission, which was initially shrouded in considerable secrecy, began slowly to open up more of its deliberations to public scrutiny. Perception and reality, however, increasingly held that the Commission had become largely discredited by politicking and selectivity. As such, it was disbanded as part of the comprehensive UN reform package championed by former UN Secretary-General Kofi Annan in 2005 and was replaced by a new UN Human Rights Council.

The Human Rights Council was intended to make advances in enforcement and implementation. To minimize the politics, a new election process for states wishing to stand for Council membership was established, requiring prospective members to make pledges as to human rights reforms they would adopt if elected. And to dissipate the selectivity that had long plagued the Commission—with some countries frequently subject to scrutiny (some, such as Israel, disproportionately so) and others, such as China, never so—a new Universal Periodic Review (UPR) process was instituted which would ensure that every country's human rights record will be examined on a rotational basis once every 4.5 years.

At the same time, first under the Commission and continued with the Council, the UN human rights system's Special Procedures have developed, a web of Special Rapporteurs, Special Representatives, Independent Experts, and Working Groups appointed by states to bring expertise and independence to the in-depth examination of thematic human rights concerns or particular country situations.

Parallel to these developments within the Commission and now Council, the advent of a growing number of Conventions over the years has brought corresponding independent bodies responsible for overseeing treaty implementation. Depending on what treaties and their Optional Protocols have been ratified by states, the Committees possess a range of powers, including periodic review of the records of state parties, receiving and offering views on individual complaints, and formulating interpretative comments offering authoritative views about particular articles of the convention. Ten such committees now exist.[37]

The architecture of the international human rights system has undoubtedly become impressively extensive. But more than seventy years on, it is safe to say that these binding legal obligations, the resolutions adopted by commissions and councils, and the words of advice offered by committees, experts, and review processes are overwhelmingly more often disregarded than respected.

And the failure to comply applies to states with abysmal human rights records as well as to states respected as strong supporters of the international human rights system. For instance, at its forty-eighth session, in May 2012, the UN Committee against Torture carried out periodic reviews of both Syria and Canada. Clearly, the scope and nature of the concerns about torture differed dramatically in the two countries. Doing its job properly, the Committee had recommendations for both governments. Syria, among many action points was, for instance, urged to "immediately cease and publicly condemn widespread and systematic practices of torture, especially by security forces."[38] Canada was urged, not for the first time, to "amend relevant laws, including the Immigration and Refugee Protection Act, with a view to unconditionally respecting the absolute principle of non-refoulement in accordance with article 3 of the Convention."[39] Five years later, neither government has acted on the Committee's recommendations. And neither faces any notable consequences for that failure, other than the likelihood of being chastised by the Committee when the next periodic review rolls around.

That same lack of consequences is apparent in the outcomes of the UPR process. All states have now been through two rounds of the UPR since it was first instituted in April 2008. There is certainly considerable real and symbolic benefit in a process that does ensure that no country—no matter how powerful or not—escapes international human rights scrutiny. But with the final decision as to which recommendations will or will not be taken up being left in the hands of the state under review, and no means of censure for failure to follow through on those accepted recommendations, UPR results also end up largely being a matter of crossing fingers in hope of compliance.

The failure of states to implement international human rights recommendations is particularly notable when it comes to reviews of state compliance with their ESC rights obligations. The Universal Declaration of Human Rights makes no distinction between civil and political rights and ESC rights. The two

Covenants which give further definition and legal weight to the rights enshrined in the Universal Declaration did, largely for Cold War–era geopolitical reasons, divide rights into the two categories. There was no indication, however, that either category was to be considered more or less enforceable than the other.[40] That has, however, very much been the fate of ESC rights, particularly in the extent to which may states from the Global North insist that those rights, dealing with such matters as education, health care, and housing, are not subject to enforcement to the same extent as civil and political rights regarding life, liberty, fair trials, and free expression, and certainly not through the courts and the justice system.

It is also clear that human rights enforcement slips completely off the table when trumped by competing interests or considerations. When national security is asserted, human rights are readily dismissed, even with respect to human rights principles such as the protection against torture, which are explicitly drafted as absolute and unconditional obligations which take precedence over such challenges as national security.[41] Similarly, human rights frequently take a back seat when trade and economic considerations are in play, and when the desire to bring belligerents together in peace talks collides with the clear human rights obligation to bring perpetrators of grave violations to justice.

Any renewed global human rights agenda must tackle this long-standing enforcement gap. Without such measures, human rights remain little more than aspirations, and public confidence that they offer real solutions to pressing problems will continue to wither. Improving enforcement requires, at a minimum, attention to UN reform, ESC rights, national security and business, and human rights.

UN Reform

Any suggestion of UN reform, regardless of which forum or body may be in the frame, inevitably draws a shudder. The fear is that at best it is a quagmire and at worst, with no shortage of naysayers and opponents of strong multilateralism in play, attempts at reform may lead to retrenchment rather than improvements. That most definitely extends to the world body's human rights system, always one of the most politically charged arenas within the UN, with any number of governments keen to undermine the independence and powers of the various rights bodies and processes. The decision to replace the Commission on Human Rights with the Human Rights Council and other substantial changes in 2005 that were adopted as part of a wider package of reforms making the UN's sixtieth anniversary was certainly marked with both controversy and compromise. But in the end, those changes did bring in a number of important advances.[42]

UN human rights reform has been getting considerable airplay recently for another reason. The Trump administration has sent a threatening message that without substantial reform, the US government may step down from its membership on the Council and withdraw or significantly cut back its financial support.[43] The US critique largely focuses on the fact that countries with disastrous human rights records, such as China, Saudi Arabia, and Egypt, have been regularly elected to Council membership, and the US government's frequent concern that the Council, like the Commission before it, devotes an inordinate amount of agenda time to human rights concerns in Israel in comparison with other countries. While it is clearly a politically motivated and selective move against the Council, it does underscore two long-standing challenges faced by UN human rights bodies: the need for greater consistency and how to exert meaningful pressure on powerful countries with poor human rights records.

Meanwhile, pressures mount elsewhere within the UN human rights system. How to improve the efficiency but strengthen the effectiveness of the growing number of expert committees set up under the UN's expanding list of human rights treaties? Where are the resources and political support for increased deployment of personnel from the Office of the High Commissioner for Human Rights on the ground, at the frontlines of human rights struggles and crises around the world? And the eternal issues around how to improve the coordination and integration of a human rights approach across the range of UN bodies, agencies, and processes?

The new UN Secretary-General, António Guterres, has set the ground for UN reforms that may certainly extend to the human rights front. He has made it clear that he intends to retool and strengthen UN bodies and mechanisms to better ensure that crises are prevented, rather than requiring responses after the fact:

> [I]t is time for the United Nations to . . . recognize its shortcomings and to reform the way it works. This Organization is the cornerstone of multilateralism, and has contributed to decades of relative peace. But, the challenges are now surpassing our ability to respond. The United Nations must be ready to change. Our most serious shortcoming—and here I refer to the entire international community—is our inability to prevent crises. The United Nations was born from war. Today, we must be here for peace.[44]

Reform is never easy or straightforward and always laced with risk; nevertheless, there may be openings ahead to once again promote a UN human rights reform agenda. This time, the focus should very much be on implementation and enforcement.

Closing the Gaps

Progress in strengthening human rights enforcement certainly requires paying close attention to some of the areas where implementation and compliance is weakest and where excuses abound for failing to live up to international obligations. These areas directly challenge and insidiously undermine the universal nature of the human rights promise.

Respect for and enforcement of ESC rights must surely be at the top of that list. It is time to leave behind outdated and misguided policies and mind-sets that treat ESC rights as second-class budgetary considerations rather than crucial and binding human rights obligations that touch on some of the most fundamental dimensions of human existence. Notably, the UN's SDGs, adopted in 2015 with a time horizon through to 2030, have a strong human rights orientation, which the Office of the High Commissioner for Human Rights has noted aligns across a number of different ESC rights. Successful implementation of the SDGs will require strengthened regard for and enforcement of ESC rights.[45]

National security arguments have been a particularly notorious challenge to human rights principles, especially since the September 11 terrorist attacks in the United States. The US government, while infamous for disregarding human rights as part of the so-called war on terror, is by no means the only state to do so; and it is certainly not a concern limited to the United States' recent experience. In some instances, national security is used as a pretext to disguise repressive measures that are clearly directed at targeting political opponents; religious, racial, or ethnic minorities; and other groups. In other cases, governments do legitimately face terrorist or other security threats, but willingly pursue responses that officially allow, or unofficially tolerate, widespread human rights violations, particularly with respect to arbitrary imprisonment, torture, fair trials, and discrimination.

In both cases, it has led us to a place where a mere reference to national security means human rights will certainly face an uphill battle: more political opposition, greater public uncertainty, and a receptive judiciary in some cases. That corrosive impact erodes the human rights framework more generally and certainly sets back efforts to encourage and strengthen implementation. Central to a new human rights enforcement agenda must be adoption of an approach to national security that embraces rights obligations as central—not antithetical—to security, security that is truly equitable and durable.

If there is one arena in which human rights advocates are consistently told to wait and be patient, it is when economic interests are on the line. Doing business should take precedence, we are told, as it will eventually and inevitably lead to greater prosperity, stronger respect for the rule of law, and more opportunities for education, training, and employment, and therefore, ultimately, human rights will flourish.

But we know that is far too simple and, more to the point, often not the case. A country's economy can grow and expand considerably while human rights violations do not abate and, in fact, even worsen. Consider China and Saudi Arabia as two glaring examples of economic boom and human rights bust. Trade policy and trade agreements that do not deliberately incorporate and commit to human rights obligations do little favor to rights and justice.

The companion to trade agreements that ignore human rights is a business world that too often shows contempt for human rights. In an ever-smaller world, companies now operate in virtually every corner, including on the edge of war zones, against backdrops of severe human rights violations, and surrounded by communities pulled down by extreme poverty.

Many companies have much more clout and greater resources than local and sometimes even national governments. But what of their human rights responsibilities? If they operate responsibly, they may help considerably in the effort to bolster human rights; but the opposite is too true too often as well—irresponsible business practices can and do cause serious human rights abuses.

For years, the debate around this vitally important area of human rights enforcement has been hamstrung by an insistence from companies and many governments that it is best to leave the corporate world to its own devices and that voluntary approaches that urge and encourage companies to comply with human rights norms are better than imposing legal requirements and concomitant penalties for failing to respect human rights in company operations. But despite an explosion in company human rights policies and corporate social responsibility programs, the voluntary approach is not working. The growing number of reports and campaigns from Amnesty International and other human rights organizations, highlighting widespread human rights concerns in industry sectors such as gold,[46] palm oil,[47] timber,[48] and cobalt,[49] or by specific companies in countries such as Nigeria,[50] Guatemala,[51] Malawi,[52] Eritrea,[53] Colombia,[54] and Myanmar[55] (to name only a small handful), makes that patently clear.

A renewed global human rights agenda that does not endeavor to make significant strides in strengthening enforcement of the human rights responsibilities of companies will truly miss the mark. A key initiative at this time, an effort to elaborate a binding treaty on business and human rights, continues to face a blend of disinterest and opposition from many governments.[56]

Conclusion

When I met Alfadil, at an isolated internally displaced persons site at the base of the Nuba Mountains in Sudan's conflict-ridden South Kordofan State, there was no denying his feeling that the international community's lauded commitment to a world of human rights protection had proven meaningless for him, his family, and his community. There was little to offer by way of response to his pained conclusion that the world's failure to take meaningful action to end the violations that were causing such suffering and loss meant that he and the Nuba people simply did not matter.

Alfadil's words, though, were far more than distressed pessimism; they were also a call to action. He certainly was not agreeing that the Nuba people did not matter—he was defiantly affirming that they do and insisting that something be done about that. That action must be to commit to forging a renewed global human rights agenda. Recognizing that the failings of the past seventy years of international human rights protection lie primarily in the yawning gap between stirring promises captured in a legion of legal instruments and the cold, hard reality that states cavalierly ignore and blatantly breach those promises without consequence, a renewed agenda must focus on concrete action, meaningful solutions, and strengthened enforcement.

This chapter has pointed to five crucial areas that must be central to renewed global efforts to protect universal human rights:

- Preventing mass atrocities by strengthening international justice, reining in the arms trade, and encouraging more principled Security Council action.
- Protecting people on the move by agreeing to a binding legal framework for equitably and globally sharing the responsibility for protecting refugees.
- Upholding the rights of women and girls by energetically championing SDG 5 dealing with gender equality.
- Defending human rights defenders by celebrating the important work they do and roundly and consistently condemning all attacks against them.
- Enforcing the countless promises already contained in international human rights instruments, including by pursuing UN human rights reform and reinforcing commitments to ESC rights; a human rights–based approach to national security; and the human rights responsibilities of businesses.

At the end of the day, all of these important measures aside, perhaps the most crucial and challenging imperative that must be addressed in the effort to revitalize global human rights protection is the need to build empathy and understanding, and foster a culture that celebrates diversity and aspires to tolerance and inclusion. That is the direct answer to Alfadil's concern that the Nuba people do not matter. It is the flipside to the waves of division and hate that have certainly always existed but have become more global and mainstream than ever.

The need for human rights empathy takes us back to Eleanor Roosevelt's powerful remarks delivered at the UN in 1958, talking of the "small places" where human rights truly take root:

> Where, after all, do universal rights begin? In small places, close to home—so close and so small that they cannot be seen on any maps of the world. Yet they are the world of the individual person; the neighborhood he lives in; the school or college he attends; the factory, farm or office where he works. Such are the places where every man, woman, and child seeks equal justice, equal opportunity, equal dignity without discrimination. Unless these rights have meaning there, they have little meaning anywhere. Without concerned citizen action to uphold them close to home, we shall look in vain for progress in the larger world.[57]

In those small places, in the streets, in refugee camps, in national capitals, and at the UN: we do all matter. And in all of those worlds, the dream of universal human rights protection can be, and indeed is, within reach.

Notes

[1] Interviewed by an Amnesty International delegation in South Kordofan, Sudan, in May 2015, Alfadil Khalifa Mohamed expressed frustration and disappointment at the international community's failure to take steps to end war crimes and other systematic human rights

violations committed by Sudanese military forces. Amnesty International, "Don't We Matter? Four Years of Unrelenting Attacks against Civilians in Sudan's South Kordofan State," July 2015, p. 6.

2 UN News Centre, "UN Aid Chief Urges Global Action as Starvation, Famine Loom for 20 Million across Four Countries," March 10, 2017. http://www.un.org/apps/news/story.asp?NewsID=56339#.WW4-0ITyuUk.

3 Human Rights Watch, "Yemen Is Suffering at the Hands of Saudi Arabia—and the UK Is Profiting," July 11, 2017. https://www.hrw.org/news/2017/07/11/yemen-suffering-hands-saudi-arabia-and-uk-profiting. Amnesty International, "South Sudan: Arms Embargo, Sanctions Fail at UN Security Council," December 23, 2016. https://www.amnesty.org/en/latest/news/2016/12/south-sudan-arms-embargo-sanctions-fail-at-un-security-council/.

4 Amnesty International, "Donors Failing Almost a Million South Sudanese Refugees in Uganda," June 19, 2017. https://www.amnesty.org/en/latest/news/2017/06/donors-failing-almost-a-million-south-sudanese-refugees-in-uganda/.

5 Rick Gladstone, "Cholera, Famine and Girls Sold into Marriage for Food: Yemen's Dire Picture," *New York Times*, May 30, 2017. https://www.nytimes.com/2017/05/30/world/middleeast/yemen-civil-war-cholera-famine-girls-marriage-united-nations.html.

6 Salil Shetty, Amnesty International, "Liu Xiaobo: A Man Who Spoke Truth to Power," July 13, 2017. https://www.amnesty.org/en/latest/news/2017/07/liu-xiaobo-spoke-truth-to-power/.

7 Amnesty International, "Turkey: Activists Worldwide Demand Release of Imprisoned Amnesty International Director and Chair," July 10, 2017. https://www.amnesty.org/en/latest/news/2017/07/turkey-activists-worldwide-demand-release-of-amnesty-international-director-and-chair/.

8 Amnesty International, "Human Rights Defenders under Threat: A Shrinking Space for Civil Society," May 16, 2017. https://www.amnesty.org/en/documents/act30/6011/2017/en/.

9 United Nations High Commissioner for Refugees, "Forced Displacement Worldwide at Its Highest in Decades," June 19, 2017. http://www.unhcr.org/news/stories/2017/6/5941561f4/forced-displacement-worldwide-its-highest-decades.html?query=global%20trends%20forced%20displacement%20in%202016.

10 Amnesty International, "'Politics of Demonization' Breeding Division and Fear," February 22, 2017. https://www.amnesty.org/en/latest/news/2017/02/amnesty-international-annual-report-201617/.

11 CBC News, "Missing and Murdered Inquiry to Forge Ahead Despite Resignation of Key Commissioner," July 11, 2017. http://www.cbc.ca/news/politics/poitras-commissioner-resignation-1.4199126.

12 Stephen Hopgood, *The Endtimes of Human Rights* (Ithaca, NY: Cornell University Press, 2013). Hopgood provocatively argues that "despite this rhetoric of rededication and hope, the ground of human rights is crumbling beneath us . . . In fact, a 150-year experiment in creating global rules to protect and defend individual human beings is coming to an end." Stephen Hopgood, "The End of Human Rights," *Washington Post*, January 3, 2014. https://www.washingtonpost.com/opinions/the-end-of-human-rights/2014/01/03/7f8fa83c-6742-11e3-ae56-22de072140a2_story.html?utm_term=.93a08f44d373.

13 International Criminal Court, https://asp.icc-cpi.int/en_menus/asp/states%20parties/pages/the%20states%20parties%20to%20the%20rome%20statute.aspx.

14 Inter-Press Service, "U.S., Russia, China Hamper ICC's Reach," July 22, 2014. http://www.ipsnews.net/2014/07/u-s-russia-china-hamper-iccs-reach/.

15 Geoffrey York, "African Union's Mass Withdrawal Strategy Mounts Pressure on ICC," *The Globe and Mail*, February 1, 2017. https://www.theglobeandmail.com/news/world/african-unions-mass-withdrawal-strategy-a-fresh-blow-to-international-court/article33869212/.

16 Human Rights Watch, "AU's 'ICC Withdrawal Strategy' Less Than Meets the Eye," February 1, 2017. https://www.hrw.org/news/2017/02/01/aus-icc-withdrawal-strategy-less-meets-eye.

17 Somini Sengupta, "Russia and U.S. Clash over Syria in Security Council Vote," *New York Times*, February 28, 2017. https://www.nytimes.com/2017/02/28/world/middleeast/united-nations-security-council-syria-sanctions-russia-trump.html. Michelle Nicholls, "U.N. Council Fails to Impose Arms Embargo on South Sudan," *Reuters*, December 23, 2016. http://www.reuters.com/article/us-southsudan-security-un-idUSKBN14C1KY.

18 United Nations Office for Disarmament Affairs, Arms Trade Treaty, as of July 18, 2017. https://www.un.org/disarmament/convarms/att/.

19 The UN Security Council has the power to refer a situation to the International Criminal Court for investigation, regardless of whether the country concerned is a party to the Rome Statute. Rome Statute of the International Criminal Court, article 13(b). https://www.icc-cpi.int/nr/rdonlyres/ea9aeff7-5752-4f84-be94-0a655eb30e16/0/rome_statute_english.pdf.

20 Euan McKirdy, "8 Times Russia Blocked a UN Security Council Resolution on Syria," *CNN*, April 13, 2017. http://www.cnn.com/2017/04/13/middleeast/russia-unsc-syria-resolutions/index .html.

21 Explanatory Note on a Code of Conduct Regarding Security Council Action against Genocide, Crimes against Humanity or War Crimes, September 1, 2015. http://www.centerforunreform .org/sites/default/files/Final%202015-09-01%20SC%20Code%20of%20Conduct%20Atrocity.pdf.

22 Global Centre for the Responsibility to Protect, List of Signatories to the ACT Code of Conduct, January 25, 2017. http://www.globalr2p.org/resources/893.

23 United Nations High Commissioner for Refugees, Figures at a Glance, as of July 18, 2017 . http://www.unhcr.org/figures-at-a-glance.html.

24 "The United Nations Convention relating to the Status of Refugees," article 1. http://www.unhcr .org/3b66c2aa10.

25 Amnesty International Canada, "The Rights of Migrants: Human Rights Regardless of Status." https://www.amnesty.ca/our-work/issues/refugees-and-migrants/the-rights-of-migrants.

26 "Considering that the grant of asylum may place unduly heavy burdens on certain countries, and that a satisfactory solution of a problem of which the United Nations has recognized the international scope and nature cannot therefore be achieved without international co-operation." Fourth preambular paragraph to UN Refugee Convention, *supra*, footnote 25.

27 World Refugee Council. https://www.worldrefugeecouncil.org/.

28 Convention on the Elimination of All Forms of Discrimination against Women, entry into force September 3, 1981. http://www.un.org/womenwatch/daw/cedaw/cedaw.htm.

29 About UN Women. http://www.unwomen.org/en/about-us/about-un-women.

30 Goal 5: achieve gender equality and empower women and girls. https://sustainabledevelopment. un.org/sdg5.

31 Daniela Rosche, "Agenda 2030 and the Sustainable Development Goals: Gender Equality at Last? An Oxfam Perspective," *Gender & Development* 24 (February 2016). http://www.tandfonline .com/doi/full/10.1080/13552074.2016.1142196.

32 "Building an Inclusive World: Canada's Feminist International Assistance Policy," June 2017. http:// international.gc.ca/world-monde/issues_development-enjeux_developpement/priorities-priorites/ policy-politique.aspx?lang=eng.

33 Malala Fund, Why girl's education? https://www.malala.org/girls-education.

34 Declaration on the Right and Responsibility of Individuals, Groups and Organs of Society to Promote and Protect Universally Recognized Human Rights and Fundamental Freedoms, UN Doc. A/RES/53/144, March 8, 1999. http://www.ohchr.org/Documents/Issues/Defenders/ Declaration/declaration.pdf.

35 "2016 was a tough year to remain positive. Almost every day we received news of another human rights defender killed because of her/his peaceful work. The scale of the repressive backlash against human rights defenders reached new heights in countries around the globe. And yet the courage and dedication of human rights defenders continues to inspire." Front Line Defenders, Dispatches 2016, April 5, 2017, p. 3. https://www.frontlinedefenders.org/en/ publications.

36 Amnesty International, "Honduras/Guatemala: Attacks on the Rise in World's Deadliest Countries for Environmental Activists," September 1, 2016. https://www.amnesty.org/en/latest/news/2016/ 09/honduras-guatemala-ataques-en-aumento-en-los-paises-mas-mortiferos-del-mundo-para-los- activistas-ambientales/.

37 Human Rights Committee; Committee on Economic, Social and Cultural Rights; Committee on the Elimination of Racial Discrimination; Committee on the Elimination of Discrimination

against Women; Committee against Torture; Committee on the Rights of the Child; Committee on Migrant Workers; Committee on the Rights of Persons with Disabilities; Committee on Enforced Disappearances; and Sub-Committee on Prevention of Torture.

[38] UN Committee against Torture, *Concluding Observations: Syria*, UN Doc. CAT/C/SYR/CO/1/Add.2, June 29, 2012, para. 22(a).

[39] UN Committee against Torture, *Concluding Observations: Canada*, UN Doc. CAT/C/CAN/CO/6, June 25, 2012, para. 9.

[40] Daniel J. Whelan, *Indivisible Human Rights: A History, Pennsylvania Studies in Human Rights* (Philadelphia: University of Pennsylvania Press, 2010).

[41] "No exceptional circumstances whatsoever, whether a state of war or a threat of war, internal political instability or any other public emergency, may be invoked as a justification of torture." United Nation Convention against Torture and other Forms of Cruel, Inhuman or Degrading Treatment or Punishment, entry into force June 26, 1987, article 2(2). http://www.ohchr.org/EN/ProfessionalInterest/Pages/CAT.aspx.

[42] Global Policy Forum, "Secretary General Kofi Annan's Reform Agenda—1997 to 2006." https://www.globalpolicy.org/un-reform/un-reform-initiatives/secretary-general-kofi-annans-reform-agenda-1997-to-2006.html.

[43] Foreign Policy, "Tillerson to U.N. Rights Council: Reform or We're Leaving," March 14, 2017. http://foreignpolicy.com/2017/03/14/tillerson-to-u-n-rights-council-reform-or-were-leaving/.

[44] "Secretary-General-Designate António Guterres' Remarks to the General Assembly on Taking the Oath of Office," December 12, 2016. https://www.un.org/sg/en/content/sg/speeches/2016-12-12/secretary-general-designate-ant%C3%B3nio-guterres-oath-office-speech.

[45] Office of the United Nations High Commissioner for Human Rights, "Transforming Our World: Human Rights in the 2030 Agenda for Sustainable Development," http://www.ohchr.org/Documents/Issues/MDGs/Post2015/TransformingOurWorld.pdf.

[46] Partnership Africa Canada, "Just Gold: A Conflict-Free Artisanal Gold Pilot Project." http://www.pacweb.org/images/PUBLICATIONS/just-gold-brochure-En-web.pdf.

[47] Amnesty International, *The Great Palm Oil Scandal: Labour Abuses behind Big Brands*, November 2016. https://www.amnesty.org/en/documents/asa21/5184/2016/en/.

[48] Global Witness, "Blood Timber: How Europe Played a Significant Role in Funding War in the Central African Republic," July 15, 2015. https://www.globalwitness.org/en/campaigns/forests/bloodtimber/.

[49] Amnesty International, "Exposed: Child Labour behind Sphone and Electric Car Batteries," January 19, 2016. https://www.amnesty.org/en/latest/news/2016/01/child-labour-behind-smartphone-and-electric-car-batteries/.

[50] Amnesty International, "One Woman vs Shell: Shell Must Face Its Day in Court over Nigeria Abuses," June 29, 2017. https://www.amnesty.org/en/latest/campaigns/2017/06/one-nigerian-widow-vs-shell/.

[51] Amnesty International, "Guatemala: Mining in Guatemala—Rights at Risk," September 19, 2014. https://www.amnesty.org/en/documents/amr34/002/2014/en/.

[52] Human Rights Watch, "'They Destroyed Everything': Mining and Human Rights in Malawi," September 27, 2016. https://www.hrw.org/report/2013/01/15/hear-no-evil/forced-labor-and-corporate- responsibility-eritreas-mining-sector.

[53] Human Rights Watch, "Hear No Evil: Forced Labor and Corporate Responsibility in Eritrea's Mining Sector," January 15, 2013. https://www.hrw.org/report/2013/01/15/hear-no-evil/forced-labor-and-corporate-responsibility-eritreas-mining-sector.

[54] Amnesty International, "Colombia Must Prioritize Rights of Indigenous People and Afro-Descendant Communities above Economic Interests," November 4, 2015. https://www.amnesty.org/en/latest/news/2015/11/colombia-must-prioritize-rights-of-indigenous-people-and-afro-descendant-communities-above-economic-interests/.

[55] Amnesty International, "Myanmar: Open for Business? Corporate Crime and Abuses at Myanmar Copper Mine," February 10, 2015. https://www.amnesty.org/en/documents/asa16/0003/2015/en/.

56 International Commission of Jurists, "Proposals for Elements of a Legally Binding Instrument on Transnational Corporations and Other Business Enterprises," October 2016. https://www .icj.org/the-icj-releases-its-proposals-for-the-content-of-a-treaty-on-business-and-human-rights/. Amnesty International, *All States Must Participate in Good Faith in the UN Intergovernmental Working Group on Business and Human Rights*, June 18, 2015. https://www.amnesty.org/en/ documents/ior40/1897/2015/en/.

57 Eleanor Roosevelt, "The Great Question," remarks delivered at the United Nations in New York on March 27, 1958. Quoted in Scott Horton, "Roosevelt on Human Rights in the Small Places," *Harper's Magazine*, December 22, 2007. https://harpers.org/blog/2007/12/roosevelt-on-human-rights-in-the-small-places/.

CHAPTER 2

The Future of
International Law

Karen J. Alter

In some ways, writing about the future of international law is a bit like writing about the future of breathing: we can safely predict that every living person will continue to breathe. This is because international law is an essential language and medium of international relations; it is the mode through which countries interact with each other. Today, international law regulates or guides a myriad of elements of our interconnected world, from the global postal service, to international travel, the shipping of products and ninety-seven other aspects of our life that we tend to take for granted.[1] Since few, if any, states are likely to trend toward a survivalist autarky, and international law is how states communicate and understand the rules of international relations, the fundamental role of international law, and the vast majority of specific international laws, is unlikely to change. But just as some people will be born and others will die, aspects of international law will change.

Since the future of international law is sound, this query is really about a different set of questions. We are wondering if the recent past will continue; will the world continue to seek multilateral solutions and promote global integration? We are wondering about the future of highly contested areas of international law, such as the promotion of human rights and the accountability of states and individuals for atrocities. And we are wondering if issues that are as yet unregulated or poorly guided by international law—the use of cyber techniques to interfere in the economy, politics, and society of other countries, the use of drones, and global climate change—will present new frontiers for international law. Finally, we are wondering whether the relationship between international law, democracy, and the international liberal order is changing.

The first part of this brief chapter explains why international law is and always will be mostly observed and sustained. The second part asks whether the past will be a guide to the future. The post–World War II (WWII) proliferation of international organizations and treaties is a product of American and European leadership in the world. Does a waning of US and European hegemony portend the end of these institutions, or at least the end of a big bang of global law genesis? The third and fourth parts consider the future of what many see as the international law project of promoting human rights and subverting war to the rule of law. The fourth part also considers emerging areas that are seen as frontiers for international law—cybersecurity, the use of drones as a tool of war, and global efforts to address climate change—to help us think about whether future use of international law will be different. The final part concludes by considering how populism threatens international law.

While I contend that international law is and will remain the primary tool of international governance, the future of certain aspects of international law—aspects associated with the international liberal order—is being questioned. If populist and authoritarian leaders manage to break public faith in the rule of law, by convincing populations that strong-man leadership is more important than rights, accountability, and political checks and balances, then the aspects of international law associated with the international liberal order will be endangered. Personally, I believe that the rule of law is morally and politically superior to authoritarian rule, and for this reason, the arc of history bends in favor of the rule of law and of international law. For this reason, I expect the international liberal order to change—as all systems change in response to public input—but to largely survive.

Why International Law Is, and Will Remain, the Primary Language of International Relations

International law is the primary tool of international governance. My focus in this chapter is on international law in both its hard and soft law forms.[2] When two or more states make a collective decision that they intend to keep for some period of time, they codify this decision as international law. States use soft international law to set and articulate joint goals in a way that is not legally binding, and therefore may not require domestic ratification. A recent example is the Paris Agreement on Climate Change, where states made commitments to address the problem of climate change.[3] These commitments were real, but they were neither legally binding nor legally enforceable. The soft-law nature of the agreement made it more politically acceptable, and for the United States, the soft-law nature meant that the president did not need to submit the agreement to Congress for ratification.

States use hard international law—formally ratified and legally binding international agreements that may or may not be enforceable—to ensure that an international agreement can bind actors within the state and future governments. An example is the Geneva Conventions, a set of treaties and protocols ratified in whole or in part by 196 countries, which define basic rights of combatants and noncombatants in war.[4] Hard-law treaties can be written to be constraining or flexible, and states will separately decide if they want to create and later use an enforcement mechanism for the international agreement.

It is true that, compared to soft international law, hard-law agreements are legally binding. But this does not mean that hard international law is more effective than soft international law. Both types of international law encapsulate the voluntary commitments of governments to a set of objectives. Soft law can be used to articulate far-reaching objectives that may later become codified in hard international law—as occurred when the United Nations General Assembly passed the Universal Declaration of Human Rights (see part III for more), the Convention on the Prevention and Punishment of Genocide, and when the General Assembly defined what constitutes coercive aggression.[5] Because hard international law is not necessarily more effective than soft international law, both legal forms are considered to be part of international law.[6]

Scholars, governments, firms, nongovernmental organizations, judges, and journalists consult international law to understand what constitutes legal versus deviant behavior. Newspapers, nongovernmental organizations, and political leaders then tout international law violations. Headlines about international law violations, in combination with the human tendency to emphasize the negative over the positive,[7] contribute to a misperception that international law is often or mostly contested and violated. This is not true. International law scholar Louis Henkin famously made a point that no one contests: "[A]lmost all nations observe almost all principles of international law almost all of the time."[8]

Henken's claim should not be surprising. Since states create international agreements they want themselves, their citizens, national and foreign firms, and others governments to follow, of course they then have a great stake in promoting adherence to these agreements. Said more concretely, when states create, sign, and ratify international agreements to guide the exchange of diplomats and the navigation of international airspace and the high seas, why would they then intentionally break these agreements? When governments create agreements to address problems they share, such as the exchange of indicted criminals who escaped to another country; the illegal trafficking of peoples, drugs, weapons, and endangered species; the spread of terrorist financing; the desire for access to citizens arrested abroad; and the generation of processes to recover children illegally taken by relatives across borders, why would governments and judges then *not* mostly follow the agreements? And why wouldn't most new governments continue to do exactly what previous governments have done: run international postal, air, and shipping services; continue importing and exporting goods as before; keep existing contracts; and follow international rules on the entry and exit of diplomats and visitors, and so forth?

But of course, there is important controversy surrounding international law. This is because certain international laws are frequently contested, and because international law gives everyone license to criticize the behavior of others. International law by definition both guides and regulates what states can and cannot do. Thus, when a state arguably violates international law, by deciding to torture suspected terrorists, by violating their citizens' or a foreign visitor's human rights, by taking an action that targets foreign imports or investors in violation of an international economic agreement, or by pursuing their national interest in ways that illegally and adversely affect another country, a wide range of actors will publicly castigate this behavior as a violation of international law. Governments dislike criticism, especially from abroad. The public is thus regularly confronted with a set of acrimonious claims and counterclaims about violations of international law.

In its crux, my argument in this section asserts that international law can be complicated and messy, but it exists and it will be mostly followed. At the same time, unfortunately, isolated breakdowns in the respect for international law will persist. Major violations of international law are costly, so international legal violations may be more visible compared with the more localized domestic legal violations, which are perhaps even more prevalent. Still, because there is no alternative to international law as a tool of international governance, and because international interactions operate within a thick web of existing laws, most international law today will continue to be sustained and obeyed.

Have We Reached the End of the International Legal Order as We Have Known It?

International law has existed for hundreds of years, but historically, much of this law was not codified. Instead, international law was surmised from the customs and actions of nations, and from scholarly treatises that articulated international law. After World War I, during the short-lived reign of the League of Nations (1920–1935), international law became more codified. The Geneva Conventions, discussed earlier, were drafted at this time, but the drafting of the conventions involved few countries, and the conventions were ratified by few countries. The outbreak and atrocities of WWII suggested to many that the international law project was itself futile.[9] Others, however, drew from the disasters of the Great Depression and WWII a sense that global governance and international law project were more important than ever. Faith won out over cynicism. The United Nations (UN) was created from the ash heap generated by WWII, and the world then experienced a big bang of international institution and international law creation. Today, there are more than thirty-seven thousand active international organizations,[10] and two hundred thousand international agreements in force in the world.[11] The vast majority of these institutions and agreements were created since 1945.

The post-WWII rapid expansion of international institutions and international law is an artifact of US global hegemony. Multilateralism and international law were integral to US foreign policy following WWII, and the United States either instigated or supported the creation of today's most important international institutions and treaties. The US embraced multilateralism and international law to build political support for its leadership and to reassure other nations,[12] to transform US domestic political choices into global rules so that American firms would not be disadvantaged,[13] and to promote American values and soft power during the Cold War contest with the Soviet Union.[14] The global regime created by the United States is known as the liberal international order. The "liberal" part of the description comes from the commitment to multilateralism—a rules-based international system[15]—and from this system's substantive commitment to democracy, human rights, and free trade. Since the end of WWII, the United States has championed these values, notwithstanding the fact that newly independent countries were much more interested in protecting national sovereignty and promoting stability and economic development in expedient ways.

For the most part, European countries were happy partners in this endeavor. European countries' liberal orientation was genuine, but their investment in the American liberal order was especially strong because living next to the totalitarian Soviet Union reinforced the virtue of democracy and human rights. Also since many European governments retained historic connections throughout the developing world, they were committed to a (relatively) open trade regime.

Following the end of the Cold War, American and European leaders became global proselytizers for democracy, human rights, and market economics, providing and at times tying the provision of aid to the signing of legal agreements that promoted these values. The post–Cold War "Washington Consensus" of American, European, and international institutional leaders coalesced around a set of market-based policies, including but not limited to free trade.[16] Neoliberal economic policies have always been contentious, and they should not be conflated with the liberal international order.[17] Ideas associated with neoliberal economics provided a veneer for many post–Cold War international economic projects, but the core of the international order has always been a commitment to multilateralism and liberal values (individual rights, democracy, and the rule of law).

The international liberal order expanded in the post–Cold War era. Countries that had avoided committing to legal agreements associated with the West—to curry favor or avoid the opprobrium of the Soviet Union—rushed to join the West's international institutions.[18] The European Community became the European Union, and membership grew from twelve countries in 1988 to twenty-seven member states that are today bound by European Union law, interpreted and applied by the Court of Justice of the European Union. The Council of Europe grew from twenty-three states in 1988 to forty-seven members that today adhere to the European Convention on Human Rights, interpreted and applied by the European Court of Human Rights. The global trade regime also expanded. In 1988, the General Agreement on Tariffs and Trade (GATT) included ninety-four "contracting members" with variegated commitments to GATT trade rules. The GATT became the World Trade Organization (WTO) in 1994, growing in size to 164 countries. WTO members had to sign a "single undertaking," agreeing to all WTO trade rules. The core trade rules are largely the same as before, but new rules for trade in services and the protection of intellectual property were added, and the WTO's dispute settlement system became compulsory, so violations of WTO rules can now be adjudicated and noncompliance can trigger legal retaliation.[19] A number of additional international institutions and international legal agreements gained new members and new signatories in the post–Cold War era. Notable post–Cold War international law advances include the following:

- The United Nations Convention on the Law of the Seas became binding in 1994. There are currently 164 state parties.

- *Ad hoc* international criminal courts for the former Yugoslavia, Rwanda, Sierra Leone, and Cambodia were created in the 1990s. States negotiated the Rome Statute, which defined war crimes, crimes against humanity, and genocide, and created the International Criminal Court (ICC).
- State parties agreed to make permanent the Nuclear Non-Proliferation Treaty (see part IV for more).
- The Paris Climate Agreement became binding in 2016, with 195 state signatories (by June 2017, 153 states had ratified the agreement).

The expansion of the international liberal order has engendered various forms of backlash. Russian president Vladimir Putin's war in Ukraine was a reaction to the Ukrainian people's ouster of a pro-Russian regime, and their desire for closer relations with the European Union. The movement for an Islamic State of Iraq and the Levant (ISIL) represents an opportunistic fundamentalist insurgency operating in the political vacuum created by the US invasion of Iraq, a war ostensibly waged to further democracy in the Middle East. More recently, China responded to a legal ruling questioning its territorial claims in the South China Sea by joining Vladimir Putin to articulate a more sovereignty-friendly vision for international law.[20]

The election of Donald Trump as US president underscores how America's commitment to the international legal order it created is fragile. While President Trump likes to suggest that everything he does is a fundamental change from what came before, in reality, antiglobalist and noninterventionists voices have always been an active part of the American policy debates. These groups have won important victories along the way, but they have generally failed to turn back the tide of global internationalism. For example, in the 1950s, US-based opponents of the International Trade Organization managed to block the adoption of a fully drafted global trade agreement that the United States had championed. This victory slowed down but did not stop the construction of a global trading system via the GATT, which later became the WTO.[21] Concerned that international human rights agreements might render America's Jim Crow laws illegal, vocal critics within the United States slowed and blocked the domestic ratification of human rights agreements that the United States had championed.[22] And conservative Americans convinced President Ronald Reagan not to sign or ratify the UN Law of the Seas Treaty that President Nixon had fought so hard to achieve.

In sum, the United States has been both the champion of the international liberal order and a reluctant participant in it. American antiglobalist and noninterventionist sentiments have long kept the United States formally outside of a number of international agreements signed by the rest of the world—including the United Nations Convention on the Law of the Seas, the ICC's Rome Statute, the International Convention on the Rights of the Child, and the Convention on the Rights of Persons with Disabilities and now the Paris Agreement on Climate Change. The rest of the world has followed the internationalist side of American foreign policy, and when necessary they have gone on without the United States. In this respect, I expect the past to be a guide to the future.

What is different now, however, is that President Trump insists that the United States will neither lead nor necessarily honor its commitments. Even President Ronald Reagan—who withdrew from the United Nations Economic and Scientific Cultural Organization, withheld dues payments to the UN, refused to participate in the International Court of Justice's adjudication of the US mining of Nicaragua's harbors, and refused to sign the fully negotiated Law of the Seas Convention—did not suggest that America would not honor its commitments. Indeed, President Reagan promised to follow the Law of the Seas in every respect except its Seabed Authority, and he relied on multilateralism and international law to negotiate his differences with others.

Many years ago, John Ruggie argued that international regimes fuse power with a social purpose.[23] Power can wane or become separated from the social purpose, as occurred when Britain became unwilling to support the global economy during the interwar period, giving rise to the Great Depression and WWII. The international order then fell apart because there was no hegemon and no real commitment to the fledgling League of Nations. But, Ruggie argues, so long as the social purpose remains, momentum can keep the extant order in place. Ruggie's argument suggests that the liberal international order can survive President Trump's inward turn so long as the social purpose it represents continues to be shared by others. The liberal international order could not, however, survive if the broader commitment to the liberal order's social purpose also changed.

Ruggie's argument is why today's populist backlash is such a threat to the global international order. The current wave of populism is squarely focused on the global liberal order, including the international commitment to global economic integration, human rights, and democracy. It is surprising that the backlash has found such strength in the United States and the United Kingdom, bastions of political liberalism that profit greatly from the very system they are rejecting.[24] Yet, recent elections in France, the Netherlands, Germany, and the United Kingdom, and growing protests on the streets in Venezuela and Russia, suggest that there is a remaining base of support for the global liberal order.

So, will the past be a guide for the future? We need to think of the prolific creation international law following WWII as a response to the dearth of codified international law in 1945. Much of this post-WWII lawmaking codified existing practice, or it was about crafting international solutions to new problems generated by the dangers of a nuclear war, the increased movement of people and goods, and the increased interdependence in the world. Because multilaterally codified international law was, before 1945, greatly undersupplied, and given the rapid growth of the global economy, international lawmaking experienced a big bang. A decline in the rate of international lawmaking is to be expected because much of the work of the big bang has been accomplished.

It is perhaps too soon to say whether global political support for the social purpose behind the global international order is truly changing. A number of countries, cities, and American states are stepping into the void President Trump has created, standing ready to defend the global liberal order. The next two sections break down the component parts of this global liberal order.

First, I consider international legal efforts to promote human rights and international criminal accountability. These largely American- and European-led projects have always been the most contested parts of the international liberal order, both within the United States and around the world (with the exception of Western Europe). Next, I consider new issues of shared concern in international law that are not *per se* related to values associated with the West. I focus primarily on cybersecurity as an illustrative example, and briefly discuss two other emerging issues (the use of drones and global climate change) to explore whether the dynamics of international law creation are changing.

The Future of Internationally Defined Human Rights and War Crimes

Not wanting a repeat of the atrocities of WWII, advocates generated an international human rights system that was forward looking and aspirational. Its forward-looking nature means that human rights advocates will always ask for a higher human rights bar. Just as the problem of crime will never be fully eradicated, promoting human rights will always be a striving project that is greatly challenged by tyrants, war, and revolutionaries.

Critics point to atrocities committed around the world as evidence of the ineffectiveness of this project, and of international human rights and war crimes laws. While mass murders, and thus violations of human rights, make front page news, the prevalence of headlines is not itself an indication that the human rights project is failing. Instead, the measure must always be whether promoting human rights through international law tools positively affects their practices.

Complicating the debate, the social science evidence supporting claims for and against the effectiveness of international human rights and mass atrocities law is not straightforward. Depending on what scholars study, the findings vary. For example, when Oona Hathaway considered the human rights records of all states that had ratified human rights treaties, the correlation between ratifying a human rights treaty and respecting human rights in practice looked very weak.[25] But when Beth Simmons disaggregated states, considering states that already were protecting human rights, states where ratification was clearly cynical, and states that were democratizing and thus hoping to improve their human rights record, she found that treaty ratification had no effect on the first two "least likely" categories, but a meaningful and significant effect on the key target of agreements—democratizing countries.[26] She thus concludes that on balance, and over time, human rights treaties improve human rights records. In a different study, Zachary Elkins, Tom Ginsburg, and Beth Simmons find that the soft law Universal Declaration on Human Rights[27] had an indirect effect in that it fundamentally reshaped national constitutions, importing human rights provisions into these constitutions.[28]

But international law can also generate unintended consequences, leading to contradictory effects with respect to violence and human rights violations. Boaz Atzili finds that international law's prohibition of the use of force for territorial change has decreased interstate war, but eliminating foreign intervention and annexation as a permitted foreign policy tool has also unwittingly contributed to the continued existence of failing states that generate instability and sustained civil conflict.[29] Daniel Krcmaric finds that the global atrocities regime has decreased the trend of political leaders committing atrocities and then fleeing into exile. Many leaders stay and improve their human rights records. But since exile is no longer a viable political option, some leaders choose to keep fighting, contributing to an increase in atrocities.[30] The negative aspects of these findings lend weight to the critics' complaints about international human rights and mass atrocities laws.

Meanwhile, when scholars extend the historical scope of their study to the pre-WWII era, they see many changes which they attribute to international law. Oona Hathaway and Scott Shapiro suggest that prior to WWI, what they call the "Old World Order," war was a legitimate tool of international relations: "It is not just that the Old World Order sanctioned war; It relied on and rewarded it."[31] It is an unquestioned truth that interstate war has declined, and so has everyday violence. Steven Pinker observes that violent death and other forms of violence used to be a normal fact of life. Pinker notes that within certain communities—what he calls "honor societies"—domestic violence, the use of violence to settle disputes, and murder rates remain high. Nonetheless, violence and violent death have notably declined around the world, for a number of reasons, including international law.[32] Recent studies correlate societies that treat their weakest members (especially women and children) poorly with more violent domestic and foreign policies. This finding means that violating women's rights, which are regulated by both domestic and international law,[33] is associated with greater national and international violence.[34]

Human rights law and international law regulating war (humanitarian law, or law of armed conflict) contribute to the decline of violence because behavior that was acceptable in the past is now prohibited by widely endorsed international law. Personally, I put my faith in large-scale trends, and in balanced social science that documents declining human rights atrocities and violence. But the counternarrative, advocated by those who dislike international human rights law and supported by isolated and smaller-scale studies, continues to support a narrative that suggests that ratification of specific treaties is not associated with improved human rights records.[35]

The point of this review is to suggest that empirical evidence alone will not resolve the debate. The question under consideration in this chapter, however, is whether the international human rights project will survive if the US commitment to it wanes? This is a harder question to answer. On the one hand, momentum favors continuation. Progress may slow, but international human rights treaties are unlikely to go away or be "unsigned" because few politicians will campaign on an anti–human rights platform. Moreover, the natural response to the atrocities of groups such as the ISIL and to violations by a political regime is to reinforce a commitment to human rights once the conflict wanes or the government leaves office.

Today, most constitutions around the world promise to respect individual rights. Constitutional provisions are backed by domestic statutes that give legal meaning to rights-promoting provisions. This means that the international human rights project has become a national human rights project. There are also networks of National Human Rights Institutions,[36] which promote best practices, monitor state compliance with international agreements, and, in some cases, investigate, advertise, and resolve human rights complaints. The international human rights project has also generated numerous human rights advocacy groups,[37] which, together with National Human Rights Institutions, create an infrastructure of support for the international human rights project.

This discussion has focused mostly on human rights as they are monitored internationally, but also entrenched and enforced within and by national systems. This is how the international human rights and mass atrocities systems are supposed to work. Human rights treaties and the ICC's Rome Statute create legal obligations with no statute of limitations, generating binding international and domestic laws with domestic (and for some countries, international) enforcement mechanisms. National enforcement is then transnationally linked, so if a perpetrator of an atrocity moves across borders, law enforcement can follow. In this respect, it is noteworthy that while governments complain that their critics are wrong, and that international criticism violates national sovereignty, no effort is being made to weaken the jurisdiction of states to prosecute foreigners for war crimes and human rights violations committed abroad.

Setbacks are a political fact of life. But the national human rights project will end only when the advocates for human rights give up. This fact makes me optimistic. Consider the case of Hissene Habré, a violent dictator who ruled Chad from 1982 through 1990. Habré went into exile and was protected by Senegal's government for a time. For many years, it looked like Habré had overcome his bloody record. But Habré's victims never gave up, raising legal cases in Senegal and Belgium, which then also went to international venues. In July 2012, the International Court of Justice ruled that Senegal had to either immediately prosecute Habré or extradite him to Belgium for prosecution. Seventeen years after he fled Chad, Habré was convicted and imprisoned in Senegal (and thus not by the ICC).

Prosecuting heads of states remains difficult; lower-level officials are easier to catch and prosecute. Meanwhile, the legal infrastructure for pursuit and accountability now exists. In this respect, the global human rights project has achieved victories that will be enduring. Indeed, it is somewhat surprising that the vision articulated during The Hague Peace Conferences—a vision of a world where waging war was illegal, where global humanitarian law existed, and where disputes would be resolved either diplomatically or through arbitration or litigation—has been largely realized.[38] This outcome is surprising because this vision was seen as utopian when it was first articulated; it failed spectacularly in the 1930s; and the combination of the Cold War and liberation movements in the developing world seemed to have made progress in the international legal order all but impossible. Yet this vision is, in essence, the liberal international order that the United States championed and the world built.

New Frontiers for International Law: Cybersecurity, Drones, and Climate Change

This section continues the investigation of how a decline in US leadership might affect international law, examining the international law project of using international law to regulate war, and the rising issue of climate change. Change disrupts, and opportunists will jump into any political vacuum that is created. We should expect international disrupters to explore what they can get away with given the unpredictability and noncommittal stance of the Trump administration. Indeed, we are already witnessing increased conflict in the world, which could easily spill into unintended wars and increasing violence.

A short-term uptick does not, however, mean that the system is permanently upended. Nearly every US president evolves to a position that recognizes that international stability is good, and that following international law is the path that generates the least resistance. Right now, President Trump mainly appears to dislike agreements that he did not negotiate. He operates on the assumption that he can get a better deal, and he presumes that others will be willing to reopen past agreements. There is a lot about the current international set of legal rules that different states dislike. In this respect, many political leaders are likely to readily profess their openness to changing existing agreements. But the Trump administration is likely to find that American Presidents and diplomats have always negotiated with a keen eye toward advancing American interests. It may not be possible to draft a new agreement that creates an even greater advantage for American firms and citizens. For some international agreements, there is room for updates and improvements that all will favor. Overall, however, a status quo bias greatly favors existing international law and the international liberal order.

Meanwhile, international problems requiring coordinated responses will continue to arise. Compared to using force, aid, bribery, and coercion, it is always more cost-effective, successful, and sustainable when countries and actors voluntarily come together to articulate collective goals and to jointly craft solutions. For this reason, international law will remain the best political tool in the diplomat's toolbox to address international problems.

The first part of this chapter explained that international solutions do not need to take the form of binding international treaties.[39] Soft law has always been an instrument of international law, one that exists alongside more informal systems of norms that are backed by coalitions of the willing. Moreover collective solutions can be crafted by actors other than heads of state. All of these pathways—nonbinding agreements, pledges created by private actors, and draft treaties awaiting ratification—plant seeds that can grow into future international law.

International law will continue to develop in a similar fashion, because international problems will not go away. One new issue—cybersecurity—offers an example of how this process is working. Cyberspace is a global entity; territorial states can block their citizen's access to the cybersphere, but they cannot regulate or control the cybersphere. Meanwhile, breaches in cybersecurity have moved from annoying to epic and transnational in their origin and scale. The impetus for transnational cybersecurity protocols is coming from firms, hospitals, electricity providers, and government agencies trying to deal with proliferating breaches of cybersecurity, including thefts of data, interference in the operating systems, pirate viruses, and spying by economic and political competitors. While most hackers and criminals fail in their objectives, it is only a matter of time until they succeed. Right now, firms, norm entrepreneurs, and states are offering competing solutions to address these problems, and governments are adopting solutions that may later be revised.[40] In other words, cybersecurity remains an area governed by norms and soft law. But once states more clearly articulate their expectations of themselves and others by drafting domestic statutes that prohibit or criminalize certain behaviors, sunk costs will be generated. Domestic laws criminalizing cyber theft provide a legal basis to extradite cyber criminals,[41] and provide indicators of emerging international customary law. Once practices converge among a large number of states, support for creating international institutions to track cybercrime will grow. These are the traditional steps through which customary international law emerges and then becomes codified. Martha Finnemore and Duncan Hollis emphasize that none of these steps happen automatically. The journey toward norm creation involves persuasion, socialization, and entrenchment, and this journey will define the content of the norms that eventually emerge. But the authors reject the idea that the processes shaping the emergent transnational cybersecurity regime are fundamentally different from what we have seen before.

The issues of drones and climate change have somewhat different dynamics, but here too one can find similarities in how international law is developing. International law bans the use of force in all situations except self-defense or a collective response to aggression. The weapons used to deliver destruction tend not to be regulated, with the important exceptions of chemical, biological, and nuclear weapons. The United States uses drone technology for targeted assassinations. Assassination may violate US and international law, but the use of drones as a tool of assassination is not itself illegal.

The situation of drones is similar to that of nuclear weapons. In 1945, the United States alone had a nuclear weapons capability. Within twenty years, five countries had nuclear capabilities: the United States, the Soviet Union, the United Kingdom, France, and China. In 1968, recognizing the dangers of nuclear proliferation, these five countries created a regime that is widely credited with slowing the spread of nuclear weapons. At its origins, the nonproliferation regime was temporary and had a limited membership. Today, the nonproliferation treaty is the most successful global arms control treaty, overseen by a permanent international agency (the International Atomic Energy Agency), with 190 state parties that convene every five years to discuss disarmament, nonproliferation, and the peaceful uses of nuclear energy.

Similar to the experience with nuclear proliferation, the United States' technological advantage contributes to its unwillingness to articulate a set of usage rules that might undercut its development of a weapon that provides the American military with a tactical advantage. Also similar, there is now a global race to match the US drone capability.[42] Meanwhile, because drones (like nuclear power) are a technology with numerous peaceful and beneficial uses, the development of drone technology will proceed. One can easily imagine how drones created for peaceful purposes can be militarized, spreading destruction, especially if drones can be based or commandeered anywhere.

Different, however, is that the United States is regularly deploying drones, whereas the United States has not used nuclear weapons since the end of WWII. Populations that experience regular drone attacks are protesting a rampage of terror from the sky. Their complaints are yet to be heeded, in large part because the victims of drone attacks tend to be marginalized populations in weak states. Should military drone capacity evolve and spread, we could begin to see pressure to regulate the use of drones as a tool of war.

Pressure will likely be insufficient so long as the United States is greatly advantaged, and so long as drone strikes do not terrorize the populations of powerful countries. American hubris in the capabilities of drones could be setting norms that others will use as they attack US forces and American territory (embassies, consulates, overseas territories, and even US territory). In refusing to discuss or regulate its own use of drones, the United States is ceding the opportunity to define a set of rules that it would like others to be held to. Whereas the nonproliferation treaty helped to stem the spread of nuclear weapons, the lack of drone regulation may accelerate the spread of armed drone capability, forever changing the face of modern war. Thus with respect to drones, we see an over-time consistent trend of powerful states being adverse to international law that might undercut their military advantage. The difference is that drone technology can more easily spread to state and nonstate militias.

The final new international legal frontier concerns climate change. There are already many treaties to manage man's usage of the biosphere. International agreements exist to limit the harvesting endangered fisheries and the transborder marketing of endangered species.[43] Bilateral and multilateral treaties coordinate usage of shared rivers and watersheds, and the International Seabed Authority oversees the mining of the deep seas. International agreements have also been a tool used to phase out domestic and global usage of ozone-depleting products.[44] These international initiatives are but a small part of a larger emerging regime complex—a set of overlapping and nonhierarchical rules—designed to address the problem of climate change.[45]

This sort of piecemeal international regulatory approach is insufficient, however, to deal with the growing threat of climate change. For numerous reasons, the challenge of climate change is hard to tackle. The change needed to stop climate change is of a much larger scale; stopping climate change requires altering behavior that is purely domestic in its origin and immediate impact; and the global distributional costs and effects of limiting carbon usage are concentrated, significant, and differentially distributed. All of these factors contribute to the current approach of creating nonbinding global pledges, some regional agreements, but little global hard international law. Transformation will come with a change in public attitudes toward cheap energy and toward politicians who prioritize carbon producers. This change exists right now at local levels, leading cities and state legislatures to adopt the policies that heads of state may, for political reasons, shun.

Of these three international law frontiers—cybersecurity, drones, and climate change—I expect the issue of cybersecurity to be the first one addressed via international law. First efforts will target nonstate actors, which means that we can expect that states will continue to enhance their cyber warfare and drone capabilities unimpeded by international legal commitments. Since management of armed forces tends to be nationally based, highly confidential, and a core national interest, significant and widespread damage will need to accrue before international law develops.

With respect to climate change, a lack of US support may slow the progress of international law. But just as the international Law of the Sea came into force despite the political opposition in the US Congress, implementation of the Paris Climate Agreement will go ahead with the support of many countries. This agreement will also be implemented by many American cities and states and by firms that adapt their products to fit the demands of a global market concerned about climate change.

Conclusion: Whither the (International) Rule of Law?

The global liberal order represents a surprising realization of The Hague Peace Conference vision. According to Christian Reus Smit, this vision succeeded because it built on the traditions that animated the American and French Revolutions, replacing absolutist right with the "self-evident" truth that "all men are created equal, that they are endowed by their Creator with certain unalienable Rights, that among these are Life, Liberty and the pursuit of Happiness. — That to secure these rights, Governments are instituted among Men, deriving their just powers from the consent of the governed."[46]

The primary political question of the day is whether populations are willing to give up on democracy, individual rights, and the rule of law. A related question is whether populations will tolerate a reversion to a political system that suppresses women's rights. The current retrenchment of women's rights, an intentional plank of ISIL strategy and a core element of modern populist and conservative movements, matters because suppressing women's rights is a hallmark of an honor society and a gateway to tolerating and even encouraging domestic violence, both of which are associated with decreasing human rights and rising international violence.

Throughout this chapter, I have put the subject of democracy to the side. Democracy cannot survive without the rule of law. In this respect, the willingness of populist leaders to denigrate and undermine the rule of law is a genuine threat to the future of democracy in specific countries. But while democracy cannot survive without the rule of law, the rule of law can exist without democracy.[47]

International law will endure as the key language and primary medium of international relations because of the presumed political and moral superiority of the rule of law; because the rule of law is associated with fundamental human values such as peace, security, economic vitality, and personal and political accountability;[48] and because the alternatives to a system of global governance governed by international law are less attractive. Popular support for international law can decline, however, if the deeply and widely shared belief in the political and moral superiority of the rule of law and legality wanes. I hope that this will not occur. I hope that populations continue to prefer governments that adhere to publicly pronounced, preexisting laws that are crafted through an accepted political process. So long as legality (the quality of being in accordance with the law) provides a first-cut legitimating justification, international law will remain a force in international relations.

But institutions are more fragile than most people believe. For the average person, the rule of law is preferable and essential. But individuals who profit from corruption and leaders who rely on fear to legitimate their rule have much to lose from the rule of law. These actors work to undermine institutions that check them, including independent judges, free elections, and the media.

Because international law draws its respect from the faith that people put in the rule of law, and because there really is no alternative for a just global order, international law will be respected by legitimate governments, and used to challenge questionable policies and governments. Because powerful actors do not like criticism or checks on their power, international law will remain a popular target of authoritarian political wrath.

But readers should not be fooled. So long as people value the rule of law, Louis Henken's famous adage remains true: "[A]lmost all nations observe almost all principles of international law almost all of the time." Should this statement ever fail to be true, the world will have to face a greater problem than a declining desire to create or abide by international law.

Notes

1 See *International Law: 100 Ways It Shapes Our Lives*, American Society of International Law. Available at https://www.asil.org/education/100-ways.
2 The difference between hard and soft law can be confusing because one cannot distinguish hard from soft international law based on the name of the agreement, and a treaty can include both soft and hard law aspects. Equally confusing is that it not clear whether hard international law is more effective than soft international law. For a discussion of how hard and soft international law are politically influential, see Kenneth Abbott and Duncan Snidal, "Hard and Soft Law in International Governance," *International Organization* 54, no. 3 (2000): 421–456; Kenneth Abbott and Duncan Snidal, "Pathways to International Cooperation," in *The Impact of International Law on International Cooperation*, Eyal Benvenisti and Moshe Hirsch, eds. (Cambridge: Cambridge University Press, 2003), 50–84.
3 The Paris Agreement has been ratified by many countries, and it has "entered into force," but its provisions take the form of nonbinding declarations of goals and self-commitments. To learn more, see http://unfccc.int/paris_agreement/items/9485.php.
4 A brief overview and history of the Geneva Conventions is available at the Legal Information Institute. See https://www.law.cornell.edu/wex/geneva_conventions.
5 The Assembly's definition has been used in rulings by international courts, and it has shaped debates regarding the ICC's future jurisdiction, which will soon include the crime of aggression. Dapo Akande and Antonios Tzanakopoulos see the inclusion of aggression in the ICC's

jurisdiction as likely to affect international law on state responsibility as well, hardening international law regarding the crime of aggression. See Dapo Akande and Antonios Tzanakopoulos, "The Crime of Aggression in the ICC and State Responsibility," *Harvard International Law Journal*, April 11, 2017. Available at http://www.harvardilj.org/2017/04/the-crime-of-aggression-in-the-icc-and-state-responsibility/.

[6] Barbara Koremenos investigates these different design features of international law in Barbara Koremenos, *The Continent of International Law* (Cambridge: Cambridge University Press, 2016).

[7] Psychologists have found that people have a greater sensitivity to negative news compared with positive news. See Hara Estroff Marano, "Our Brain's Negative Bias," *Psychology Today*, June 20, 2016. Available at https://www.psychologytoday.com/articles/200306/our-brains-negative-bias.

[8] Louis Henkin, *How Nations Behave* (New York: Columbia University Press, 1979), 47.

[9] This was the view of early international relations realists. See Edward Hallett Carr, *The Twenty Years' Crisis, 1919–1939; an Introduction to the Study of International Relations* (London: Macmillan, 1940).

[10] See https://www.uia.org/yearbook?qt-yb_intl_orgs=3#yearbook_pages-page_yb_faq-0.

[11] Oona Hathaway and Scott J. Shapiro, *The Internationalists* (New York: Simon & Schuster, 2017), xviii.

[12] G. John Ikenberry, *After Victory Institutions, Strategic Restraint, and the Rebuilding of Order after Major Wars* (Princeton, NJ: Princeton University Press, 2001).

[13] Anne-Marie Burley, "Regulating the World: Multilateralism, International Law, and the Projection of the New Deal Regulatory State," in *Multilateralism Matters*, John Ruggie, ed. (New York: Columbia University Press, 1993), 125–156.

[14] Joseph S. Nye, "Public Diplomacy and Soft Power," *The Annals of the American Academy of Political and Social Science* 616 (2008): 94–109. doi:10.1177/0002716207311699.

[15] John Ruggie, "Multilateralism: The Anatomy of an Institution," in *Multilateralism Matters*, John Ruggie, ed. (New York: Columbia University Press, 1993), 3–47.

[16] John Williamson, "What Washington Means by Policy Reform," in *Latin American Adjustment: How Much Has Happened*, John Williamson, ed. (Washington, DC: Institute for International Economics, 1990).

[17] The terms "neoliberal" and "liberal," have become political hot-potatoes, sowing popular confusion. Liberalism is a long-standing political tradition associated with individual rights, limited government, political and legal checks on the exercise of government power, and the rule of law. This is the tradition associated with the liberal international order. Both liberalism and neoliberalism embrace private property as a cornerstone individual right, but neoliberalism elevates the protection of private property over other public goals, and it presumes that market-based solutions will inevitably be superior to solutions crafted by government. In the 1990s, neoliberalism was heavily pushed by the same countries that have long promoted the liberal international order. Hypermarket neoliberalism has become the fulcrum of criticism in the developing world and among the political left, and the economic inequality that neoliberal policies have created are fueling the political backlash against globalization.

[18] Karen J. Alter, "The Evolving International Judiciary," *Annual Review of Law and Social Science* 7 (2011): 387–415.

[19] These figures were compiled by the author. In my book *The New Terrain of International Law: Courts, Politics, Rights,* I discuss how the end of the Cold War put into motion a series of political changes in the United States, Europe, and at a global level that led to the proliferation of international courts and international legal rulings, from six permanent international courts that had collectively issued 3,276 binding rulings by 1989 to twenty-five operational international courts that as of 2015 had collectively issued over 49,000 legal rulings. See Karen J. Alter, *The New Terrain of International Law: Courts, Politics, Rights* (Princeton, NJ: Princeton University Press, 2014), Chapter 4. The litigation data in my book ended in 2011. I have updated the data through 2015 for this chapter.

[20] See Kenneth Anderson, "Text of the Russia-China Joint Declaration on Promotion and Principles of International Law," *Lawfare*, July 7, 2016. Available at https://www.lawfareblog.com/text-russia-china-joint-declaration-promotion-and-principles-international-law.

21 John H. Barton, Judith H. Goldstein, Timothy Edward Josling, and Richard H. Steinberg, *The Evolution of the Trade Regime* (Princeton, NJ: Princeton University Press, 2006).

22 Elizabeth Borgwardt, *A New Deal for the World: America's Vision for Human Rights* (Cambridge, MA: Belknap Press of Harvard University Press, 2005).

23 John Ruggie, "International Regimes, Transactions and Change: Embedded Liberalism in the Postwar Economic Order," in *International Regimes*, Stephen Krasner, ed. (Ithaca, NY: Cornell University Press, 1983), 195–232.

24 We must remember, however, that voter turnout was only 58 percent in the 2016 election (about the same as in 2012), and that President Trump lost the American popular vote by almost 2.9 million votes (2.1 percent)—only two other US presidents were elected with a smaller percentage of the votes than President Trump. See Carl Bialik, "No, Voter Turnout Wasn't Way Down from 2012," *FiveThirtyEight*, November 15, 2016. Available at https://fivethirtyeight.com/features/no-voter-turnout-wasnt-way-down-from-2012/; and Gregory Krieg, "It's Official: Clinton Swamps Trump in Popular Vote," *CNN*, December 22, 2016. Available at http://www.cnn.com/2016/12/21/politics/donald-trump-hillary-clinton-popular-vote-final-count/index.html.

25 Oona Hathaway, "Do Treaties Make a Difference? Human Rights Law and the Problem of Compliance," *Yale Law Journal* 111 (2002): 1935–2042. A number of studies replicate these findings, focusing on a single treaty or a single legal provision.

26 Beth Simmons, *Mobilizing for Human Rights: International Law in Domestic Politics* (Cambridge: Cambridge University Press, 2009).

27 Adopted by the United Nations, December 10, 1948.

28 Zachary Elkins, Thomas Ginsburg, and Beth Simmons, "Getting to Rights: Treaty Ratification, Constitutional Convergence, and Human Rights Practices," *Harvard International Law Journal* 54, no. 1 (2013): 61–94.

29 Boaz Atzili, *Good Fences, Bad Neighbors: Border Fixity and International Conflict* (Chicago and London: University of Chicago Press, 2012).

30 Daniel Krcmaric, "Dilemmas of Globalized Justice: International Criminal Accountability, the Exile Option, and Civil Conflict" (forthcoming).

31 Hathaway and Shapiro, *The Internationalists*, xvii.

32 Steven Pinker, *The Better Angels of Our Nature: The Decline of Violence in History and Its Causes* (London: Allen Lane, 2011).

33 See Convention on the Elimination of All Forms of Discrimination against Women (ratified by 189 countries) and the Convention on the Rights of the Child (http://www.ohchr.org/EN/ProfessionalInterest/Pages/CRC.aspx) (ratified by 195 countries).

34 Pinker notes that "honor societies" are as violent as ever (Pinker, *The Better Angels of Our Nature*, 686–689). His findings draw on and are deepened by the work of Valerie Hudson, who shows a link between violence against women and a broad range of behaviors that affect world peace (Valerie M. Hudson, *Sex and World Peace* [New York: Columbia University Press, 2012]).

35 See, e.g., Eric A. Posner, *The Twilight of Human Rights Law* (Oxford: Oxford University Press, 2014).

36 These nationally based institutions are coordinated and networked via the United Nations Human Rights Office of the High Commissioner. See http://www.ohchr.org/EN/Countries/NHRI/Pages/NHRIMain.aspx.

37 Margaret E. Keck and Kathryn Sikkink, *Activists beyond Borders: Advocacy Networks in International Politics* (Ithaca, NY: Cornell University Press, 1998).

38 Christian Reus-Smit, "The Constitutional Structure of International Society and the Nature of Fundamental Institutions," *International Organization* 51, no. 4 (1997): 555–589.

39 Abbott and Snidal, "Pathways to International Cooperation."

40 Martha Finnemore and Duncan B. Hollis, "Constructing Norms for Global Cybersecurity," *American Journal of International Law* 110 (2017): 425–479.

41 Extradition requires double criminality, meaning the behavior must be considered a crime in the extraditing and the receiving state.

42 See "The Unstoppable Spread of Armed Drones," *Stratfor*, October 25, 2016. Available at https://worldview.stratfor.com/article/unstoppable-spread-of-armed-drones.

43 Since fish do not respect borders, fisheries agreements are side-agreements under the Law of the Seas Convention. Bilateral and regional fisheries agreements also exist. In addition, a separate regime governs whaling. The monitoring of endangered land-based species is overseen by the Secretariat of the Convention on International Trade in Endangered Species of Wild Fauna and Flora.

44 The Montreal Protocol, often cited as the single most effective global environmental agreement, orchestrated the phase-out of chlorofluorocarbons. In 2016, a new agreement replicated the format of the Montreal Protocol to oversee the phase-out of hydrofluorocarbons. See Warren Cornwall, "Nations Sign Major Agreement to Curb Warming Chemicals Used for Air Conditioning," Science, October 15, 2016. Available at http://www.sciencemag.org/news/2016/10/nations-sign-major-deal-curb-warming-chemicals-used-air-conditioning.

45 Robert O. Keohane and David G. Victor, "The Regime Complex for Climate Change," Perspectives on Politics 9, no. 1 (2011): 7–23.

46 This history of the United States Declaration of Independence is discussed in Christian Reus-Smit, The Moral Purpose of the State: Culture, Social Identity and Institutional Rationality in International Relations (Princeton, NJ: Princeton University Press, 1999), 127–154.

47 This understanding is reflected in a 2012 book that looks at international and transnational efforts to promote the rule of law. See Michael Zürn, André Nollkaemper, and R. P. Peerenboom, Rule of Law Dynamics: In an Era of International and Transnational Governance (Cambridge and New York: Cambridge University Press, 2012).

48 Stephan Haggard, Andrew Macintyre, and Lydia Tiede, "The Rule of Law and Economic Development," Annual Review of Political Science 11, no. 1 (2008): 205–234. doi:10.1146/annurev.polisci.10.081205.100244; John K. M. Ohnesorge, "The Rule of Law," Annual Review of Law and Social Science 3 (2007): 99–114; Guillermo O'Donnell, "The Quality of Democracy: Why the Rule of Law Matters," Journal of Democracy 15, no. 4 (2004): 32–46; John Ferejohn and Pasquale Pasquino, "Rule of Democracy and Rule of Law," in Democracy and the Rule of Law, Jose Maria Maravall and Adam Przeworski, eds. (Cambridge: Cambridge University Press, 2003), 242–259; Gary Goertz, The Puzzle of Peace: The Evolution of Peace in the International System, Paul F. Diehl and Alexandru Balas, eds. (New York: Oxford University Press, 2016).

CHAPTER 3

Revitalizing the International Response to Forced Migration
Principles and Policies for the "New Normal"
T. Alexander Aleinikoff

The pictures are graphic and heart-rending; the numbers beyond easy comprehension. The first two decades of the twenty-first century have produced crises of persons forced from their homes by violence and conflict at a scale not seen since the middle of the last century. New emergencies pile on top of long-standing unresolved situations of displacement, with the total number of forced migration now exceeding sixty-five million people.[1] This is the *new normal*—one for which the international legal instruments and institutions established just after World War II (WWII) are no longer "fit for purpose." The future appears no brighter. In coming years, flows due to natural disasters and climate change are predicted to exceed those currently caused by conflict.

The boats arriving in Europe—as well as the boats sinking in the Mediterranean and Aegean—occasioned demands that "something must be done" and led to several international summits in 2016 and an instruction from the United Nations General Assembly (GA) to the United Nations High Commissioner for Refugees (UNHCR) to draft a Global Compact on Refugees by 2018. The challenges that threaten to overwhelm the international system, however, began long before, and the most intractable aspects of the problem are present not in Europe but rather reside in the Global South, where the vast number of forced migrants are located.

Origins of the Refugee Protection System

The international refugee regime we see today grew from *ad hoc* efforts in the early twentieth century[2] and international organizations created during and just after WWII. With more than a million persons still displaced in Europe and elsewhere several years after the end of the War, the (newly minted) GA established the Office of the High Commissioner for Refugees in 1950 and called for the drafting of a general convention on refugees. A year later, the Convention Relating to the Status of Refugees was adopted in Geneva.

The modern international refugee regime is a partnership of member states and international organizations, based on the norms of the Convention. The Convention (and its 1967 Protocol)—now with more than 150 state members[3]—provides a definition of "refugee" and establishes a robust set of rights for refugees that state parties commit to protect. Central among these is the right not to be returned to a state that will persecute a refugee (the right to *non-refoulement*). The Convention, however, establishes no international body for adjudicating refugee claims or allocating state responsibilities necessary for the system's success. The fundamental responsibilities of the system fall to member states, who are charged with the recognition of refugees and guaranteeing their rights, and who are expected to provide funds to UNHCR[4] and other international organizations and nongovernmental organizations (NGOs). Under the GA statute, the High Commissioner is charged with "providing international protection," "seeking permanent solutions," and "supervising [the] application" of international conventions relating to refugees[5]; but UNHCR can undertake activities only where states have authorized them to be present.

Implicit in the Refugee Convention are compromises that mediate the pursuit concerns of humanitarian relief and rights for the displaced and preservation of state control over the entry of noncitizens. The document establishes no right to enter a state to claim asylum—its key guarantee is the right not to be returned. Nor does it provide an international mechanism for enforcing Convention rights—leaving enforcement to (the vagaries of) the domestic laws of hosting states. The Convention also fails to guarantee a right to a solution (local integration or resettlement) or to commit signatory states to any formal system of international burden-sharing.

Despite these embedded and structural limitations, refugee protection and assistance have grown considerably as the international system has evolved. Most significantly, persons fleeing civil disorder and violence generally are recognized as refugees (or can benefit from some other form of international or domestic protection) even if they do not come within the specific language of the Convention's definition (which requires a well-founded fear of persecution on account of race, religion, nationality, political opinion, or membership in a particular social group).[6] Thus, virtually all Syrians who have fled the violence in their home country receive international protection without specifically demonstrating that they or groups they belong to have been targeted for persecution. Furthermore, legal scholars maintain that the norm of *non-refoulement* has attained the status of customary international law, with the result that it binds all states—even those who are not signatories to the Convention or the Protocol.[7] As to assistance, the resources devoted to relief for displaced persons have grown exponentially. UNHCR's expenditures in 1971 (twenty years after the agency's establishment) were just $9 million; ten years later, they had increased to nearly $500 million; in 1992, they passed the $1 billion level, and by 2015, they had exceeded $3 billion annually.

How the Current System Is Broken

The goal of the international refugee regime is to provide safety to those forced to flee over international borders, to help them rebuild their lives and to find solutions that will mean that they are no longer refugees. Thus, to function adequately (and as intended), the international system requires (1) *asylum space*—a cross-border place for persons fleeing persecution (coupled with a right not to be returned), (2) *refugee rights*—to protect rights lost in being a refugee and to help refugees attain self-reliance and begin to rebuild their lives, (3) *solutions*—to "reattach" refugees to political communities that provide membership and the rights of citizenship, and (4) *international cooperation*—in responding to, funding, and resolving refugee situations.

Today, each of these elements of a successful regime is under severe pressure. The central challenges include the following.

Growing Denials of Access

As noted above, neither the Refugee Convention nor other international law instruments establish a right to enter a country to apply for asylum. But refugee protection cannot exist if states do not permit access; and in this regard, the international system has been largely successful: states neighboring countries in conflict have generally left their borders open to persons fleeing violence. Thus, South Sudanese refugees have found safe haven in Uganda, Sudan, and Ethiopia; Nigerians fleeing Boko Haram have been accepted into Cameroon and Chad; refugees from Mali have freely entered Niger, Algeria, and Burkina Faso. There are, however, a growing number of examples of the restriction of asylum space. Most significantly, the countries bordering Syria (Jordan, Lebanon, Turkey, Iraq)—after accepting more than four million refugees—have now largely closed their borders to further flows. States not contiguous with refugee-producing countries have adopted policies of deterrence, with the European Union's (EU's) response to Syrian and other asylum seekers being the most publicized today. The United States (regarding forced migrants from the Northern Triangle countries), Australia (to stop boats carrying asylum seekers from Bangladesh, Burma, and elsewhere), Israel (building a wall and opening a detention center directed at asylum seekers from Northern Africa), and non-EU European states (e.g., Macedonia) have all adopted policies and practices aimed at denying asylum space to putative refugees.[8]

Denial of Rights

Despite the fact that the Refugee Convention guarantees a rich set of human rights, some of the largest refugee-hosting states (Pakistan, Thailand, Lebanon, Jordan[9]) are not signatories to the Convention. This does not necessarily render refugees rightless, as they may receive protections under domestic law; but inevitably, those protections are less robust than those guaranteed by the Convention. And ratification of the Convention is hardly a guarantee that a state will respect its rights-granting provisions. Refugees are routinely denied the right to work or start businesses and excluded from labor law protections and social safety net programs; refugee children are often excluded from schools; states frequently restrict the right to free movement—all in contravention of international law. States justify these restrictions because of perceptions that refugees would take jobs from citizens and would overburden social protection programs that already struggle to meet the needs of the local communities.

Long-Term Refugee Status/Lack of Solutions

The international refugee regime never contemplated that persons would remain in refugee status for long periods of time. Yet solutions to refugee situations have declined dramatically in recent years. Out of more than sixteen million refugees worldwide,[10] only 552,200 returned to their home states in 2016.[11] Refugee resettlement totaled fewer than 200,000 for 2016, and formal local integration has been negligible for a number of years. Quite simply, protracted refugee status is now the rule, not the exception. The impacts of protracted refugee situations on refugees—particularly refugee children—are obvious,[12] as are the consequences for hosting states.

No Framework for Responsibility-Sharing

The preamble to the Refugee Convention states that "a satisfactory solution" to refugee situations "cannot . . . be achieved without international co-operation." However, it provides no guidance on how such cooperation should be organized or proceed. A form of practice has emerged over the past number of decades that approximates a framework for responsibility-sharing, with donor states supporting multilateral organizations (e.g., UNHCR, United Nations Children's Fund [UNICEF], World Food Programme [WFP], International Office on Migration) and NGOs (such as Save the Children, Oxfam, International Rescue Committee) involved in refugee operations[13] and also providing direct support to hosting states. A relatively small number of states participate in UNHCR's resettlement process. States may also cooperate at a regional level.[14] But the overall paucity of solutions and shortfalls in funding make clear the inadequacies of the informal system of burden-sharing.

Rise of Xenophobia Makes Protection Rights and Achievement of Solutions Difficult

Most European states and developed states elsewhere have witnessed the rise of far-right/populist political movements that have fundamentally altered the domestic discourse on refugees. Countries generally quite favorable to refugee relief and admissions in the past have adopted tough new measures, constructing border fences, limiting admissions, changing rules for recognizing refugees, and restricting refugee rights. One of President Trump's first actions in office was to freeze the US refugee admissions program and cut the number of refugees to be resettled in the United States by more than half (as of this writing, these measures have been partially put on hold by judicial decisions).

Together, these elements have coalesced to seriously undermine the ability of the international refugee system to deliver on its basic goals. Denials of access mean that people will be forced to reside in unsafe places. Denials of refugee rights, coupled with a lack of solutions, produce refugee dependency (what I have termed elsewhere a "second exile"[15]). The lack of an adequate responsibility-sharing framework contributes to all these challenges: states are less likely to keep borders open and countries of first asylum are less likely to recognize refugee rights if other states do not contribute to refugee assistance and the resolution of situations of displacement. A system seen as unresponsive and out of control fans the flames of xenophobia, which in turn can restrict political will to expand funding, resettlement, and other programs aimed at ameliorating the current deficiencies.

What Is to Be Done?

Simply making the system function as it was intended to is, in the current climate, daunting. But even this will not be enough, if—as will be suggested—the "refugee problem" is of a different scope and character than it was when the founding documents of the international regime were adopted.

Making the System Work as It Was Intended To

A program to get the international refugee system back on track would include the following:

- affirming state commitments under the Convention and Protocol and seeking additional ratifications;
- ensuring that borders remain open to asylum seekers and that the principle of *non-refoulement* is rigorously respected;
- increasing funding for refugee assistance in countries of first asylum;
- increasing—and coordinating—development assistance to hosting states;
- making progress on solutions, through support for voluntary returns and a significant increase in resettlement;
- launching antixenophobia campaigns worldwide and in targeted states; and
- initiating a legal campaign to enforce refugee rights, focusing on rights guaranteed by the Refugee Convention (such as freedom of movement, right to work, and right to education).

Changes for the Coming World

The measures just described are *the minimum necessary* for a serious effort to rescue the *current* international system of refugee protection. But given the "new normal" in global forced migration, ensuring that the original system is functioning well is, it may be asserted, too unambitious a goal. It would be like rebuilding urban or highway infrastructure intended for living patterns and means of transportation of the last century. The features of today's world that make last century's solutions less efficacious include the following:

- an anticipated regular or increasing flow of forced migrants (instead of episodic and decreasing flows, as seen from the mid-1990s to about 2010);
- the rise and persistence of protracted refugee situations;
- the increase in the number of noncamp refugees;
- causes of forced migration not foreseen by the original legal instruments, including climate change and threats from gangs and organized crime;
- far larger budget requests from multilateral organizations;
- concerns about international terrorism;
- concerns about the demographic impact of significant refugee flows;
- mixed migration flows;
- larger and more sophisticated smuggling and trafficking organizations; and
- a decline in American leadership on refugee issues.

If migration flow numbers continue to stay high or increase, if solutions remain limited, and if there is little likelihood of ending current major conflicts any time soon, then simple math makes clear that we will be facing an increasing number of refugees worldwide each year for the foreseeable future. Making progress will require a major redirection of program and policy as well as institutional change.

Programmatic Changes in Countries of First Asylum

Ameliorating the accumulating harms of protracted displacement situations must be a top priority. The preferred outcome, of course, is a durable solution. But when solutions are not available, then the practice of *care and maintenance* must be replaced with *policies of inclusion* in the economic and social life of local communities. Hosting states in the developing world, however, are unlikely to adopt robust policies of inclusion without additional support from the international community, as inclusion is costly (if refugees are given access to schools, medical care, and other forms of social protection) and is usually opposed by local populations (who see refugees as competition for jobs and responsible for overcrowded schools, rising rents, and other social and economic ills).

There is growing recognition that development actors are more appropriate funders and implementers of these activities than humanitarian agencies. Recent initiatives by the World Bank are crucial—indeed, likely game-changers—in this respect. What is needed is a concerted effort among development agencies (international and national) to make responding to and resolving displacement a funding priority.

Once it is recognized that development actors have a crucial role to play in the initiation and support of new programming, it becomes clear that a new operational model for multilateral actors is necessary. The New York Declaration for Refugees and Migrants, adopted by the GA in September 2016, acknowledges the need for a new "business model." It calls on UNHCR to develop a Comprehensive Refugee Response Framework (CRRF) for inclusion in a Global Compact on Refugees. The CRRF would provide for a mechanism for a comprehensive and coordinated response to refugee emergencies and protracted situations—adopting a "multistakeholder approach" that would include national and local authorities, international organizations, international financial institutions, regional organizations, regional coordination and partnership mechanisms, and civil society partners, including faith-based organizations and academia, the private sector, media, and the refugees themselves. A plan developed under the CRRF would provide emergency aid and protection to displaced persons, offer assistance to hosting communities, support policies of inclusion, and plan for solutions.[16]

A final piece for a transformed system of response is an enhanced role for the private sector and civil society. This would expand participation beyond programs of "corporate social responsibility" (for businesses) and the role as implementing partners (for NGOs). Private investment in refugee-hosting areas would complement the new joined-up humanitarian-development business models, and web-based networks that match refugees and employers, provide educational resources to refugees, and support virtual communities would materially advance efforts at self-reliance and sustainable resettlement.[17]

The preceding paragraphs have used the term "inclusion" to describe policies and programs that would permit forced migrants to participate in the local economy and social services provided generally to citizens of the hosting state. "Inclusion" may be distinguished from "integration," which is generally identified as one of the traditional durable solutions for refugees. Hosting states often reject integration as a goal because, in their view, refugees should return to their countries of origin when conditions permit. This circle can be squared by seeing inclusion as a step in the "progressive realization of solutions"—one that may ultimately lead to more sustainable returns (as refugees gain skills and education that are transferable back home) or perhaps to local integration.[18]

Programmatic Changes in Other Affected States

Refugees often move beyond countries of first asylum, seeking protection and opportunities in a third country. Movement based on other visas (labor, family unity) or offers of resettlement raise few concerns,[19] as they are consistent with the domestic immigration law of the third country. However, spontaneous onward movements have (since post–Cold War days) been viewed as problematic. Generally, well-functioning asylum systems can handle a reasonable flow of spontaneous claimants, but large flows—as seen during the Balkan Wars, the Haitian and Cuban movement to the United States, and now with the Syria situation—raise difficult policy issues and frequently spawn harsh administrative measures aimed at deterring and deflecting the flows.

Effective management of moderate flows (Afghans to Europe, Central Americans to the United States, Bangladeshis to Malaysia) will require a holistic approach that understands refugee protection as one part of an overall response to migrant movements. It will need to combine fair procedures for extending protection to refugees and other vulnerable migrants, new avenues for increased legal migration,[20] and efficient mechanisms for the return of migrants who do not qualify for admission. This requires thought and work—and advocacy to ensure public support[21]—but these policies can largely be accomplished within the domestic immigration systems of receiving states.

Large-scale movements implicate the international community as a whole if the number of refugees is of a magnitude that (1) is beyond the resources of states disproportionately affected due to their proximity to the source country or (2) should trigger responsibility-sharing norms as part of the international solidarity required for the refugee regime to function effectively. It is precisely these movements that have generally met with restrictive practices in developed states. Policy options have, in the past, fluctuated among: deterrence (US interdiction of Haitians; Australian "pushbacks"), mass admission (German response to Syrian asylum seekers; US handling of Cuban flows in earlier decades), programs establishing temporary protection (as adopted for the Balkan flows in the 1990s), returns to "safe countries" (the EU–Turkey deal), and establishment of "offshore" processing or safe havens without refugee processing (Australia and the United States, respectively).

It is clear that more effective advocacy against deterrent policies is urgently needed. Refugees should not be turned away, detained for long periods of time, or sent to other places that do not provide protection for rights guaranteed by the Convention and other international law instruments. But to be persuasive, advocates will need to propose alternative approaches and policies that can assure domestic populations that large-scale flows are being responsibly managed. These could include (1) granting blanket status to members of large-scale movements, perhaps linked to "temporary status,"[22] (2) development of formal and robust sharing arrangements among resettlement (and other) states, and (3) creation of regional processing centers that provide adjudications according to international law, reach timely decisions, and allocate "screened-in" refugees according to an agreed-upon sharing arrangement.

Legal and Policy Changes

It may come as a surprise that the vast numbers of persons now being protected and assisted as refugees in Turkey, Lebanon, Jordan, and Iraq have never been officially adjudicated to be "refugees"—that is, their claims to protection have not been assessed under the definition of "refugee" in the 1951 Convention. For decades, this has been the practice of both multilateral organizations (most particularly, UNHCR) and hosting states that face large flows of persons fleeing violence and conflict in their home states. (UNHCR calls such persons *prima facie* refugees, but they in fact are treated as if they have been recognized as refugees after status determination proceedings.) Regional instruments provide a legal basis for providing protection to persons fleeing conflict and disorder,[23] but international legal norms have not caught up with international practice.[24]

There are other classes of forced migration, however, who have no color-able claim to protection and assistance under the current international refugee regime, such as persons fleeing severe economic deprivation, serious abuse of human rights (not based on the grounds specified in the Refugee Convention), natural disaster, or the effects of climate change. Individuals in these categories may benefit from other legal norms and international relief efforts. Thus, persons at risk of torture in prison are entitled to *non-refoulement* under the Torture Convention and the EU Convention on Human Rights; severe drought, famine, and epidemics are likely to trigger an international response from multilateral organizations (WFP, UNICEF, World Health Organization [WHO]) and NGOs (Save the Children, Médecins Sans Frontières [MSF], Oxfam).

The question is whether new norms protecting additional classes of forced migrants would now be advisable. There is general consensus among refugee and human rights advocates that it is not an opportune time to "open up" the definition of refugee in the 1951 Convention—for fear that a number of states might in fact seek a narrower definition. So what has been proposed is a set of guidelines—perhaps modeled after the Guiding Principles on Internal Displacement—or a new protocol to the Convention,[25] although serious work on what new classes should be protected and how remains to be done.

The Global Compact on Refugees could be a vehicle for new norms. It could include a protocol—based on the refugee definition in the Organisation of African Unity (OAU) Convention—to provide protection for persons displaced because of violence and civil disorder. It could also amend the UNHCR statute or adopt a resolution stating that UNHCR's mandate runs to all displaced persons in need of international protection. Finally, the Compact could establish a process for drafting norms that would fill existing gaps in protecting persons forced over international borders due to natural disasters and climate change.[26]

Institutional and Structural Changes

The problems identified above, and the necessary solutions, suggest two different kinds of structural change: (1) structural reform in pursuit of a new operational model that better combines humanitarian and development analysis, planning, and implementation and (2) establishing a formal framework for responsibility-sharing.

The need for the first is now well-recognized in the Secretary-General's reports for the World Humanitarian Summit and for the September Summit on Large-Scale Movements of Migrants and Refugees,[27] although precisely what structural changes are being recommended remains undefined—and the New York Declaration made no proposals on this subject. This lack of a plan for institutional reform is no doubt due to sensitive issues of agency "turf" associated with particular funding streams (often from the same donor). So, what we have seen from the international conferences are calls for better coordination and "empowered leadership"—with no specification as to how this might happen. There are several possibilities, such as: UNHCR becoming the "lead agency" on displacement with overall accountability for developing and coordinating a comprehensive plan that includes humanitarian and development elements; the Resident Coordinator, as head of the UN country team, assuming a leadership role with greater authority and accountability; or the creation of a new "Agency for Forced Migration" that would combine functions.

Equally important would be the establishment of a formal framework for responsibility-sharing in mass flows and crises. James Hathaway and R. Alexander Neve have developed a proposal for allocating refugees and costs based on a sharing formula agreed to in advance of a crisis. The proposal separates a refugee's place of arrival from the eventual place of asylum—a distinction Hathaway believes makes his model both more fair and more acceptable to participating states.[28] If it is unlikely that states will sign up in advance for such commitments, an alternative would be a "stand-by arrangement" under which states would precommit to developing a sharing agreement early in a crisis—as opposed to the current situation, where resettlement and other solutions come much later. Under either option, the system would move from the current practice of *ad hoc* arrangements to a protocol or some other instrument binding states to work collectively on solutions. As a number of commentators have suggested, these kinds of arrangements may best be pursued at a regional level.[29]

None of these efforts will succeed without a change in the level and source of funding. The kind of "step-up" required could be accomplished by establishing a *Global Fund for Refugees* (GFR)—a multistakeholder organization, constituted by donor and host states, multilateral organizations, and experts on analysis, planning, and finance. Initial capitalization for the fund could come from foundations, donor states, bond issuances, and other financial vehicles.[30] A GFR could provide support to both of the structural changes described above—the adoption of new business models by actors on the ground and the creation of a formal responsibility-sharing framework among states. It could drive change by funding only those plans that meet criteria specified in advance.

Conclusion

The best way to deal with large-scale flows of forced migrants is of course to deal with the underlying causes of such flows: conflict and violence, economic privation, climate change. "Prevention," "early warning," and "preparedness" are regularly featured in UN documents, donor reviews, and NGO studies, and it is well-recognized that the costs of preventing and preparing for crises are far less than those of responding to them (particularly when responses—in the form of continued assistance for the displaced—continue indefinitely). Secretary-General Guterres has announced "preventing conflict and sustaining peace" as the top priority for the UN.[31] A comprehensive approach to prevention must be based on sustainable development, security, peace building, human rights, and other approaches; and it must include effective mechanisms to hold accountable those responsible for inciting and sustaining conflict.

This chapter has limited itself to proposing improvements in responding to forced migration emergencies and protracted situations. It has stressed the inadequacy of simply requesting increases in resources for humanitarian agencies and their partners.[32] New approaches must bring a wider range of actors together (including civil society and the private sector) who adopt new operational models; new legal norms will need to be developed; advocacy to shape public opinion (both to fight xenophobia and to support the necessary changes in the international system) will be an important element; and fairly dramatic institutional change will be necessary to address the "new normal" in forced displacement.

Animating these recommendations are core principles that derive from the international refugee regime's founding instruments and which have evolved over sixty years of practice:

- Persons forced from their homes because of violence and conflict should not be returned to a risk of serious harm and violations of human rights (*non-refoulement*).
- In order to ensure *non-refoulement*, states must provide "asylum space" to forced migrants.
- The international community has a responsibility to assist countries to which refugees flee in order to ensure the continued provision of asylum space and to show international solidarity.
- Norms of due process apply to refugee status determinations; detention of asylum seekers is not generally permitted and should not be used to deter other asylum seekers.
- Persons recognized as refugees have rights under international law; those rights—if respected—will help refugees rebuild their lives and will also permit them to contribute to the states that have granted them protection.
- Refugee status should not continue indefinitely; the international community has a responsibility to actively seek and provide durable solutions.
- The responsibility to provide protection for, and assist, refugees and to find solutions for refugee situations must be shared among members of the international community; to operate most efficaciously, responsibility sharing should be "regularized."
- Refugee protection cannot thrive in societies whose populations do not support it; affirmation of these principles and support for the "refugee cause" requires conscientious advocacy and political commitment.

Above all else, laser-like focus must be kept on the overarching goal of this exercise: to protect the lives of refugees. To be sure, discussions may need to address issues of security and state control, turf battles among multilateral organizations, ineffective leadership in major states and the EU, the failures of conflict prevention and solution processes, funding shortfalls, and the lack of true international solidarity. But what is crucial is that *refugees' lives matter.* More than sixty years ago, the international community came together to create a system to resolve refugee crises created by WWII and to ensure that future crises would be resolved through the guarantee of rights and international responsibility-sharing. That system is today under severe challenge. It is not able to adequately provide protection or restore the lives and communities of millions of displaced people around the world. All signs point to continued refugee flows and unresolved protracted situations. The world can continue to stumble along, lurching from crisis to crisis, relying on *ad hoc* responses. Or it can now begin a process of serious operational, legal, and institutional reform.

Notes

This chapter is based on a paper, "Revitalizing the International System of Refugee Protection," written for a conference sponsored by the Social Change Initiative, June 19–21, 2016, in Dublin.

[1] UN High Commissioner for Refugees (UNHCR), *Global Trends: Forced Displacement in 2016* ("Global Trends 2016"), June 19, 2017, p. 5.

[2] Examples include the international response to one million Russians who fled the Russian Civil War and assistance in population "transfers" between Greece and Turkey and elsewhere.

[3] As of April 2015 (UNHCR stats): 142 states have ratified both; 145 Convention, 146 Protocol.

[4] Almost all of UNHCR's funding comes from "voluntary contributions" (public and private). Less than 5 percent are from assessed contributions that fund the UN.

[5] UN General Assembly, *Statute of the Office of the United Nations High Commissioner for Refugees*, Annex to General Assembly Resolution 428 (V) of December 14, 1950, Chapter I (6).

[6] UN High Commissioner for Refugees (UNHCR), *Guidelines on International Protection No. 12: Claims for refugee status related to situations of armed conflict and violence under Article 1A(2) of the 1951 Convention and/or 1967 Protocol relating to the Status of Refugees and the regional refugee definitions*, December 2, 2016, HCR/GIP/16/12.

[7] Technically, objecting states would not be bound.

[8] For a full discussion, see James Hathaway and Thomas Gammeltoft-Hansen, "Non-Refoulement in a World of Cooperative Deterrence," *Columbia Journal of Transnational Law* 53 (2015): 235.

[9] Turkey, the world's largest refugee-hosting state, has ratified the Convention but has maintained its original scope as applying only to refugees from Europe.

[10] This figure does not include the nearly five million Palestinian refugees in the Occupied Territories, Lebanon, Jordan, and Syria.

[11] UNHCR, "Global Trends 2016," 25–27. Of these returns, about 381,000 were Afghans repatriating from Pakistan. Human Rights Watch issued a scathing report in 2017 asserting that deportation threats and police abuses were a significant cause and labeling the returns "the world's largest unlawful mass forced return of refugees in recent times." Human Rights Watch. "Pakistan Coercion, UN Complicity," February 13, 2017. https://www.hrw.org/report/2017/02/13/pakistan-coercion-un-complicity/mass-forced-return-afghan-refugees.

[12] See T. A. Aleinikoff and S. Poellot, "The Responsibility to Solve: The International Community and Protracted Refugee Situations," *Virginia Journal of International Law* 54 (2014): 195.

[13] These organizations also receive significant funding from private sector and individual sources.

[14] For example: (1) "regional processes" (such as the Bali process, with forty-eight members) that focus on migration, enforcement, and protection; (2) regional free trade/free movement agreements (e.g., Economic Community of West African States [ECOWAS], Mercosur); (3) UNHCR-sponsored regional solutions plans, such as the Addis Ababa Commitment on Somali Refugees and the Solutions Strategy for Afghan Refugees; (4) the Nairobi Declaration on Durable Solutions for Somali Refugees and Reintegration of Returnees in Somalia (March 25, 2017); and (5) the Brazil Declaration and Plan of Action (December 3, 2014), a product of the region's "Cartegena+30" conference.

[15] T. A. Aleinikoff, "Rethinking the International Refugee Regime," The Gruber Distinguished Lecturer in Global Justice delivered at Yale Law School, February 8, 2016.

[16] Annex I (Comprehensive Refugee Response Framework) to the New York Declaration on Refugees and Migrants (September 13, 2016).

[17] The White House, "Fact Sheet: White House Announces Commitments to the Call to Action for Private Sector Engagement on the Global Refugee Crisis," National Archives and Records Administration. September 20, 2016. https://obamawhitehouse.archives.gov/the-press-office/2016/09/20/fact-sheet-white-house-announces-commitments-call-action-private-sector; Report

of the Special Representative of the Secretary-General on Migration ("Sutherland Report") (February 3, 2017), paras. 57–59.

[18] Consider the Nairobi Declaration, an agreement of the Intergovernmental Authority on Development states to promote refugee returns to Somalia. An important part of the approach is advancing refugee education and skills training to enhance self-reliance and prepare them for gainful employment in host countries and upon return (part IV).

[19] Although there may be domestic controversy over the appropriate level of resettlement offers and concerns regarding the effectiveness of integration programs.

[20] These could include, e.g., private sponsorship of resettlement, increased labor migration, and mobility under regional trade agreements (e.g., ECOWAS and MERCOSUR).

[21] Including persuading the public that security concerns have been addressed.

[22] J. Hathaway, "A Global Solution to a Global Refugee Crisis," *Open Democracy* (February 29, 2016).

[23] The OAU Convention governing the specific aspects of refugee problems in Africa, the Cartagena Declaration, the EU Subsidiary Protection directive, Temporary Protected Status under US law.

[24] UN High Commissioner for Refugees (UNHCR), *Guidelines on International Protection No. 12: Claims for refugee status related to situations of armed conflict and violence under Article 1A(2) of the 1951 Convention and/or 1967 Protocol relating to the Status of Refugees and the regional refugee definitions*, December 2, 2016, HCR/GIP/16/12.

[25] See J. Golenziel, "Displaced: A Proposal for International Law to Protect Refugees, Migrants, and States," *Berkeley Journal of International Law* (forthcoming).

[26] On protection gaps for persons displaced due to climate events, see W. Kalin and N. Schrepfer, "Protecting People Crossing Borders in the Context of Climate Change: Normative Gaps and Possible Approaches" (UNHCR, 2012), 28–43.

[27] *One Humanity, Shared Responsibility*, Secretary-General Report for the World Humanitarian Summit, paras. 124–142 (collective outcomes; "from delivering aid to ending need"); *In Safety and Dignity: Addressing Large Movements of Refugees and Migrants*, Secretary-General Report in preparation for the high-level plenary meeting on addressing large movements of refugees and migrants, paras. 71–86 (UNHCR "to initiate and coordinate a comprehensive refugee response plan").

[28] J. Hathaway and R. Neve, "Making International Refugee Law Relevant Again: A Proposal for Collectivized and Solution-Oriented Protection," *Harvard Human Rights Journal* 10 (1997): 115.

[29] See, e.g., the Nairobi Declaration.

[30] In formulating a GFR, it would be important to take a careful look at the design and performance of GAVI and the Global Fund to Fight AIDS, Tuberculosis, and Malaria.

[31] António Guterres, "Remarks to the Security Council Open Debate on 'Maintenance of International Peace and Security: Conflict Prevention and Sustaining Peace' Secretary-General," United Nations, January 10, 2017. https://www.un.org/sg/en/content/sg/speeches/2017-01-10/secretary-generals-remarks-maintenance-international-peace-and.

[32] Indeed, there is a serious question whether the existence of a system of robust humanitarian response actually gives incentives to those who would spark conflict because they know that affected people will be cared for externally by the international community.

CHAPTER 4

Women Rebuilding Societies
Resiliency from the Bottom Up
Laurie Adams

> In peace and in war, women are the glue that hold societies together. The world cannot afford to miss out on women's voices and roles. For peace, freedom and development to be lasting and sustainable, women must be an essential part of all peace negotiations and peace building processes. The world needs to do that not only for women's sake, but for the larger good for all.
>
> —*Zainab Salbi*

Twenty-five years after Women for Women International (WfWI)[1] was founded by Zainab Salbi to serve women survivors of war, the world has woken up to the critical role of women in everything from building peace to the global economy. The International Monetary Fund now talks about the billion-dollar dividend that will come from women's participation in the labor market. The World Bank has launched a $1 billion fund for women's economic development. Canada, the Netherlands, and private donors have radically increased their funding to reproductive rights and services in the face of the United States cutting back. The Sustainable Development Goals (SDGs), which commit to "Leaving No One Behind" not only have a stand-alone goal on gender equity, but have mainstreamed gender equity throughout all the SDGs.

That women's political and economic potential has been recognized at the highest levels is no small feat, but there is still not enough attention on two critical issues:

1. How to reach the most impoverished—women whose lives have been so shattered or their opportunities so limited that development and humanitarian interventions exclude them or do not address their needs and potential.
2. How to leverage and support the agency these very same destitute women have in rebuilding societies and economies due to their deep resilience and the critical role they play at the grassroots level in their families and communities.

Fostering Resilience

Not only do women overwhelmingly bear the brunt of both conflict and poverty, but conflict itself drives women further into poverty and isolation, exposes them to various forms of gender-based violence, and worsens discriminatory social attitudes. Both directly and indirectly, conflict erodes women's health and well-being, decreases educational opportunities for them and their children, and fosters extreme poverty.

Yet women survivors of conflict and poverty need not be condemned as passive victims. To the contrary, they are resilient, and they have the potential to become agents of change in their homes and communities. Globally, we need to acknowledge this resilience and understand it in order to effectively support it. When we speak about resilience, we mean women striving for change, for better lives, and for more peaceful societies in the face of challenges posed by poverty, conflict, and patriarchal structures and behaviors. We mean women who are resilient to both economic shocks and constant, discrimination.

We know that with the right support, even the most marginalized women will run for leadership positions, educate other women on their rights, organize community actions, and stop violence against themselves and others.[2] According to data collected by WfWI, following our one-year program, earnings triple, practice of family planning goes from 30 percent to 87 percent, and sharing knowledge of rights goes from 10 percent of women to 89 percent of those we serve by the end of a year. Take, for example, the story of just one of the nearly half a million women we have served:

> Hosai Bayani lives in rural Afghanistan, a country where 87% of women have reported facing verbal, physical, or sexual violence. One day about a decade ago, Hosai's husband announced he was leaving. With no explanation, and no divorce; he simply abandoned her. For the sake of her two children, she moved in with her in-laws and was forced to depend on them. She joined WfWI one year training and support program where she cultivated her innate passion and skill for helping survivors of violence. After graduation, she got a job as a trainer with Women for Women International. She gained the respect of her in-laws and the community. With this respect, she ran for local government office and won.

And it's not just the women served by WfWI globally whose lives have been changed with access to resources and support and their realization of their own agency. The authors of a study into the trauma experiences of undocumented and refugee women now living in the United States write, "Women noted the confluence of individual, familial, and social supports and resources that they were able to garner as important to developing coping and resilience . . . In developing resilience and coping, women noted the importance of external supports and their situatedness in terms of accessing these supports."[3]

Key Lessons for a New Global Agenda

WfWI's conviction that investing in and believing in women is an efficient and underutilized route to change was groundbreaking when we developed our strategy twenty-five years ago. This belief is increasingly accepted; however, interventions have not been sufficient so far. Even today, no country has achieved full gender equality, there are still more than one hundred countries with discriminatory laws on the books, and a third of all women still experience violence, to name just a few alarming statistics. Committing to and adopting the methods and principles below will help us all do more to support women affected by conflict and poverty, and enable them to reach their full potential.

Women Bring Returns

Investing in women is investing in families and communities. Strong women build strong nations. As Esther Duflo says in "Women Empowerment and Economic Development,"[4]

> [P]overty and lack of opportunity breed inequality between men and women, so that when economic development reduces poverty, the condition of women improves on two counts: first, when poverty is reduced, the condition of everyone, including women, improves, and second, gender inequality declines as poverty declines, so the condition of women improves more than that of men with development.[5]

WfWI data[6] consistently prove this point, which has also been backed by the World Bank, the McKinsey Global Institute,[7] UN Women,[8] and countless nongovernmental organizations.

Cash Is Efficient and Effective

As we learned in Elizabeth Kiewisch's "Looking within the Household: A Study on Gender, Food Security, and Resilience in Cocoa-Growing Communities,"[9] families contributed to household expenses based on what they were able to farm and sell. She writes, "While each household member managed income from his or her own crops, he or she also had obligations to the household and contributed to common expenses. An individual's income was subject to limited sharing obligations to meet these common expenses." Giving women cash, enabling them to make their own choices about relative investments, is a very effective development and humanitarian intervention, as are savings and lending groups. At WfWI, we offer women cash transfers for them to invest in their small businesses, pay school fees for children, or use in other ways they think is valuable to their household. After they graduate from the program, women triple their income, proving that cash infusions at a critical time in a woman's life can change her stances dramatically in the long run.

Engage Men to Support Women's Rights

WfWI first piloted a men's engagement program in Nigeria in 2002. Since then, we have worked with more than fifteen thousand men across six countries to support women's rights. We place a particular focus on training leaders in local communities (including religious, traditional, military, and civil society leaders) so that they can use their influence to help protect and promote women's rights and gender equality. The results have been transformative. Globally, the men we trained in 2016 alone reported a 34 percent increase in the number of actions they took in support of women's rights and participation.

Localization

Top-down development solutions fail. WfWI, while headquartered in the United States, uses a global approach, employs local staff wherever we work, and adapts our program to the needs and the realities of the lives of the women we serve locally. Global actions on issues such as food security and inequality need to go hand in hand with local interventions. The solution to entrenched global problems, such as increase in conflict, the linked increase in terrorism, and the refugee crisis, requires a local as well as global response. Solutions must rise from the bottom up; we must reach women where they are.

Take a Holistic Approach

According to a field experiment in Afghanistan, to empower women through development aid, it is essential to consider the multifaceted needs and the many obstacles women face. Therefore, economic interventions and social interventions are most effective when they are combined.[10] Building women's economic resilience is dependent on social capacity, such as their health and ability to influence decisions, particularly financial decisions. Women's social empowerment is supported through economic empowerment and independence. A woman given economic skills and resources, with no self-confidence or efficacy, and without networks of support, is unlikely to leverage those resources, nor draw on the resilience to withstand inevitable shocks. A woman supported to understand her rights, without the ability to maintain her livelihood or invest in her or her family's education or health, is less likely to have the tools to defend those rights. And without the voices of men who use their privileged positions in communities to defend women's rights, reaching gender equity is harder, if not impossible.

Bridge the Humanitarian/Development/Rights Divide

We must meet women where they are. Especially during or in recovery from a crisis, support for vulnerable women needs to provide integrated service solutions. Their lives are not divided—unlike international organizations' programs and funding streams, which too often are—between "humanitarian," "development," or "rights" compartments, any more than they are divided between economic or social parts of their lives. Well-intentioned interventions addressing women's needs in isolation can be ineffective. Women need urgent assistance—such as emergency cash—at the onset of a crisis. Yet, as many of the crises facing the world today are not short term, we need to integrate longer-term approaches into meeting immediate needs as well. In conflict, women's rights and development are often deprioritized in favor of an emergency response to create "stability," but our experience has shown us that women's rights need to be addressed immediately for any sustainable solution to any crisis or conflict. Women need to be included from the beginning to enable them to meaningfully participate in decision-making at all levels so that interventions are designed to respond to their needs.

Priorities: Call to Action

As a global community, we now have the SDGs as our shared framework. We present our recommendations therefore in the context of commitments to fulfill these SDGs and meet their target indicators:

Deliver the SDGs

Whatever their limitations, the SDGs, with their stand-alone goal on gender equality, and the gender lens embedded across all the SDGs, are a powerful step forward for the world's most disadvantaged women. As global advocates in leaders of civil society, WfWI will in 2020—alongside many other organizations— use our data and our connection with the most marginalized women to track and report on progress five years in. Let us, as citizens, continue to show that we care about the world's poorest and most disadvantaged people—women survivors of conflict. We must hold governments accountable for these goals that we collectively worked for several years to set and agree upon.

Identify and Listen to the Most Marginalized

We are committed to listening to and learning from the most marginalized women. We do this through a combination of our monitoring, evaluation, and learning, as well as by building women's capacity through our programs. The success of the SDGs is dependent on listening to those left furthest behind and supporting them to drive forward the changes that they want to see. We must amplify the voices of those most marginalized so that they can be front and center to both the implementation and the review of the SDGs, for example, through meaningful consultation, representation, and sharing of lessons learned.

Identify and Invest in the Most Vulnerable

Women bear the brunt of increased conflict, natural disasters, and economic shocks, not only because they are most vulnerable themselves, but because it is women who are tasked with the responsibility of finding ways to support their children and families when they are left with nothing. Investing in those left furthest behind should be an immediate priority, as they require greater and longer-term support to catch up with the average earners in their community (e.g., someone living on $0.70 a day will require more support to reach $1.25 a day). There are many ways to invest—whether it be individuals supporting direct programs or businesses investing additional resources in reaching and training the most marginalized women for employment. When governments step back, civil society and the private sector must step forward.

Provide Comprehensive and Long-Term Support

The SDGs present a comprehensive framework which recognizes the complex needs faced by the most marginalized people. The women we work with are faced with the legacy of conflict that poses multiple and intersecting challenges: post-trauma illness and injury, impoverishment, forced displacement. Comprehensive support that works across sectors (economic, social, etc.) is essential to addressing these needs, along with long-term services supporting behavioral changes and women's empowerment.

Increase Funding for Women's Empowerment

We welcome the recognition in the SDGs that improving women's representation and participation is crucial for progress of all Goals. Increasing women's participation requires a monumental increase in funding for women's empowerment, particularly to support change to break down the barriers that women face in accessing economic and political opportunities as well as services (such as health and education).

Include Data That Reflect the Challenges of the Most Vulnerable

Data collection needs to better capture women's needs and better share their stories. The revisions we make to our monitoring and evaluation instruments are designed to more accurately measure progress in what matters for the women we work with and serve. We are adapting our processes to include more indicators and other, more qualitative feedback mechanisms. The SDGs' emphasis on vulnerable, marginalized groups, and on inequality, provides an opportunity to rethink what and how data are collected, and to look for information that is more relevant to those left furthest behind. More qualitative indicators on women's empowerment, and indicators that capture women's exclusion, such as lack of access to social networks, are examples of data that should be collected and widely disseminated in the future.

Conclusion

Our agenda is guided by the most marginalized, vulnerable, and ultra-poor women in countries affected by conflict. We believe that any global agenda needs to have women's needs right at the center to ensure that we do not leave anyone behind. We know that women are in danger of being forgotten; their voices are unheard and their needs are unmet. And yet, their resilience and direct contribution to creating more peaceful societies serve to inspire and illuminate a global agenda in which all women lead lives of dignity and fulfillment.

Notes

[1] Since 1993, WfWI has served more than 462,000 women survivors of war in Afghanistan, Bosnia and Herzegovina, Democratic Republic of Congo, Kosovo, Nigeria, Rwanda, South Sudan, and the Kurdistan Region of Iraq. With a long-term vision for sustainable change and development, WfWI works with the most marginalized and socially excluded women so that they have the skills, networks, and tools they need to rebuild their lives, communities, and nations. Through WfWI's comprehensive twelve-month program, women learn about their rights and health, and gain key life, vocational, and business skills to access livelihoods and break free from trauma and poverty.

[2] 2016 global averages (baseline/enrollment vs. endline/graduation at twelve months after enrollment, n/a excluded): leadership positions 8.7–12.2 percent; educating other women on their rights 6.7–20 percent; organizing community actions 40.8–61.4 percent; stopping violence being committed against them 18.4–54.5 percent.

[3] R. D. Goodman, C. K. Vesely, B. Letiecq, and C. L. Cleaveland, "Trauma and Resilience among Refugee and Undocumented Immigrant Women," *Journal of Counseling & Development* 95 (2017): 309–321. doi:10.1002/jcad.12145.

[4] Esther Duflo, "Women Empowerment and Economic Development," *Journal of Economic Literature* 50, no. 4 (2012), 1051–1079.

[5] Ibid., 1052

[6] wfwi-summary-report-effective-wps-approach-nov-2015.pdf.

[7] The McKinsey Global Institute, *The Power of Parity: How Advancing Women's Equality Can Add $12 Trillion to Global Growth*, September 2015.

[8] UN Women, *Progress of the World's Women 2015–2016: Transforming Economies, Realizing Rights*, 2015.

[9] Elizabeth Kiewisch, "Looking within the Household: A Study on Gender, Food Security, and Resilience in Cocoa-Growing Communities," *Journal of Gender and Development* 23, no. 3 (2015): 497–513.

[10] A. Beath, F.Christia, and R. Enikolopov, "Empowering Women through Development Aid: Evidence from a Field Experiment in Afghanistan," *American Political Science Review* 107, no. 3 (August 24, 2013): 540–557.

CHAPTER 5

Global Press Freedom in the Crosshairs

Joel Simon

The threats to press freedom, free expression, and the rights of journalists around the world are unprecedented, even as technology has transformed the way in which people communicate and share news. Until journalists are free to do their work without violence, censorship, and intimidation, the true potential of the information revolution will never be realized.

This is the most deadly and dangerous period for journalists in modern history. At least forty-eight journalists were killed in relation to their work between January 1 and December 15, 2016, the Committee to Protect Journalists found in its annual analysis.[1] (Additionally, at least twenty-seven more journalists were killed during 2016, though it is not confirmed that their deaths were work related.) Deaths in combat or crossfire ticked to their highest number since 2013 as conflicts in the Middle East dragged on. More than half of the journalists killed in 2016 died in combat or crossfire, for the first time in decades. The conflicts in Syria, Iraq, Yemen, Libya, Afghanistan, and Somalia claimed the lives of twenty-six journalists. Political groups, including Islamist militant organizations, were responsible for more than half of the killings.[2]

As of mid-July, at least eighteen journalists have been killed in 2017.[3]

Furthermore, as of December 2016, more journalists were jailed around the world—259—than at any time since Committee to Protect Journalists (CPJ) began keeping detailed records in 1990.[4] The previous record was 232 journalists in 2012. The top five jailers—Turkey, China, Egypt, Eritrea, and Ethiopia—accounted for 68 percent of imprisoned journalists worldwide. Turkey alone accounted for nearly a third of the global total, with at least eighty-one imprisoned journalists. All the journalists jailed in Turkey face anti-state charges.[5]

Wasn't technology—the global Internet, social media, phones with the potential to turn every eyewitness into a reporter—supposed to help create an information utopia? To make censorship obsolete? Why is press freedom in decline around the world, and violence and repression against the media on the rise? And why does it seem unlikely that this dynamic will change anytime soon?

Let me seek to answer this question by sharing my own experience.

I got my start in journalism working as a freelance reporter in Central America and Mexico in the 1980s. I covered the civil wars in Guatemala and El Salvador, the debate over the North American Free Trade Agreement in Mexico, as well as immigration and environmental issues.

Like any good journalist, I always tried to report as much as I could first-hand. I traveled extensively and interviewed all sorts of people from all walks of life. But there was no way international reporters like me could cover such vast and complex stories without relying on the help and support of local reporters. This included well-connected columnists in the capitals, who would offer advice and insights over a beer. It also included the local police reporters, who would show you around their towns and literally know where the bodies were buried.

Here's a dirty little secret: many foreign correspondents—myself included—spent a good deal of time re-reporting what was in the local press. Every journalist I knew would start their day by obsessively reading the local newspapers, watching the local news, listening to the radio. While the media in these counties was not always as free or independent as we would have liked, it was a vital source of information, and the starting point for much of what we transmitted to the world.

Being an international journalist—even a lowly freelancer like myself—was an exalted existence. If a politician, a criminal, a celebrity, or a business person wanted to communicate with the world, he or she pretty much had to talk to us. There was simply no other way to reach a large audience.

And this also meant that no one wanted to mess with us—at least not too much. That would instantly lead to increased public scrutiny and negative attention, something that even guerrillas and cartel leaders were looking to avoid. In fact, it was the collective monopoly that we journalists exercised over information that gave us our power and kept us safe.

And I should also note that there were a lot of us. Why? Because every decent newspaper in the United States and Europe wanted its own network of foreign correspondents. Covering the world with a local angle was seen as a civic responsibility and a way to increase prestige and win journalism prizes. Most local newspapers back in the 1980s and 1990s had lots of ads, including classifieds, so they had hefty profits and the resources to take on global reporting.

How does the media cover the world now? It's pretty different and in some ways much better. As I noted, international correspondents spent a lot time monitoring and reporting what was in the local media. Well, now you can do that from your desk, wherever you are. Don't speak the local language? No problem, you can use Google Translate. Looking for an eyewitness account or diverse perspectives on a global news event? No need to get go the scene and track down observers. You can also do that from your desk using social media and hashtag searches, and this will only get easier as these platforms become even more ubiquitous and Internet access expands.

These technologies mean that more information is available to more people than at any time in human history. But at the end of the day, the news is made by human beings who gather and share experiences, observations, and analysis that determine what we know about the world. And those individuals are more vulnerable than ever.

Yes, the seasoned foreign correspondents are still out there. But there are fewer of them because the revenue model for local newspapers has collapsed. Most new organizations give away their content online, while the advertising revenue goes to Google and Facebook. As a result, international reporting in the United States and many other countries is now the purview of a few large established media organizations, such as Reuters, Bloomberg, the Associated Press, the *New York Times*, and the *Washington Post*, along with upstarts such as VICE News and BuzzFeed. Freelancers and local journalists fill in the gaps.

Journalists used to be the gatekeepers. Collectively, they decided to a large extent what the public knew and didn't know. That meant if you were a corrupt dictator, or the leader of a drug cartel, or the leader of al-Qaeda and you had a message for the world, you pretty much had to talk to the press. Osama Bin Laden used to convene press conferences and give interviews to international journalists. This didn't mean that journalists were necessarily liked or respected; it just meant that they were useful and had a certain power.

Today, that power is diminished. We live in a much more dynamic and diffuse information environment. And this is why journalists are being killed and imprisoned in record numbers. According to CPJ data, most journalists who are killed are murdered and deliberately targeted. They are killed in their homes, or at their office, or while traveling between the two. The vast majority of them, 90 percent, are local reporters, killed in their own country.

While there are a wide range of threats to journalists around the world, Jihadi militants were responsible for a significant percentage of the killings in recent years. Again, the majority of these victims are local reporters in places such as Syria, Iraq, Somalia, and Pakistan, journalists largely unknown outside their countries. But there are also those whose names may be more widely known than others—like the journalists at the satirical weekly *Charlie Hebdo* in Paris, who were killed in an attack on their offices, and the American freelancers James Foley and Steven Sotloff, who were murdered by Islamic State (IS) militants in the summer of 2014.

Many of these Jihadi groups—particularly al-Qaeda and IS—are exploiting the same information technologies that have disrupted traditional media in order to build their own alternative networks. They use websites, chat rooms, and social media to communicate with their followers and supporters. And they use high-production videos uploaded to YouTube and shared on Twitter when they have a message for the world. Quite simply, these groups no longer need journalists to get their message out. Having lost their utility, journalists have become dispensable, sources of ransom payment and props in terrorizing videos.

This impacts and severely constricts the news and information that people receive from many parts of the world. For example, much of Syria has been off limits to the international media—it has been just too dangerous for reporters to travel there. This is certainly true of Raqqa, the city in the arid northwest of the country that was, until very recently, the capital of the IS and where there was a military offensive in 2016 and 2017. In order to fill in this information void, a group of citizen journalists set up a media collective they call Raqqa is Being Slaughtered Silently,[6] or RBSS, which relies on an underground network of collaborators who smuggle information out, information that is incorporated into global media coverage. These activists are not impartial. They are trying to draw attention to the plight of their city, and the cruelty and deprivations that define daily existence under the IS. This is dangerous work. At least four members of the RBSS have been murdered, and some were even hunted down after fleeing to Turkey.[7] These are among the many local reporters—many of them unconventional—who are dying to bring news to the public.

This is the way in which the technological transformation of the global information environment is linked to violence against journalists.

But what about repression? The dynamic is different, but technology is also crucial to the analysis.

Throughout history, every totalitarian system has been based on the control of information. This was certainly true in the Soviet Union, where information was managed from the top down through state control of the media. For the most part, government bureaucrats decided what the people in the Soviet Union could and could not know.

But information is much harder to control in the Internet era. Hierarchical systems of censorship and control are less effective once a significant portion of the population is online. As a result, government strategies of information management have become much more sophisticated. And from the point of view of these repressive states, recent events have demonstrated what can happen when information is not managed effectively.

Governments have seen the disruptive power of the social networks, particularly linked to street protests. These technologies were at the heart of the 2009 Green Revolution in Iran—which was ultimately crushed—and helped fuel the Arab Spring revolts that toppled entrenched autocracies in Egypt and Tunisia in 2011.

Repressive governments took note. They understood that they couldn't just unplug the Internet without suffering significant economic consequences, so they developed more sophisticated strategies of information control. In the last five years, we have seen a tremendous crackdown on online speech worldwide, a crackdown that, if it continues, has the potential to undermine the Internet as a shared global information resource, splintering it into a series of national systems, each with its own rules and limits.[8]

China has led the way, deploying surveillance technology, online blocking, and an army of paid trolls who root out critical commentary. When these measures fail, targeted repression is the next step. Dozens of Chinese journalists are behind bars.

When a delegation from CPJ met in October 2014 with President Recep Tayyip Erdogan of Turkey, he told us that he is "increasingly against the Internet every day." He was referring to the way the IS uses the Internet to recruit new followers, but he has lashed out as his own citizens have used online tools to share information that the government wants to keep from the public. Social media also helped fuel the Gezi Park protests in 2013, when tens of thousands of people in

Istanbul flooded the city's central square to oppose the latest urban development plan.[9] The Turkish government has been cracking down ever since. Following the aborted coup in 2016, Turkey has become the world's leading jailer of journalists.[10] Other countries with Internet crackdowns, combined with intensive media repression, include Ethiopia, Egypt, and Cameroon.

Another leader concerned about the disruptive power of information is Vladimir Putin of Russia, although he has taken a different, and perhaps innovative, approach not only to managing information domestically but deploying it against his enemies.

Putin's greatest fear is of a "Color Revolution," like the mass protests that toppled pro-Russian regimes in Georgia in 2003 and Ukraine in 2005. When people pour into the streets to protest corruption and repression, Putin never sees citizens claiming their democratic rights. Instead, he sees successful information operations carried out by Western governments that manufacture grievances and then spread them using both traditional and social media. He believes that the Obama administration—and in particular, Hillary Clinton—used this strategy to foment a social revolution to topple his government following a disputed election in 2012.

Putin views every negative story about Russia—from high-level corruption in the Kremlin to the Olympic doping scandal—through this lens, as part of a Western-led coordinated effort to weaken and ultimately undermine his regime. This is one reason he has taken dramatic steps to curtail free expression in Russia, both online and offline. When Putin first came to power in 1999, the Russian broadcast media was controlled by leading oligarchs but was relatively open. Putin tolerated this arrangement until the broadcast networks ran one too many critical stories, and then he moved against them, using tax audits, regulatory action, and legal pressure to bring the networks under Kremlin control. Today, the original media oligarchs are in exile or dead, replaced by a new generation of Putin loyalists.

Also dead are quite a few critical reporters, including Anya Politkovskaya, Paul Klebnikov, and Natalia Estemirova, all of whom were murdered while investigating the nexus between the Kremlin, pro-Putin paramilitary forces in Chechnya, and the massive fraud around the redevelopment funds used to rebuild a region decimated by civil conflict.

For awhile, Putin tolerated more open discourse online, but as Internet penetration has grown in Russia, the government has taken additional efforts to rein in critical websites and social media commentators, taking legal action for posting "extremist content" and instituting an onerous registration process.

But what makes Russia unusual is that it has responded to what it believes is information warfare directed against its interests by developing offensive capabilities it can use to target its adversaries. Essentially, Putin believes Russia can play at the same game. This is known as the Gerasimov Doctrine, which posits that "deception and disinformation, not tanks and planes, [are] the new tools of power."[11] Russia has used false news to stir up unrest in the Balkans, and in Ukraine, where it planted stories of attacks on ethnic Russians that paved the way for the annexation of Crimea in March 2014.

These strategies have now been extended to the United States. State-sponsored Russian hackers targeted the Democratic National Committee and the personal e-mail of Clinton's campaign manager John Podesta. This information was first leaked by someone who adopted the moniker Guccifer 2.0 and has been publicly linked to the Kremlin. The information eventually ended up in the hands of WikiLeaks, and Julian Assange made it public at the most politically damaging moments, on the eve of the Democratic Convention and as an October surprise.

As of this writing, there is no concrete evidence of active collusion between the Trump campaign and the Russian government, but this possibility is being investigated by the US House Permanent Select Committee on Intelligence as well as by many, many journalists looking to land a big scoop. We don't know what's true, and what's real, but we do know that any journalist who breaks new ground is likely to be labeled a liar or "fake news" by President Trump or his surrogates.

What is the relationship between President Trump lashing out at critical media in the United States and the safety of journalists reporting in high-risk environments? What is the relationship between press freedom in the United States and press freedom in the rest of the world?

The threat to journalists in the United States is not one of life or death. The United States has the First Amendment, which protects freedom of the press, and an independent judiciary to back it up. It has strong, diverse media that continues to evolve and adapt in response to new and disruptive technologies. Violence against journalists in the United States is extremely rare.

But there is plenty of cause for concern. Under the administration of President Barack Obama, particularly in the first term, Americans saw systematic efforts to limit media access and stamp out leaks by aggressively prosecuting whistleblowers. In fact, there were more prosecutions during the Obama administration under the 1917 Espionage Act than during all previous administrations combined. This is not something that went unnoticed around the world.

These negative trends have been accelerated under the current US president. Donald Trump ran a campaign that sought to marginalize and at times delegitimize the role of the press. He has called reporters "dishonest" and "scum," excluded critical reporters from his events, and threatened to make it easier to sue the media. He has insulted reporters, unleashing the most vile and disgusting trolls, who sought to intimidate and demean the journalists whom Trump had singled out. White House press briefings are no longer broadcast.

Trump is not the first candidate to run a campaign against the press. What is more troubling is that he has not changed his behavior since moving into the White House. President Trump has continued to lash out at the media at every turn, declaring them—twice—the "enemy of the American people." He routinely accuses journalists of lying, and has appropriated the term "fake news," which originally meant "news that was made up" and now means "news that President Trump does not like." Trump is not the only political leader using this kind of aggressive language. President Duterte of the Philippines, the leaders of Saudi Arabia and Egypt, and the prime minister of Cambodia have used some of the same rhetoric and tactics to describe the press in their own countries, often with a nod to the current US administration.

It is true that journalists are not being hauled off to jail in the United States and that the president, like every other citizen of this country, is free to express his views about what the media is reporting. But words matter, and when President Trump denigrates, demeans, and deplores the work of the press, he not only undermines the work of the media in the United States but also makes it more difficult for journalists working in dangerous and repressive environments around the world do their job. That's bad news for everyone, because in today's interconnected world, the public relies on the work of these local journalists to keep informed.

One of the key strategies of press freedom organizations such as CPJ and others around the world has been to engage with the US government and urge that they defend the rights of journalists around the world and stand up for press freedom as a key US value. The US record has never been perfect—far from it. But the United States does have tremendous influence, and has used it to make a difference. This has been the case in both Democratic and Republican administrations.

To give some examples, during the Clinton administration, at the start of the 1995 negotiations that led to the Dayton Peace Accords in Bosnia, US diplomat Richard Holbrooke told Serbian president Slobodan Milosevic that talks could not begin as long as US journalist David Rohde was in the custody of the pro-Serb Bosnian forces, who had detained him in Bosnia. Rohde was released after around a week. More recently, in July 2015, when President Obama visited Ethiopia, CPJ raised both publicly and privately the issue of the large number of local journalists jailed in that country. Several were released prior to the presidential visit.

In comparison, the Trump administration is delivering a different message on the global stage: journalists are contemptible, and governments that crack down on the media face no consequences in terms of their relationship with the United States. In his first one hundred days in office, Trump completed the press freedom violators' trifecta, meeting with President Recep Tayyip Erdogan of Turkey, President Abdel Fattah el-Sisi of Egypt, and President Xi Jinping of China. As noted above, these three countries are the world's leading jailers of journalists and together account for more than half of all journalists imprisoned around the world. No one knows what Trump said behind closed doors in his meetings, but he has praised both Xi, whom Trump hosted at Mar-a-Lago, and Sisi, whom he claimed is doing a "fantastic job." Secretary of State Rex Tillerson all but institutionalized this position when he noted in a May 3, 2017, speech to all State Department employees that an "America First" agenda means deemphasizing human rights.[12]

Along with the ceaselessly hostile rhetoric toward the US media, Trump's embrace of the world's leading press freedom violators, and his administration's willingness to make press freedom of secondary importance in foreign diplomacy, is serving to normalize media repression. This is terrible news not only for the journalists languishing in jail, but for all those around the world seeking to report independently in places where the government claims the power to determine the truth, and those who report otherwise may be killed.

Of all the things President Trump has said about the press—his rants about fake news, failing news organizations, and journalists as "enemies of the American people"—this may be one of the most chilling in its implications for global press freedom:

> TRUMP: When people call you "brilliant" it's always good, especially when the person heads up Russia.
>
> HOST JOE SCARBOROUGH: Well, I mean, also is a person who kills journalists, political opponents and . . .
>
> WILLIE GEIST: Invades countries.
>
> SCARBOROUGH: . . . and invades countries, obviously that would be a concern, would it not?
>
> TRUMP: He's running his country, and at least he's a leader, unlike what we have in this country.
>
> SCARBOROUGH: But, again: He kills journalists that don't agree with him.
>
> TRUMP: Well, I think that our country does plenty of killing, too, Joe.[13]

Scarborough's question is not terribly precise. There's no evidence that Putin kills journalists. However, there is plenty of evidence that he is indifferent to their murders. Still, Trump's answer is staggering. In a single stroke, he greatly reduces the moral leverage that the United States has exercised in defense of journalists and press freedom throughout decades. Since taking office, Trump has demonstrated no interest in the tradition of standing up for the rights of persecuted journalists. To the contrary, through his statements and behavior, he has undermined his ability to do so.

The damage to the global press freedom movement is hard to overstate. The anti-press rhetoric and actions of the US president and his surrogates send a signal around the world that the United States is no longer willing to lead on defending press freedom, leverage its bilateral relations to demand the release of imprisoned journalists, or rally its allies to support progressive norms and policies globally. Instead, the US administration is creating a new normal, with "fake news" providing the perfect framework for repression.

For example, in February 2017, Venezuela shut down the broadcast of CNN in Spanish, alleging that the network "instigates religious, racial and political hatred."[14] The trigger was the broadcast of an investigative story alleging that the Venezuelan Embassy in Iraq was selling passports to suspected terrorists. In normal times, one would expect the president of the United States to decry such action, and stand up for the rights of the journalists to report the news and inform the public in a country experiencing massive social upheaval. But at a time when President Trump was blasting CNN for reporting "fake news," he was not in a position to press the case. Indeed, he said nothing.

How should journalists respond? There has been much debate but some suggestions include the following.

First, don't allow themselves to be considered the opposition. Second, don't focus on access. Third, double down on the work, which is to report the news. Finally, recognize the limits of solidarity. And how should the broader international community respond? Individual members and leaders of civil society should support, demand, and insist on free and independent media.

There is a significant and real threat to the media in the United States, but the challenge is even larger than that. What is at stake is the global information system—that jury-rigged and imperfect mix of technology and people on which we depend to stay informed. Brussels-based journalist Jean-Paul Marthoz likes to say that the American journalists are the world's journalists—meaning that the whole world depends on journalists in the United States to do their job in order to keep them informed about the events taking place in the United States that have a significant effect on their lives.

The converse is also true. The world's journalists are America's journalists, and they are depended on to keep people in the United States informed about the global events that impact Americans' lives. Dozens have given their lives to do so.

The world's journalists deserve the support of US society and government. American journalists in particular need to stand up and defend their right to their job, not just out of solidarity but out of self-interest. They also need to stand together to defend the global information system. That is why everyone— journalists and average citizens—who believes in the power of information, who believes that the people and not the government, and certainly not violent forces, should determine what we know, everyone needs to stand up and embrace this obligation to protect press freedom as a new global agenda priority.

Notes

[1] https://cpj.org/killed/.

[2] Ibid.

[3] https://cpj.org/killed/2017/.

[4] https://cpj.org/imprisoned/2016.php.

[5] Ibid.

[6] https://cpj.org/blog/2015/07/how-islamic-state-uses-killings-to-try-to-spread-f.php; https://www.democracynow.org/2017/7/6/raqqa_is_being_slaughtered_silently_syrian; http://www.newyorker.com/news/news-desk/telling-the-truth-about-isis-and-raqqa.

[7] https://cpj.org/blog/2016/01/for-journalists-fleeing-islamic-state-turkey-is-as.php   http://www.independent.co.uk/news/world/middle-east/isis-beheads-raqqa-is-being-slaughtered-silently-activist-and-friend-in-turkey-a6714911.html.

[8] For an overview of online censorship, see Justin Clark, Robert Faris, Ryan Morrison-Westphal, Helmi Noman, Casey Tilton, and Jonathan Zittrain, *The Shifting Landscape of Global Internet Censorship* (Berkman Klein Center for Internet & Society Research Publication, 2017).

[9] Constanze Letsch, "Turkey Protests Spread after Violence in Istanbul Over Park Demolition," *The Guardian*, May 31, 2013.

[10] https://cpj.org/imprisoned/2016.php.

[11] https://www.nytimes.com/2016/07/26/world/europe/russia-dnc-putin-strategy.html.

[12] https://www.state.gov/secretary/remarks/2017/05/270620.htm.

[13] Philip Bump, "Donald Trump Isn't Fazed by Vladimir Putin's Journalist-Murdering," *The Washington Post*, December 18, 2015.

[14] https://cpj.org/2017/02/venezuela-suspends-cnn-en-espanol-broadcasts.php.

CHAPTER 6

Digital Information Access

Courtney C. Radsch

Internet governance has become one of the most important issues impacting media and press freedom in the modern era. From censorship and the free flow of information, the role of bots, algorithms, and artificial intelligence (AI) to big data and surveillance, the forces affecting media and journalism are becoming inseparable from those of the digital age. The future of Internet governance can also be considered the future of media and press freedom. The way that governments, companies, and individuals communicate and get their news is reconfiguring the information ecosystem and challenging the hegemony of the state over the media ecosystem. This, in turn, is reconfiguring the contours of the public sphere, with profound implications for public policy and geopolitics. The journalistic field has traditionally played a central role in constructing and maintaining the public sphere, but technology companies are becoming increasingly influential and even determinative by setting the boundaries and terms of visibility.

The role of states and traditional concepts of sovereignty and power are in a state of flux amid tensions about the power of Internet giants and social media firms, tussles over national law and its applicability online, and concerns about what shifts in dominant information and communication trends mean for the future of journalism and press freedom, and thus for politics more broadly.

Striking the right balance between government regulation, self-regulation by tech companies, and the role of the public will define the future of information in the digital age. At the core of this balancing is the question of who should decide what content is permissible and what is not. A look at the abuse of media laws by authoritarians around the world is a clear warning against government regulation of information. At the same time, relying on Internet platforms to filter or verify information could result in the privatization of censorship. This is particularly concerning, as online activity and information is consolidated across a few hegemonic platforms, nearly all of which are based on the West Coast of the United States.

Internet and mobile phone penetration continues to rise in every region of the world, and about 2.8 billion people globally use social media on a monthly basis, with more than 91 percent of them doing so via mobile devices.[1] According to Reuters, more than half of all online users across thirty-six countries (54 percent) say that they use social media as a source of news each week.[2] Facebook, with over two billion users, has become a dominant publishing platform and, in some cases, is synonymous with the Internet.[3] Internet platforms depend upon quality journalism to populate their feeds and give their platforms value. As Klint Finley wrote in 2016 in *Wired* magazine, telecommunications companies are becoming media companies, and media companies are becoming telecoms.[4]

The dominant communications platforms of any particular era configure the potentiality for expression and power dynamics in the public sphere. Mass media, for example, enabled the formations of publics by portraying the normative and constitutive rules of the collective, whereas the networked, AI-inflected, personalized nature of new information and communications technologies facilitate the formation of public spheres shaped by contestation between agents actively involved in constructing, shaping, and creating norms.

Therefore, how these platforms are governed and the ability of journalism to adapt to their logic must be at the center of the global agenda. They enable or favor certain forms of communication and practices over others, as those that conform to or leverage the properties of the dominant platforms are more likely to succeed than those that do not. Institutional, cultural, and social factors also exert influence, and ultimately the forms of organization, power, authority, and trust that emerge depend on decisions about how these platforms are governed and the way people are able to use them.[5]

For example, scholars have argued that printing ushered in new sociocultural and politico-economic practices, such as industrialization, nationalism, and vernacularization, and enabled the development of new forms of political organization—the nation-state—and new ways of thinking—such as the Enlightenment and self-determination.[6] The process by which a particular medium, such as TV or the Internet, becomes a dominant force in a given society includes compelling other institutions, such as the press or the political class, to conform to that medium's logic, resulting in new political forms and social practices, such as cable news or electoral campaigns focused on raising money.[7] Harold Innis, who argued that the medium of writing was essential to the extension of government and military power across vast distances, believed that modes of communication are fundamental to understanding the development of cultural forms and their consequences, whether they be the division of political power, the organization of the economy, or the evolution of social practices such as journalism. Similarly, social media and the ubiquitous Internet have ushered in an era in which finding and disseminating information, communicating across vast distances, and personalizing one's information diet is easier, faster, and cheaper than at any point in human history.

The Internet era has forced the journalism field to adapt to a new logic in which journalists and the media are no longer the gatekeepers and values such as immediacy, personalization, affinity, and hyperbole have become dominant. Revolutionary change in the economics of the news business has upended traditional paradigms of advertising, dissemination, and production. In 2016, Google and Facebook took the lion's share of online advertising dollars at 49 percent and 40 percent, respectively, according to the Interactive Advertising Bureau. Much has been written about the economic reconfiguring of the news industry as digital platforms decimated profit margins; suffice to say that choices about online advertising, tracking, cookies, and revenue models were made at each step of the Internet era, from websites to social media platforms to the Internet of Things. Early options to offer online content for free on a website or later on social media platforms created a path to dependency and expectation from the audience that content, particularly news content, regardless of its quality, should be free.

The ubiquity of the Internet and the increasing prevalence it plays in news consumption habits, including via mobile and various apps, mean that people are carrying portable news devices around with them wherever they go. Facebook, Google, Yahoo, and so forth deliver news they think you'll like based on your previous viewing and engagement habits and those of your friends. They use collaborative filtering, algorithmic personalization, and AI to serve up a menu of news and information they think will resonate most with a given user. The assumption at the heart of their newsfeeds and news apps is that you should get more of what you and your friends like, not necessarily what is in the public interest, or what you might not like but need to know. The result is filter bubbles and echo chambers that foster insulated communities at risk of becoming increasingly isolated from those who hold different views.[8]

Media convergence, audience fragmentation, algorithmic personalization, new media players, and the intersection of copyright, intellectual property, and expressive freedom with algorithms are just a few of the forces at work impacting the logic of how journalism functions and what "press freedom" means in the digital age. The technologies through which we make, impart, receive, and engage with journalism and other forms of information and communication have shifted considerably, at once democratizing media but also leading to new forms of media capture and censorship.

The so-called Right to Be Forgotten (RTBF), online extremism, and combating fake news have become some of the most important issue areas impacting how the Internet is governed and by whom. How these debates play out will have significant impact on our communications system, and the values on which it is premised: privacy versus transparency, free speech versus illegal speech, freedom of expression and surveillance, and the AI and algorithmic design versus human curation. The role of big data runs through each of these, as do questions about state sovereignty and the privatization of censorship. Yet despite the great promises of the Internet era, the technologies that have liberated journalism have also been turned against free and independent reporting amid pervasive surveillance, censorship, and online harassment.

Around the world, journalists and bloggers have turned to social media as the publication platform of choice. But the past few years have seen a proliferation of cybercrime legislation, anti-terrorism laws that target online speech, and prohibitions against spreading "false news." Additionally, the more traditional criminal defamation and blasphemy laws are being expanded to the Internet, often with more severe penalties than offline speech. In many less developed countries and illiberal democracies, vaguely worded laws and a lack of basic technological understanding by policymakers and judicial branches have created an increasingly perilous situation for journalists and activists. Such deliberate ambiguity serves the interests of authorities seeking to restrict independent reporting and criticism, and enables them to equate such speech with terrorism or crime. Criminalizing the creation and dissemination of a range of vaguely defined content opens up journalists, activists, and others to prosecution for engaging in standard reporting and commentary, and restricts the topics that can be discussed in the public sphere.

Nearly half of the 259 journalists imprisoned in 2016 worked online. The majority were jailed on anti-state charges such as terrorism or undermining national security, and at least nine of them were jailed on false news charges. Turkey, the leading jailer of journalists, closed down several online news outlets, destroyed the digital archives of one of the country's leading newspapers, and arrested a journalist in part because he had encrypted information on his computer. In Ethiopia, the Zone 9 bloggers[9] were sent to prison on charges of terrorism, in part for participating in an email encryption training session. Jordan has prosecuted dozens of people who posted messages that the government viewed as supportive of the Islamic State and arrested at least four journalists for reporting or commenting on anti-terrorism operations.[10] More than 110 journalists and activists in Egypt were targeted in what appeared to be a state-sponsored surveillance and hacking operation known as NilePhish.[11] Also in Egypt, a recent anti-terrorism law makes it illegal for journalists to contradict official accounts of terror attacks, imposing fines of up to $65,000 and a minimum of five years in prison for reporting information that differs from that of the Egyptian Defense Ministry.[12] In the United Kingdom, police used anti-terrorism legislation to demand communication between a BBC journalist and a man in Syria who said he was an Islamic State member, to obtain information on journalists' confidential sources, and to require Internet Service Providers to do more to track and take down extremist content. Draft UK legislation would oblige telecommunication companies to enable real-time surveillance and remove encryption.[13] But such attempts by governments to control the public sphere and punish those who digress are only half the equation.

The other half is shaping the dominant narratives in the public sphere. Russia has a host of media organizations dedicated to disseminating propaganda, interacting with news and its users, and perpetuating a certain worldview that is not hospitable to journalists or press freedom. Its Internet Research Agency reportedly employs hundreds of people to engage on social media platforms and promote a pro-Russian perspective, and appears to operate a network of pro-Kremlin websites, including the Federal News Agency. With a reported budget of at least 20 million rubles (roughly $400,000) a month and competitive salaries, it surpasses that of many news organizations; the Internet Research Agency has "industrialized the art of trolling."[14]

In the European Union (EU), the European External Action Service's StratCom team, which is charged with countering and uncovering what it calls Russian disinformation, received a boost in its 2017 budget. East StratCom maintains the EU Mythbusters Twitter account and distributes the *Disinformation Review*, a weekly bulletin highlighting examples of pro-Kremlin mis- and disinformation.[15]

Politics has always blended with the dominant media of the era. From the use of papyrus by the ancient Egyptians to extend their empire, to the role of the printing press in the secularization of politics in Europe, to the use of TV commercials by political candidates in contemporary America, to geopolitics in the era of social media.[16] In this era of social media and the networked society, one would expect that more governments will set up departments to counteract fake news/propaganda in the near future, even though there is little evidence that government-funded counternarratives have an impact, which will make it harder for democratic governments to criticize countries such as Russia, China, and Iran that already fund bot farms and pay Internet commentators to promote their views and sow disinformation.

But even as governments seek to govern the Internet, they need the help of tech companies. Internet intermediaries face increasing pressure to get involved in deciding what information should flow through their networks or platforms or in moderating the content available through their services. In many cases, states are outsourcing some of their oversight and censorial power to private companies in which there is a lack of public oversight or democratic input. This is not just the case in repressive regimes or illiberal democracies, but is in fact being led by Europe and other Western countries. And in these cases, they are often responding to public pressure.

An example is the delisting requirements mandated by European law. The RTBF ruling in the EU required that Google remove "personal data" from search results when requested, under certain exceptions, with no requirement for truth or public interest. The ruling was vague and left it up to Google to create and enforce the implementation mechanism, which it did by interpreting the ruling narrowly as applying to the relevant country-level domain rather than its entire platform. This tactic has come under fire from EU officials, who have called for a much broader interpretation of the ruling. Meanwhile, in Canada, a judge ruled that Google had to delist instances of copyright infringement across the full set of domains, irrespective of whether that country was subject to Canada's laws or not. The RTBF set a precedent for other delisting efforts, with the approach spreading to Brazil, Indonesia, Argentina, and elsewhere, led by both government and civil society. The RTBF exemplifies tensions between governmental, public, and private sector approaches to balancing privacy with openness and the free flow of information.

There is tension between normative, regulatory, and legal approaches that in some cases is tipping the balance away from state control. Governments of all stripes have called for increased surveillance powers and encryption backdoors following terrorist attacks, and are increasingly seeking to hold social media firms responsible for the monitoring and removal of extremist propaganda and accounts that promote radicalization or violence.

In early 2015, following the deadly attacks on the satirical French newspaper *Charlie Hebdo*, France, EU interior ministers, the United States, and Muslim-majority states called for greater restrictions on online extremism, including holding social media platforms partially responsible for content.[17] That same year, the UN Security Council's Counter-Terrorism Committee called for Internet platforms to be held liable for hosting or indexing extremist content. Australia has said that it will treat extremist content in the same way it treats child pornography and actively seeks its removal.[18] Several Western governments have set up Internet Referral Units specifically designed to get alleged terrorist material offline and often leverage a tech company's own Terms of Service to justify removal requests, rather than a court order. And more than 90 percent of these requests appear to be honored.[19] But governments are not content with having to do all the work to flag problematic content and demand that tech companies do more, and do it more quickly and proactively.

The same dynamic has been seen with the issue of "fake news." Fake news, like terrorism, is rarely defined but used by the public, tech firms, and policy-makers alike. The trouble with this is that "fake news" has become a catch-all term encompassing both false information portrayed as news, disinformation and misinformation, counterfeit news, and propaganda, as well as news or information someone disagrees with or doesn't like. Revelations about hacking and the scourge of "fake news" online during the 2016 US election, the United Kingdom's Brexit vote, and concerns about Russian influence in a range of European elections have put the issue of combating fake news and propaganda online front and center of the international agenda. How governments and tech firms respond will favor certain species of thought, organization, authority, and truth over others, with significant epistemological and ontological repercussions that will influence our ways of knowing and the evaluative means for establishing veracity and authority.

China has led the way in seeking to restrict news and rumors, and to deter journalists and bloggers from reporting breaking news as its leaders strive to maintain their power. But it is the more recent debates emanating from the United States and Europe that have provided cover for governments of all stripes to crack down on what they consider fake news.[20] False news restrictions are used to shutter critical outlets, censor content, and send a chilling message to the media more generally that is likely to encourage self-censorship. The proliferation of cybercrime bills has exacerbated this trend, as legislation often includes language prohibiting and even criminalizing the publication or sharing of false news and/or information.

A rash of arrests in recent years related to spreading false news, rumors, or insults on social media has been seen throughout Asia, Africa, and the Middle East, including in more liberal countries such as Jordan and Lebanon. In Cameroon, the government launched a campaign against the spread of false news via social media and proposed a social media bill that limits the dissemination of what the government considers to be rumors and "defamation of facts."[21] At least twenty countries in the world have some type of restriction on the circulation of false news, information, or rumors, according to a review of Freedom House's annual *Freedom of the Press* survey.[22] In Egypt and Ethiopia, at least nine journalists were jailed in 2016 for violating such statutes and several others detained or harassed for spreading false information, when in fact they were doing journalism.[23] Thus, in Western democracies, the issue of fake news has risen to the top of the Internet governance agenda because of

Brexit and the US elections, with repressive countries happy to use this as cover for their own practices.

If national government oversight and regulation becomes the dominant norm, then the approaches of tech platforms will have no choice but to adapt. There are now precedents for requiring Internet giants to ban or remove particular categories of content. The European Commission's Code of Conduct for Countering Illegal Hate Speech Online commits Facebook, Twitter, Microsoft, and YouTube to removing reported hate speech within twenty-four hours from their consumer-facing properties. Similarly, the so-called RTBF created a mechanism for individuals to request content removal. Thus, mechanisms for handling, assessing, and implementing complaints are in place. Although well-intentioned, this outsources responsibility to private companies to determine what is legal or permitted, without sufficient guidance from the courts, even as they decry the size and power of these Internet giants and call for efforts to break what they see as a monopoly. Regulations also appear to be increasingly broad and interpreted to apply not only to the national context, but to the entire platform. This creates the opportunity for authoritarian governments who would seek to control the online narrative through censorship to make similar demands.

Many of the Internet giants say that they don't want to be in the position of having to decide what speech is legal or not, and dispute that they play the role of publisher. But the major tech platforms such as Facebook, Google, and Yahoo all exert some form of editorial control over news content. They have adopted practices that are more similar than not to publishing, such as creating partnerships with journalistic organizations, fact-checking, removing or restricting content, and curating news. Other tech companies appear less concerned about making normative decisions about what information should be allowed in the public sphere. The web-hosting service GoDaddy, Google, and CloudFlare kicked the neo-Nazi site *Daily Stormer* off their services. But, whereas the former claimed it violated their terms of service, the latter called the decision arbitrary and that of the CEO, who wrote in an e-mail to staff that he "woke up in a bad mood" and called the people behind the offending site an expletive.[24] He also cautioned against the danger of this power to decide who could be online or not, noting in a blog that "a small number of companies will largely determine what can and cannot be online."[25] He could make that decision, he said, "because I'm the CEO of a major Internet infrastructure company." As one tech journalist wrote, the company has "helped to establish an industry-wide norm that some content is too offensive to be hosted by any mainstream technology company." [26]

Putting subjective decisions about what constitutes extremist content, fake news, or hate speech in the hands of corporate actors without providing them with sufficient guidance, ensuring effective remedy, or requiring transparency about how such decisions are made and remedies implemented risks privatizing censorship and infringing on protected speech and due process, and could unwittingly provide a tool to repressive governments or tech leaders to retaliate against unwanted criticism or opposition.

Intermediary Liability and the Privatization of Censorship

Technology companies, unlike media companies, are shielded from legal responsibility for content that appears on their platforms—otherwise know as *intermediary liability*. The core issues of the debate over legal responsibility hold significant implications for what role Internet and social media companies play in journalism and the free flow of information. Should social media firms be legally responsible for removing hate speech, "fake news," or extremist content? Germany thinks so, and in 2016, it passed a law that would compel social media companies to remove illegal content within a very short time frame or risk fines as high as €50 million.[27] While the law applies to "social media networks" with more than two million users and includes an exception for "platforms with journalist content for which the platform operation takes full responsibility," overly broad language could affect a range of platforms and services and put decisions about what is illegal content into the hands of private companies that may be inclined to overcensor in order to avoid potential fines.

This concern is not hypothetical. The former associate general counsel at Google, Daphne Keller, told *BuzzFeed News* that Internet platforms "take down perfectly legal content out of concern that otherwise they themselves could get in trouble."[28] Such measures could make it more difficult for journalists, media, and civil society more broadly in repressive countries, where they rely on social media to disseminate news and engage in the public sphere, because of concerns that legitimate critique would be interpreted as extremism. "Governments should set the boundaries through laws about what is illegal, not leave it up to the companies, this is not a principled approach and leads to questions over why something is or is not terrorism," said one Internet company official in an interview.

Nonetheless, as companies are under fire to scrub extremist content, fake news, and hate speech from their platforms in order to head off government regulation, they are censoring content and offending accounts, reconfiguring economic incentives, and experimenting with new approaches. For example, Twitter not only removed offending "fake news" accounts, including those belonging to the so-called alt-right in the United States, but it also refused to verify some accounts, or even removed their verification status, a symbol of authenticity.[29] Online app stores removed some alt-right news sites and the Twitter accounts of several people associated with the alt-right, including a technology journalist for *Breitbart News* and an executive at *Business Insider*.[30] Facebook, Google (YouTube), Twitter, and Microsoft have created a shared database of content they deem to be "extremist" and removed from a given platform, demonstrating how hashes, essentially a form of digital fingerprinting, can be used to facilitate content removal across multiple platforms.[31] The Association for Progressive Communications said that such an approach showed that "Google/Jigsaw is openly venturing into selling ideologies, with little transparency or oversight of its methods."[32] As Nicholas Lemann wrote in the *New Yorker*, "one relatively new private company, which isn't in journalism, has become the dominant provider of journalism to the public, and the only way people can think of to address what they see as a terrifying crisis in politics and public life is to ask the company's billionaire CEO to fix it."[33]

Tech firms are also seeking to rejigger the economic incentives that have fueled many counterfeit news or disinformation sites, and are experimenting with new approaches to signal veracity. Google and Facebook announced that their advertising systems would ban sites that traffic in misinformation and disinformation, and both have implemented new tools to identify and combat "fake news." Facebook's tool allows users to flag "hoaxes" and has partnered with a handful of third-party fact-checking organizations to flag "disputed" news. On some Google news pages, a "fact-check" tag has been included. Deciding who decides what news is fake is a governance question, one that will empower some actors over others, and affect the dynamics of the public sphere.[34]

The approaches that companies take and the solutions they build influence what governments can mandate they do.[35] Currently these initiatives are voluntary, but they could be made mandatory, which would set a troubling "precedent for cross-site censorship," according to the nonprofit Center for Democracy and Technology.[36] For example, tech companies argued against creating a shared database for content removal related to the RTBF, but put one in place for extremist content. Now that such a shared database exists and coordination between companies is taking place, this could be expanded to include other types of objectionable content—such as "fake news"—and create legal "knowledge" among participating companies about such content. What happens when repressive governments want companies to use these mechanisms to pursue objectives such as clamping down on dissent? For example, Turkey could make the same case for Gulenist content, as could Egypt about Muslim Brotherhood content.

Journalists and media organizations are getting caught up in removal efforts by Western tech firms. When tech platforms make choices about what content to remove, they rely on automated processes. Although most claim human review at some point, they inevitably end up censoring journalistic material, with little recourse for those affected. Tech companies must automate some aspect of content removal because of the scale and scope of content being created and shared. This results in what I call *algorithmic censorship*, a particular type of privatized censorship.

After YouTube announced an automated review for "violent extremist" content, the pages of several Syrian news sites and sites documenting human rights abuses were closed and accounts deactivated, according to several reports. As Google executives were blogging about the accuracy of their AI program and the fact that 75 percent of videos "removed for violent extremism over the past month were taken down before receiving a single human flag," *Orient News* appeared to have had its account closed and *Middle East Eye* had several videos from Syria removed for violating community standards.[37] Evidence used in the Chelsea Manning case was also reportedly removed. Facebook suspended the account of a French journalist because a 2013 post included an Islamic State flag,[38] and the citizen journalism group RBSS told me that their accounts on

Facebook and Twitter were shut down for several weeks because of reported terms of service violations, though they provided the only coverage of Raqqa to counter Islamic State propaganda. Requests through the automated system received no response, and it was not until someone intervened directly with the companies that those RBSS accounts were reinstated. But even with human review, errors or judgment will be made that require consideration of context and interpretation in deciding on the permissibility of any content. Thus, Facebook defended its decision to remove a post of the Pulitzer Prize–winning *Napalm Girl* photo because it violated its community standards. The decision to cleanse the Internet of violent extremism means journalists, intelligence analysts, and researchers will also lose access to the content. What if the United States sought to extend its prohibition against showing the flag-draped coffins of soldiers being returned from Iraq or Afghanistan to the Internet? As Arendt observed, "appearances are realities, and that which does not appear is politically insignificant."[39]

Search algorithms and social networking feeds determine what you see at the top of results and effectively bury whatever is decided to be less relevant or recommended to you based on unknown criteria. They configure the public sphere by making some things visible. Algorithmic personalization and collaborative filtering, such as recommendations about which content you might like based on your previous consumption patterns, are perfectly suited to and a product of the dominant communications ecosystem. The convergence of AI and algorithmic design will influence the information ecosystem in ways that are as yet unknown.

Conclusion

Information and events rarely have inherent meaning or importance; they must be interpreted, framed, and contextualized before becoming imbued with significance and import, a process in which gatekeepers such as journalists and media owners traditionally played a central role. That is why Internet governance as media regulation matters. The way tech companies and governments grapple with "fake news" and terrorist content online will have significant political and public policy repercussions that will impact the Internet and information flows in the years to come. It is essential, therefore, that self-regulation by tech companies be transparent, subject to independent oversight, and include some sort of path to remedy.

An algorithmic ombudsperson could assess the policies of private tech companies and the assumptions on which algorithms are based to ascertain the impact on the public interest. And any remedy must be more effective than the black box that online complaint mechanisms currently invoke.

How Internet giants decide to implement policies around what type of information flows through their platforms can have unintended consequences that may serve to restrict or facilitate press freedom and the free flow of information. As new technologies emerge, the public, policymakers, and the private sector must grapple with how to govern the global public sphere.

Notes

[1] https://wearesocial.com/special-reports/digital-in-2017-global-overview.

[2] https://reutersinstitute.politics.ox.ac.uk/sites/default/files/Digital%20News%20Report%20 2017%20web_0.pdf.

[3] https://qz.com/333313/milliions-of-facebook-users-have-no-idea-theyre-using-the-internet/; http://www.zdnet.com/article/who-really-wins-from-facebooks-free-internet-plan-for-africa/.

[4] https://www.wired.com/2016/10/att-buying-time-warner-future-google/.

[5] Ronald Diebert, *Parchment, Printing, and Hypermedia* (New York: Columbia University Press, 1997); Neil Postman, *Amusing Ourselves to Death: Public Discourse in the Age of Show Business* (London: Penguin, 2006).

[6] Benedict Anderson, *Imagined Communities: Reflections on the Origin and Spread of Nationalism* (London and New York: Verso, 1991); Innis Harold, *Empire and Communication* (Toronto UP, 1950); Marshall McLuhan, *The Gutenberg Galaxy: The Making of Typographic Man* (Toronto: University of Toronto Press, 2011).

[7] Pierre Bourdieu, *Practical Reason: On the Theory of Action* (Palo Alto, CA: Stanford University Press, 1998); David L. Altheide, *Media Logic* (New York: John Wiley & Sons, 1979).

[8] Castells, Sunstein.

[9] A collective of Ethiopian bloggers.

[10] http://www.theguardian.com/world/2014/nov/27/-sp-courts-jordan-crush-support-isis; https://cpj .org/2015/07/jordanian-court-orders-arrest-of-journalist-over-t.php.

[11] https://cpj.org/blog/2017/06/how-surveillance-trolls-and-fear-of-arrest-is-affe.php.

[12] https://cpj.org/2015/08/egypts-new-anti-terrorism-law-deepens-crackdown-on.php.

[13] https://cpj.org/2017/05/expanded-surveillance-powers-could-threaten-work-o.php.

[14] https://www.nytimes.com/2015/06/07/magazine/the-agency.html?_r=0.

[15] https://twitter.com/EUvsDisinfo; https://euvsdisinfo.eu/.

[16] Deibert.

[17] http://www.wired.co.uk/news/archive/2015-01/12/charlie-hebdo-isp-internet-surveillance; http:// www.bloomberg.com/news/2015-01-27/france-seeks-to-sanction-web-companies-for-posts-pushing-terror.html; http://www.msnbc.com/msnbc/senators-introduce-social-media-bill-after-terror-attacks.

[18] http://www.abc.net.au/news/2015-02-20/brandis-announces-program-to-combat-terrorist-propaganda/6160406.

[19] http://cima.ned.org/wp-content/uploads/2016/10/CIMA-CVE-Paper_web-150ppi.pdf; http://www .theverge.com/2015/1/28/7931043/european-union-flag-terrorist-youtube-videos.

[20] https://www.cpj.org/blog/2011/10/china-confronts-internet-rumors-and-trashy-tv.php; https://www .cpj.org/2011/08/chinese-microblog-suspends-accounts-for-false-rumo.php.

[21] https://fronteranews.com/news/africa/can-equate-social-media-terrorism-cameroon-thinks/; http://internetwithoutborders.org/fr/cameroonian-governments-dangerous-stance-against-a-free-and-open-internet/.

[22] https://freedomhouse.org/.

[23] https://cpj.org/imprisoned/2016.php.

[24] https://arstechnica.com/tech-policy/2017/08/cloudflare-ceo-the-people-behind-the-daily-stormer-are-assholes/.

[25] https://blog.cloudflare.com/why-we-terminated-daily-stormer/.

[26] https://arstechnica.com/tech-policy/2017/08/cloudflare-ceo-the-people-behind-the-daily-stormer-are-assholes/.

[27] http://fortune.com/2017/06/30/germany-law-social-media-hate/.

[28] https://www.buzzfeed.com/hamzashaban/eus-online-hate-speech-deal-prompts-fears-of-censorship?utm_term=.wxxqZ1NQVN#.al68gLjZnj.

[29] https://cpj.org/blog/2017/03/deciding-who-decides-which-news-is-fake.php.

[30] https://www.washingtonpost.com/news/morning-mix/wp/2016/11/16/a-great-purge-twitter-suspends-richard-spencer-other-prominent-alt-right-accounts/;http://fortune.com/2016/11/16/twitter-ban-alt-right/.

[31] https://blog.google/topics/google-europe/partnering-help-curb-spread-terrorist-content-online/.

32 https://www.apc.org/en/news/question-day-how-protect-human-rights-online-while.
33 http://www.newyorker.com/news/news-desk/solving-the-problem-of-fake-news It%E2%80%99s.
34 https://cpj.org/blog/2017/03/deciding-who-decides-which-news-is-fake.php.
35 https://cpj.org/blog/2012/02/twitter-google-selective-blocking-censorship.php.
36 https://cdt.org/blog/takedown-collaboration-by-private-companies-creates-troubling-precedent/.
37 http://www.middleeasteye.net/news/youtube-criticised-after-middle-east-video-taken-down-over-extremist-content-1244893230.
38 https://rsf.org/en/news/rsf-deplores-suspension-french-journalists-facebook-account.
39 Jeffrey C. Goldfarb, *The Politics of Small Things: The Power of the Powerless in Dark Times* (Chicago, IL: University of Chicago Press, 2007), 14.

PART II

SOCIETY

CHAPTER 7

An Economy in Service to Life

L. Hunter Lovins

David Brower, the founder of the modern environmental movement, once asked, "What do you want the earth to look like in 50 years?" "Let's do a little dreaming. Aim high," he said. "Navigators have aimed at the stars for centuries. They haven't hit one yet, but because they aimed high they found their way."

Is our future one of empowered entrepreneurs and innovators building a resilient society that works for everyone? Will clean energy and regenerative agriculture roll climate change backwards,[1] create millions of high-wage jobs, and empower sustainable livelihoods for people around the world?[2] Will a commitment to ensuring well-being[3] for all the world's people displace the cold-hearted neoliberalism that is now the default global economic narrative?[4] Will we build a society that is regenerative, one that restores the environment and repairs the damage caused by inequality?

It's a dream worth working for. But to get there, we'll need to create a new story of who we are, what we want, and how to achieve a finer future.

The story that defines us today is based on the belief that people are selfish and our economy is the single most important thing that society needs to protect. Acting on this narrative has brought humanity to a cliff's edge, to the risk of total system collapse.[5] The international community must recognize that there's nothing to guarantee that the human species will make it. In what is rapidly becoming an existential crisis, survival means embracing the principles of living systems; it means crafting an economy in service to life. This transformation goes far beyond older framings of sustainable development to regenerative economics.

Collapse Is a Risk

Think about it: total civilizational collapse.
The loss of everything that you care about.
Impossible?

For millions of people around the globe, collapse is already common-place: from beggars on the streets in major cities,[6] to infrastructure crumbling,[7] to one in ten people the world around without safe water,[8] and millions of Chinese,[9] Indians,[10] and Americans[11] dying every year from acute air pollution.

Ours is a very brittle system; its vulnerability evident in everything from offshored jobs to organized crime going global, to the fact that the failure of a bank no one had ever heard of on Cyprus threatened the financial stability of the Eurozone.[12] Frustrated young men with nowhere to go, no jobs, and no prospects are radicalized, and launch predictable attacks against which there is no defense.[13] International diplomat Christiana Figueres warned,

> People have lost trust that their lives can get better and that institutions are on their side. This in turn is leading to apathy, depression, despair and in some cases to the development of radical views. This cycle must be stopped, before it consumes our collective future.[14]

Today, sixty-five million refugees are on the move, more than at any time since World War II.[15] Mercy Corps estimates that twenty-four more people become migrants every minute.[16] Threatening the stability of the European Union,[17] this flood of humanity is driving xenophobic populism around the world.[18] Twice that many people face conflict or disasters, and need an estimated $35 billion each year in humanitarian assistance.[19] Collectively, this is exhausting even the most generous donor nations. And these numbers don't count the estimated $1.4 trillion needed each year to implement the Sustainable Development Goals.[20]

In 2015, a group of applied mathematicians studied the phenomenon of collapse throughout human history.[21] They concluded that cases of severe civilizational disruption "due to precipitous collapse—often lasting centuries—have been quite common." The title "Human And Nature DYnamical Study (HANDY)" was clearly chosen for the acronym, but the subtitle, "Is Industrial Civilization Headed for Irreversible Collapse," sets forth the thesis. The authors did not claim to make short-term predictions, but their conclusion is stark: under conditions "closely reflecting the reality of our world today . . . we find that collapse is difficult to avoid."

Collapses throughout history inflicted massive misery, often for centuries following. They caused population decline, economic deterioration, intellectual regression, and the disappearance of literacy (Roman collapse); serious collapse of political authority and socioeconomic progress (repeated Chinese collapses); disappearance of up to 90 percent of the population (Mayan); and some losses so complete that forests swallowed any trace until archaeologists rediscovered the ruins of once-complex societies (many Asian collapses).

The study argued, however, that collapses are neither inevitable, nor natural; they have two underlying causes:

1. "*the stretching of resources* due to the strain placed on the ecological carrying capacity" (emphasis added)
2. "*the economic stratification of society* into Elites [rich] and Masses (or 'Commoners') [poor]" (emphasis added)

These causes, the study concluded, have played "a central role in . . . the process of the collapse." This was their finding across cases drawn from over "the last five thousand years."

Rebuttals on ideological websites[22] objected that the study's use of mathematical models made collapse seem unavoidable. To be fair, the HANDY authors stated, in terms, that collapse is not inevitable. But in a time in which every major ecosystem on earth is threatened, and inequality has soared to pre-Depression levels, the warning is timely.

It is especially timely given that the HANDY authors are not alone in prophesying looming ruin. From the 1972 book *Limits to Growth*[23] to Dr. Graham Turner's 2014 report *Is Collapse Imminent?*,[24] many have warned that business as usual will drive collapse. (The 1972 book anticipated it in the 2030s.) At that point, the books and reports warn, human activity and, indeed, populations will decline, in some cases precipitously. Historian Peter Turchin now predicts that humanity will collapse within ten years.[25] Social instability and political violence, he says, will peak even earlier.[26]

The woes of the world are not an accident. Nelson Mandela once said, "Like Slavery and Apartheid, poverty is not natural. It is man-made and it can be overcome and eradicated by actions of human beings."[27]

The story on which our current economy rests began with Adam Smith and the other "liberal" economists. Their concept of capitalism displaced the feudal systems of the Middle Ages and unleashed the greatest prosperity the world has even known. Captured by robber barons, however, it corrupted into the crony capitalism that created the first gilded age and the Great Depression.

Whirled between the New Deal and a world at war, economic theory came to rest in 1947 with thirty-six men. Gathered at Mont Pelerin, a hotel in Switzerland, they sought to return economic thinking to Smith's pure form of capitalism.[28] Arguing that markets are perfect and that individual liberty is the single most important value, they agreed that the only legitimate role of government is to maintain a military, enforce contracts, and protect an individual's ability to amass private wealth. Following a severe form of neo-Darwinism, they saw people as greedy, desiring only personal gain. Money, they said, is the best metric of success. If the rich are rich, it is because they clawed their way to the top of the food chain. The rest of us, therefore, because we're inherently inferior, are properly relegated to the role of servants to what these neoliberals believed was a just economy. Our purpose is to work to secure enough money so that we can buy things and thereby participate meaningfully in their all-important, consumer society.

The small band, including Milton Friedman, Ludwig von Mises, and Friedrich Hayek, was remarkably successful. Their Mont Pelerin Society placed its members as advisors to every head of state on the planet, with several of them serving as central bankers and three of them becoming heads of state themselves. They took control of the Chicago School of Economics, used the newly created "Nobel Prize in Economic Science" to legitimize their approach, and spread their ideology to economics departments and companies around the world.

The framers of neoliberal ideology saw humans as uncaring, and narrowly self-interested. And that's OK, they said: the magic of the market means that people individualistically pursuing their greed will aggregate to deliver the greatest good for the greatest number.

The only trouble is that the real world doesn't work that way. Supremely self-interested people do exist. Science tells us that about 1 percent of the population, individuals that psychologists label as psychopaths, accurately fit this description.

Most of us, however, are not like that. We yearn for more than just acquiring money.

The view of human nature and how to achieve success is dogmatically taught in most economics courses and in business schools around the world.[29] A *Forbes* magazine article blamed this version of economic theory for the problems facing the world today:

> [T]he fault lies not with the rich, not with corporations, not with China, not with the Illuminati, not with Al Qaeda, but with the economics discipline. Bad ideas have done at least as much damage to our world as anyone's bad intentions. Decades of misguided policy from both political parties and in other nations has critically weakened the core of our economy and left us in a situation where, despite our tremendous level of technological achievement, we seem to be regressing. Just as in the Great Depression, we have the ability to solve these problems practically overnight. What we lack is sound theory to guide our actions.[30]

Worse, politicians and many other economic actors interpret the discipline and base their political decision-making on half-baked theories. As Milton Keynes, one of the more famous economists, stated, "Practical men who believe themselves exempt from any intellectual influences are usually the slaves of some defunct economist."[31] The myths and half-truths to which politicians routinely fall prey include the beliefs that: we can have infinite growth in a finite world; markets are inherently fair; prices tell the truth; salaries reflect value; and more income equals more happiness. These fallacies contribute significantly to the malfunctioning of the current economic system.

Rethinking how economics is taught, and how it is used by politicians, is vital to achieving the systemic change we need. Oxford professor Kate Raworth describes how to do this in her work on Doughnut Economics.[32] Student groups across the world are meeting to rewrite the discipline.[33]

Because professional economists, and the politicians they advise, get the social science wrong, the economy doesn't work for most people on earth. We have created a system that seeks to meet nonmaterial needs with material things, celebrating consumerism and stripping the earth like locusts. It's called "shopping therapy" or "He who dies with the most toys wins."

As Ellen Goodman puts it,

> Normal is getting dressed in clothes that you buy for work and driving through traffic in a car that you are still paying for in order to get to the job that you need to pay for the clothes and the car and the house that you leave vacant all day so you can afford to live in it.[34]

"Too big to fail" crushes local self-determination, and millions of people reportedly hate their jobs.

And we grow lonelier.

Pope Francis warned, "The external deserts in the world are growing, because the internal deserts have become so vast."[35] He quotes the Earth Charter that challenges humanity to do better:

> As never before in history, common destiny beckons us to seek a new beginning . . . Let ours be a time remembered for the awakening of a new reverence for life, the firm resolve to achieve sustainability, the quickening of the struggle for justice and peace, and the joyful celebration of life.[36]

To get there, we will have to overcome a well-financed strategy to deliver precisely the world we have today. In 1971, Lewis Powell, a Washington lawyer, soon to become Supreme Court Justice, was asked by the head of the US Chamber of Commerce to set forth how to relegitimize business after the cultural transformation of the 1960s. Powell wrote the "Confidential Memorandum: Attack on American Free Enterprise System"[37] that laid out a strategy to enable corporatism to embed itself in every influential sector of society, including high schools and universities, media, judiciary, and town councils. On the strength of this strategy, wealthy foundations and individuals such as the Koch Brothers founded and endowed such institutions as the Heritage Foundation, American Legislative Exchange Council (ALEC), American Enterprise Institute, Cato Institute, and the other organs of neoliberal ideology that are ascendant today. It is worth reading Powell's Memorandum, and reflecting on the extent to which his strategy succeeded. Within nine years, Ronald Reagan was president of the United States and Margaret Thatcher was prime minister in the United Kingdom; neoliberalism had captured the Western world. With the fall of the Berlin Wall and communism thereafter, it dominated the globe.

The institutions founded by the Powell Memorandum are still at it. When resurgent populism swept a new administration into the White House, the new president was handed a playbook and list of nominees by the Heritage Foundation.[38] ALEC continues to provide legislation for, among other things, suppressing voters and democracy across the world.

Neoliberalism, built to defend personal freedom from the evils of fascism and communism, has become the tool of the new oppressors. Before the elections of Reagan and Thatcher, all classes of people were rising together. After 1980, only the top 1 percent prospered. In 2016, Oxfam estimated that eighty-five people had as much wealth as the poorest 3.5 billion. By 2017, that number had become eight men owning the same as half of humanity. The richest 1 percent in the world now has more than the other 99 percent of humanity.[39] Meanwhile, billions of people struggle and every major ecosystem on earth is threatened.[40]

It's a Mess

Or if it's not, as the actor Tommy Lee Jones said, "It'll do til the mess gets here."[41]

So what do we do?

Some people look at these statistics and say, "There's nothing I can do, so I'll just quit trying and party until it's over."[42] This is perhaps the most profoundly irresponsible thing you can do. You are the result of four billion years of evolutionary history. Act like it.

Further, it is intellectually dishonest. There IS a route forward. Rabbits freeze when threatened. Humans invent a new solution. Throughout human history, we have bonded to create a better world.

The first step is to commit, personally, that you are going to act. Courageous citizens are stopping at least some of the destruction facing us: human rights activists[43] fight inhumane conditions in Bangladeshi factories[44] or biopiracy[45] in India. Professors,[46] scientists,[47] businesspeople,[48] and young people[49] risk arrest to stop the mining of coal and the construction of pipelines to ship fracked oil.[50] Students and clergy[51] demand that their universities and churches divest from ownership in fossil fuels.

Conservationists save remnants of intact ecosystems,[52] and agency personnel enforce pollution regulations.[53] Practitioners of corporate social responsibility elicit enhanced profits from cutting harmful business practices[54] and ensure that workers and communities are treated decently.[55] Green developers create less wasteful, more delightful buildings to deliver higher productivity because employees do better in cleaner environments.[56] Aid agencies from United Nations (UN) High Commissioner for Refugees and the World Food Programme to nongovernmental organizations such as CARE and Oxfam overcome vast odds to feed and comfort the millions struggling with famine and dislocation.

Organizations such as CDP[57] set standards and measure reduction in impacts. They show that companies that are managing their carbon emissions and are mitigating climate change enjoy 18 percent higher returns on their investment than companies that aren't, and 67 percent higher returns than companies that refuse to disclose their emissions.[58]

New accounting systems such as the Global Reporting Initiative,[59] the International Integrated Reporting Committee,[60] the Sustainability Accounting Standards Board,[61] and other metrics groups measure and prove the business case for more responsible behavior.

All of these proponents of "sustainability" strive to bring the system back to neutral. By definition, sustainable means the system, or an enterprise, is able, unlike now, to endure indefinitely without collapse. The disparate efforts for change are essential foundations. They place "sustainability" as a necessary midpoint of the climb.

But where are we going?

The world's collective progress toward sustainability is more than noble; it's essential if we are to preserve life as we know it. But increasingly, even those doing this work sense that it is failing to meet the crises accelerating around us. The conventional definition of sustainable development, meeting the needs of the present without compromising the ability of future generations to meet their needs,[62] is essential and necessary, but it is insufficient.

It has become fashionable to denigrate sustainability because it isn't enough. Some fault "green" activities as being only "less bad," "uninspiring." But this circular firing squad is worse than silly. It confuses and disheartens people facing a world rushing to economic and ecological catastrophe.[63] As Jo Confino, executive editor of the *Huffington Post*, puts it, "The status quo is a huge beast with claws sharpened and teeth bared. All the new models that people are pushing are like mice running around bumping into each other."[64]

Imagine a pool of muck. This isn't far off from a description of the collapse coming at us. Every bit of the work that we are doing to lift humanity toward sustainability is a rung on the ladder we are building to ascend up out of the degenerative world in which we now live.

All of the work that we are doing to accelerate green practices, to maximize sustainability, and to build a regenerative world is essential to the structural integrity of our ladder. Take away the lower rungs and we all sink deeper into the muck. What is missing is a shared story of a common commitment.

In the wake of the 2016 US election, a resistance movement, the largest in human history, rose across the globe.[65] Activists woke from a forty-year somnolence to demand a world based on caring for each other, on abundance and equity, on community integrity and ensuring that citizens have a say over how their lives will unfold. What can you do? Join the resistance.

A New Narrative Rising

At the same time, recognize that doing the same thing and expecting a different outcome is insanity. Yes, redouble your efforts to integrate sustainability throughout your business and your community. Implement green practices, build the business case for whole-system sustainability, and rally your neighbors and coworkers to appreciate the value of work together for the common good. But realize that until we change the story of who we are, and where we want to get to, the best we'll achieve is to keep the current system from collapsing.

Humanity is hungry for "a vision all living things can share."[66] To supplant the prevailing neoliberal myth, we need a new narrative that portrays a world that works for 100 percent of humanity, as Buckminster Fuller put it. Our goal must become the equitable distribution of resources in ways that deliver well-being for everyone within planetary limits: shared well-being on a healthy planet.

The future is founded on our vision. The stories we tell ourselves are the runways to that future. Or they become the locks that trap us into dead ends. In that sense, the future is now: what we do today delivers the reality of tomorrow.

A fresh vision for the future is emerging.[67] Born of a new narrative, it says that humans are happiest when we are interconnected.[68] Money matters and is a useful tool, but the health of our home and families matters more.[69] Equity throughout society and resilience are better starting places for a global economy.[70] We can, says this new vision, "entrepreneur" our way to a finer future.

The new story starts with a more sophisticated understanding of who we are as human beings. The best modern science tells us that we are not simply the rugged individuals that the neoliberal myth would have us believe. The evolutionary biologists now know that when hominids came down out of the trees in Africa, we were naked, our claws were pretty inadequate, our teeth were pretty puny, we weren't as fast as a lion. Archeologists tell us that before we were even fully human, we nearly died out: the population was reduced to only a few thousand individuals.[71] They survived, and we are here, because they weren't greedy bastards, in it only for themselves.

Instead, these few individuals, our ancestors, bonded. Because they cared more for each other, they prevailed. They cared more for their whole group than any individual cared for his or her personal success.[72] We, say the evolutionary biologists, are alive today because our ancestors created solutions together. In our DNA, they say, are these genes: the fierce longing to work together, to care for one another, and to begin again. All animals have a drive to acquire what they need to live, and to defend this. What makes us uniquely human, says Dr. Paul Lawrence of Harvard, as Darwin himself noted, is an equally powerful drive to bond. And a drive to comprehend, to create, to innovate. To be happy, says Lawrence, humans need to fulfill each and all of these drives.

The best science shows that many of the underlying assumptions of the old narrative are wrong. Most people are not the greedy individualists we've been told we all are. Rather, we seek goodness, caring, and connection first. All people need basic material support, but few of us are motivated primarily to acquire wealth. We seek lives that mean something, to leave the world a little better than we found it. And we long to bond with others who do the same. This is why organizations that respect dignity and implement more sustainable practices better engage workers, increasing productivity. The companies that create purpose-driven, sustainable brands deliver higher profitability.[73]

The Regenerative Economy

John Fullerton spent eighteen years at J. P. Morgan, leaving as managing director. In 2001, he walked away to create a new approach. Realizing that the essence of life and the evolutionary process is regeneration, he pointed out that sustainability is the result, not the means, of getting development right. Nature, he says, is sustainable *because* it is regenerative (see figure 7.1).

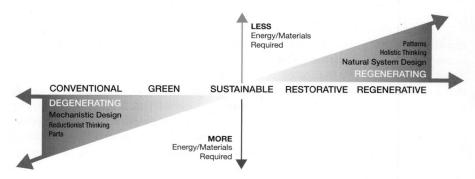

Figure 7.1   An Economy: Place—Culture—Enterprise—Government—Commons

Source: Adapted from Bill Reed's "Trajectory of Ecological Design." Graphic courtesy of Capital Institute.

Yes, it is critical to buy time by fighting the degenerative aspects of the current system and reach a sustainable plateau, but to go beyond that, we need to build a better one. Fullerton outlined what he calls Regenerative Capitalism,[74] articulating what an economy aligned with natural systems and the laws (not theories) of physics would look like. Leading evolutionary theorists agree,[75] and are now cataloguing the patterns and principles that nature (living and non-living alike) uses to build stable, healthy, and sustainable systems throughout the world.

Fullerton sets forth eight principles:

1. *Right relationship*: Holding the continuation of life sacred and recognizing that the human economy is embedded in human culture, which is itself embedded in the biosphere. All systems—from molecular scale all the way to cosmic scale—are nested, interconnected, and defined by overarching relationships of mutualism within which any exchange takes place.

2. *Innovative, adaptive, and responsive*: Drawing on the innate ability of human beings to innovate and "create anew" across all sectors of society. Humans are innately creative and entrepreneurial. Even in failure, we "begin again."

3. *Views wealth holistically*: True wealth is not money in the bank. It is defined in terms of the well-being of the "whole," achieved through the harmonization of the multiple forms of capital, with system health only as strong as the weakest link. Well-being depends on belonging, on community, and on an array of community-stewarded assets.

4. *Empowered participation*: All participants of the system must be empowered to participate in and contribute to the health of the whole. Therefore, beyond whatever moral beliefs one may hold, financial and nonfinancial wealth must be equitably (although not necessarily equally) distributed in the context of an expanded understanding of systemic health. All people long to be part of something bigger than themselves.

5. *Robust circulatory flow*: Like the metabolism of any healthy system, resources (material and nonmaterial) must circulate up and down the system efficiently and effectively. Circular economy[76] concepts for material and energy are one important aspect of this principle at work in a Regenerative Economy.

6. *"Edge effect" abundance*: In nature, the most abundant places are where two ecosystems come together: where a meadow meets a forest, or a river the sea. Creative collaborations across sectors of the economy increase the possibility of value-adding wealth creation through diversity of relationships, exchanges, and resiliency.

7. *Seeks balance*: Balances resilience, the long run ability to learn and grow stronger from shocks, with efficiency, which, while more dynamic, creates brittle concentrations of power. Living within planetary boundaries, without collapse, requires economic systems that are designed for a balance of efficiency and resilience, and are built on patterns and principles that mirror those found in healthy natural systems.

8. *Honors community and place*: Operating to nurture healthy, stable communities and regions, both real and virtual, in a connected mosaic of place-centered economies. We can have a global exchange of goods and services so long as it ensures the unique integrity of each place.

Organizations such as Capital Institute,[77] Savory Institute,[78] Natural Capitalism Solutions,[79] and leading companies across the world[80] are beginning to implement these principles to align economics with the way the rest of the world works.

Fullerton's principles are not absolutes. They are part of the emerging field of holistic thinking. They are interconnected and necessarily work together to sketch a complex pattern that is beyond linear description. They draw from the best thinking in ecological economics,[81] economic democracy, positive psychology,[82] evolutionary biology,[83] and the emerging discipline of Humanistic Management[84] to offer a new story of who we are as human beings, and how we can craft a finer future.[85]

Pragmatic examples of a Regenerative Economy[86] are emerging in community cohousing projects,[87] and the rise of green development[88] and community ownership movements.[89] Its glimmerings can be seen in the triumph of the sun,[90] as distributed, renewable energy becomes cheaper[91] almost everywhere than fossil fuels and industrial control of our power systems.[92] In late 2016, Bloomberg New Energy reported that solar now costs less than wind, which costs less than any fossil energy, noting, "The world recently passed a turning point and is adding more capacity for clean energy each year than for coal and natural gas combined. Peak fossil-fuel use for electricity may be reached within the next decade."[93] Meanwhile, renewables also generate twelve times the new jobs of any fossil energy. The International Energy Agency reported that in 2015, renewable energy jobs increased by 6 percent, while employment in oil and gas decreased by 18 percent.[94]

Such agencies as the UN Conference on Trade and Development,[95] and Food and Agriculture Organization[96] now recognize that organic, smallholder agriculture is the only feasible way to feed the world's people. The success of holistic planned grazing in returning carbon to the world's grasslands through regenerative agriculture[97] is showing how we can roll climate change backwards, profitably solving one of humanity's worst crises.

Scholars look at the prospect that automation will destroy most current jobs[98] and turn to alternatives such as basic income guarantees.[99] This is being recognized as a way to eliminate profound poverty in developing countries,[100] at the same time that it confers dignity on people previously stigmatized by being trapped in welfare.

Corporate leaders are learning that not only is there an undeniable and robust business case for adopting more regenerative practices,[101] but it's also the right thing to do. As corporate sustainability icon Ray Anderson showed,[102] doing this enhances every aspect of shareholder value.[103] More recently, Paul Polman, CEO of Unilever, showed that the company's brands that are committed to sustainability drive 60 percent of the company's profits, and are growing 50 percent faster than the rest of the company.[104]

California,[105] which has committed to cut its carbon emissions to 40 percent below its 1990 levels by 2030, and 80 percent by 2050, already employs more people in the solar industry (sixty-four thousand people) than all coal mines in the United States (fifty-three thousand people).[106] Fans of irony chuckled when the Kentucky Coal Museum installed solar panels on its roof because doing that was cheaper than buying the electricity sold by its coal-fired utility.[107] California's green economy has expanded manufacturing and the economy is booming, with state gross income increasing by 17 percent from 2003 to 2013, even as greenhouse gas emissions fell by 5.5 percent. It is now considering committing to be 100 percent renewably powered by 2050,[108] as the statistics showed that this course lifted it from the world's eighth largest economy to the fifth.

The science fiction writer William Gibson said, "The future is already here, it's just not widely distributed." Our movement is already here, it's just not self-aware and interconnected.

Most fundamentally, it has lacked a coherent narrative: a story of who we are, what we stand for, and how we are going to achieve it.

But the people of the world are awakening. In 2015, essentially all UN member nations agreed to two landmark global treaties. First, the UN General Assembly unanimously adopted the seventeen Sustainable Development Goals. These include ending hunger and poverty, reducing inequality, preserving marine and terrestrial ecosystems, taking urgent action on climate change, and inclusive and sustainable economic activity. This broad global consensus on societal goals is unprecedented in human history.[109] Then, as the year closed, 196 nations agreed to the Paris Accord to limit climate change to no more than 2°C (and preferably no more than 1.5°C). At perhaps the last moment, and despite recent Federal backsliding in the United States, a global commitment to climate action is emerging.[110]

In 2016, several hundred people from two dozen nations joined to frame a new narrative. Working together as Leading for Wellbeing,[111] we are ordinary people: workers, scholars, business leaders, mothers, bankers, activists, faith leaders, farmers, and more. To counter the Powell Memorandum, we created the Meadows Memorandum[112] to offer the following alternative:

> True freedom and success depend on creating a world where individuals flourish and we all prosper. Governments serve humanity best when they recognize our individual dignity and enhance our interconnectedness. To thrive, businesses and society must pivot toward a new purpose: shared well-being on a healthy planet.

Working groups are outlining the steps needed to transform the following and other aspects of our society:

Culture	Civil society
Business	Consciousness
Finance	Media
Education	Agriculture
Political system	Energy

The world has become unstable economically, environmentally, and socially. The demand for a new economic model is growing louder in coalitions around the world.[113] The work to fashion a finer future needs us all.

Advocates of an economy in service to life must settle on a theory of change, and then a strategy of change, as Lewis Powell did in 1971. Coalitions are emerging[114] to replicate in new terms what the framers of the neoliberal paradigm did at Mont Pelerin. We are beginning to create a strategy of change similar in impact to the one Lewis Powell created in 1971.

Our job is to create a powerful movement for this new economy based on the core values of human dignity, the common good, and stewardship, an economy resonant with the ancient wisdom we have forgotten. This will be a movement of collaborating networks that draw on civil society, on research and policy communities, on business, on multifaith groups, on cultural icons, and on new economics practitioners. They will operate at the level of values and principles and articulate a compelling story of possibility. We need courage to commit to the entrepreneurial experiments that will help us regain safety, respect for the sacred, and a sense of home again. The necessary values shift will not happen unless there is a powerful new story, one that tells how we want to live. If we are to avoid collapse, enough people must live this story and demand that their governments change policies and practices.

We don't have all the solutions. But we have the beginnings.

We're changing stories. We're giving people a place to stand, a place to hold on to.

Achieving this is the challenge for every human alive today. It is our great work, and, as Bucky also said, our final exam.

We invite you to join us.

Notes

[1] Adam Sacks, "Putting Carbon Back in the Ground—The Way Nature Does It," 2013. http://www.climatecodered.org/2013/03/putting-carbon-back-into-ground-way.html.

[2] "Countries Turn to Green Jobs for Economic Growth," Worldwatch Institute, 2016. http://www.worldwatch.org/node/6006.

[3] http://www.oecd.org/statistics/oecd-workshop-on-measuring-business-impacts-on-peoples-well-being.htm.

[4] George Monbiot, "Neoliberalism—The Ideology at the Root of All Our Problems," *The Guardian*, April 15, 2016. https://www.theguardian.com/books/2016/apr/15/neoliberalism-ideology-problem-george-monbiot.

[5] Safa Motesharrei et al., "'Human And Nature DYnamical' Study (HANDY): Human and Nature Dynamics: Modeling Inequality and Use of Resources in the Collapse or Sustainability of Societies," *Ecological Economics* 101 (May 2014): 90–102. http://www.sciencedirect.com/science/article/pii/S0921800914000615.

[6] http://www.endhomelessness.org/library/entry/the-state-of-homelessness-in-america-2015.

[7] Jordan Golson, "It's Time to Fix America's Inrastructure," *Wired Magazine*, January 23, 2015. http://www.wired.com/2015/01/time-fix-americas-infrastructure-heres-start/.

[8] Water.org, "The Water Crisis," https://water.org/our-impact/water-crisis/. Even major American cities are unable to supply safe drinking water to their citizens: Matthew Dolan, "Flint Crisis Could Cost U.S. a \$300B Lead Pipe Overhaul, Agency Warns," *Detroit Free Press*, March 5,

2016. http://www.freep.com/story/news/local/michigan/flint-water-crisis/2016/03/04/flint-crisis-could-cost-us-300b-lead-pipe-overhaul-agency-warns/81316860/.

[9] Dominique Mosbergen, "Air Pollution Causes 4,400 Deaths in China Every Single Day: Study," *Huffington Post*, August 14, 2015. http://www.huffingtonpost.com/entry/air-pollution-china-deaths_us_55cd9a62e4b0ab468d9cefa9.

[10] Reuters, "More Indians than Chinese Will Die from Air Pollution: Researcher," *The Financial Express*, August 18, 2016. http://www.financialexpress.com/economy/india-air-pollution-death-rate-to-outpace-china-researcher/351209/.

[11] Tony Brown, "Americans Still Dying from Air Pollution," *Medscape*, June 28, 2017. http://www.medscape.com/viewarticle/882240.

[12] Graeme Wearden and Ben Quinn, "Eurogroup Head Says Cyprus Shows Future of Bank Rescues—As It Happened," Eurozone crisis live, *The Guardian*, March 25, 2013. https://www.theguardian.com/business/2013/mar/25/eurozone-crisis-cyprus-bailout-deal-agreed.

[13] Gregor Aisch, Adam Pearce, and Bryant Rousseau, "How Far Is Europe Swinging to the Right?" *New York Times*, July 5, 2016. http://www.nytimes.com/interactive/2016/05/22/world/europe/europe-right-wing-austria-hungary.html?_r=0.

[14] Christiana Figueres, "Restoring Hope," *Huffington Post*, July 14, 2016. http://www.huffingtonpost.com/christiana-figueres/restoring-hope_b_10974734.html.

[15] Aryn Baker, "How Climate Change Is behind the Surge of Migrants to Europe," *Time Magazine*, September 7, 2015. http://time.com/4024210/climate-change-migrants/.

[16] "A Global Crisis: Life in Fragile States and the Effects of Mass Migration," *Global Washington*, 2016. http://globalwa.org/issues/2016-2/fragile-states-mass-migration/.

[17] Daniel Bilefsky and Alison Smale, "Dozens of Migrants Drown as European Refugee Crisis Continues," *New York Times*, January 22, 2016. http://www.nytimes.com/2016/01/23/world/europe/valls-france-eu-warns.html.

[18] Nagaire Woods, "Populism Is Spreading: This Is What Is Driving It," *World Economic Forum*, December 9, 2016. https://www.weforum.org/agenda/2016/12/populism-is-spreading-this-is-whats-driving-it.

[19] "Report of the High Level Panel on Humanitarian Financing," January 12, 2016. https://www.worldhumanitariansummit.org/whs_finance/HLPhumanitarianfinancing.

[20] Mark Anderson, "$1.4tn a Year Needed to Reach Global Goals for World's Poorest," *The Guardian*, November 18, 2015. https://www.theguardian.com/global-development/2015/nov/18/14tn-dollars-a-year-needed-to-reach-global-goals-for-world-poorest.

[21] Motesharrei et al., "Human and Nature Dynamics," 90–102.

[22] E.g., Ian Angus, "What Did That 'NASA-Funded Collapse Study' Really Say?" *Climate and Capitalism*, March 31, 2015. http://climateandcapitalism.com/2014/03/31/nasa-collapse-study/.

[23] Donella Meadows et al., *The Limits to Growth*, The Club of Rome, 1972. https://www.clubofrome.org/report/the-limits-to-growth/.

[24] Graham Turner, "Is Global Collapse Imminent?" Melbourne Sustainable Society Institute, 2014. http://sustainable.unimelb.edu.au/sites/default/files/docs/MSSI-ResearchPaper-4_Turner_2014.pdf.

[25] Mary Papenfuss, "Society Could Collapse in a Decade, Predicts Math Historian," *Huffington Post*, January 6, 2017. http://www.huffingtonpost.com/entry/peter-turchin-cliodynamics-society-collapse_us_586f1e22e4b02b5f85882988.

[26] Peter Turchin, "Social Instability Lies Ahead, Researcher Says," *UConn Today*, December 27, 2016. http://today.uconn.edu/2016/12/using-social-science-to-predict-the-future/.

[27] Nelson Mandela Speech at Trafalgar Square, https://www.youtube.com/watch?v=tevKVIcHscw.

[28] Philip Mirowski, *The Road from Mont Pelerin* (Cambridge, MA: Harvard University Press, June 2009). http://www.hup.harvard.edu/catalog.php?isbn=9780674033184.

[29] https://www.forbes.com/sites/johnharvey/2016/10/31/five-reasons-you-should-blame-economics/#4f1b61d8cccd.

[30] John T. Harvey, "Five Reasons You Should Blame the Economics Discipline for Today's Problems," Forbes, October 31, 2016.

[31] John Maynard Keynes, *The General Theory of Employment, Interest and Money* (United Kingdom: Palgrave Macmillan, 1936).

[32] Kate Raworth, "Exploring Doughnut Economics," https://www.kateraworth.com/videos/.

[33] Rethinking Economics, http://www.rethinkeconomics.org/.

[34] Ellen Goodman, speeches and conversations with the author.

[35] Pope Francis, *Laudato Si*, https://w2.vatican.va/content/dam/francesco/pdf/encyclicals/documents/papa-francesco_20150524_enciclica-laudato-si_en.pdf.

[36] The Earth Charter, http://earthcharter.org/.

[37] Lewis Powell, "Confidential Memorandum: Attack on American Free Enterprise System," Washington and Lee University School of Law, August 23, 1971, http://law2.wlu.edu/deptimages/Powell%20Archives/PowellMemorandumPrinted.pdf.

[38] Alex Shepherd, "The DC Think Tank behind Donald Trump," *New Republic*, February 22, 2017. https://newrepublic.com/article/140271/dc-think-tank-behind-donald-trump.

[39] "62 People Own the Same as Half the World, Reveals Oxfam Davos Report," January 18, 2016. https://www.oxfam.org/en/pressroom/pressreleases/2016-01-18/62-people-own-same-half-world-reveals-oxfam-davos-report.

[40] Global Biodiversity Outlook 3, Secretariat of the UN Convention on Biodiversity, 2010. http://www.cbd.int/doc/publication s/gbo/gbo3-final-en.pdf.

[41] Cormac McCarthy, *No Country for Old Men* (Alfred A. Knopf, 2005 [book]; Ethan Coen and Joel Coen, 2007 [movie]).

[42] Dark Mountain, http://dark-mountain.net/.

[43] International Labor Rights Forum, http://www.laborrights.org/creating-a-sweatfree-world/sweatshops.

[44] Carole Cadwalladr, "Inside Avaaz—Can Online Activism Really Change the World?" *The Guardian*, November 16, 2013. https://www.theguardian.com/technology/2013/nov/17/avaaz-online-activism-can-it-change-the-world.

[45] Vandana Shiva, India, http://www.navdanya.org/.

[46] Bill McKibben, Author, Educator, Environmentalist, http://www.billmckibben.com/.

[47] Nature Specials, Planetary Boundaries, http://www.nature.com/news/specials/planetaryboundaries/index.html.

[48] Jeremy Grantham, "Be Persuasive, Be Brave. Be Arrested (If Necessary)," *Nature*, November 14, 2014. http://www.nature.com/news/be-persuasive-be-brave-be-arrested-if-necessary-1.11796.

[49] Idle No More, Canada, http://www.idlenomore.ca/.

[50] Sarah Jaffee, "Standing Firm at Standing Rock: Why the Struggle Is Bigger Than One Pipeline," *Moyers and Company*, September 28, 2016. http://billmoyers.com/story/standing-firm-standing-rock-pipeline-protesters-will-not-moved/.

[51] 350.org, We're building a global climate movement, http://350.org/.

[52] https://wilderness.org/.

[53] http://www.eea.europa.eu/.

[54] http://www.wbcsd.org/Overview/About-us.

[55] http://www.ilo.org/global/about-the-ilo/lang--en/index.htm.

[56] http://www.usgbc.org/articles/leed-dynamic-plaque-diaries-alliance-center.

[57] https://www.cdp.net/en.

[58] Carbon Disclosure Project, https://www.cdp.net/CDPResults/CDP-SP500-leaders-report-2014.pdf.

[59] https://www.globalreporting.org/Pages/default.aspx.

[60] http://integratedreporting.org/the-iirc-2/.

[61] http://www.sasb.org/.

[62] *Our Common Future*, http://www.un-documents.net/ocf-02.htm.

[63] Brito Lidia and Smith Stafford, "State of the Planet Declaration," Planet under Pressure, March 26–29, 2012. http://www.planetunderpressure2012.net/pdf/state_of_planet_declaration.pdf.

[64] Personal communication, Jo Confino, Conference on Beyond Business as Usual, DNV-GL, Copenhagen, November 16, 2013.

[65] http://www.voanews.com/a/thousands-protest-globally-against-trump-travel-ban/3706760.html.

[66] Kate Wolf, "Brother Warrior," http://www.katewolf.com/.

[67] http://leading4wellbeing.org/.

[68] Michael Pirson, *Humanistic Management* (Cambridge: Cambridge University Press, 2017).

69   Introductory video, Humanistic Management Network, http://www.humanetwork.org/.

70   Richard Wilkinson and Kate Pickett, *The Spirit Level* (London: Bloomsbury Press, 2010). https://www.amazon.com/dp/B003TWOK70/ref=dp-kindle-redirect?_encoding=UTF8&btkr=1.

71   Robert Krulwich, "How Human Beings Almost Vanished from Earth in 70,000 B.C." *Krulwich Wonders*, NPR, October 22, 2012. http://www.npr.org/sections/krulwich/2012/10/22/163397584/how-human-beings-almost-vanished-from-earth-in-70-000-b-c.

72   Anne Minard, "Early Humans Were Prey, Not Predators, Experts Say," *National Geographic News*, March 7, 2006. http://news.nationalgeographic.com/news/2006/03/0307_060307_human_prey.html.

73   Freya Williams, *Green Giants* (New York: Amacom, 2015). http://www.greengiantsbook.com/.

74   John Fullerton, *Regenerative Capitalism* (Greenwich, CT: Capital Institute, 2015). http://capitalinstitute.org/wp-content/uploads/2015/04/2015-Regenerative-Capitalism-4-20-15-final.pdf.

75   Eric J. Chaisson, *Cosmic Evolution, The Rise of Complexity in Nature* (Cambridge, MA: Harvard University Press, 2002). http://www.hup.harvard.edu/catalog.php?isbn=9780674009875.

76   *Towards a Circular Economy*, http://www.ellenmacarthurfoundation.org/about/circular-economy/towards-the-circular-economy.

77   www.capitalinstitute.org.

78   http://www.savory.global/.

79   http://www.natcapsolutions.org.

80   We Mean Business, https://www.wemeanbusinesscoalition.org/.

81   Costanza, Robert, *Flourishing on Earth*, https://www.youtube.com/watch?v=PZkTlVPgqG4&feature=relmfu.

82   Christopher Peterson, "What Is Positive Psychology and What Is It Not," *Psychology Today*, May 16, 2008. https://www.psychologytoday.com/blog/the-good-life/200805/what-is-positive-psychology-and-what-is-it-not.

83   Edward O. Wilson, *The Social Conquest of Earth* (New York: Liveright, 2013). https://www.amazon.com/Social-Conquest-Earth-Edward-Wilson/dp/0871403633.

84   Michael Pirson et al., *From Capitalistic to Humanistic Business* (United Kingdom: Palgrave, 2014). http://www.palgrave.com/page/detail/from-capitalistic-to-humanistic-business-michael-pirson/?.

85   Natural Capitalism Solutions, www.natcapsolutions.org/finerfuture.

86   Capital Institute, http://fieldguide.capitalinstitute.org/.

87   http://www.cohousing.org/.

88   www.usgbc.org.

89   Michael Shuman, The Local Economy Solution (White River Junction, VA: Chelsea Green, 2015); see also Ryan Coonerty, "The Local Economy Solution," *Solutions Journal*, November 2015. https://www.thesolutionsjournal.com/article/the-local-economy-solution/.

90   Hunter Lovins, "The Triumph of Solar in the Energy Race," *Unreasonable.is*, August 7, 2015. https://unreasonable.is/triumph-of-the-sun/.

91   Tony Seba, *Clean Disruption—Energy & Transportation* (Colorado Renewable Energy Society, June 9, 2017). https://www.youtube.com/watch?v=2b3ttqYDwF0.

92   Michael J. Coren, "2016 Was the Year Solar Panels Finally Became Cheaper Than Fossil Fuels. Just Wait for 2017," *Quartz*, December 26, 2016. https://qz.com/871907/2016-was-the-year-solar-panels-finally-became-cheaper-than-fossil-fuels-just-wait-for-2017/.

93   Tom Randall, "World Energy Hits a Turning Point: Solar That's Cheaper Than Wind," *Bloomberg Technology*, December 14, 2016. https://www.bloomberg.com/news/articles/2016-12-15/world-energy-hits-a-turning-point-solar-that-s-cheaper-than-wind.

94   Renewable Energy World, "Renewable Energy Job Growth Unique in Global Energy Sector," May 27, 2016. http://www.renewableenergyworld.com/articles/2016/05/renewable-energy-job-growth-unique-in-global-energy-sector.html.

95   Wake Up Before It's Too Late, UNCTAD, 2013. http://unctad.org/en/PublicationsLibrary/ditcted2012d3_en.pdf.

96   "FAO calls for 'paradigm shift' towards sustainable agriculture and family farming," Food and Agriculture Organization, September 29, 2014. http://www.fao.org/news/story/en/item/250148/icode/.

97   http://savory.global/assets/docs/evidence-papers/restoring-the-climate.pdf.

[98] Claire Miller, "The Long-Term Jobs Killer Is Not China. It's Automation," *New York Times*, December 21, 2016. https://www.nytimes.com/2016/12/21/upshot/the-long-term-jobs-killer-is-not-china-its-automation.html?_r=0.

[99] Patrick Kulp, "Universal Basic Income Could Find More Mainstream Traction in 2017," *Mashable*, January 2017. http://mashable.com/2017/01/05/universal-basic-income-2017-year-ahead/.

[100] Byrd Pinkerton, "What a Kenyan Village Can Teach Us about a Universal Basic Income," *Vox*, May 12, 2017. https://www.vox.com/2017/5/12/15600280/kenyan-village-universal-basic-income-give-directly-podcast.

[101] Andrew Winston, "Whiteboard Session: The Business Case for Sustainability," *Harvard Business Review*, HBR video, April 28, 2017. https://hbr.org/video/5415413929001/whiteboard-session-the-business-case-for-sustainability.

[102] Ray Anderson, The Business Logic of Sustainability, TED, February 2009. https://www.ted.com/talks/ray_anderson_on_the_business_logic_of_sustainability.

[103] Hunter Lovins, *The Way Out: Kickstarting Capitalism to Save Our Economic Ass* (New York: Hill & Wang, 2012). https://www.amazon.com/Way-Out-Kick-starting-Capitalism-Economic/dp/0809034697.

[104] Personal communication from Kees Kruythoff-tielenius, "Future of Value & Values Business Model" conference, June 27, 2017, Englewood Cliffs, NJ.

[105] Gabriel Kahn, "Did California Figure Out How to Fix Global Warming? The Golden State's Accidental History," *Mother Jones*, March/April 2016. http://www.motherjones.com/environment/2016/03/california-cuts-greenhouse-gas-jerry-brown-growth-energy.

[106] Justin Worland, "Coal's Last Kick," *Time Magazine*, May 2017. http://time.com/coals-last-kick/.

[107] Alexandra Larkin, "Kentucky Coal Museum Switching to Solar Power," *CNN*, April 6, 2017. http://www.cnn.com/2017/04/06/us/coal-museum-goes-solar-trnd/index.html.

[108] Chris Megerian, "It's Time to Talk 100% Renewable Energy, California Senate Leader Says," *Los Angeles Times*, January 19, 2017. http://www.latimes.com/politics/essential/la-pol-ca-essential-politics-updates-california-renewable-1484864454-htmlstory.html.

[109] http://www.un.org/sustainabledevelopment/sustainable-development-goals/.

[110] Historic Paris Agreement on Climate Change, UN Framework Convention on Climate Change, 2015. http://newsroom.unfccc.int/unfccc-newsroom/finale-cop21/.

[111] http://natcapsolutions.org/L4W/resources/videos/.

[112] Named after the great systems thinker Donnella Meadows: http://leading4wellbeing.org/wp-content/uploads/2017/05/Meadows-Memorandum-with-Cover-V8.1.pdf.

[113] http://leading4wellbeing.org.

[114] http://leading4wellbeing.org.

CHAPTER 8

Engaging Business and Civil Society for Sustainable Development

Lars Fogh Mortensen and Karen Lund Petersen

The adoption of the United Nations (UN) 2030 Agenda and the Sustainable Development Goals (SDGs) in September 2015 was a remarkable achievement. In the outcome document,[1] heads of state, government, and high representatives commit to full implementation: "We have adopted a historic decision on a comprehensive, far-reaching and people-centered set of universal and transformative goals and targets. We commit ourselves to working tirelessly for the full implementation of this Agenda by 2030."

With this UN 2030 Sustainable Development Agenda combining development, poverty alleviation, and sustainability agendas, the ability to create coherence between and within each of these very broad policy areas is both a huge challenge and an absolute necessity for success.[2] Implementation of the 2030 Agenda thus requires full attention to the links and coherence in policies between and within many sectors, policy areas, and initiatives.[3] Moreover, not only countries but also various societal organizations and private businesses will need to embark on a profound transformation to achieve durable, long-term change.[4] As a recent study involving a number of international think tanks concludes, the importance of engaging non-state actors in implementation of the SDGs, including civil society and the private sector, is vital to success.[5] The challenging question is, however, who those actors are and who should be targeted in such a strategy on policy coherence for sustainable development.

This question is challenging precisely because it requires considering who has the authority or the power to create policies on sustainability and, in effect, who is responsible for doing so. The main obstacle today is that "policy coherence for sustainable development" is addressed mainly as a question of improving national policies, implementing national policies, and defining the right legal measures for governments to act. Yet, rather than being stakeholders of governments and international institutions, increasing global interaction and communication technologies requires a broader perspective on policy and governance: to recognize that policies are (also) created and governed by transnational corporate and civilian actors.[6] These transnational policies are neither fully dependent on nor detached from national policymaking, but they are nevertheless shaping the current political environment.

To broaden the horizon, take a step away from nationalism, and suggest a more transnational cosmopolitan view on policy coherence, three steps are required. First, the "policy coherence" debate and the implied meaning of policy must be considered. Second, a good solution on policy coherence for sustainable development requires an understanding of the sustainability policies of key global economic and social actors. Last, one must understand how two types of actors, private companies and civil society groups, each govern sustainability, and how their practices limit and support the aims of greater sustainable development.

The Policy Coherence Agenda

In spite of sustainable development entering the global agenda as early as 1986 with the Report of the Brundtland Commission,[7] the field of studying policy coherence for sustainable development is by no means a long-standing independent research field. Elements have been studied in research on sustainability transitions, sustainability governance, and environmental governance, among others, but it is mostly within the field of Policy Coherence for Development that the concept has been academically targeted as an issue for development studies, in the context of development cooperation and aid effectiveness.[8]

With sustainable development being defined much more broadly by the 2030 Agenda than by previous global agendas for development, studying the coherence of sustainable development policies can be considered a new area of study. That being said, however, the 2030 Agenda does very little to explain what is meant by "policy coherence for sustainable development." It merely states that "[w]e commit to pursuing policy coherence and an enabling environment for sustainable development at all levels and by all actors" and identifies one policy coherence target, SDG 17.14[9]: "Enhance policy coherence for sustainable development," without providing additional details.[10]

In establishing global indicators for the SDGs, definitions become rather narrow, focusing on national implementation. Meeting its mandate to define indicators for the 17 SDGs and their 169 targets, the UN Statistical Commission agreed in March 2016 on an indicator for the policy coherence target which focuses solely on national policy mechanisms.[11] The indicator is defined as: "Number of countries with mechanisms in place to enhance policy coherence of sustainable development."[12] It might seem banal to observe that we need to move beyond such a national focus and that an approach to measuring policy coherence that focuses exclusively on national policy mechanisms is insufficient.

Other organizations have recently defined policy coherence for sustainable development. The Organization for Economic Co-operation and Development (OECD), for example, argues that policy coherence is "an approach and policy tool to integrate the economic, social, environmental and governance dimensions of sustainable development at all stages of domestic and international policy making."[13] The tool aims to increase governments' capacities to achieve

- political commitment and policy statements that can help translate commitment into action;
- policy coordination that can resolve conflicts or inconsistencies between policies; and
- systems for monitoring, analysis and reporting on the impacts of policies to provide evidence to inform decision-making.[14]

It is clear that the OECD, like the UN 2030 Agenda, sees the economies of individual states as the main (or only) actors of policy coherence. Policy interlinkages are specified between the social, economic, and environmental pillars of sustainability, and policy effects distinguish between national and international effects.

The private sector, international organizations, civil society, and nongovernmental organizations (NGOs) are grouped together as "other actors."

Who Are the Important Actors?

Nation-state policies on sustainable development are increasingly challenged "from above" by structures of transnational capital (e.g., multinational enterprises), global media, and international institutions, and "from below" by a diffusion of local resistance through the informal economy, social media, and grassroots activism. These trends have given rise to new social and economic hybrid actors—actors that are neither fully global nor entirely national. On the one hand, they are "national" in the sense that they refer to national law and make attempts to influence state policies through lobbying.[15] On the other hand, they are also not exclusively national, as their actions affect and are affected by global-level interactions independently of their national affiliation, through their choices of investment, corporate policies on sustainability, grassroots activities, civil action, and so forth.

In the discipline of International Political Economy, key scholars have similarly argued that a new corporate elite has emerged in global affairs, and that they are important for understanding how today's global order has surpassed the Westphalian state-centric one.[16] However, as critics have argued, such descriptions of the current order miss out on the importance of the complex interdependence that exists not only between public and private actors,[17] but also between the local and global levels in international politics. Many of today's powerful actors operate both within and beyond national political spheres as hybrid actors.

From a more solutions-oriented perspective, this problem of diversity and interdependency is recognized in the governance literature, where numerous attempts have been taken to map all levels and actors relevant for economic, social, and environmental implementation of sustainability.[18] Yet, while such mappings often include a wide range of dependencies and links between levels, actors, and policies, the questions of importance tend to stand in the background, avoiding the question of who and what are the most important to success. While there is much truth to the description of complexity, politically it often works against prioritization and thus decision and change, as everything and all actors tend to be seen as equally relevant and important. In fact, we need some prioritization and understanding of responsibility in order to avoid a sense of despair among policymakers or to become a tool that simply justifies a "business as usual" approach to sustainability issues. The same is true when talking about policy coherence for sustainable development and the role of the nation state versus other actors. If these other actors are not defined in terms of who they are and how they matter to success, the direction of progress becomes clouded.

An alternative way to approach these actors and their influence on sustainability is to study how key non-state actors, through their actions and definitions of sustainability, render some political solutions possible and others impossible. In other words: who are these powerful global actors, how do they define new possibilities of sustainable action, and how do they limit other forms of action?

To answer these questions, one must consider how transnational actors impact the understanding of national sustainability policies in particular, and concepts of policy coherence in general. Zooming in on the role of two kinds of hybrid actors, private companies and global civil society groups, helps to define these influences.

Private Companies

Large multinational enterprises generally grow both economically and in terms of their number of employees. As they grow, they become more international, with subsidiaries or/and large markets in many countries. They develop increasingly complex value chains, with multiple suppliers and customers spread across many countries and regions of the world.

In today's global corporate sphere, corporate decision-making is increasingly defined and implemented beyond national control. Although companies are subject to national law and engage in national policymaking through lobbying and by participating in various public–private partnerships (PPPs), the role of private networks and self-initiated norm-building works to detach corporate policies from national affiliations. As Michael Power explains in his seminal work on risk management, companies are increasingly setting up self-imposed norms and governance structures to manage an increasingly uncertain environment and to steer away from government interference.[19]

Currently, there are many kinds of corporate policymaking that affect sustainability outside the realm of nation-states and legal regulation. Three of the most defining ones include: self-regulating reporting and compliance regimes, consumer/citizen mobilization, and new business models.

Voluntary reporting and compliance regimes are increasingly used as tools for self-regulation among companies. In this respect, sustainability reporting and reporting on corporate social responsibility (CSR) are important as tools for communication and tracking ways in which large companies take sustainability into account in their business operations. Another way is the increasing use of compliance systems, such as the ISO 14000 standards. These systems of reporting and self-imposed compliance have, by and large, become the new norms defining sustainable business. Even though CSR reporting is often criticized for being merely a reporting mechanism for large companies to show and advertise all the good things they do, rather than a core activity of the company, CSR is still an important norm that forces companies to defend and sustain their environmental and sustainability strategies and actions.[20]

Sustainability reporting has gained ground since the 2012 Rio+20 Sustainable Development Conference, with the outcome document containing a paragraph on the importance of sustainability reporting and the Group of Friends of Paragraph 47 formed after the conference as a political group with government representatives.[21] The main actor in sustainability reporting is the Global Reporting Initiative, which produces sustainability reporting guidelines used by approximately 5,800 companies worldwide, including the majority for the world's largest 250 companies.[22] Other guidelines and frameworks have been prepared by the UN Global Compact and the OECD.[23] Many companies have in recent years adopted sustainable strategies and/or grouped together with other companies or engaged in dialogues to strengthen their sustainability efforts. And some private companies have already taken initiatives to incorporate elements of the UN 2030 Agenda into their corporate strategies.

The second group of corporate sustainability policies are those relating to consumer groups and markets. Expectations from citizens toward the private sector, including but not limited to their role as consumers, is another defining factor for understanding changes in sustainable corporate practices. When groups of citizens are unhappy with the behavior of certain private companies, new technology has enabled organized campaigns on social media, which can be devastating for the public image of a private company.

A third kind of activity that defines the sustainability practices of private companies is private business innovation and changes in production and consumption. This is happening through the implementation of new and innovative business models that stem, in most cases, from private companies and a way to understand corporate sustainable practices. One example is the current trend toward the leasing of goods and services—a trend we see in many sectors. A well-known and established system is, for example, the leasing of cars. But the leasing of other goods and services is also rapidly expanding in many countries, including leasing schemes for mobile phones, clothing, furniture, and electricity, to name a few.[24] The pace of innovation and diffusion of new ideas and business models will play a key role in driving systemic transitions toward sustainability and meeting the SDGs.[25]

A meeting of twenty-five stakeholders from science, business, policy, and civil society orchestrated by the European Environment Agency identified four clusters of innovation with potential to support sustainability transitions in the systems that provide Europe's food, mobility, and energy. These are essentially new business models that can play a key role in moving toward sustainability.[26] They are the following:

- Collaborative consumption in which consumers can obtain goods or services more effectively and efficiently, for example, through leasing or sharing goods and services, rather than owning them.
- "Prosumerism," in which consumers also become producers, for example, through producing and selling extra energy (from solar panels), or food produced in their gardens.
- Social innovation entails developing completely new concepts, strategies, and organizational forms to better meet societal needs.
- Eco-innovation and eco-design go further than purely technological innovation and incorporate environmental considerations by reducing the life-cycle impacts of a product or by increasing its reusability through design.

In regard to the private sector, it seems to be beyond doubt that developments in the practices of networks governed by self-regulation, consumers, and new business models will affect the implementation of the UN 2030 Agenda and the SDGs, despite the fact that the relationship between the private sector, governments, and public policymaking is informal and often subtle.

Global Civil Society Groups

Since 1992,[27] the role of major groups (women, children and youth, indigenous people, NGOs, local authorities, workers and trade unions, business and industry, the scientific community, and farmers) in policy processes has gradually increased. The adoption of the UN 2030 Agenda and the SDGs, to a large extent, results from a very broad consultation and involvement of such major groups throughout the process.

NGOs are probably the most widely recognized civil society groups and epistemic communities in the field of global sustainability policy. Many large NGOs are recognized and consulted by governments and international organizations. Thus, in many respects, these groups are accepted as established actors in the international system.

Another kind of global civil actors are those united via social media on often-shifting topics. These are less formally organized, yet increasingly important. We see that among consumers who target the national origin of certain goods, services, or companies, in resistance to regimes, or in surveillance. Common to these civil society groups is their paradoxical relation to the state, state governance, and policymaking. Like the private companies described above, these groups draw their legitimacy by claiming to be more than a state (in fact often by opposing or resisting state policies), yet each citizen is still a citizen somewhere. As many scholars have pointed out, the term "global civil society" is an attempt to overcome the statist bias present in the concept of civil society.[28] This also means that these groups gain legitimacy by speaking "on behalf" of some kind of (global) public ethics, and not by being citizens in a state. Or, as Olaf Corry concludes, "'global' in global civil society relates to the emergence of a global consciousness, espousing the non-particularity or worldwide interests."[29] Thus, environmental NGOs speak on behalf of nature, development NGOs on behalf of the weak, and Anonymous on behalf of privacy. And in doing so, they make politics.

This reference to a global public consciousness and ethics can be very powerful, yet it also makes the future very unpredictable and hard to govern through national policy coherence regimes. The development of a global civil society creates uncertainty about who the important stakeholders are, and how they can be represented in policymaking. This problem of uncertainty seems reinforced by the rapid change of information technologies witnessed in the past decades. "Globalization" and "network society" are the usual terms used to describe the trends that enable citizens to share information and to act in unity, in certain directions, in huge numbers, and within days or sometimes hours of one another.[30]

Besides installing uncertainty about the effectiveness of national sustainability policies, there are also positive effects of this development, as many of these global civil society groups work to expose the limits of current policymaking. According to Scholte, civil society groups do so by (1) giving voice to minority stakeholders, (2) enhancing public awareness and education, (3) raising public debate, (4) creating transparency on established policy solutions, and (5) helping to monitor implementation.[31] These NGOs have evolved considerably, shifting in recent years from efforts to affect government and intergovernmental processes to developing environmental standards and monitoring trends.[32]

Solutions

Global economic and civil actors make up an increasingly important context for national and international policymaking—a context that must be considered when discussing policy coherence for sustainable development. The core sustainability practices of these actors should be strengthened in future approaches to policy coherence on sustainable development.

Recognizing that companies and civil society groups are hybrid actors that sometimes escape national policy and independently shape policies is key to any solution on sustainability and policy coherence. Moreover, we need to start to define those powerful stakeholders and their modus operandi on sustainability.

The informal and self-regulating nature of these corporate and civil actors makes it difficult to monitor their effects by traditional means of national regulatory mechanisms. Instead, one might suggest that we start to systematize and increase the use of organizational forms such as PPPs to facilitate and support new possibilities of sustainable action by global nongovernmental groups and companies.

PPPs entail "promising a promise," or that of voluntarily agreeing on making the future in the image of a desired future.[33] These partnerships are thus not about the state (system) losing power, but rather about how it governs at a distance by making societal groups and organizations hold to future commitments.[34] This idea of partnering can thereby be seen as a kind of metagovernance, where the state strategically governs companies and societal groups to self-regulation by appealing to the virtue of voluntary, responsible, and "appropriate" behavior. As such, steering is not only understood as something directed toward particular actors, but, in the context of PPPs, a variety of perspectives (economic, social, environmental, and legal) can be brought to the table in an attempt to anticipate societal, local, and global dependencies and find better solutions. Only in this way can we make sense of "policy coherence for sustainable development" in an increasingly globalized and transnational world.

Along these lines, we also need to recognize the limitations of the current UN indicator on policy coherence. The agreed indicator for measuring UN SDG goal 17.14 (enhance policy coherence for sustainable development) is, as mentioned previously, defined as the "number of countries with mechanisms in place to enhance policy coherence of sustainable development."[35] This indicator is weak, as it simply measures how many countries do something to tackle a particular issue, and does not provide any information on how much or what they do. Therefore, it has little or no value.

Instead, something like a UN work program on policy cohesion for sustainable development is needed. Such a work program should support and facilitate transnational collaboration and PPPs on sustainable development, to help secure the development of norms and actions that support precautionary and responsible measures. The recently established Partnership for Enhancing Policy Coherence for Sustainable Development could be used as a source of inspiration to develop this dialogue further.[36]

The corporate practices identified above should be included in such a UN work program as well, including establishing norms for different forms of private–public collaboration, creating framework conditions for voluntary reporting and compliance regimes, and by sharing information on innovation and changes in consumption and production through the implementation of new business models.

In the case of global civil society groups, key decisions are much more difficult to locate, yet no less important. The practices of global civil society movements (NGOs or less formalized groups) are based on voluntary networks and draw legitimacy from a rather vague idea of public consciousness, rather than from a representation of interest. A work program should therefore create awareness about new forms of civil action, groups, and trends in order to support policy coherence at the national and international levels. This can help to develop standards for civil society and corporate participation in the decision-making process,[37] and to provide information about changes in the role of civil society as a global megatrend.

Conclusion

In the UN 2030 Agenda, the goal and concept of "policy coherence for sustainable development" emphasize national political and legal solutions to sustainable development, and tend to overlook innovative policies in the wider transnational corporate and civilian spheres. In order to find solutions to the current lack of sustainable development policy coherence, world leaders and decision makers must understand how a wider range of powerful (global) stakeholders in business and civil society are crucial to the success of policy coherence.

Instead of focusing on national legislation and implementation only, policies made by non-state actors that operate outside or across the borders of national legal regulation should also be considered. This includes corporate norms and compliance systems, the rise of new business models, new trends in the formation of civil society groups, the use of social media, and so forth.

Policy coherence needs to be governed by new means. The establishment of PPPs can make room for policies and solutions that cut across national and functional boundaries to create solutions that anticipate societal, local, and global dependencies. A UN work program to support development of such norms and actions would encourage precautionary and responsible actions and measures. Ultimately, business and civil society are critical to sustainable development policy coherence, and ultimately to meeting the seventeen SDGs.

Notes

[1] This chapter has been adapted from an earlier version previously published as "Extending the Boundaries of Policy Coherence for Sustainable Development: Engaging Business and Civil Society," *Solutions Journal*, 8, no. 3 (May 2017).United Nations, *Transforming Our World: The 2030 Agenda for Sustainable Development*. A/RES/70/1 (New York: United Nations, 2015).

[2] Policy Coherence of the Sustainable Development Goals—a Natural Resource Perspective, International Resource Panel (Paris: UNEP DTIE, 2015); D. Le Blanc, "Towards Integration at Last? The Sustainable Development Goals as a Network of Targets," UN Department of Economic and Social Affairs, DESA Working Paper No. 141, ST/ESA/2015/DWP/141 (March 2015).

[3] R. Costanza et al., "The UN Sustainable Development Goals and the Dynamics of Wellbeing," *Solutions* 7, no. 1 (2016): 20–22.

[4] United Nations, *Transforming Our World*.

[5] D. O'Connor et al., "Universality, Integration, and Policy Coherence for Sustainable Development: Early SDG Implementation in Selected OECD Countries" (World Resource Institute [online], 2016).

[6] U. Beck and N. Sznaider, "Unpacking Cosmopolitanism for the Social Sciences: A Research Agenda," *The British Journal of Sociology* 57, no. 1 (2006): 1–23.

[7] United Nations, *Report of the World Commission on Environment and Development: Our Common Future* (New York: United Nations, 1986).

[8] M. Carbone and N. Keijzer, "The European Union and Policy Coherence for Development: Reforms, Results, Resistance," *European Journal of Development Research* 28 (2016): 30–43.

[9] https://sustainabledevelopment.un.org/sdg17.

[10] United Nations, *Transforming Our World*, 31.

[11] Ibid.

[12] United Nations, Report of the Inter-Agency and Expert Group on Sustainable Development Goal Indicators. E/CN.3/2016/2/Rev.1 (New York: United Nations Economic and Social Council, February 2016).

[13] *Policy Coherence for Sustainable Development in the SDG Framework: Shaping Targets and Monitoring Progress* (Paris: OECD, 2015).

[14] *Better Policies for Sustainable Development 2016: A New Framework for Policy Coherence* (Paris: OECD, 2016).

[15] M. P. Smith and L. E. Guarnizo, *Transnationalism from Below. Comparative Urban and Community Research*, Volume 6 (New Brunswick: Transaction, 1998).

[16] S. Strange, *The Retreat of the State. The Diffusion of Power in the World Economy* (Cambridge: Cambridge University Press, 1996).

[17] R. Falkner, "Private Environmental Governance and International Relations: Exploring the Links," *Global Environmental Politics* 3, no. 2 (2003): 72–87.

[18] L. Meuleman and I. Niestroy, "Common but Differentiated Governance: A Metagovernance Approach to Make the SDGs Work," *Sustainability* 7, no. 9 (2015): 12295–12321.

[19] M. Power, *Organised Uncertainty: Designing a World of Risk Management* (Cambridge: Oxford University Press, 2005).

[20] M. Friedman, "The Social Responsibility of Business Is to Increase Its Profits," *New York Times* [online], September 13, 1970. Accessed May 31, 2016. http://www.colorado.edu/studentgroups/libertarians/issues/friedman-soc-r; P. Heugens and N. Dentchev, "Taming Trojan Horses: Identifying and Mitigating Corporate Social Responsibility Risks," *Journal of Business Ethics* 75 (2007): 151–170.

[21] United Nations, *The Future We Want*, 66/288 (New York: United Nations, 2012); T. Fogelberg, "How to Make Business Accountable? The Contribution of Sustainability Reporting," in *ASEF Outlook Report 2014/2015*, Ch. 8 (Singapore: Asia-Europe Foundation, 2015).

[22] T. Fogelberg, "How to Make Business Accountable?"

[23] UN Global Compact [online] (2016). https://www.unglobalcompact.org/what-is-gc/mission; Policy Framework for Policy Coherence for Development, Working paper no. 1. OECD Office of the Secretary-General, Unit for Policy Coherence and Development (Paris: OECD, 2012).

[24] *Environmental Indicator Report 2014: Environmental Impacts of Production-Consumption Systems in Europe* (Copenhagen: European Environment Agency, 2014).

[25] *European Environment—State and Outlook 2015: Synthesis Report* (Copenhagen: European Environment Agency, 2015).

[26] Ibid.

[27] United Nations, *Report of the United Nations Conference on Environment and Development*, Rio de Janeiro, June 3–14, 1992 (New York: United Nations, 1992).

[28] M. Kaldor, "The Idea of Global Civil Society," *International Affairs* 79, no. 3 (2003): 582–593; J. Bartelson, "Making Sense of Global Civil Society," *European Journal of International Relations* 12, no. 3 (2003): 371–395.

[29] O. Corry, "Civil Society and Its Discontents," *Voluntas* 17 (2006): 303–324.

[30] Z. Bauman, *Globalization: The Human Consequences* (Cambridge: Polity Press, 1998); M. Castells, *The Rise of the Network Society* (Oxford: Blackwell, 1996).

[31] J. A. Scholte, "Civil Society and Democracy in Global Governance," *Global Governance* 8 (2002): 281–304.

[32] Policy Framework for Policy Coherence for Development, Policy Coherence and Development; D. H. Cole, "From Global to Polycentric Climate Governance," *Climate Law* 2, no. 3 (2011): 395–413.

[33] N. Å. Andersen, "To Promise a Promise: When Contractors Desire a Life-long Partnership," in *Hybrid Forms of Governance: Self-suspension of Power*, N. A. Andersen and I. Sands, eds. (New York: Palgrave, 2012), 205–231.

[34] A. La Cour and N. A. Andersen, "Metagovernance as Strategic Supervision," *Public Performance and Management Review* 39, no. 4 (2016): 905–925.

[35] United Nations, Report of the Inter-Agency and Expert Group on Sustainable Development Goal Indicators.

[36] United Nations, PCSD Partnership—A Multi-stakeholder Partnership for Enhancing Policy Coherence for Sustainable Development, Partnerships for SDGs [online] (2017). https://sustainabledevelopment.un.org/partnership/?p=12066.

[37] B. Gemmill and A. Bamidele-Izu, "The Role of NGOs and Civil Society in Global Environmental Governance," in *Global Environmental Politics* D. C. Esty and M. H. Ivanova, eds. (New Haven, CT: Yale Center for Environmental Law & Policy, 2002).

CHAPTER 9

New Frontiers of Health Access

Pape Amadou Gaye and Gracey Vaughn

By 2030, there will be 8.5 billion of us.[1] The global demand for health care will only continue to rise as our populations grow—and get older. And as the economies of low- and middle-income countries (LMICs) mature, more leaders are looking to health as a powerful investment, not just for well-being, but for economic development.

This chapter focuses on key drivers that must be addressed in the next decade in order to meet the new global agenda. It describes the evolving profile of the health sector, including global epidemiological changes, new players in the sector, and the critical role of technology for stronger health systems. It examines the obstacles that prevent access to health care, and the ways we can overcome them. It looks at the new frontier of health and how health markets can help populations not only become healthier, but also thrive. Finally, it makes the case for the critical role of health systems research and implementation science as key elements for ensuring that future health interventions are responsive to the needs of individuals, families, communities, and nations.

Health Access in the Context of the Sustainable Development Goals

In 2015, the world jumped from the unfinished Millennium Development Goals (MDGs) agenda to the Sustainable Development Goals (SDGs). The SDGs build on lessons learned from the MDGs, which catalyzed fifteen years of progress in health and development. In 2000, when the MDGs were adopted, those goals seemed impossible. And while we did not achieve them all, some countries saw truly astounding results, including in maternal health, child mortality, and HIV. Today, the SDGs set forth 17 goals and 169 associated targets. These are the result of 193 United Nations member states uniting with a plan for a healthier, more prosperous world. Goal 3 addresses health, stating that countries will "ensure healthy lives and promote well-being for all at all ages." This includes a target to achieve universal health coverage (UHC).

UHC covers a full spectrum of health services, including health promotion, disease prevention, treatment, rehabilitation, and palliation. UHC is not possible without universal access, which has three dimensions:[2]

1. *Physical access*: The availability of health systems, including workforce, care, and services, must be within reasonable reach of those who need them. It includes the provision of primary care and adjustment for demographic and epidemiological shifts.
2. *Sociocultural barriers and breakthroughs*: To achieve UHC, we must overcome the challenges of gender discrimination and inequality, geographic and remote rural reach, and the digital divide. We must influence clients' willingness to seek services by tailoring health interventions and messages to address the social and cultural barriers that may deter them from accessing services.
3. *Financial access and capacity*: People must have the ability to pay for health services without financial hardship, including the price of the services and the indirect and opportunity costs (e.g., transportation and time away from work). We must innovate through partnerships, financing, governance, and systems development to realize this dimension of UHC.

In addition to SDG 3, several other goals offer targets with important implications for health and UHC, in particular, SDG 17 (focused on partnerships) and SDG 8 (focused on decent work and economic growth). Goal 17 declares that the world must strengthen partnerships to make progress. In the health sector, many nontraditional players have stepped into bigger roles. A growing number of private-sector actors want to do social good and break into emerging markets while they are doing it. More social entrepreneurs and robust civil society organizations have entered the arena. In the last few years, academic institutions have increased their efforts to provide opportunities for students to engage in research and find long-lasting solutions to global health problems.

Goal 8 prioritizes decent jobs for all. Our sector has been challenged to focus on job creation in the health workforce by the World Health Organization's (WHO's) High-Level Commission on Health Employment and Economic Growth report.[3] In 2006, the WHO World Health Report first put the global health workforce crisis on the map with its sober assessment of endemic health worker shortages. The WHO and the World Bank estimate that if we are to have any chance of attaining universal access to health care by 2030, we will need to fill about forty million new health-sector jobs by 2030, mostly in middle- and high-income countries.[4] The SDGs include only one vague mention of the health workforce, in Target 3c, which is neither specific nor measurable. Yet health workers and access to them must become integral to the plan for achieving the SDGs. And countries must commit their own resources to solve the crisis.

Access through Health Systems & Workforce Development

Critical for Universal Health Access

A shortage of health workers leads to greater inequities in access to health services and, in turn, more preventable illness, disability, and death. This is precisely why government leaders, nongovernmental organizations (NGOs), and civil society came together to create the first-ever Global Strategy on Human Resources for Health: Workforce 2030, released at the World Health Assembly 2016. This strategy sets out a vision of "accelerating progress towards UHC and the SDGs by ensuring equitable access to health workers within strengthened health systems." It also outlines milestones for 2020 and 2030 to advance mechanisms such as health training institutions, health workforce registries, and national health workforce accounts.[5]

High-income countries such as Germany, Japan, and Turkey are paving the way to UHC and all the positive health and economic outcomes it brings.[6] Yet a looming shortage of eighteen million skilled health workers in LMICs stands between us and the promise of global UHC—and the economies it could help stimulate. This shortage is greatest in countries that experience the highest burden of disease, and where health systems are weak and vulnerable. To achieve UHC—meaning that every person is able to secure the health services they need without jeopardizing their finances—growing and strengthening our global health workforce is essential.

As early as 2006, the WHO deemed all twenty countries with the highest child mortality rates to also be health workforce "crisis countries."[7] A 2013 report by the US President's Emergency Plan for AIDS Relief indicated that fourteen of its focus countries all cite a lack of adequate staff or staff turnover as their top barriers to providing consistent HIV care to clients.[8] Only four of the seventy-three countries that comprise 96 percent of maternal deaths have adequate midwives to deliver essential sexual, reproductive, maternal, and newborn health interventions.[9] And prior to the 2014 Ebola epidemic, Guinea, Liberia, and Sierra Leone each had fewer than three doctors, nurses, and midwives per ten thousand people—far short of WHO's recommendation of at least twenty-three per ten thousand people to provide essential health services.[10]

Education and training are at the heart of solving our health workforce shortage. The following are some steps we must take to expand access to health workers and health care:

- *Put primary and secondary education* within reach for more children to augment the future pool of candidates for health education and training. This includes investing in education infrastructure, enlarging teaching faculty, and regulating public and private education and learning institutions to ensure high standards and alignment with public goals.[11]
- *Reform preservice education*: This will ensure an adequate pipeline of health workers and establish stronger ties between preservice education

and the service delivery systems, resulting in less time spent on in-service training to avoid duplicative, redundant efforts.

- *Focus on primary health care (PHC)*: Too often, health education focuses on specialized, hospital-based care instead of primary health. We need both. Adding health system leadership and governance to curricula will help countries build fit-for-purpose workforces.
- *Optimize the mix of skills within the health workforce*: Task-sharing—or reorganizing health workers' scopes of practice—improves access to services, reduces clients' wait times, and leads to more satisfied patients.

Health Systems Development

The WHO Health Systems Framework provides six foundational building blocks for a strong health system that will increase health access and coverage.[12] Our sector has used these building blocks to guide research, programming, implementation, and measurement of health systems performance (see figure 9.1).

These building blocks have been criticized for failing to sufficiently address behavior change. Behavioral economics—a hot topic in global health right now—focuses on generating demand for access to high-quality services by changing certain behaviors.

But behavior change in clients is not the only necessary component to expand access to health services. Our health systems must be resilient and responsive to both clients and health workers. This calls for

- innovative research;
- more nuanced frameworks;
- flexible learning tools;
- translation of evidence to action;
- research embedded within policymaking processes and practice; and
- improved implementation science.

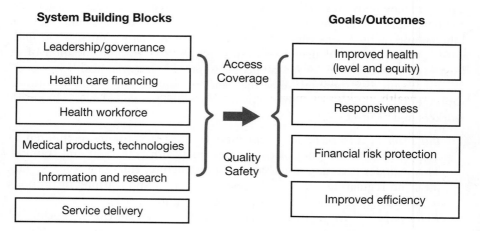

Figure 9.1 WHO Health Systems Framework

Despite wide recognition that we need stronger health systems everywhere in order to achieve UHC, there is limited direct funding for research in this area. Most available research funding is bundled into service delivery. The Alliance for Health Policy and Systems Research[13] was founded as part of the WHO to foster this burgeoning research field to help us better understand and improve how societies organize themselves to achieve collective health goals, and how different actors interact in the policy and implementation processes.

More research institutions are stepping up their collaboration between the North and Global South to increase research opportunities and capacity. The Medical/Nursing Education Partnership Initiatives, for example, drove education reforms in medical and nursing education in a number of African countries, in partnership with other institutions in Africa, the United States, and the United Kingdom, and funded by the US government through the US President's Emergency Plan for AIDS Relief and the National Institutes of Health. Annual symposiums helped countries promote health professional education, link health systems and other initiatives, and share experiences.[14]

Service and Care Delivery: Revitalizing Primary Health Care

We are witnessing a revitalized focus on PHC around the world. During the 2015 UN General Assembly, the Primary Health Care Performance Initiative was officially launched to improve PHC in LMICs through better measurement and knowledge sharing.[15] And the World Economic Forum has initiated the Primary Care Coalition to bring together partners to provide sustainable global PHC. The coalition helps align partner efforts and focuses on financially sustainable models for public–private primary care delivery, well-functioning primary care innovations, and matching government needs with private-sector offerings.[16]

Emergency surgical treatment is an essential component of PHC. Yet the G4 Alliance estimates that over five billion people globally lack access to safe, affordable, reliable surgical and anesthesia care. This comes with a high price tag: low-income countries face $12.3 trillion in gross domestic product (GDP) losses by not investing in essential surgical and anesthesia care,[17] and nearly seventeen million lives are lost annually due to lack of access to surgical care.[18] That is why the G4 Alliance advocates policy priority for surgical, obstetric, trauma, and anaesthesia care as part of the global development agenda. Its member organizations work to make safe surgical care accessible for all.

Our health workforces must include not only specialized cadres, but also generalists who can provide emergency surgery and anesthesia services on the front lines of care. UHC will never happen without the nurses, midwives, community health workers, and others who provide PHC and essential life-saving services every day. Ultimately, we must make the case that successful PHC will not only save lives, but also lead to a more solid health-care system and competitive marketplace.

We are seeing a renewed focus on integrated, people-centered service delivery as a strategy to achieve UHC, especially in reaching underserved and marginalized populations. Integration is a strategy to eliminate inefficiencies, improve coordination of care, and build resilient systems prepared to respond to public health crises. It is especially important as we experience demographic and epidemiological shifts to aging populations and chronic diseases. Lithuania, for example, has launched a program that coordinates and integrates cardiovascular services to reduce the hospital-centric delivery of care, minimize inefficiencies, and equalize the provision of urban and rural services. Shifting to a primary care–centric model translated to a drop in mortality from heart attack and stroke. Lithuania also worked to prevent and manage risk factors such as high blood pressure, cholesterol, and diabetes, and made essential medicines more available. Not only has access in the country improved, but costs have dropped.[19]

Demographics and Epidemiological Shifts: Youth, Displaced Migrants, and Noncommunicable Diseases

Our global health landscape and epidemiological profile are changing with the size and demographics of our populations. And many of these changes are complex. Epidemiologically, our disease burden is shifting from infectious diseases such as HIV, tuberculosis, and malaria to noncommunicable diseases (NCDs) such as cancer, diabetes, and heart disease. The complexities of NCDs and aging are becoming more apparent as well, as people live longer. We cannot afford to ignore NCDs, as these diseases cost LMICs about 5 percent of their GDP.[20]

NCDs are responsible for 70 percent of all deaths, killing forty million people annually. Fifteen million of these deaths are premature, occurring between the ages of thirty and sixty-nine, mostly in LMICs. The big four groups of NCDs—cardiovascular disease, cancers, respiratory diseases, and diabetes—account for over 80 percent of all premature deaths. Unhealthy lifestyle choices, including tobacco use, physical inactivity, alcohol misuse, and unhealthy diets, all elevate the risk of dying from an NCD. We must improve detection, screening, treatment, and palliative care for NCDs, and focus on poverty as a socioeconomic factor. NCDs are costly to treat and quickly drain household resources or result in the loss of breadwinners.[21]

Target 3.4 of the SDGs calls for the reduction by one-third of premature mortality from NCDs by 2030 through prevention and treatment. Collaborations and efforts such as the WHO's Global Action Plan for the Prevention and Control of NCDs can serve as road maps. Government leadership—such as Kenya's cancer strategy[22] crafted in partnership with professional organizations and civil society—is also key.

Population shifts also include urbanization and the so-called youth bulge. More and more of us are moving to cities, contributing to urban health challenges related to pollution, water, sanitation, and more. The health needs of young people are looming larger, as today there are more people under the age of twenty-five than ever before, particularly in LMICs.

Theoretically, this young generation will have the technological and financial resources to reduce rates of infectious disease and child and maternal mortality to universally low levels by 2030, and to achieve UHC. But this will require investing today in the world's 1.2 billion adolescents. A *Lancet* report found that spending $5.20 per capita each year across seventy-five LMICs to improve health and reduce injuries among young people will show economic and social benefits at ten times those costs by saving 12.5 million lives, preventing more than thirty million unwanted pregnancies, and averting widespread disability.[23]

As our numbers of young people grow, so does our need for long-term employment. Unemployment among young people is on the rise worldwide, but the health sector can be a huge employer for those who have access to education and training.[24] Expanding that access and creating more jobs for young people who want to become health workers will yield sustainable returns.

Young people also make powerful ambassadors for health. The Civil Society for Family Planning Project, for instance, engages dynamic young people from across francophone West Africa to educate and mobilize their peers around reproductive health and family planning, thus expanding access to these services in the region. The youth ambassadors not only serve as role models in their communities, but also help hold governments accountable for the family planning commitments they made to Family Planning 2020 (FP2020)[25] and the Ouagadougou Partnership.[26] FP2020 was launched in 2012 as a global commitment among governments, civil society, multilateral organizations, donors, the private sector, and the research and development community to enable 120 million more women and girls to use contraceptives by 2020. The Ouagadougou Partnership is a coalition working to give 2.2 million more people in the francophone West African region access to family planning by 2020.

Children make up over half of sixty-five million forcibly displaced migrants worldwide.[27] There are up to one billion migrants globally, including twenty-one million refugees. Many refugees and migrants (forcibly displaced or not) have no access to health services nor financial protection for health needs, and too often, they face discrimination in health-care systems. Protecting their human rights—including the right to health—has risen on the international agenda in the last decade.

Many governments are working to integrate migrant health needs into their national plans, policies, and strategies. For instance, Sri Lanka and the Philippines have designed insurance schemes for overseas migrant workers. Brazil, Spain, and Portugal have adopted a policy of equal access for all migrants regardless of their legal status.[28]

Within those billion migrants are health workers, although their migration is often driven by demand for their employment in high- and middle-income countries—which often leaves lower-income countries with even more severe shortages of health workers. We need to advance international recognition of health workers' qualifications to optimize skills use, maximize the benefits and minimize the negative effects of health worker migration, and safeguard migrants' rights.[29]

Access through Sociocultural Determinants: Gender, Acceptability, Geography, Technology

Gender Equality and Health Access

Gender is just one dynamic, layered determinant that intersects with many others—such as ethnicity, poverty, race, migratory status, level of ability, age, sexual orientation, income, education, and place of residence—to affect access to health care. Gender norms influence access to and control over health resources on many levels: economic, social, political, even subconscious. This means the health-care experience is often drastically different for men and women.[30]

For survivors of gender-based violence, many barriers can stand between them and health care—shame, guilt, fear of the perpetrator, stigma, worry over their children's safety and custody, an irregular immigration status, and lack of financial resources.

Many standards, strategies, and road maps have been developed in the past decade for gender analysis and planning, mainstreaming gender in corporate functions, and establishing accountability.[31] Government leaders, civil society, the private sector, and communities must all act to improve gender equality and thus increase access to health care.

It is imperative that countries and institutions do more to empower women and maximize their economic participation, including placing them in meaningful leadership roles in the health sector and addressing gender biases and inequities in education and technology, the health labor market, and health reform processes.[32]

Acceptability

Cultural and social factors often determine whether people will access services. Are the services available perceived to be of good quality or poor? Are most of the health workers male or female, and how might this affect accessibility? (In some societies, for example, casual physical contact between unmarried men and women is unacceptable.)[33] Do some clients feel excluded or judged by the health workers? What treatments or health interventions have traditionally existed in the community?

These were important questions, for example, when the human papillomavirus vaccine was introduced in Latin America and the Caribbean. Health workers' interpersonal communication skills became crucial during this effort, as some parents worried that the vaccine could encourage their daughters to become sexually active earlier than they otherwise might. And the benefits of the vaccine are often delayed until adulthood, when it can prevent cervical cancer in women.[34]

This effort—as with any new health intervention or technology—called for clear messages for the medical, scientific, and lay audiences; collaboration with the media to raise awareness; and coordination with professional associations and institutions. It takes targeted qualitative research to understand what people already know and think about a particular disease, vaccination, and the link between the two, in order to prevent misinformation, confusion, and negative reactions.

Ultimately, we must create patient-centered health systems to make services more acceptable to the entire population.

Rural Access: Community Health Workers Can Reach the Last Mile

To achieve UHC, we must reach the last mile—those remote, sparsely populated areas that have few or no health workers. As more people move to cities, people living in hard-to-reach rural areas need new solutions for health access to ensure they are not left behind. Many governments, businesses, nonprofits, and foundations are investing in community health workers to reach the poorest, often forgotten, people with the health services they need. Here are a few examples:

- *Last Mile Health* in Liberia helped train more than 1,300 health workers and community members to prevent and contain the spread of Ebola so they could "keep safe, keep serving" in the midst of the 2014 outbreak. Now Last Mile Health is expanding its efforts through a community health worker academy.[35]

- *The Ethiopian government* improved access to high-quality health care through its Health Development Army, which trained young women with at least a tenth-grade education to deliver babies, provide immunizations, and offer family planning services and other basic health skills as health extension workers.[36] In 1990, one in five children died before the age of five in Ethiopia, one of the highest child mortality rates in the world. Thanks to the government's pledge to achieve the MDGs—and its careful measuring of progress and needs—the under-five death rate dropped by 66 percent. Now over fifteen thousand health posts provide PHC to rural areas, staffed by thirty-eight thousand health workers.[37]

- *India's* long-time investments in frontline health care have resulted in advanced service policies and guidelines, including the Rural Health Mission,[38] which delivers services to remote areas. Communization, flexible financing, improved management through capacity building, monitoring progress against standards, innovations in human resources management—these are all strategies India has employed to expand access to high-quality health care.

- *The Frontline Health Workers Coalition*, an alliance of US-based organizations, urges greater and more strategic US investment in frontline health workers as a cost-effective way to save lives. The coalition advocates for community health workers and their contributions to health systems around the world—particularly in the most vulnerable regions and in containing outbreaks and epidemics.[39]

The Promise of Digital Health

Digital technologies are transforming our health sector, though the context in high-income countries varies greatly from that in many LMICs. For instance, mobile broadband costs eat up 11–25 percent of average monthly incomes in LMICs, compared to only 1–2 percent in high-income countries.[40] This digital divide disproportionately affects women and those in the most remote areas—those who could benefit most from its ability to expand access to care.[41] As information and communication technology (ICT) infrastructure in LMICs matures, we can overcome the digital divide by designing digital health interventions that are properly resourced; are regulated; are in line with individual countries' principles, values, and health system maturity; and address the greatest health needs.

There are plenty of existing and forthcoming tools to improve health access—telemedicine, electronic health (e-health), mobile health (m-health), social media, massive open online courses, webcasts, podcasts, high-fidelity simulation decision-support tools, electronic medical records, electronic systems for disease surveillance, and laboratory and pharmacy information systems. These tools are becoming more relevant even in the lowest-resourced countries. To ensure these innovations flourish, ministries of health must provide a rigorous governance framework to vet and provide clear guidance on norms and standards as part of their national health strategies.[42]

Health officials today can collect more and better data on the health system and its beneficiaries than ever before. These data help countries plan for the future, pinpoint emerging health threats, and determine how best to allocate health system resources and commodities. To remain accessible, the health information systems must be interoperable—meaning able to communicate with one another through common standards. Adopting these common standards as part of a national health strategy reduces long-term operating costs and makes health information more accessible and valuable. Global goods[43] and reusable open-source software (e.g., OpenMRS,[44] DHIS2,[45] HL7 FHIR,[46] OpenHIE[47]) make it easier for countries to adopt such digital technologies.

Technology also plays an important role in expanding health care from hospitals into community settings. It can be used, for example, to train less-skilled cadres of health workers to offer certain treatments that leave more highly trained health professionals to attend to more problematic cases. Engaging health workers in designing these solutions is crucial. When communities—and community health workers—are empowered with tools they understand and can master, they will apply their own creativity and ingenuity.

Digital health interventions are most successful when they are contextually appropriate and use existing infrastructure and health system investments. During the 2014 Ebola outbreak, for example, a new technology called mHero[48] allowed government officials in Liberia to reach faraway, even isolated frontline health workers and rally them during the crisis. The collaborators behind mHero used existing systems (iHRIS,[49] OpenHIM,[50] RapidPro,[51] and DHIS2), many of which were already deployed in Liberia, to create this tool.

Globally, countless digital health solutions have been designed to improve access to, and quality of, maternal and child health services. The Mobile Obstetrics

Monitoring program in Indonesia and the Wired Mothers program in Tanzania have reduced mortality rates through better coordination of care. Programs such as MAMA Bangladesh and MomConnect[52] in South Africa have allowed for quicker, better access to health information for clients and better birth outcomes.[53]

Networks—at the national, regional, and global levels—also promote better use of ICT to increase health access. An exemplary model of South–South collaboration is the Asia eHealth Information Network.[54] It builds capacity for e-health, health information systems, and civil registration and vital statistics nationally and regionally; utilizes effective networking to increase peer assistance and knowledge exchange and sharing; promotes standards and interoperability within and across countries; and enhances leadership, sustainable governance, and monitoring and evaluation.

The promise of digital health tools to improve health outcomes, expand coverage, and reduce costs abounds. A PricewaterhouseCoopers research found that between 2013 and 2017, m-health could give 15.5 million more people in Mexico access to health services—and reduce public and private health care spending by $3.8 billion. In Brazil, it could increase access for 28.4 million people and cut public and private health care spending by $14 billion.[55]

To capitalize on these opportunities, countries must build a solid foundation that includes adopting e-health strategies and appropriate governance models, adhering to open international standards, and using human-centered and open-source digital health tools.

Access through Financial Affordability and Capacity Building

Financing is critical to enable universal health access. To realize the potential impact of health investment on the world economy, we must ask some tough questions:

- How do we move from the prevalent pay-as-you-go systems, in which relatively few of us have health coverage, to coverage for 100 percent of the population?
- How do we ensure that people do not lose their farms or their businesses when they fall sick and can no longer pay out of pocket?
- What will it take for private companies to go from low-volume/high margins to high-volume/low margins?
- How do we achieve disruptive innovation at scale while alleviating potential risks that are so often the main cause of resistance to change?

Changing Economies

Today, the African continent has the fastest-growing economies in the world. By 2034, it could have a workforce larger than India or China. This growth translates to $2.6 trillion in African business opportunities by 2020.[56] And globally, there is a growing middle class with greater purchasing power than ever.

Soon, we should see more domestically financed health systems and mixed markets where the public and private sectors offer multiple points of access to an array of comprehensive health services. More and more, the demand will come from communities that are educated and able to focus on self-care, while supply comes from health workers who provide high-quality, sustainable, client-centered services to all those in need.

But how will we reach this future? And how can we afford it?

The first step will be investing in the health workforce, where huge funding gaps remain. For every dollar invested in community health workers, for example, we see returns as high as $10. Eighty percent of populations rely on them for PHC and yet many in the global health and development community continue to see them as volunteers. Governments, donor agencies, and others must budget and plan for their integration into the formal health system.

There are two billion people worldwide who still lack access to essential medicine.[57] Pharmaceutical companies can be part of the solution by focusing on how they deploy their products and collaborating to develop strong health systems. The mission of the Access to Medicine Foundation is to stimulate and guide pharmaceutical and vaccine companies to do more for the people living in LMICs without access to medicine or vaccines. The foundation is employing five strategies from 2017 to 2021 to shift pharmaceutical company practice, including embedding pro-access governance, mainstreaming inclusive business models, improving industry responsiveness to public health priorities, employing "access-thinking" in product deployment, and addressing unmet needs through research and development.

Pharma companies must reduce barriers to access, be trendsetters in the supply chain, and directly contribute to unlocking growth in emerging markets. Accenture Research learned that the top ten pharmaceutical companies for increasing access to medicines in LMICs grew 20 percentage points of stock price annually over their peers.[58]

Countries must also lead efforts to increase access to medicines. Senegal's government, for example, drastically improved the country's supply chain for family planning products by implementing the Informed Push Model nationwide. By improving logistics and reinvesting proceeds from contraceptive purchases back into the public contraceptive supply system, Senegal ensures a constant flow and availability of products, allowing women to more freely choose the methods they want at affordable prices. The model reduced contraceptive stockouts to less than 2 percent. And in a single year, from 2012 to 2013, the number of women and girls using modern methods of contraception rose by 8.4 million.[59]

Innovative Financing Models for Health and Resource Mobilization

If Coca-Cola can deliver its products to the most remote communities in the world, surely we can deliver health care there, too.

Today, a new architecture for collaboration among the public and private sectors is taking shape in global health and development, including innovative financing models for health. Companies such as Pfizer, Johnson & Johnson, and GE are joining the traditional global development actors and pioneering a shift from a corporate social responsibility model to a shared-value approach, meaning they are finding business opportunities while addressing social problems. And with the help of NGOs, governments, and other stakeholders as partners, businesses have the power to create real change on monumental social problems such as access to health care.

The Clinton Global Initiative (CGI) offered another innovative model to convene and catalyze private-sector initiatives and partnerships. From 2005 to 2016, members of the CGI community made more than 3,600 commitments, which are estimated to have improved the lives of over 435 million people in more than 180 countries.[60] This model was unique: CGI, rather than directly implementing projects, facilitated action by connecting public, private, and government members to make effective and measurable commitments together. Other innovative examples include the following:

- Gavi, the Vaccine Alliance, is an international organization created in 2000 that brings together the public and private sectors to improve access to new and underused vaccines for children in the world's poorest countries. Seventy-three Gavi-supported countries have saved $18 in health-care costs and losses in productivity and wages for every $1 spent on immunization. The benefits of people living longer, healthier lives could increase the return on investment to $48 per $1 spent. By 2015, Gavi had immunized over five hundred million additional children and prevented more than seven million deaths. It plans to reach an additional three hundred million children between 2016 and 2020, averting a further five to six million deaths.[61]

- The Global Fund is a partnership organization founded in 2002 to accelerate the end of AIDS, tuberculosis, and malaria as epidemics. Governments, civil society, and the private sector collaborate to reach people affected by the diseases by raising and investing nearly $4 billion annually to support programs run by local experts, where the disease burden lies. By the end of 2015, it supported programs that saved more than twenty million lives.[62]

- Creating Shared Value through Partnerships, launched in 2015 by the Australian government's Department of Foreign Affairs and Trade, is the government's first aid policy specifically targeting the private sector as a fundamental partner; it recognizes that the private sector has the means and, increasingly, the motivation to contribute to development outcomes as part of its core business.[63]

- The US Global Development Lab was created in 2014 as an innovation hub to take smart risks and test new ideas, in partnership with the US Agency for International Development (USAID) and others.[64]

- USAID's Grand Challenges for Development, a program that has funded more than eighty-five solutions—a third of which came from LMICs—to global development problems and leveraged nearly 5:1 in funding from non-USAID sources, is a cost-effective investment for the US taxpayer.[65]

Governments are slowly becoming more open to outsourcing and contracting certain functions to the private sector—and to bringing economists, financiers, and other new stakeholders into the fold. Africa, in particular, has great potential for new market solutions. And some health financing models with track records in US urban settings are now being tested and adapted in LMICs. Examples of public–private models include the following:

- The Challenge Initiative,[66] an urban reproductive health project funded by the Bill & Melinda Gates Foundation that engages municipalities and requires mayors who want to participate to commit their own resources while also leveraging local philanthropists and other private-sector actors.
- The Abraaj Group's investments in networks of private-sector health facilities linked with frontline health workers.[67]
- Living Goods, an NGO working in Uganda and Kenya that empowers women to serve as both businesswomen and frontline health workers. A large-scale randomized trial in Uganda found that Living Goods' community health promoters helped reduce child mortality by 27 percent and infant mortality by 33 percent.[68]

It is also possible to raise revenue for the health sector through so-called sin taxes, such as on alcohol and tobacco. WHO modeling predicts that raising the tax on cigarettes by one "international dollar" per pack would raise cigarette excise revenue worldwide by about $141 billion and decrease global cigarette consumption by about 18 percent.[69]

The International Monetary Fund estimates that sin taxes helped low-income countries, in aggregate, increase their tax revenue from 13 percent to 17 percent of GDP between 1990 and 2011. For LMICs, in aggregate, the percentage increased from 16 percent to 20 percent, and for upper middle-income countries, it increased from 22 percent to 28 percent.[70]

Governments see the returns in economic growth when they invest tax revenue in health. A review of historic microeconomic and macroeconomic studies found that about 11 percent of economic growth in LMICs during 1970–2000 resulted from reductions in adult mortality.[71]

After 189 world leaders adopted the Millennium Declaration in 2000, African leaders pledged to allocate at least 15 percent of their annual budgets to the health sector in the Abuja Declaration, though Tanzania is the only nation that has achieved the goal. Twenty-six countries increased their government expenditures allocated to health, while eleven reduced their contributions, and nine showed no upward or downward trend.[72]

To close the financing gap, donor countries must develop new sources of funds, improve the efficiency of health spending, prioritize health in general budget/debt relief funds in recipient countries, and encourage innovative funding sources to supplement traditional bilateral assistance for health.[73]

Capacity Strengthening

To ensure that every investment in global health and development leaves behind a legacy of stronger institutions and people, we should recommit to capacity building and keep it at the core of the development paradigm. Donors can help by funding efforts within individual countries to build a culture of data—including collecting and using human performance data and improving measurement and analytics. Technology is making such transformational education more widely available through self-paced courses, individually tailored/modular training curricula, and new digital tools for learning, data collection, and decision support.

New procurement reforms from multilateral, bilateral, and private donors should include deliberate and clear indicators and deliverables on capacity strengthening, including built-in requirements for stronger exit/transition strategies.

Improving Governance of Health Systems

The SDGs call for a paradigm shift in order to achieve UHC. For LMICs in particular, that paradigm shift needs to include strong governance of PHC as a necessary step toward UHC.

More countries today are working to make lifesaving health services available closer to the people who most need them. Decentralization—or the process of shifting greater authority to manage health care from the central to the local level—has been a key governance mechanism in many countries. In Kenya, decentralization is transforming health care in areas such as Turkana County, one of the country's poorest. This improvement is largely due to its booming health workforce, attracted and retained through a new incentive framework. Greater governance over data has helped the Dominican Republic to reinvest over $6 million in its health system after eliminating "ghost workers," revealed through a payroll analysis, and hiring new health workers to increase access to services. And Senegal is making great progress toward this shift as well, in part by investing in community health workers and integrating them into the overall health system.

The countries that have had the greatest success in family planning, for example, have taken these services to the people, in part by giving local health officials more control over health care. Indonesia, Thailand, and Singapore have all created favorable policy environments, relaxed the laws that were holding their programs back, and invested greatly in their community health workforces. Thailand has essentially destigmatized family planning and made it a mainstream way of life. And now many African countries that are working to emulate these Asian achievements—such as Senegal and Rwanda—are seeing success as well. In Rwanda, the use of modern contraception rose from 4 percent in 2000 to almost 50 percent in 2007.

Botswana provides a good example of how domestic resource mobilization and good governance can lead to large-scale success in a mass antiretroviral therapy (ART) program. With the country's overwhelming HIV epidemic, many eligible citizens did not have access to ART. So the government decentralized ART distribution, which was initially only available in urban centers, and began providing it free to all eligible citizens. As a result, nearly 87 percent of eligible citizens had access to ART, and AIDS-related deaths decreased from

21,000 to 5,800 between 2003 and 2013. The government financed 68 percent of the total domestic and international AIDS spending of $374 million.[74]

South-to-South Collaboration Increases Access to Health Care

When countries in the Global South do not share ideas and successes with each other, it is a missed opportunity that comes at a high cost—namely, lost lives and weaker societies. But more forums and partnerships are now making such sharing possible—for example, transmitting the family planning successes of Asia to sub-Saharan Africa.

Partners in Population and Development, a global intergovernmental initiative, serves as a South–South knowledge-sharing platform in the areas of reproductive health, population, and development. Member countries reach over half of the world's population.[75]

Haiti and Lesotho, two resource-poor countries, offer another good example. Haiti had developed a model of HIV care that, through an exchange of knowledge and collaboration, was adapted and expanded in Lesotho, enabling the effective scale-up of HIV and other treatment services in a rural African setting.[76]

Conclusion: Racing toward 2030

Attaining the SDGs (in particular SDG 3), achieving universal health access, revitalizing PHC, realizing the economic benefits of health investments—these are the challenges we now face. They are daunting, but all are achievable. To do so will require advocacy and action on all of the key drivers outlined in this chapter. We will need to create more partnerships and innovative models, achieve scale on digital health solutions, and attract more donors, private-sector actors, and governments to increase their investments and commitments to the new frontier of health and health markets.

Strengthening the health workforce, a critical pillar of the health system, must remain central to all of these efforts—for without adequate numbers of skilled health workers stationed where they are needed most, none of these ambitious achievements will be possible. Attainment of this lofty goal will be easier if development partners from civil society, faith-based organizations, and the private sector work with governments to address the already well-documented challenges, and prepare for new and future ones that achieving universal health access will require.

Notes

[1] United Nations Department of Economic and Social Affairs/Population Division, *World Population Prospects: The 2015 Revision, Key Findings and Advance Tables*, Working Paper No. ESA/P/WP.241 (New York, 2015).

[2] David Evans, Justine Hsu, and Ties Boerma. "Universal Health Coverage and Universal Access," *Bulletin of the World Health Organization* 91 (2013): 546–546A. doi:http://dx.doi.org/10.2471/BLT.13.125450.

[3] World Health Organization, *Working for Health and Growth: Investing in the Health Workforce* (Geneva: High-Level Commission on Health Employment and Economic Growth, 2016).

[4] World Health Organization, "Health Workers: A Triple Return for Health, Economic Growth, and Employment" (World Health Organization, 2016). Accessed June 1, 2017. http://www.who.int/mediacentre/news/notes/2016/health-workers-triple-return/en/.

[5] World Health Organization, *Global Strategy on Human Resources for Health: Workforce 2030* (Geneva, 2016).

[6] Mark Pearson et al., *Universal Health Coverage and Health Outcomes* (Paris: OECD, 2016). https://www.oecd.org/els/health-systems/Universal-Health-Coverage-and-Health-Outcomes-OECD-G7-Health-Ministerial-2016.pdf.

[7] United Nations, "Under-Five Mortality Rate (per 1,000 Live Births)," *Human Development Reports.* Accessed June 10, 2017. http://hdr.undp.org/en/content/under-five-mortality-rate-1000-live-births.

[8] Heather Bergmann et al., *Linkage and Retention in Pre-ART Care: Best Practices and Experiences from Fourteen Countries* (Arlington, VA: USAID's AIDS Support and Technical Assistance Resources, AIDSTAR-One, Task Order 1, 2013).

[9] United Nations Population Fund, *The State of World's Midwifery 2014* (New York, 2015).

[10] Frontline Health Workers Coalition, *Cost of Scaling up the Health Workforce in Liberia, Sierra Leone, and Guinea amid the Ebola Epidemic: FHWC Costing Analysis* (Washington, 2015).

[11] http://www.who.int/hrh/com-heeg/en/.

[12] World Health Organization, *Everybody's Business: Strengthening Health Systems to Improve Health Outcomes: WHO's Framework for Action* (Geneva, 2007). Accessed July 8, 2017. http://www.who.int/healthsystems/strategy/everybodys_business.pdf?ua=1.

[13] http://www.who.int/alliance-hpsr/en/.

[14] https://2009-2017.pepfar.gov/partnerships/initiatives/mepi/index.htm; https://www.pepfar.gov/partnerships/initiatives/nepi/.

[15] http://phcperformanceinitiative.org/.

[16] https://www.weforum.org/projects/global-platform-for-access-to-care.

[17] G4 Alliance, *G4 Alliance Annual Report 2015–2016* (New York: G4 Alliance, 2017). Accessed June 9, 2017. https://static1.squarespace.com/static/5435b2b9e4b0e1fd29fa9d26/t/57fec2f4e-6f2e11a01c58c2c/1476313847131/G4_Annual+Report_V14.compressed+%281%29.pdf.

[18] John G. Meara et al., "Global Surgery 2030: Evidence and Solutions for Achieving Health, Welfare, and Economic Development," *The Lancet* 386, no. 9993 (2015): 569–624.

[19] World Health Organization, *Lessons from Transforming Health Services Delivery: Compendium of Initiatives in the WHO European Region* (Copenhagen, 2016).

[20] David Bloom et al., *The Global Economic Burden of Noncommunicable Diseases* (Geneva: World Economic Forum, 2011).

[21] http://www.who.int/mediacentre/factsheets/fs355/en/.

[22] Ministry of Health Kenya, *National Cancer Control Strategy: 2017–2022* (2017).

[23] Peter Sheehan et al., "Building the Foundations for Sustainable Development: A Case for Global Investment in the Capabilities of Adolescents," *The Lancet*, 4 (2017). doi:10.1016/s0140-6736(17)30872-3.

[24] International Labour Organization, *World Employment Social Outlook: Trends for 2016* (Geneva, 2016).

[25] http://www.familyplanning2020.org/microsite/about-us.

[26] https://partenariatouaga.org/en/about-us/the-partnership/.

[27] United Nations High Commissioner for Refugees, *Global Trends: Forced Displacement in 2015* (Geneva, 2016).

[28] United Nations High Commissioner for Refugees, *War's Human Cost: Global Trends 2013* (Geneva, 2014).

29 World Health Organization, *Working for Health and Growth: Investing in the Health Workforce* (Geneva, 2016).

30 Veronica Magar, "Gender, Health and the Sustainable Development Goals," *Bulletin of the World Health Organization* 93, no. 11 (2015): 743. doi:10.2471/blt.15.165027.

31 http://genderstandards.org/authors/; http://www.who.int/mediacentre/factsheets/fs403/en/.

32 World Health Organization, *Working for Health and Growth.*

33 Jean-Frederic Levesque, Mark F. Harris, and Grant Russell. "Patient-Centred Access to Health Care: Conceptualising Access at the Interface of Health Systems and Populations," *International Journal for Equity in Health* 12, no. 1 (2013): 18. doi:10.1186/1475-9276-12-18.

34 Jennifer L. Winkler et al., "Determinants of Human Papillomavirus Vaccine Acceptability in Latin America and the Caribbean," *Vaccine* 26 (2008). doi:10.1016/j.vaccine.2008.05.027.

35 http://lastmilehealth.org/.

36 "The Health Extension Program of Ethiopia," *Harvard Health Policy Review*, December 30, 2016. Accessed June 9, 2017. http://www.hhpronline.org/articles/2016/12/17/the-health-extension-program-of-ethiopia.

37 Bill Gates. "Strong Coffee, Stronger Women," *Gates Notes* (web log), May 9, 2017. Accessed May 25, 2017. https://www.gatesnotes.com/Health/Strong-Coffee-Stronger-Women.

38 http://nhm.gov.in/.

39 https://www.frontlinehealthworkers.org/.

40 http://www.itu.int/en/ITU-D/Statistics/Pages/default.aspx.

41 Broadband Commission for Sustainable Development, *Digital Health: A Call for Government Leadership and Cooperation between ICT and Health*, 2017. Accessed June 11, 2017. http://www.broadbandcommission.org/Documents/publications/WorkingGroupHealthReport-2017.pdf.

42 https://www.measureevaluation.org/his-strengthening-resource-center/resources/his-strategic-plan.

43 National Academies of Sciences, Engineering, and Medicine, "Global Health and the Future Role of the United States," 2017. doi:10.17226/24737.

44 http://openmrs.org/.

45 https://www.dhis2.org/.

46 https://www.hl7.org/fhir/.

47 https://ohie.org/.

48 http://www.mhero.org/.

49 http://ihris.org/.

50 http://openhim.org/.

51 http://rapidpro.io/.

52 http://www.health.gov.za/index.php/mom-connect.

53 Pablo Iacopino and Mike Meloan, *Scaling Digital Health in Developing Markets: Opportunities and Recommendations for Mobile Operators and Other Stakeholders* (GSMA, 2017).

54 http://www.openhealthnews.com/resources/asia-ehealth-information-network-aehin.

55 PricewaterhouseCoopers Private Limited, *Socio-Economic Impact of mHealth: An Assessment Report for Brazil and Mexico* (2013).

56 Jacques Bughin et al., *Lions on the Move II: Realizing the Potential of Africa's Economies* (New York: McKinsey, 2016).

57 Access to Medicine Foundation, *The 2016 Access to Medicine Index Methodology* (Haarlem, 2015).

58 Thomas Ebel, Erik Larsen, and Ketan Shah, *Strengthening Health Care's Supply Chain: A Five-Step Plan* (New York: McKinsey, 2013). Accessed June 25, 2017. http://www.mckinsey.com/industries/healthcare-systems-and-services/our-insights/strengthening-health-cares-supply-chain-a-five-step-planT.

59 Leah Hasselback et al., "Understanding and Addressing Contraceptive Stockouts to Increase Family Planning Access and Uptake in Senegal," *BMC Health Services Research* 17, no. 1 (2017). doi:10.1186/s12913-017-2316-y.

60 https://www.clintonfoundation.org/clinton-global-initiative/commitments.

61 http://www.gavi.org/.

⁶² https://www.theglobalfund.org/en/.

⁶³ Commonwealth of Australia, Department of Foreign Affairs and Trade, "Creating Shared Value through Partnership: Ministerial Statement on Engaging the Private Sector in Aid and Development," 2015. Accessed June 30, 2017. http://dfat.gov.au/about-us/publications/aid/Pages/creating-shared-value-through-partnership.aspx.

⁶⁴ https://www.usaid.gov/GlobalDevLab.

⁶⁵ https://www.usaid.gov/GlobalDevLab/documents/2015-lab-year-review.

⁶⁶ https://tciurbanhealth.org/.

⁶⁷ Elizabeth MacBride, "The Story behind Abraaj Group's Stunning Rise in Global Private Equity," *Forbes*, November 5, 2015. Accessed June 7, 2017. https://www.forbes.com/sites/elizabethmacbride/2015/11/04/the-story-behind-abraajs-stunning-rise/#53199e2520ac.

⁶⁸ https://livinggoods.org/.

⁶⁹ Mark Goodchild, Anne-Marie Perucic, and Nigar Nargis, "Modelling the Impact of Raising Tobacco Taxes on Public Health and Finance" (WHO, 2016). Accessed June 30, 2017. http://www.who.int/bulletin/volumes/94/4/15-164707/en/.

⁷⁰ Dean T. Jamison et al., "Global Health 2035: A World Converging within a Generation," *The Lancet* 382, no. 9908 (2013): 1898–1955. doi:10.1016/s0140-6736(13)62105-4.

⁷¹ D. T. Jamison, L. J. Lau, and J. Wang, "Health's Contribution to Economic Growth in an Environment of Partially Endogenous Technical Progress," in *Health and Economic Growth: Findings and Policy Implications*, G. Lopez-Casasnovas, B. Rivera, and L. Currais, eds. (Cambridge, MA: MIT Press, 2005), 67–91.

⁷² World Health Organization, "The Abuja Declaration: Ten Years On," 2011. Accessed May 20, 2017. http://www.who.int/healthsystems/publications/abuja_declaration/en/.

⁷³ Taskforce on Innovative International Financing of Health Systems, *More Money for Health, and More Health for the Money* (WHO, 2009). Accessed July 15, 2017. http://www.who.int/tobacco/economics/en_tfi_economics_final_task_force_report.pdf.

⁷⁴ Amanda Glassman and Miriam Temin, *Millions Saved: New Cases of Proven Success in Global Health* (Washington, DC: Center for Global Development, 2016).

⁷⁵ http://www.partners-popdev.org/.

⁷⁶ Louise C. Ivers et al., "South–South Collaboration in Scale-Up of HIV Care: Building Human Capacity for Care," *AIDS* 24, Suppl. 1 (2010). doi:10.1097/01.aids.0000366085.14064.

CHAPTER 10

Bodies of Water
The Role of Hydration in Health, Wellness, and Wealth
Gina Bria

The purpose of this chapter is to explore the role of hydration in creating human health, wellness, and material wealth. We highlight hydration as the most potent health promotion strategy we have, interrupting and preventing the spiral of ever-growing disease states, and illuminating what the capital of health can mean.[1] In addition, we bring to this discussion breakthrough findings from the new research on water enabling improved health through more efficient hydration, and improved water quality through natural self-purification processes. These new research findings offer innovative approaches to our growing water scarcity dilemmas, and suggest practical and widespread solutions in our water-challenged world. In particular, water scientists are discovering more efficient hydration strategies that actually reduce liquid consumption, and multiple ways to activate and even accelerate water's molecular capacity to purify itself from contaminants, both natural and synthetic. This will allow us to reintroduce purified water back into contaminated environments and contaminated bodies to self-repair and restore vitality. We conclude with a discussion of successful approaches to accelerate the formation of water's molecular capacity, spanning ancient practices and cutting-edge research laboratories.

Why Hydration Is the Most Potent Health Intervention

"Promotion of healthy practices is our most urgent health intervention. Many of the risk factors underlying the top causes of disease and disability are modifiable through lifestyle changes."[2] Wise words indeed, yet rarely is hydration listed as the first optimizing recommendation for health promotion and lifestyle changes. Here is why we should make hydration our top priority: our bodies and our planet are mostly water. This affects everything.

Yet, while it is often stated that the human body is, by volume, 60–70 percent water, even the common use of this statistic doesn't seem to land hydration first on the list of priority health promotion strategies and needs. Perhaps, we can motivate a reprioritization by calculating in another, more compelling, way. By molecular count, the human body is 99 percent water.[3] That is to say, if you line up all the molecules inside you, of every one hundred counted, ninety-nine of them would be water and only one of those molecules would be of another material. This and other astounding new research is surfacing from labs in the United States, Japan, Italy, Russia, and China.[4] It makes sense, then, that water solutions should be the most potent health support in our bodies. Simple and affordable, optimal hydration becomes the most effectual and upstream intervention for ensuring health, and the wealth that comes with it. This wealth comes in two ways: first, the reduction in cost burdens of illness and second, the increase in our capacity and productivity, through the restoration of inner resources for self-regulation, resilience, and performance.

The Wealth in Hydration

Hydration is critical for the human brain and overall function; even a 2 percent loss in hydration leads to measurable cognitive loss and a reduction in human performance.[5] Let's just take that 2 percent alone and add it back to our wealth-generating capacities in terms of productivity, performance, and cognition. Hydration is an untapped treasure. The positive impact of healthful living on the care of ourselves and others through being well hydrated with untainted water can be truly capitalized now that we know the sheer volume of water molecules inside our own human bodies.

Moreover, our planet is a body of water, as are we. Its pollution is our pollution; its purity our purity. Hydration with pure water is health embodied to sustain, enhance, and build capacity for both our bodies: planetary and human. As water flows and makes its circuit around the globe, whether through the vapors of the air, the world's ocean currents, the aspirations of trees, or underwater rivers, it flows and comes back to us wherever we are. Our place in this, besides protecting the waters that surround us, is to become alert to the power of the water inside us. And to develop new pathways to solutions, ideally local, based on the new science of water.

This new science has identified a fourth phase of water, a fluid gel phase existing past vapor, between liquid and ice. This form of water is always potentially ready to activate, can be induced to expand, and has tremendous potency that we are only beginning to more fully understand. There are two major applications of this new phase of water, referred to in the growing literature alternately as structured, liquid crystalline, coherent, ordered, gel, or Exclusion Zone (EZ) water. The first is that this new understanding of water at this molecular state or phase allows us to more efficiently hydrate *using less liquid water*. While we cannot yet definitively measure how great that percentage is, we surmise it to be substantial, extrapolating from desert and *in extremis* environments, where this form of hydration has been in use since ancient times. Second, this molecular phase is water's own *self-purifying state* using its intrinsic molecular processes.[6] Better health through more efficient hydration, reduction in water use, and restoration of water purity are, each and all, good things to activate in our current conditions.

New and Revolutionary Science of Water

Water is H_2O. We have long known that as the indisputable chemical expression of a single molecule of water. However, it is not the expression of water molecules linked together. Surprisingly, water is not always H_2O. When water molecules come together, water becomes H_3O_2, a revolutionary discovery of Dr. Gerald Pollack, bioengineer and water scientist from the University of Washington, Seattle. Why is this so groundbreaking? The implications of discovering a new state of water promise to transform our entire relationship to water: how we think about, use, apply, absorb, conserve, distribute, purify, and enjoy water.

How do we understand the significance of this new state of water? First, we can review how we got here. It's the story of simple, straightforward, laboratory experiments which identified H_3O_2, or what he calls EZ water, which stands for Exclusion Zone. EZ water is indeed a far-reaching new discovery, and while it has always been there, we are just now identifying its surprising and unique properties. It is nothing short of water's own specialized purifying stage. Yes, water has the capacity to cleanse itself, and we can either interfere with that or we can help it along. Dr. Pollack's truly breakthrough work came by noticing a difference in water if you looked at not just the single water molecule, but how the molecules linked up over time and space. Together, they became more and more tightly knit, forming interlinking crystals, still in fluid state, much like lace or crocheted netting. This is called the liquid crystalline state, also known as EZ, gel water, or structured water. In this "exclusionary zone" where the crystals form, Pollack saw how water molecules linking or cohering together squeeze out any other molecules, becoming pure water. It is, simply put, water filtering itself. This specialized state of water has been theoretically kicking around for over one hundred years. We knew it could be there, but no one had actually seen it until Pollack found a way to show it happening in his lab. This is just the innovative science news we need as we face water contamination threats worldwide.

H_3O_2 inside Cellular Structure

On top of that, further testing of H_3O_2 identified just the same self-purifying phase of water found inside every human cell. Indeed, *all* living cells hold H_3O_2, or EZ, water. While we may drink H_2O, molecular processes work inside us to eventually turn the intercellular water into H_3O_2. Scientists and physicians have long thought all water in the body was in the H_2O stage, never guessing that much of that 99 percent inside us was in this special form of EZ water. H_3O_2 water also drives cellular function in a way H_2O does not, and helps explain why we need better hydration (rather than simply more water) to accomplish health.[7] New cell research confirms that the liquid crystalline water found inside cells is necessary for efficient function of molecular processes, including protein folding and electrical conduction.[8] In short, EZ water is what hydrates our cells, our bodies, and all living things. When all those molecules link together as H_3O_2, we receive the hydration that is vital for cellular function, health, and wellness.

How EZ Water Forms

If recent breakthroughs have discovered a new state of water—more potent, hydrating, and renewably self-purifying—how do we activate and access it? Pollack's explanation for how water goes EZ or turns to the liquid crystalline, or gel-like, phase is simple. The transformation, that is the linking up of the water molecules, or their cohesion, is activated in two ways: contact with hydrophilic surfaces, or sunlight. The first activation happens when there is molecular contact with hydrophilic or nonrepelling surfaces; these interfaces grow the crystals that turn water into liquid crystalline, EZ state.[9] But the second activation is much more powerful: exposure to light waves. Sunlight in the form of UV rays, and the unseen light of infrared, induces separation of charges, which, like magnets, push, pull, or hold things in place. Light waves split the water molecule into positive and negative charges. Charge separation begins to line up solitary H_2O connections into more complex, ordered ones: H_3O_2, named for its shared hydrogen atom.[10]

What Pollack saw was the beginning of this process happening in water molecules, those oh so many, many water molecules. That's a lot of electric charge turning liquid water into a more cohesive gel. To our eyes, we can't see this difference happening where the molecules actually link up to each other, but we can taste the difference from liquid water. Indeed, gel water can seem as thin as liquid, just slightly silkier, or it can develop to be as thick as Jell-O, depending on the amount of light exposure or other activators.

As mentioned earlier, this charge separation can also happen when water comes into contact with hydrophilic surfaces. This highly charged, highly ordered or structured water is in all sorts of foods, but more importantly, it is the medium inside you that helps keeps your cells and tissues in the proper shape, function, and buoyancy. We hear all the time that we are made of water, but we don't think about how it is packaged in the body, what kind or phase of water our bodies contain. The percentage of gel water in your body is immensely important. Why? Because this structured water, EZ, gel water, or H_3O_2 hydrates differently. In this different phase of water, water organized in such a way is able to retain moisture longer, drive cell function more effectively, and conduct electricity at a higher speed. The density and purity of water found in its H_3O_2 state dramatically improve efficient conduction and efficient hydration, so we can do much more with much less water. The issue of water for health and wealth shifts from one of resource scarcity to hydration quality. The key question becomes how to activate and access the most potent phase of water.

Methods to Activate Structured Water: H_3O_2

How do we access water in its more efficient state for hydration and decontamination? Emerging strategies to formulate H_3O_2, structured or EZ water, take us out of the realm of laboratory chemicals, expensive science equipment, or energy draining machinery, and into collaboration with natural biological processes. We can begin to transform our relationship with water by working with sunlight, infrared light, vortexing, minerals and clay, electromagnetism, and plants. All of these resources offer accessible, affordable, sustainable methods to produce the structured water which is essential for hydration. This form of hydration was naturally available until widespread decontamination, coupled with more time spent indoors, away from the sun.

Hello Sunshine: Sunlight

Sunlight is the first and foremost method of transforming H_2O to H_3O_2. As light waves hit water molecules, they split into positive and negative charges, which drives the molecular process of natural water self-purification and enhancement. Many cultures around the globe use the sun to purify water and plant materials with techniques as simple as setting vessels in the sun for variable durations. With our new science, we can now explain why this has an effect.

Shine the Light: Infrared Light

Like the sun, light waves from infrared, found indoors as well as outdoors, have also been shown to transform H_3O_2.[11] Light treatment of both water for decontamination and also to treat health conditions such as cardiovascular risk are beginning to show up strongly in clinical and practical work, with simple heat lamps showing reported efficacy.

Shake It Up: Vortex or Spiral Agitation

Vortex or spiral agitation methods, identified by Viktor Schauberger's observations in the early twentieth century, are detailed in his *Living Water* books. His research archive remains open sourced even today and remains among the earliest, and rivaling da Vinci's, documentation of water fluid properties. These methods are now finding application in reforestation and de-desertification projects, especially in Eastern Europe. Recovered folk techniques using spiral or vortex strategies, for example, in biodynamic agriculture, are gaining use. Effects of vortexed water show indications of higher yield in agricultural productivity as evidenced in the wine industry. Current research from Vitorio Elia and his team at the University "Federico II" of Naples, Italy, confirms H_3O_2 formulation in perturbation techniques and vortexing, as well as contact with hydrophilic surfaces.[12]

Down to Earth: Minerals and Clays

Biotite, a liquid crystal mineral concentrate, originated in Japan, with a patent from water scientist A. Shimanishi, in 1986. It has tested effective for the removal of lead, arsenic, and other tainting materials, including industrial synthetics. In addition, biotite has been shown in tests to remove *Escherichia coli*, *Staphylococcus aureus*, and *Salmonella*. This is important because many decontamination efforts to clean water by removing lead and arsenic discover that the treated water becomes reinfected with *E. coli* contaminates once the water has been transported to homes, ultimately failing to deliver pure water at the site of use. Many water aid agencies report this widespread problem. A water which becomes structured or EZ, as with biotite or other minerals, addresses this two-part problem, reducing heavy metals contamination, while at the same time preventing recontamination at another site.[13] The use of hydrophilic clays, another ancient (clay decontamination pellets were found on the Ice Man) and widespread practice, was common in ceramic-making communities, where silt making and water mixing had observable effects on water purity.

Electromagnetic Methods

Clays, which are powdered minerals, are activators of H_3O_2 precisely because of their electromagnetic properties. Once activated, with the addition of water, minerals supply the very charge separation which leaps from molecule to molecule at superconductor speed. Clays for water purification use are experiencing a resurgence, though they had remained in common use in traditional cultures until disrupted by migration and urbanization. A new material made of inexpensive clay and papaya seeds "easily removes harmful metals from water and could lower the cost of providing clean water to millions of people in the developing world," according to chemist Emmanuel Unuabonah. Both papaya and clay had been separately used in water purification in the past, but until now, they had not been combined in what Unuabonah calls a "hybrid clay."[14] The use of minerals, such as in copper pots or in ceramic amphores, is a time-honored tradition for purifying water. We now have super-sophisticated laboratory experiments confirming that electromagnetic methods do indeed produce H_3O_2 water.[15] The water treated by hybrid clay had not been tested for H_3O_2; likely no one suspected it was anything but purified H_2O. However, with our current understanding, we can now apply the new value of H_3O_2 for the cellular health of all living things: people, animals, and plants.

Green Water: Plants Methodology

We save plants for last to make special mention. Understanding plants as an underutilized source of water can radically reshape our approach to water scarcity and water decontamination. It may come as a surprise that we can ingest plants to hydrate more fully, exploiting the H_3O_2 already in their cells; we can also find ways to use plant H_3O_2 to purify water, such as the example of papaya seeds in hybrid clays. Plants are bodies of water too, easily ranging between 80 percent and 98 percent water by volume. Now that we know what to look for, scientific data provide proof that the water locked in plants is H_3O_2. This has many implications. Foremost being that eating a high plant diet brings in hydration that is not only pure, or purer, but deeply hydrating, and full of nutrition and minerals to boot. Leafy greens are literally a form of *green water*. Water is not only blue; it's green.

This returns us to many ancient traditions that use plants as sources of hydration or hydration enhancement. Anthropologists have long identified food strategies among desert dwellers as a central source of hydration.[16] Desert roots and seeds have been utilized as a source of hydration for centuries—we just didn't realize the kind of water, H_3O_2, that was at work. Cactus, yucca, and chia are examples of three plants that have tested positive for their high H_3O_2 contents. Ghee is another surprise food in use since ancient times that produces high-volume H_3O_2, also recently confirmed through lab testing. The use of fats to activate hydration can be traced to mainly high-altitude cultures, such as Tibetans or Incas.[17] It is only recently that we have laboratory confirmation that fats act as a key component of hydration by transforming H_2O to H_3O_2.[18]

As Stefano Mancuso and Alessandra Viola remind us, "Today, plants make up more than 99 percent of biomass on the planet. Think about that: this means all the world's animals—including ants, blue whales, and us—make up less than one percent."[19] Plants can be our most powerful ally in shaping solutions to our hydration strategies, not only in hydrating ourselves from the water locked in plants, but rehydrating our planet using plants in multifaceted ways. Plants have already offered instrumental strategies and solutions, and they can be used for future water purification, agricultural irrigation, and hydration through foods, as they did for many traditions around the world. The hope for our bright future may very well lie in this green water.

Physicist and 2014 Prigogine Medal winner Mae-Wan Ho reflects on the science behind sun, water, and plant interaction, stating, "Green plants and especially blue-green bacteria have been splitting water according to the equation $H_2O \rightarrow H^+ + OH^-$ for billions of years, in order to obtain energy from the sun; and in the process fixing carbon dioxide to make carbohydrates and other macromolecules to feed practically the entire biosphere." The separation of charges in the formation of liquid crystalline water is essentially the same process.

Agriculture and Freshwater Use

As early as 2007, we already had the data exposing agriculture as the largest consumer of freshwater, accounting for more than 70 percent of the world's water use.[20] After freshwater has been processed for industrial agricultural use, it is more likely contaminated than not. In 2009, according to the US Environmental Protection Agency, 46 percent of American rivers and streams were in poor quality, even with protective controls in place.[21] Given global practices with even less oversight, that number can only be rising. This has a direct and profound implication for the depletion of freshwater resources and for the biodiversity dependent on freshwater. In 2016, the World Wildlife Fund reported that over the last forty years, we've witnessed over 50 percent reduction in mammals on the planet, 78 percent if they live near freshwater. "Populations of vertebrate animals—such as mammals, birds, and fish—have declined by 58% between 1970 and 2012. And we're seeing the largest drop in freshwater species: on average, there's been a whopping 81% decline in that time period."[22] While this is grave news indeed, further severe impact could be intercepted with simple steps, including irrigation innovations, biodynamic farming, and permaculture. All of these practices use, or can be enhanced by using, H_3O_2 to transform agriculture with radically efficient water usage.

Agricultural practices are being modified all over the world as water issues become critical. New forms of irrigation are being tested. A brilliant experiment with sunflower crops was conducted recently in China in a semi-arid region using pinpointed irrigation techniques.[23] Small adjustments such as these can have a great impact on water use, with success furthered by using or adding H_3O_2. Many of these techniques are recoverable from ancient traditions, and many of these actually used water in the H_3O_2 form. For example, biodynamic farming, which uses an adaptive living systems approach, incorporates recovered traditional techniques for extraordinary yield and land restoration. Biodynamic techniques make H_3O_2 widely available for irrigation, relying on liquid crystalline structures found in natural materials, using both hydrophilic materials and sun exposure. A sister technique to biodynamic farming, permaculture, makes use of the H_3O_2 methodology simply by planting in curves rather than straight lines.[24] Alchemy indeed.

Conclusion

Our purpose here is to magnify for our readers the first-order importance of hydration in human health and its potential to raise our well-being and wealth by the diminishment of disease, and the increase in capacities. In addition, we provide new science to support the increase in pure water techniques, both new and old, for the water we drink must be of a higher quality and efficacy to meet the challenges of today. The discovery of H_3O_2 could not come at a better time. As Ban Ki-moon, former secretary-general to the United Nations, says, "We must connect the dots between climate change, water scarcity, energy shortages, global health, food security and women's empowerment. Solutions to one problem must be solutions for all." We provide here new and innovative pathways for activating hydration and water purity for all.

Notes

[1] OECD Workshop on Measuring Business Impacts on People's Well-being, Paris, February 23–24, 2017. http://www.oecd.org/statistics/oecd-workshop-on-measuring-business-impacts-on-peoples-well-being.htm.

[2] G. Christie and D. Yach, Personal conversations and review of draft chapter with coauthors.

[3] Gerald H. Pollack, *Cells, Gels, and the Engine of Life* (Seattle: Ebner and Sons, 2010).

[4] Notably, Mae-Wan Ho, *Living Rainbow H₂O* (London: Institute of Science in Society, 2012); R. Saykally et al., "Energetics of Hydrogen Bond Network Rearrangements in Liquid Water," *Science* 306, no. 5697 (October 29, 2007): 851–853; E. Del Giudice, V. Voeikov, A. Lomonosov, and A. Tedeschi, "The Widespread Properties of EZ Water," in *Fields of the Cell: The Origin and the Special Role of Coherent Water in Living Systems* (Kerala, India: Research Signpost, 2015).

[5] Ana Adan, "Cognitive Performance and Dehydration," *Journal of the American College of Nutrition* 31 (2012): 71–78; L. Armstrong et al., "Mild Dehydration Affects Moods in Healthy Young Women," *Journal of Nutrition* 142 (February 2012): 382–388.

[6] G. Pollack, *Beyond Solid, Liquid, Vapor: The Fourth Phase of Water* (Seattle: Ebner and Sons, 2013).

[7] A. Disalvo et al., *Membrane Hydration: The Role of Water in the Structure and Function of Biological Membranes* (New York: Springer Verlag, 2015).

[8] G. Pollack, *Beyond Solid, Liquid, Vapor.*

[9] According to quantum electrodynamics (QED), liquid water is a two-phase system in which one of the phases is in a coherent state where all molecules are phase correlated, whereas the other is made up of uncorrelated molecules in a gas-like state. Recent data demonstrate that interfacial water adjacent to hydrophilic surfaces exhibits peculiar anomalous properties, e.g., it is electrically charged and the sign of its charge is the same as that of the charge of the contiguous hydrophilic surface. It is known as "Exclusion Zone water" (EZ water) because it excludes solutes. These properties of interfacial water can be derived from the properties of coherent water and are relevant in living systems, where water is almost entirely interfacial, being close almost everywhere to some macromolecular backbone or to some surface. We conclude that all the above properties of EZ water are the consequence of the coherent collective oscillations occurring within liquid water and on its boundaries. From E. Del Giudice et al., "The Widespread Properties of EZ Water," 2015.

[10] According to Pollack, the H_3O_2 process begins with the splitting of water, into H^+ and OH^-. The OH^- units form the EZ lattice, which is hexagonal. If you count the number of oxygens and hydrogens in a unit cell, i.e., in one hexagon, then you get H_3O_2. The "trick" in counting is that oxygens and hydrogens are *shared* by adjacent unit cells. For example, each oxygen atom is shared by three contiguous hexagons, which means that a given hexagon contains only one-third of that oxygen. Using this algorithm, you go around the hexagon and add up all of the fractional hydrogen and oxygen contributions, and you get H_3O_2. Pollack, private correspondence, 2017.

[11] As evidenced from experiments by Pollack, but also by R. Tsenkova and her team at the University of Kobe. R. Tsenkova, Z. Kovacs, Y. Kubota, "Aquaphotomics: Near Infrared Spectroscopy and Water States in Biological Systems," Subcell Biochemistry 71 (2015): 189–211.

[12] V. Elia, "Spiral Perturbation of Water: Iterative Procedures to Highlight the Formation of Molecular Aggregates of Water Molecules in Pure Perturbed Water," Dept. of Chemical Sciences, University "Federico II" of Naples, Italy, presented at 11th Annual Biology, Chemistry and Physics of Water Conference, 2010.

[13] Envirotek Laboratories, Inc., Antibacterial Test Report #14-206 for Liquid Biotite.

[14] E. Unuabonda et al., "Hybrid Clay: A New Highly Efficient Adsorbent for Water Treatment," *ACS Sustainable Chemistry & Engineering*, May 9, 2013, 966–973.

[15] Q. Ren identifies electromagnetic processes as a method of producing EZ water: "A loop of electric current, an electron, an atomic nucleus and a molecule all can have magnetic moments. Developments of quantum biology also indicate that spin magnetic moment may have a direct impact on the biological process. Inspired by these researches, we studied the effects of the magnetic field and spin magnetic moment on EZ. A spinor field was generated using the magnetic rotator, which can be described as a magnetic field of a spiral structure. It is shown that spin magnetic moment profoundly expands these zones in an irreversible manner." Quansheng Ren, School of EECS, Peking University, on the effect of magnetic rotator on the exclusion zone of water.

[16] G. Bria, *How to Grow Water: It's Not Only Blue, It's Green* [video file], November 2016. Retrieved from https://www.youtube.com/watch?v=kAiCeRZLCoE.

[17] R. Bria, forthcoming dissertation, Vanderbilt University, Department of Anthropology, 2018.

[18] A. Disalvo et al., *Membrane Hydration*.

[19] Stefano Mancuso and Alessandra Viola, *Brilliant Green, The Surprising History and Science of Plant Intelligence* (Washington, DC: Island Press, 2015).

[20] D. Molden et al., *Water for Food, Water for Life: A Comprehensive Assessment of Water Management in Agriculture. Pathways for Increasing Agricultural Water Productivity* (London: Earthscan and International Water Management Institute, 2007), 279–310.

[21] US Environmental Protection Agency, "Rivers and Streams," *National Water Quality Inventory: 2000 Report* (2002).

[22] Living Planet Report, 2016. https://www.worldwildlife.org/pages/living-planet-report-2016.

[23] L. Qin et al., "Field-Based Experimental Water Footprint Study of Sunflower Growth in a Semi-Arid Region of China," *Journal of the Science of Food and Agriculture* 96 (2016): 3266–3273.

[24] Permaculture Research Institute, Greening the Desert project, 2009.

CHAPTER 11

The Next One Hundred Years of Vitality
Partnering for Healthy Impact
Derek Yach and Gillian Christie

From 100+ Years Ago: The Commission on Vitality

In 1908, United States President Theodore Roosevelt appointed the National Conservation Commission to evaluate the conservation of the country's natural resources. A year later, the Commissioners, led by Yale Professor Irving Fisher, released their "Report on National Vitality: Its Wastes and Conservation." The report outlined the state of the nation's health and examined how lengthened lives could improve economic earnings at the turn of the twentieth century.[1]

Life expectancy in the United States in 1909 was forty-five years of age. Though this number was increasing due to advances in vaccinations (particularly smallpox) and sanitation, there was widespread agreement that public health efforts could improve life expectancy and quality of life. The Commissioners believed that this could be achieved by tackling risk factors that affected health and longevity in the 1900s: (1) the hygiene of the environment, including air, soil, dwellings, and clothing; (2) the hygiene of nutrition, including the immoderate intake of food; (3) drug habits, including alcohol and tobacco use; and (4) activity and sex hygiene. It also meant avoiding the detrimental effects of tobacco, alcohol, and diet: "Of all poisons in ordinary use, alcohol and tobacco are the most common," and "[t]he diet has a distinct relation to endurance . . . avoidance of overeating, and especially of excess in protein, and thorough mastication, are wholesome rules." Many of the risk factors identified in 1909 still persist, and contribute to major causes of disease, disability, and death.

In realizing the underlying determinants of health, the 1900s were marked by broad support for public health policies and programs in the United States. A lack of progress in the basic sciences also meant fewer interventions to treat disease. Since then, the scientific basis of pharmaceutical drugs, complex surgeries, imaging techniques, genetics and genomics, and other health-care treatments have progressed and proliferated to dominate resources and funding over public health. Although this has led to treatments that cure disease, it has also resulted in a deep-pocketed *treatment industry* that overshadows the impact of promoting health. Health care, rather than wellness and vitality, has come to dominate health in the United States.

By contrast, in many other countries, health and health-care operations are seamlessly tied together. Across Scandinavia, for example, spending on social services and health-care delivery are integrated. For every dollar spent on health-care treatment services in Scandinavian countries, two dollars are spent on social services that support healthy individuals and society. For every dollar spent on health care in the United States, only 55 cents is spent on similar social services.[2] The result is that Scandinavians generally live longer and in better health than their American counterparts.

Despite differences in spending in various countries, the past century has witnessed tremendous global health, economic, and business gains. These developments, however, have largely been at the expense of nonrenewable resources, which have been pushed beyond environmental limitations.[3] As originally proposed by the National Conservation Commission, the far-reaching changes that are occurring to the structure and functioning of the Earth's natural resources are a growing threat to human health.[4] Health care alone, both in the United States and around the world, will not be able to solve the challenges posed by continued environmental degradation and a warming climate. It will require adapting previously held beliefs, practices, and systems for the next one hundred years.

This chapter aims to provide a brief overview of the state of health and health care in the United States, with a view to better understanding these domains in an international context. We examine the beginnings of public health one hundred years ago, and subsequently adopt a long-term perspective to examine what has changed during this time. We conclude by proposing a few suggestions on the path forward for vitality and longevity over the next one hundred years.

100+ Years Later: What Has Changed in Health and Longevity?

Human Health and Longevity

People are living longer. A baby born in the year 1900 could not expect to live beyond 45 years of age. A baby born in 2015 could expect to live to an average of 71.4 years of age.[5] Despite living longer—a tremendous feat for human civilization—people are living longer in poorer health. In the United States, between 1990 and 2010, life expectancy increased from 75.2 to 78.2 years (3 years), though healthy life expectancy (a measure of the number of years of life in good health at a given age) increased from 65.8 years to 68.1 years (only 2.3 years). As these epidemiological changes play out in the United States and around the world, it is clear that the risk factors underlying leading causes of disease, disability, and death are converging.[6]

Table 11.1 and Table 11.2 demonstrate the convergence in risk factors underlying major causes of death and disability. A majority of these risks are

TABLE 11.1   Convergence of Risk Factors Underlying Leading Causes of Death, 2015

	Ranking	Global	US	China	India
Risk factor underlying cause of death	1	Dietary risks	Dietary risks	Dietary risks	Dietary risks
	2	High BP	Tobacco	High BP	Air pollution
	3	Tobacco	High BP	Tobacco	High BP
	4	Air pollution	High BMI	Air pollution	High FPG

Note: BP = blood pressure; BMI = body mass index; FPG = fasting plasma glucose.

TABLE 11.2   Convergence of Risk Factors Underlying Leading Causes of Disability, 2015

	Ranking	Global	US	China	India
Risk factor underlying cause of disability	1	Dietary risks	Dietary risks	Dietary risks	Air pollution
	2	High BP	Tobacco	High BP	Dietary risks
	3	Malnutrition	High BMI	Tobacco	Malnutrition
	4	Tobacco	High FPG	Air pollution	High BP

Note: BP = blood pressure; BMI = body mass index; FPG = fasting plasma glucose.

modifiable through behavioral interventions. These include maintaining a healthy diet and weight, engaging in regular physical activity, avoiding tobacco use and excess alcohol intake, and adhering to prescribed medications.

Although these risk factors are not dissimilar to those presented in the Commission on Vitality, age-related diseases that do not have equivalent prevention interventions will increase as populations live longer. It is expected that poor mental health (contributing to various dementias such as Alzheimer's disease) and musculoskeletal disorders (associated with the body's movement, including rheumatoid arthritis) will rise in prevalence over the coming decades.[7] Similar interventions are needed to address the impact of these age-related diseases.

Global Health Financing

The scenario of people living longer, but in poorer health, poses substantial financial and social challenges for global health funding and partnerships. It is estimated that the growing cost of chronic diseases globally will total $30 trillion by 2030.[8] Chronic diseases are costly to treat, but cost-effective to prevent by reducing risk factors. And yet, in recent years, less than 10 percent of the $30 billion budget of the US National Institutes of Health has been allocated toward studies on behavioral interventions that target modifiable risk factors.[9] This number is likely to decrease with proposed National Institutes of Health budget measures by the Trump administration. This means funding to reduce chronic diseases in the United States and elsewhere will have to be diversified from traditional sources of health financing.

In a major analysis of funds and partners in global health, Chelsea Clinton and University of Edinburgh Professor Devi Sridhar recently concluded that monetary assistance from international development agencies and foundations to fight infectious diseases is unmatched by funding to address chronic diseases. The leaders in funding sources were country donor programs and the Bill & Melinda Gates Foundation, while the main recipients of these funds were the World Health Organization; the World Bank; the Global Fund to Fight AIDS, Tuberculosis and Malaria; and the Global Alliance for Vaccines and Immunisation. All of these global health players principally support work on infectious diseases, with not one working on chronic diseases. This is despite chronic diseases being the leading cause of death and disability worldwide, extending far beyond the death toll of infectious diseases.[10]

With funding for global health largely allocated toward infectious diseases, and increasingly threatened due to political uncertainties, from where will additional financing be generated to address the growing cost of chronic diseases? We propose the following three areas:

Individuals

New funds may be realized in savings from people living healthier lives and living longer. This means introducing initiatives that incentivize individuals to take control of their health through engaging in behaviors that prevent disease.

Corporations

Many businesses are realizing the economic value and spillover effects of investing in prevention activities within the workplace, marketplace, and community. This entails investing in workplace health programs that facilitate behavior changes among employees, modifying the healthiness of products and services offered in the marketplace, and investing in community partnerships to improve the health of community members. The insurance industry (along with governments) is a leading stakeholder that can materially and monetarily benefit from improvements in health and lengthened lives.

Governments

Governments will realize financial gains by structuring their tax policies and regulations to make healthy choices the easy choices, as originally proposed by the Ottawa Charter for Health Promotion. The Ottawa Charter was signed by delegates at the World Health Organization's First International Conference on Health Promotion held in Ottawa, Canada, in 1986 and foreshadowed the role of behavioral economics in promoting health and longevity.[11]

Without major changes in health financing, the funding landscape to tackle chronic disease is unlikely to change substantially in coming decades. This means that currently unrealized sources of financing will be needed to address the growing toll of chronic diseases in both the United States and globally.

Business and Government in Society

Time-related trade-offs have existed throughout history in the ability of stake-holders to promote societal and economic benefit. Economists too easily assume that humans make rational decisions, though as Bill Foege, a previous Centers for Disease Control and Prevention (CDC) Director and Senior Advisor to Bill Gates on Global Health, reminds us, "the urgent too often crowds out the important." Our flaws in decision-making mean that our inherent preference is for action today and not tomorrow. Businesses act no differently. As a result, the perceptions and roles of business and government within society have evolved over the past one hundred years.

Businesses impacting health and longevity—from big food to big soda to big alcohol—have historically been viewed as contributors to ill health, and not part of the solution. The elaborate and well-financed strategies employed by tobacco companies served to foster distrust of the private sector among the public health community.[12] This was followed by food, beverage, and alcohol producers being viewed as contributing to the obesity epidemic.

Empirical evidence is emerging that shows the profitability of embedding health and sustainability criteria into business practices.[13] Entire investment funds that only invest in health- and sustainability-related businesses have also emerged. As companies realize the importance of addressing societal values, consumers—and particularly millennials—have become more active in demanding more from the companies with which they interact. In turn, companies have become more socially aware and politically active.

As businesses adapt to newly activated consumers, governments are being pushed to change. With the number of people over sixty years of age expected to increase from nine hundred million in 2015 to two billion in 2050 (a change from 12 percent to 22 percent), aging populations are increasingly straining government budgets, particularly social security and pension bene-fits.[14] The Organisation for Economic Co-operation and Development and the International Monetary Fund have outlined the impacts of people living longer on long-term financing and the stability of the global financial system.[15] Both of these organizations demonstrate the importance of leveraging government and other institutional investment opportunities to generate financial gains to support the needs of aging populations. Governments are also increasingly leveraging insights from behavioral economics such as incentives, rewards, and discounts, which have traditionally been spearheaded by business, to prevent disease and encourage healthy behaviors.

Technology Advancements

Human health and longevity are being transformed by technology in ways unimaginable one hundred years ago. New tools enable people to track the number of steps walked in a day, alert a loved one if an elderly person has fallen, or monitor the amount of carbon dioxide emitted by a vehicle. These new technologies are personalized, preventive, and predictive in scope.[16] With sustained engagement, these technologies have the potential to reduce costs attributed to the leading causes of health-care spending in the United States: diabetes ($101 billion), heart disease ($88 billion), and low-back and neck pain ($86 billion).[17]

Realizing the potential of technology, the Institute for the Future identified economic and social catalysts for impact on health and longevity to the year 2030. The catalysts draw upon new advances in technology such as smaller, more powerful, and cheaper sensors; artificial intelligence, robotics, predictive analytics, and machine learning; the Internet of Things; and additive manufacturing/three-dimensional printing.[18] The World Economic Forum has additionally spearheaded the notion of the Fourth Industrial Revolution, which is predicated on advancements in technology and data. While it is evident that health and longevity will continue to be transformed by changes and advances in technology, it is not certain in what ways and how.

With technologies becoming more embedded within our everyday lives—and soon likely to be embedded within our bodies—ethical, legal, and social challenges must be proactively addressed. Frameworks that target privacy and confidentiality concerns associated with data from biotech devices must be cocreated between business and government partners.[19] This must ensure strong protections for consumers, and tough consequences for companies that do not support these principles. Similarly, challenges related to automation will need to be reconciled. While automation in health care may not have the same negative impact on employment (health care [and particularly long-term care] is among the fastest-growing job categories that is less impacted by automation), other sectors with high automation will inevitably result in changes to physical and emotional well-being.[20] With the acceleration of technology, including big data and artificial intelligence, new opportunities will be created to develop healthier societies. These opportunities, however, must be balanced with impending data and employment concerns.

The Next One Hundred Years: New Models for Capitalizing on the Triumph of Longevity

Shared Value Business Models

New business models are emerging that capitalize on behavior changes in health vitality and the lengthening of lives. These progressive business models are often embedded in the notion of "shared value." Proposed by Harvard Business School professors Michael Porter and Mark Kramer, shared value business models refer to those that generate both economic profit and societal benefit. They rest on the premise that companies must generate societal benefit at profit. According to Porter and Kramer, shared value can "lead to new approaches that generate greater innovation and growth for companies—and also greater benefits for society."[21]

Insurance is among the purest forms of a business model that can create shared value.[22] The South African insurer Discovery Limited is one company that is promoting *shared value insurance*. Over its twenty-five-year history, Discovery has pioneered Vitality, an incentive-based health promotion program. The program leverages advancements in behavioral economics, personalized technologies, and data analytics to target major modifiable behavioral risk factors. Premiums are reinvested to provide compelling rewards for members. Independent research on the effectiveness of Vitality in South Africa has shown Vitality-integrated policies with a 42 percent improved mortality rate and up to 76 percent reduced rate for highly engaged members. On average, Vitality members live fourteen years longer than the insured South African population.[23]

Increasingly, models that generate shared value leverage technology and principles of behavioral economics. Within the technology landscape, many companies that are aspiring to create shared value are partnering with wearables and smartwatch companies to develop anticipatory guidance to address privacy and confidentiality issues. Similarly, these companies are leveraging behavioral economics to incentivize consumers to make the healthy choice the easy choice through a range of rewards and incentives.

Business models that prevail in the future will require a convergence of shared value, technology, and behavioral economics. Efforts by government and industry also need to be better aligned for health, and will require closer interaction and smart policies that support social and environmental goals with government and business objectives.

Corporate Disclosures of ESG + H

In 1970, the American economist Milton Friedman contended that the primary aim of business was to maximize profits. Friedman believed that a company's value was predicated on its economic value to shareholders. Over time, companies have realized the imperative to invest and report on nonfinancial performance measures that impact their bottom line. Corporate reporting platforms such as the United Nations (UN) Global Compact and the Global Reporting Initiative have emerged that encourage companies to report on their environmental, social, and governance (ESG) activities. This is because a company's business activities affect ESG metrics, which in turn contribute to a company's financial performance.

In the United States, President Donald Trump has rolled back many of the environmental protections that were introduced by his predecessor, President Barack Obama. In a compelling op-ed in the *New York Times*, Michael Bloomberg contends that the United States will reach its climate-related commitments outlined in the Paris Agreement by businesses taking the lead, regardless of the Trump administration.[24] Almost half (more than 250) of the total number of coal plants in the United States will shut down or switch to cleaner fuels in the coming years. They are closing not because of Trump's policies, but because consumers are demanding affordable energy from clean sources. In 2010, thirteen thousand Americans died because of airborne coal pollution. This number is estimated to be 7,500 today. Even as the Trump administration eliminates President Obama's Clean Power Plan, the United States will still likely meet its Paris commitments to reduce greenhouse gas emissions by 26 percent below 2005 levels by 2025.

With so many companies reaffirming their environmental pledges, they should also be supported in reporting on their health impacts. Because business activities affect health in a variety of ways, businesses must be held accountable, encouraged, and incentivized by both corporate reporting platforms and investors to disclose their health impacts.[25]

Longevity as an Opportunity for Investment and Victory for Development

Many efforts exist to lengthen and enhance human lives by tinkering with the core aging process. Contemporary quests for the proverbial fountain of youth are often well-endowed by Silicon Valley venture capitalists aspiring to develop homo-cyborgs and human immortality. While potentially disruptive in the long term, these investments can distract and take away from shorter-term gains in improving the quality of life of older adults today. Shorter-term solutions exist that are possible and can be made available to all. We focus on the latter in this section.

Recognizing the triumph of longevity, a growing number of financial stakeholders are beginning to realize the potential gains in supporting and investing in companies and initiatives that encourage healthy aging. For example, in the private sector, BlackRock, the world's largest asset manager, has developed a dedicated retirement institute to focus on financial decision-making in later life. Bank of America Merrill Lynch's corporate investment division has created thematic investing spotlights on companies working to support "the silver economy." The division has estimated that the spending power of consumers aged 60+ is expected to reach $15 trillion by 2020. SwissRe, the second-largest reinsurance company in the world, has released its "Who Pays for Ageing" report that outlines opportunities for providing a better financial safety net for seniors. Public and nonprofit stakeholders as diverse as the International Monetary Fund, the World Health Organization, the Milken Institute, and AARP all support initiatives addressing longevity. Finally, companies are designing products to support older adults, particularly at the intersection of health and wealth— termed *whealthcare*. With financial reasoning being among the first cognitive abilities to decline with the onset of various dementias, companies are aiming to develop solutions that prevent both financial insecurity and cognitive decline.[26] While the world's longevity is a tremendous achievement for human development, its gains will be threatened if older adults are not living engaged, healthy, and vital lives.

The commonality underlying each of these initiatives is a clear demonstration of the need for a greater focus on the prevention, adaptation, and mitigation of unhealthy aging. What is needed is dedicated and guided investment in the development and deployment of interventions that facilitate and optimize healthy aging. This also entails generating the necessary research to fill in gaps in evidence related to longevity, by including older adults in the design, testing, and implementation.[27]

Conclusion: Partnerships for Health and Longevity

Following the culmination of the UN Millennium Development Goals in 2015, a new set of global goals, the UN Sustainable Development Goals (SDGs), came into force in January 2016. The SDGs comprise seventeen goals focused on ending poverty, protecting the planet, and ensuring prosperity for all.[28]

Many of the SDGs focus on health. SDG3 focuses directly on "good health and well-being," while others indirectly focus on health. These include SDG11 (sustainable cities and communities), SDG12 (sustainable consumption and production), SDG8 (decent work and economic growth), SDG5 (gender equality), SDG10 (reduced inequalities), SDG4 (inclusive and quality education for all and lifelong learning), and SDG17 (multistakeholder partnerships for the goals).

For the first time, international development goals proposed by the UN explicitly call out the private sector as part of the solution in attaining the goals. The SDGs actively encourage partnerships between the private sector, along with governments, nonprofits, and the broader UN system. In order to capitalize on the gains in health and longevity that we have witnessed over the past one hundred years, and see continued improvements in the next one hundred years, including achievement of the targets of the SDGs, concerted and coordinated actions by a variety of stakeholders will be needed. We propose a few ideas that could be undertaken across sectors within the framing of the SDGs through to the year 2030 and beyond:

Public Policy Recommendations

For governments, improving health and longevity means introducing regulations and policies that support the health, financial, technological, and other needs of older adults. These regulations would be predicated on paternal and nonpaternal (behavioral economics) levers of change, and would enable and ensure the dignity and quality of life of older populations as they age.

Corporate Recommendations

For business operating in any sector, this entails visionary leaders will place health, longevity, and sustainability goals at the center of their shared value agendas. Advancing health and longevity will require additional evaluation of efforts as well as disclosures on performance. Similarly, investors should adopt a long-term and socially conscious investment thesis while demanding more information and data on societal impacts from companies. Corporate reporting bodies should work to develop additional metrics for companies and stock exchanges on health-related impacts.

Philanthropic Recommendations

For philanthropic and nonprofit organizations, criteria that integrate health and longevity measures should be developed and used when making organizational strategy, grant-making, and program-related decisions. Health and longevity should be indicators to be used when engaged in decision-making and operational practice.

Civic Recommendations

And last, for civil society, every day is an opportunity to improve one's health! Civil society leaders should be encouraged to spearhead activities that promote health and prevent disease within their own communities on a regular and ongoing basis. As individuals prioritize healthy choices, they not only improve their own vitality and longevity, but serve as active contributors and supportive role models in their communities.

Infuse Longevity with Vitality

In 1910, President Theodore Roosevelt declared, "The health and vitality of our people are at least as well worth conserving as their forests, waters, lands, and minerals."[29] In order to support this declaration, health and longevity must continue to be improved and the environment preserved over the next one hundred years. SDGs offer one strategy to help realize this vision. To harness this opportunity and turn strategy into results, we need to galvanize public, corporate, philanthropic, and civic resources committed to infuse human longevity with health and vitality.

Notes

[1] I. Fisher, *A Report on National Vitality: Its Wastes and Conservation* (Washington, DC: Govt. Print Office, 1909).

[2] E. H. Bradley and L. A. Taylor, *The American Health Care Paradox: Why Spending More Is Getting Us Less* (New York: Perseus Books Group, 2013).

[3] D. L. Heymann et al., "Global Health Security: The Wider Lessons from the West African Ebola Virus Disease Epidemic," *The Lancet* 385 (2016): 1884–1901.

[4] S. Whitmee et al., "The Rockefeller Foundation–Lancet Commission on Planetary Health: Safeguarding Human Health in the Anthropocene Epoch: Report of The Rockefeller Foundation–Lancet Commission on Planetary Health," *The Lancet* 386 (2015): 1973–2028.

[5] National Institute on Aging, *Global Health and Aging: Living Longer* (National Institute on Aging, 2011). Accessed December 19, 2016. Available at https://www.nia.nih.gov/research/publication/global-health-and-aging/living-longer.

6   Global Burden of Disease, *GBD Compare, Viz Hub* (Global Burden of Disease, 2015). Accessed April 3, 2017. Available at http://vizhub.healthdata.org/gbd-compare; GBD 2015 Mortality and Causes of Death Collaborators, "Global, Regional, and National Life Expectancy, All-Cause Mortality, and Cause-Specific Mortality for 249 Causes of Death, 1980–2015: A Systematic Analysis for the Global Burden of Disease Study 2015," *The Lancet* 388 (2016): 1459–1544.

7   Alzheimer's Association, "Alzheimer's Disease Facts and Figures," *Alzheimer's & Dementia: Journal of the Alzheimer's Association* 13 (2017): 325–373.

8   D. E. Bloom et al., *The Global Economic Burden of Noncommunicable Diseases* (Geneva: World Economic Forum, 2011).

9   C. Calitz, K. M. Pollack, C. Millard, and D. Yach, "National Institutes of Health Funding for Behavioral Interventions to Prevent Chronic Diseases," *American Journal of Preventive Medicine* 48, no. 4 (April 2014): 462–471.

10 C. Clinton and D. Sridhar, "Who Pays for Cooperation in Global Health? A Comparative Analysis of WHO, the World Bank, the Global Fund to Fight HIV/AIDS, Tuberculosis and Malaria, and GAVI, the Vaccine Alliance," *The Lancet* 390, no. 10091 (2017): S0140-6736(16)32402-3.

11 World Health Organization, *Ottawa Charter for Health Promotion* (Geneva: WHO, 1986).

12 S. Kunkle, G. Christie, C. Hajat, and D. Yach, "The Role of the Private Sector in Tilting Health Systems toward Chronic Disease Prevention," *Global Heart* 11, no. 4 (2016): 451–454.

13 R. Fabius et al., "Tracking the Market Performance of Companies That Integrate a Culture of Health and Safety: An Assessment of Corporate Health Achievement Award Applicants," *Journal of Occupational & Environmental Medicine* 58, no. 1 (2016): 3–8.

14 World Health Organization, *Media Centre: Ageing and Health* (2015). Available at http://www.who.int/features/factfiles/ageing/ageing_facts/en.

15 OECD, Institutional Investors and Long-term Investment: Project Report (2014); International Monetary Fund, *Global Financial Stability Report: Potent Policies for a Successful Normalization* (2016).

16 G. Christie, A. Holzhausen, J. Kvedar, A. Martin, R. Palacholla, and D. Yach, *Technological Innovations for Health and Wealth for an Ageing Global Population* (World Economic Forum, 2016). Accessed April 3, 2017. Available at: http://www3.weforum.org/docs/WEF_Global_Population_Ageing_Technological_Innovations_Health_Wealth_070916.pdf; Institute for the Future, *Technology Catalysts for Human and Economic Vitality 2030* (Institute for the Future, 2014); K. Schwab, *The Fourth Industrial Revolution* (World Economic Forum, 2016), accessed April 3, 2017, available at http://www3.weforum.org/docs/Media/KSC_4IR.pdf.

17 J. Dieleman et al., "US Spending on Personal Health Care and Public Health, 1996–2013," *JAMA* 316, no. 24 (2016): 2627–2646.

18 Institute for the Future, *Technology Catalysts Map* (Vitality Institute & Institute for the Future, 2014).

19 G. Christie, K. Patrick, and D. Yach, *Guidelines for Personalized Health Technology* (New York: Vitality Institute, 2016). Accessed April 3, 2017. Available at http://www.thevitality-institute.org/ELSI.

20 R. Susskind and D. Susskind, *The Future of the Professions: How Technology Will Transform the Work of Human Experts* (Oxford: Oxford University Press, 2016).

21 M. Porter and M. Kramer, "Creating Shared Value," *Harvard Business Review*, 2011; R. Taylor and F. Amankwah, Exploring Shared Value in Global Health and Safety: Workshop Summary (Institute of Medicine, 2016).

22 A. Gore, P. Harmer, M. Pfitzer, and N. Jais, "Can Insurance Companies Incentivize Their Customers To Be Healthier?" *Harvard Business Review*, 2017. Available at https://hbr.org/2017/06/can-insurance-companies-incentivize-their-customers-to-be-healthier.

23 FSG & Shared Value Initiative, Insuring Shared Value: How Insurers Gain Competitive Advantage by Better Addressing Society's Needs (FSG & Shared Value Initiative, 2017). Available at http://www.sharedvalue.org/groups/insuring-shared-value-0.

24 M. Bloomberg, "Climate Progress, With or Without Trump," *New York Times*, 2017. Accessed at https://www.nytimes.com/2017/03/31/opinion/climate-progress-with-or-without-trump.html?smprod=nytcore-iphone&smid=nytcore-iphone-share&_r=0.

[25] D. Malan, S. Radjy, N. Pronk, and D. Yach, *Reporting on Health: A Roadmap for Investors, Companies, and Reporting Platforms*, (Vitality Institute, 2016).

[26] J. Karlawish, "Whealthcare: Preventing Financial Fraud and Promoting Cognitive Health and Wealth," *Forbes*, 2016. Accessed at https://www.forbes.com/sites/jasonkarlawish/2016/06/04/whealthcare-preventing-financial-fraud-and-promoting-cognitive-health-and-wealth/#e2652403317b.

[27] C. Hajat, A. Selwyn, M. Harris and D. Yach, "Preventive Interventions for the Second Half of Life: A Systematic Review," *American Journal of Health Promotion* (2017): 1–18.

[28] United Nations, Sustainable Development Goals (2016). Available at http://www.un.org/sustainabledevelopment/sustainable-development-goals.

[29] T. Roosevelt, "New Nationalism" (speech), 1910. Available at http://teachingamericanhistory.org/library/document/new-nationalism-speech.

CHAPTER 12

Designing the University of the Future
A New Global Agenda for Higher Education

Mary R. Watson

What is the role of higher education in moving forward a New Global Agenda for change? As has been clearly articulated elsewhere in this volume, there are many pressing global challenges facing our world today: escalating consequences of climate change, inequality, political conflict, forced migration, and rising intolerance, among others. None of these dynamics are new, of course. Yet, we find ourselves now at a perceived tipping point, where, in the aggregate, these issues seem existential in their force and magnitude. We seem to be challenging the continued existence of the earth itself.

Agendas have been set and reset to focus our global and local efforts to address these systemic problems. The Sustainable Development Goals are one laudable example, and they provide us with a rich typology of challenges in which to situate our efforts. Yet no agenda, including the Sustainable Development Goals, can capture the human imagination and will that is required to face forward into the winds of sea change ahead. For this, we need living, breathing human beings who will enact that change themselves. Many of them spend time studying in universities.

One of things that inspires deep hope in me is seeing young people around the world advocating for, and then creating, a new way forward. As a university dean, professor, and researcher myself, I play a role in building on the long history of higher education as an instrument to advance social progress. I am privileged and inspired by partnerships with students who lead us along the way. But the larger higher education system as a whole is in trouble: it is deeply atrophied, with learning mechanisms developed for a generation that has now passed, and with a purpose that no longer fits the energy of those who seek learning. Our current system was designed for knowledge acquisition and life preparation, concepts that focus on success in the status quo system, drawing on principles of the dominant disciplinary canon that are no longer relevant. Now is the time to reset the purposes of higher education to meet calls for learning in action that include diverse voices and viewpoints suitable for understanding the complex challenges we face.

My purpose in this chapter is to propose how we should redesign the system of higher education to meet learners in our current global moment. Many young (and not so young) leaders, activists, and innovators embody an emergent bias toward change, and they form the very force that is needed to advance our collective progress. To be sure, we do see some institutional change unfolding, especially in networks of universities that currently constitute a powerful force in moving the higher education system forward. To animate how we might imagine the university of the future, I draw on interviews with global colleagues whose networks are remaking education as we speak, and together with them, I propose a New Global Agenda for higher education.

The Current Context for Higher Education

Our global challenges are complex and enormous, and many of the institutions we have come to rely upon have increasingly failed us. We see young people in the global media, turning away from formal institutions and taking to the streets to speak out against what they see as a dysfunctional world they inherited from us, full of strife and without adequate resources to keep it alive. They see faltering economies, rising unemployment, and increasing inequality. We experience this as a crisis of governance, of leadership, and of progress.

In many countries around the world, higher education has long played a key role in the ascendance of young people along the trajectories of their work lives and upward through social class. When I was young, the education benefit was clear. Success in obtaining a college degree was a sure way to inculcate knowledge that would enable progress for oneself within the larger society. Over the past decades, dedicated university faculty and higher education leaders spent their careers in universities, researching the dynamics of social challenges, designing courses that provide context and critique, promising new insights for action, and designing pathways through which students followed their learning progress. But despite those efforts, the connection between education and success is more dubious now, as career paths have become disrupted, student debt is high, and the value of university education itself is being challenged.

Universities have conventionally been designed in three general forms: liberal, research, and professional, but those forms now need integration and reanimation. Our current siloed and disciplinary-bound system sets pedagogy, learning agendas, and types of learners apart. We can debate whether the current higher education system was a good design a century, or even fifty years ago, but it is clear that today we need a new way forward. Our university types must be blended in order to shape the interdisciplinary education required for the future. Our definitions of successful outcomes must move into the shared space of problem-solving on pressing challenges. Our canon must be diversified with the voices of those affected by, embedded in, and working to address the world's challenges. These changes are necessary to ensure the viability of universities as a place where young people will invest time and money to achieve the kinds of learning they seek.

Case Study: The Frame of US Higher Education

The US approach to higher education has played a key role in shaping global higher education, and as such, it deserves a short review to help explain how we got to this moment. The flow of students is one piece of evidence that the United States has been a desirable destination: in 2016, the number of international students attending US universities rose to nearly a million, contributing about $30 billion to the US higher education economy, with the largest share coming from China.[1] Knowledge creation is another indicator: academic journals in the United States, at least for those who publish in English, have been important outlets for global academics seeking credibility, including promotion and tenure. I leave it to other global experts to comment on other countries and their influence on global higher education, but the US system's outsized influence deserves a brief historical exploration.

In the United States, education has focused on differentiating our learning approach by disciplines and the types of learners who studied. These contours were set in motion hundreds of years ago, and their assumptions still drive our university system today (see table 12.1).

Many of the first colleges in the United States followed a tradition of liberal arts education, an approach that dates back to conceptions by ancient Greeks of the way citizens should be prepared for life. In its earliest forms, liberal arts education focused on elements of logic, grammar, and rhetoric, later adding mathematics and science. At colleges founded early in the United States in the mid-1600s through mid-1700s, Harvard College, King's College (now Columbia), and the College of New Haven (now Yale) and at liberal arts colleges that were established in small bucolic towns, including Williams College, referred to as the "Athens of the New World," a liberal education focused on civic preparedness and a religious moral foundation.[2] A liberal arts education was *a place to retreat to*—away from the distractions of the "real world" and *toward a development of one's full actualization*. It was a place to read, write, discuss, and reflect; to contemplate citizenship and meaning; to bring ancient cultures alive in one's own imagination; and to be exposed to new ideas through

TABLE 12.1   Forms of Education

	Aim	Process	Outcome
Liberal	Prepare (elite) citizenry	Seminar: reading, writing, discussion, reflection	Broadly educated moral citizen
Research	Advance (scientific) progress	Lecture/Lab: concepts, computation, experimentation	Discovery and knowledge creation
Professional	(Mass) produce industrial and public actors	Practicum/ Studio: methods, analysis, craft, design	Alignment of skills with societal role specialties

a general learning approach and sharpening of the mind. It was a place to make connections and join new networks of privilege; it was a place to repose and experiment, to become an adult, while awaiting "real life" to begin, and for (mostly) men[3] to be developed civically and morally, before they would move toward the earliest genteel professions of law or medicine. The ideas were very large, and expansive, the intellectual distances vast; there were always more questions. The liberal arts college was about *individual development*, something that could not be measured but was imagined as infinite.

For others, there was the research university. Following on from the German tradition of science and research, the research university was a place of knowledge creation, of exploration of unexamined frontiers, of the application of specialized skills to discovery and advancement. Johns Hopkins and the Massachusetts Institute of Technology were among the first research universities in the United States. By the late 1800s, research had become a primary aim for some universities. By the Second World War, research universities had developed many discoveries that proved useful for direct application, and by the 1950s, the US university was a multifaceted place that was organized around disciplines and research fields. It was funded by philanthropic and government money that underwrote its discoveries, for those discoveries were central to the advancement of state and country.[4] Learning occurred in laboratories and lecture halls. The central focus was on *knowledge advancement* and on the modern promise of progress, activities in which faculty led and students engaged. The purpose was *discovering*, or learning to research, rather than learning for development.

For others, there was vocational learning, following on from a tradition of apprenticeship and morphing into what became known as *professionalism*. Those in professional education did not necessarily experience universities as havens of reflection or crucibles of discovery: for professional learners, universities were pathways of promise. Unlike their sometimes tonier counterparts, many students came from lower- or middle-class families who dreamed of a life for the next generation that had not been possible for them. The belief was that if they studied hard and long, stayed focused and specialized, and developed new talents in fields that held opportunities going forward, they too would achieve the promise of a higher education. Their aspiration was specific: a stimulating and productive career, a means to fiscally and professionally advance themselves, and a stable life for their family and broader communities. The education was specialized, the distances traveled narrow but deep; there were answers, solutions, and methods. Exploration of learning focused on learning tools of analysis, methods of inquiry, with a focus on skill acquisition. The ideas were to be locally applied, to a defined problem in an organization or profession. The purpose was *alignment* to emerging industrial needs, and as the twentieth century moved on, the need for mass production of a professional class accelerated.

Once the nearly exclusive domain of the elite, over the past one hundred years, access to higher education in the United States has now greatly expanded, both in terms of the number of students who are educated and the number of colleges and universities in which they study.[5] Today, there are about 4,700 colleges and universities in the United States, enrolling about twenty million students.

Nearly 60 percent of US adults over eighteen have attended some college, with 33 percent holding a bachelor's or master's degree.[6] Popularity among US undergraduate majors continues to be bifurcated between liberal and professional pursuits, with low priority on the purest research fields of science and technology. As of 2015, at the undergraduate level, business majors outnumber all others, staying stable at about 20 percent of degrees granted since the mid-1990s; humanities and social sciences (16–17 percent) remain very popular; natural science and math are low (about 8 percent, down from 10 percent in 1970); and education has seen the largest decline (7 percent, down from 21 percent in 1970). At the graduate level, business is way up (25 percent, up from 11 percent in 1970) and education is popular but declining (24 percent, down from 37 percent in 1970).[7]

However well intentioned, the expansion of higher education in the United States has been uneven and, despite assertions of meritocracy, outcomes are still tied to class, gender, and race. First, education in the United States remains the domain largely of the economically elite: about 80 percent of young people from families in the top quartile of income distribution earn college degrees, compared with about 11 percent of those from the bottom quartile who earn a bachelor's degree.[8] Second, from a history of higher education systems designed largely for men, women are ascending to meet graduation rates of male US students in higher education. In 1969, US census data show that about 12 percent of women held college degrees or higher; by 2015, this rose to about 33 percent. As a sign of gender progress, 60 percent of students in graduate school in the United States are women.[9] But outcomes by race continue to be persistently uneven: rates of graduation are proportionally higher for whites and Asians (62 and 63.2 percent, respectively) than for black and Hispanic students (45 percent and 38 percent, respectively) with far larger proportions of white and Asian students achieving academic degrees.[10]

Students and their families across the higher education system weigh learning, outcomes, and cost when making college choice. Students increasingly prioritize future employment as a primary reason for attending college. One survey of college freshmen in 2016 reported that 85 percent of students say getting a better job is a top reason for attending college (up from 68 percent in 1976). This focus on job outcomes may stem from pragmatism related to the high cost of US higher education; 68 percent of students who graduated in 2015 had student debt, with an average loan of $30,000, with the poorest students borrowing the most: in 2012, 84 percent of those receiving Pell Grants[11] borrowed an average of $30,000,[12] and the current total US student loan debt is a staggering $1.3 trillion.[13] Yet despite career interest, there is consistent evidence that learning matters to students: in 2015, 84 percent of entering freshmen students indicated a primary reason for attending college was to learn more about things that interest them, the highest score for this item since 1971.[14]

Facing challenges of relevance, access, and cost, the US system of higher education is in need of reform. Education continues to be differentiated by type, sequestering the liberal from the research and professional in ways that prohibit real-world problem-solving. Interdisciplinary learning is experienced by only some students, and only in some fields, limiting the animation of their learning experience. Increased access has only been partly successful, leaving many private university classrooms mostly white and upper middle class, while public universities are flooded with too many students and too few resources to support them. The cost of private education is too high.

Significant pressures for reform of higher education are leaving universities little option but to change. New universities are being started in places where demand is high; existing universities are being challenged to prove their value proposition to students and families. Faculties and university leaders are exploring ways to reimagine their learning environments so they can be more relevant to the demands of our world and more appealing to the global marketplace of prospective students. Many governments are increasing demands for accountability. Universities are being asked to demonstrate effectiveness in increasing access to students from low-income families, affordability by lowering tuition, and outcomes as evidenced by graduation rates and career outcomes.

A New Global Agenda for Higher Education

Education is undergoing a period of transformation, and many institutions are changing the rules through which they engage learners. I set out three agenda items for universities: they must be designed to leverage the *interdisciplinary* systems changes we need, they must be both *global and local*, and they must be *inclusive* by class, race, gender, and other identities (see table 12.2). I culled these three agenda items from my own research and in my discussions with seven global leaders working in Africa, Asia, Europe, and the Americas (specifically Canada, China, Japan, South Africa, the United Kingdom, and across the United States).[15] I organize the next section around three agenda items.

TABLE 12.2   A New Agenda

	Aim	Process	Outcome
Interdisciplinary, liberal, research, and professional	Relevance with scholarly and societal meaning	Interdisciplinary, multimethod, reflective, theory and practice	Engaged citizens with talents leveraged around the world
Globally connected	Accelerate higher education reform through networks	Partnerships, shared practice across boundaries	Systems change with capacity to address global challenges
Locally embedded	Build on and value local talents and cultural context	Deep local cocreation and embedded practice	New forms of learning with impact on communities
Critically inclusive	Engage voices and histories to reshape canon	Question assumptions, witness, and reflect	Inclusive body of shared knowledge relevant to all

Agenda #1: Build Higher Education Networks Designed for Interdisciplinary Systems Reform

The first principle of change is interdisciplinary systems innovation across the conventional boundaries of liberal, research, and professional learning. My interviews were full of stories about leading networks that bridge across universities and other institutions to facilitate collective change. Here, I focus on interdisciplinary work in social innovation education, one of many examples I discovered, highlighting Ashoka U (the United States/Latin America/Europe/Asia) and the J. W. McConnell Family Foundation (Canada).

The Ashoka U Changemaker Campus[16] network is a consortium of universities dedicated to advancing social innovation education. Cofounded by graduates of Stanford University, and launched by the global social entrepreneurship organization Ashoka: Innovators for the Public, it has advanced an idea to form a network of innovative universities that could model new forms of education and organizing, creating systems change together. Nine years later, the now forty-two universities have modeled interdisciplinary and purpose-oriented education, shaped joint initiatives, engaged thousands of students in positive social change, and advanced education in social innovation across universities more broadly. The network includes universities from Australia, Canada, Colombia, Ireland, Mexico, the United Kingdom, Singapore, and the United States. The goals are focused on advancing an interdisciplinary field: teaching and research in social innovation education that bridges programs in liberal arts, business, social sciences, engineering, and more, bringing liberal, research, and professional approaches together.

Speaking with Marina Kim, cofounder and Director, at a recent convening of leaders of the network, I heard that the Ashoka U network has the not-so-humble aspiration to reform the entire system of higher education. They are leveraging new models and activating existing leaders in the Ashoka U campus network to inspire others to adopt ideas, and they aim to advocate to higher education networks and influencers about ways to stay relevant in the future. How did she create this network and lead this change? By encouraging students and faculty to work on what they had the "intrinsic motivation and the talents to do," and "by seeing the opportunity for higher education to innovate itself from the inside out." As Marina describes it, building a field is "like climbing a mountain. You must pace yourself, get water and food, and build a team." Most importantly, she says, higher education reform must be at its core relational. The key is to build a high level of voluntary engagement among individuals who have institutional-level support to innovate new educational approaches to redefine the role of higher education in the twenty-first century.

Field reform requires resources, financial and otherwise. One example of this kind of network of innovation is in the J. W. McConnell Foundation, which has launched Project RECODE, designed to advance innovation in universities across Canada. Through grant-making and other activities, the McConnell Foundation aspires to strengthen "Canadian institutions and communities in which they operate [to] face contemporary issues such as climate change, rising inequality . . . First Nations reconciliation." The foundation aspires to build a "social infrastructure" of organizations, universities and other types, to advance progress in Canadian communities through what they call a "solutions ecosystem" that requires interdisciplinary work that crosses institutional boundaries.[17]

Agenda #2: Set the Global Context as the Most Critical Learning Lab, Connecting Deeply to the Local Context

The second principle that emerged from my conversations was the connection between a global perspective and the local context, embedding learning in both domains simultaneously. Here, I focus on a story of global collaboration to build a new sustainability- and peace-focused university, Project HELIO (Human Ecology Lab in ōsakikamijima in Hiroshima, Japan), in collaboration with and modeled on the College of the Atlantic (COA) in Bar Harbor, Maine.

COA was founded in 1969 on Mount Desert Island outside Acadia National Park. Conceived during an important time in the environmental movement, the college epitomizes small and local: it has only 350 students and thirty-five faculty, and it is committed to economic development of the island. Despite its size, the student community is deeply global, coming from forty countries and forty states. All students have the same major, human ecology, but each student's progress is self-designed and unique. Students and faculty cogovern the college, and they work on locally embedded change projects.

Jay Friedlander, Sharpe-McNally Chair of Green and Sustainable Business at COA, shared some of the secrets of the college's success, citing the deep connection between each individual's passion and the needs of the local community. He spoke of the motivation that brought him to COA, saying he "was in the Peace Corps in Mauritania in the early 1990s where they had abolished slavery in 1980s." There, he said, he realized that "business is the most ubiquitous activity on the planet and to make positive change it is the biggest lever you can pull." He moved to COA to "plant the seed of ideas to have a multiplier effect, combining theory and practice." Today, Jay expands the connections between student passions and economic development of the island through a sustainable business incubator called the Diana Davis Spencer Hatchery.[18] As Jay told me, the key is to "not let sustainability and economics be pitted against one another." He offers what he calls the "abundance cycle"[19] as a model for economic development and social progress to happen in tandem.

After the Fukushima disaster in Japan, a former Japanese university president and educational reformer, Hiromi Nagao, reached out COA to seek their advice on a global aspiration to create a new university on a small island off the coast of Hiroshima. This university, they aspire, will upend the Japanese model of education and focus on locally embedded problem-solving rather than on knowledge mastery of narrow fields. Their motivation, and Jay's enthusiasm, led to the launch of Project HELIO,[20] a new university experiment in Japan that is currently being codesigned with students who have spent the past two summers there. The island context, ōsakikamijima, will be home to a new university modeled on COA, connecting students and faculty with local communities for both learning and economic development. I visited the island earlier this year and participated in the meeting held with community representatives, local government officials, and visitors from other universities. What I experienced is the deeply local reaching out globally to another deeply local community in ways that bridge space. Cultural context differs, yet the models of one region can be accepted in another when dialogue and discourse are the methods.

But doing global learning requires more than community dialogic process—it also requires critically reflective understanding that draws on intellectual traditions from around the world and across time. One network of universities aspiring for such intellectual change is the Critical Edge Alliance,[21] a network of universities aspiring to expand critical global reflection into higher education. According to cofounder L. H. M. Ling, we must "bring non-Western cultures, histories, and languages" into our academic discourse, research, and teaching. Drawing on histories of alternative and reform universities, and building on the central principle of student self-determination and governance, this network aspires to advance active citizenship in communities and the world at large.

Agenda #3: Build Deep Relationships, Critical Theory, and Inclusion at the Center of Learning

The last theme is community and inclusion, elements that were shared with me from a variety of perspectives about who and what should be included. This agenda item requires openness to a diverse set of voices that come together to critically examine the current issues around which education is centered. Here, the central point is that academic canon, developed with input from a limited group of individuals from a narrow range of experiences, is not a broadenough conception for the global challenges we now face. Thus, we must question our extant assumptions, and we must do so with the full engagement of a new, inclusive set of voices. I report here stories from the Globally Responsible Leadership Initiative (GRLI; the United Kingdom/South Africa/global), the Posse Foundation, Creating Connections Consortium, Bold Women Lead, and OutHistory.org (all US).

The GRLI is a global network of universities that, in partnership with the United Nations Global Compact, focuses on the reimagination of leadership education worldwide. This network represents universities in Europe, South Africa, and the Americas. This network's goals aim for system transformation to reimagine education with a lens that incorporates the "I, the we, and the all of us."[22] As Claire Maxwell, associate director of the Oasis School of Human Relations and chair of the GRLI board, told me, "[H]igher education needs to work at a deeper level on values, beliefs, and individual development beyond the intellect and [make] this part of the whole rather than an occasional experience." The GRLI espouses three "laws of globally responsible leadership:" that we are part of a natural system, that we are interconnected, and that we must engage in problem-solving of the pressing world dilemmas. John North, Executive Director of the GRLI told me that he feels "we are disconnected from ourselves, from nature, and from others due to the way we have defined progress," a legacy he has experienced himself in his home context of South Africa.

What John says we need is to reconnect to our humanity in ways that transform how leadership education is taught.

As we have learned from the networks discussed above, aspirations for deep human connection are not enough; to achieve the inclusiveness to which we aspire, we must change the faces of those in the room. In the United States, this means actively engaging people of color, who have been historically under-represented in the university ecosystem. Shirley M. Collado, newly in place as the ninth president of Ithaca College, is one such imaginative leader who has built access pathways and networks. After a decade in leadership at the Posse Foundation,[23] building access to liberal arts colleges for underrepresented groups, Shirley turned to leadership roles in universities. Among her field accomplishments is a network called Creating Connections Consortium,[24] a cross-institutional network of liberal arts colleges and research universities designed to create strategies for more inclusive campuses, and a new leadership initiative called Bold Women Lead.[25] Shirley now takes her vision to the college presidency, where she aspires to create "brave spaces" that embrace the "messiness" of higher education.[26] As she told me, "Institutional transformation requires intentionally activating and sustaining issues of equity, diversity, and inclusion into the DNA and hardwiring of organizations." Her leadership challenges all of us to advance inclusion by not leaving these issues at the periphery.

The content of what is being taught also requires deep revision toward inclusion, across the histories of race, ethnicity, religion, and gender, among other areas. I highlight one example here: emerging conceptions of gender identity matter deeply to the current generation of students, many of whom identify as nonbinary, transgender, or gender fluid. We must take action to include these voices of the LGBTQ[27] community, both historical and present, and their legacies of learning into our higher education curriculum. Claire Potter, codirector of OutHistory.org,[28] aspires to do just this, by making LGBTQ history accessible to all. Building on work from the United States of AIDS project and the ACT UP Oral History project, OutHistory provides a platform to lift up stories of the movement, including features on one hundred activists and other leaders as well as important documents and visual history. The platform is curated by an executive board, and its connections to universities and students expand available material to learners in all spaces. It is an exciting model that is changing the content of the histories we teach and learn.

The Way Forward

In closing, I want to add my own experience to affirm the themes gathered from the voices I have shared here, aiming to propel higher education forward. In my roles at The New School, I have been deeply involved in field-building that crosses academic disciplines, institutional boundaries, and forms of pedagogy. The New School, founded in 1919 by legendary progressives including John Dewey, has long been committed to unconventional, boundary-crossing learning that is designed to stimulate both social progress and advance careers that lead to productive, creative lives. The college which I lead is the current incarnation of the founding college of the university, and it carries this boundary-spanning, interdisciplinary spirit to this day.[29] We are reshaping our educational design in the context of the future of work, while we also build on the deep assets of our legacy. It is a complex, and sometimes contested, process.

As collaborator, codesigner, and leader in many university-wide initiatives, I have seen firsthand the power of field-crossing academic development. One case in point at The New School is a university-wide management initiative that brings together programs in design, the arts, social justice, media, government, and creative industries. Working with university and program leaders, faculty colleagues, motivated students, and industry-experienced university trustees, we are shaping the integration of more than a dozen academic degree programs, university-wide platforms, and an academic center. Our aim is no less than the reinvention of management education, bringing the liberal arts and research into what has been previously seen as mostly a professional domain, and doing so with the purpose of reimagining industries and systems to address the most pressing of the world's problems, while building capacity in our creative economies.

In this initiative, and many others, we are bridging divides, disciplinary and others. We enact this approach more easily because many of our students and faculty expect it; they joined us because they believe that what is seen as impossible in other places is possible here. We engage with a global agenda, we continue to press for more inclusion of different voices in the academic canon with our 40 percent international students, we are steeped in the traditions of critical scholarship,[30] and we are infused by design and creativity.[31] But to really make change in higher education, we must harken back to the fact that we need the "all of us," that is, our universities, communities, governments, businesses, and more to make this agenda realized at scale. It is not easy, or reasonable, to expect quick progress, and there is no consensus on a clear pathway. But the struggle is profoundly necessary.

A field shift in higher education is rapidly underway, and we must actively shape it. If we follow the global agenda laid out here, spiriting systems change, engaging local and global learning contexts, and including a variety of student learners, we can better align our universities with the elements that students seek, organizations need, and world problems require. The result will be a system of universities that can face the future and engage learners in the existential challenges of our time.

So I ask you to imagine what a redesigned higher education for the future would look like. In my view, it is already within sight. It will be interdisciplinary, blending the liberal, research, and professional. It will respond to the demands of pressing world problems, such as climate change and global urbanization, through embedded problem-solving. It will meet young people, and the organizations where they will work, where they are: wanting to explore progress in the context of researching and designing solutions in socially grounded scenarios. It will be inclusive, diverse, and challenge the status quo. It will be more affordable and flexible in delivery format so that more learners can participate. It will be alive and purposeful.

We must begin now, we must act quickly, and we must be resilient in our advancement of the way ahead.

Notes

1. "How International Students Are Changing U.S. Colleges," *Wall Street Journal*, 2017. http://graphics.wsj.com/international-students/. At the time of this writing, there are questions about the continued desirability of US universities, given the recent political climate. Although there has been a decline in applications to some universities/fields, the general trend still remains up.

2. Christopher J. Lucas, *American Higher Education: A History*, 2nd ed. (New York: Palgrave MacMillan, 2006).

3. In this chapter, I regretfully use the binary language men/male and women/female to conform to the data-reporting conventions of educational and government agencies. However, I fully recognize the uncounted nonbinary, fluid, and trans individuals who make up a substantial and vital voice in our university communities.

4. Björn Wittrock, "The Modern University in Its Historical Context; Rethinking Three Transformations," *NAUKA*, no. 2 (2014).

5. This chapter is too brief to review a full history of colleges in the United States; historically, black colleges and universities, normal schools, tribal colleges, women's colleges, and community colleges are notable examples of expanded access. Yet, they too can be characterized as liberal, research, and professional.

6. Camille L. Ryan and Kurt Bauman, *Educational Attainment in the United States: 2015* (Washington, DC: U.S. Census Bureau, 2016). https://www.census.gov/content/dam/Census/library/publications/2016/demo/p20-578.pdf.

7. *The Condition of Education, Undergraduate Degree Fields*, Institute for Educational Sciences: National Center for Education Statistics, 2017. https://nces.ed.gov/programs/coe/indicator_cta.asp.

8. *Digest of Education Statistics*, Institute of Education Sciences: National Center for Education Statistics, 2017. https://nces.ed.gov/programs/digest/d16/tables/dt16_322.10.asp.

9. Ryan and Bauman, *Educational Attainment in the United States*

10. D. Shapiro et al., *A National View of Student Attainment Rates by Race and Ethnicity – Fall 2010 Cohort* (Signature Report No. 12b) (Herndon, VA: National Student Clearinghouse Research Center, 2017).

11. Federal grants for low-income undergraduate students.

12. Mark Huselman, *The Debt Divide: The Racial and Class Bias Behind the "New Normal" of Student Borrowing* (New York: Demos, 2013); Debbie Cochrane and Diane Cheng, *Student Debt and the Class of 2015* (Institute for College Access and Success, 2016). http://ticas.org/sites/default/files/pub_files/classof2015.pdf.

13. Zack Friedman, "Student Loan Debt in 2017: A $1.3 Trillion Crisis," *Forbes*, February 21, 2017.

14. Kevin Eagan, Ellen Bara Stolzenberg, Hilary B. Zimmerman, Melissa C. Aragon, Hannah Whang Sayson, and Cecilia Rios-Aguilar, *The American Freshman: National Norms Fall 2016* (Los Angeles: Higher Education Research Institute, UCLA, 2017).

15. Stories drawn from Shirley M. Collado, president, Ithaca College; Jay Friedlander, Sharpe-McNally Professor, College of the Atlantic; Marina Kim, director, Ashoka University; L. H. M. Ling, cofounder, Critical Edge Alliance; John North, executive director, and Claire Maxwell, board chair, Globally Responsible Leadership Initiative; and Claire Potter, codirector, OutHistory.org.

16. Ashoka U Changemakers: http://ashokau.org/changemakercampus/.

17. Coro Strandberg, *Maximizing the Capacities of Advanced Education to Build Social Infrastructure for Canadian Communities (RECODE)* (Vancouver, CA: The J. W. McConnell Family Foundation and Simon Frasier University, 2017).

18. College of the Atlantic Diana Davis Spencer Hatchery: https://www.coa.edu/hatchery/.

19. Abundance Cycle: http://www.abundancecycle.com/about.

20. College of the Atlantic Project HELIO: http://aust.jp/HELIO-SS/.

21 Critical Edge Alliance: http://www.criticaledgealliance.com/.

22 Globally Responsible Leadership Initiative: http://www.grli.org.

23 The Posse Foundation: https://www.possefoundation.org/.

24 Creating Connections Consortium (C3) (http://c3transformhighered.org/partners/#sthash .jKxqwY5M.dpbs) is funded by the Andrew W. Mellon Foundation.

25 Bold Women Lead: http://www.boldwomenlead.org/.

26 Nick Corasaniti, "At Ithaca College, A President Focused on Diversity," *New York Times*, June 7, 2017. https://www.nytimes.com/2017/06/07/education/ithaca-college-shirley-collado-diversity.html.

27 LGBTQ stands for lesbian, gay, bisexual, transgender, queer.

28 OutHistory.org: http://outhistory.org/.

29 My portfolio as executive dean includes applied graduate schools (policy, international affairs, writing, media, environment) and an undergraduate liberal arts program designed for adult students.

30 History timeline, The New School: http://www.newschool.edu/about/history/.

31 Parsons School of Design inspires design thinking and practice across the university at The New School: http://www.newschool.edu/parsons/.

CHAPTER 13

A New Leadership Agenda
Expanding the Practice
of System Leadership
Russ Gaskin

New Leadership for New Types of Problems

The problems our society faces today are qualitatively different than those we've encountered in the past, in part because they are fueled less by our failures than by our success.

The success of our species at turning new knowledge into a dizzying array of new products, services, and solutions has also produced a host of serious unintended consequences. The more our economies grow and provide us with valuable goods, the greater our climate impact; the more we increase industrial productivity, the greater our gaps in wealth and income; the more affordable our goods and services become, the higher certain social and environmental costs rise. While some social measures, such as average educational and poverty levels, are systematically improving, others are systematically worsening, driven by our own innovation and productivity. In other words, the more we succeed, the worse some things get.

This is the very definition of *systemic*, in that the system we have designed to so effectively produce our goods and services also systematically produces negative outcomes as it expands. These problems are not random outcomes of the operation of individual parts of the system; they stem from the design of the solutions themselves.

That makes today's problems even more intractable and difficult to solve. The interdependent nature of our success, and its side effects, means that we as a species must deal with the fact that many things we love, and want more of, are harming us. To truly solve them, we not only need to advance technical and policy responses to the problems themselves, but we must also discover ways to continue producing the same benefits with fewer side effects or reduce our appetites for the products of our success. Either path is incredibly complex and challenging, and it may be that both are needed.

Solving this new type of problem requires a new type of leadership, what Peter Senge, Hal Hamilton, and John Kania have termed "System Leadership."[1] It's not the leadership of one brilliant scientist or inventor making a new

164

discovery, nor the leadership of great social or political leaders who organize the political will to address social ills such as racism or poverty. While these forms of leadership have been and continue to be critical to human success and survival, they are simply not enough. The complex challenges we face today are multifaceted, composed of political, social, economic, technological, and educational elements. One policy change won't fix them. Even entire sectors, whether public, private, or social, can't fix them alone. These systemic problems require a whole new level of collective insight and behavior change that crosses organizational, cultural, and sectoral boundaries.

The leadership needed to bring people together across these boundaries, help them see and understand their complexities, while also moving to effective action, is what we mean by System Leadership. This is leadership that is about fundamentally redesigning the system we've developed so that it systematically produces meaningful and positive outcomes for the whole system, and all its parts, for the long term, not just for some of its parts in the short term.

Four Critical Competencies

Those of us who have worked on diverse social and environmental issues across sectors have developed some initial insights into what System Leadership looks like. Some of us, including the Academy for System Change (the United States), Tamarack Institute (Canada), the Collective Leadership Institute (Germany), and my firm, CoCreative, have designed training programs specifically around this type of leadership. While none of us would argue that we have the answer, and our approaches vary in focus and content, there are four common denominators that seem to reflect the core competencies that system leaders need:

1. convening across boundaries;
2. building empathy;
3. leading across competing values; and
4. leading through complexity to meaningful action.

I'll illustrate each of these critical competencies with a representative story, share examples of leadership initiatives that are already advancing them, and end with a few proposals that may inform how we can grow system leadership globally.

Convening across Boundaries

We collaborate because the challenges we face in business and society are interdependent: They can only be solved by groups working productively together. However, it is also true that our potential for collaboration remains largely unrealized. The world may be boundless and flat, but we remain bounded and confined by powerful limits.

—Chris Ernst and Donna Chrobot-Mason, *Boundary Spanning Leadership*

In June 2002, my colleagues Susan Davis and Alisa Gravitz convened a unique collaboration to explore together how solar electricity production might play a critical role in reversing global climate change.

The Solar Circle network, as the collaboration came to call itself, was convened by Davis and stimulated by Gravitz's team at Green America (known as Co-op America at the time), who had crunched the numbers and realized that to reach a carbon neutral economy, assuming we didn't want to also grow the risk associated with nuclear power production, solar energy had to account for at least 50 percent of total energy supply. That was a challenging insight at a time when the global energy production from solar was less than that from one nuclear power plant.

In the launch meeting of the new network, Gravitz posed a problem to the group: "We know that the solar industry has been growing fast, somewhere around 20 to 30% a year," she began as she popped a slide of solar industry growth on the screen. "That's great, but here's the problem," she continued as she revealed two trend lines on a fifty-year chart. "When you look at the growth of carbon outputs globally, you're not going to make any difference in saving this planet. Despite your extraordinary growth as an industry, we will hit climate change tipping points long before we have enough solar in place to change the climate trend."

That challenge launched a fifteen-year collaboration that has catalyzed massive innovation and growth in the global solar industry.

The Solar Circle network was diverse by design, representing the entire spectrum of both the challenges and the opportunities. Among its members were a senior executive at the US National Renewable Energy Lab, heads of independent solar companies, as well as corporate solar divisions, academics, investors, representatives from US state governments, technology consultants, solar technicians, grid operators, civil society leaders, and a Chinese political leader.

By 2004, this diverse group had settled on an extraordinary goal: "By 2050, solar energy would account for at least 50% of the global energy supply."

Over the next ten years, operating largely through the market and behind the scenes to avoid political pushback, the network developed four policy studies showing the economic and job growth potential of solar; conceptualized and drafted policy templates to support solar in China, the United States, and several other countries; negotiated the merger and program alignment of the then-four solar trade associations in the United States; developed several state revolving loan funds to fund solar projects; devised and spun off a number of companies and nonprofits to address missing parts of the market development ecosystem; headed off a price surge by helping silicon producers anticipate the growing supply needs of solar producers; and organized dozens more interventions.

While it would be impossible to directly attribute the massive success of the solar electric industry to the actions of a single collaboration, even one as productive as the Solar Circle, the group's initiatives were certainly key to removing specific policy, market, and cultural barriers along its path. And the movement has indeed been massive, with recent scenarios that dramatically exceed the group's target goal,[2] largely because of the dramatic fall in the cost of solar, now lower than coal in some parts of the world.[3]

The ability to identify, gather, and lead an effective microcosm of an entire system is the most critical competency of the four I describe here. In a sense, the other four competencies are irrelevant unless we can bring together a collaboration that represents the whole system we're working to change.

Why is this competency so foundational? As we saw in the Solar Circle example, both the analysis and the strategy that emerged from the group were multifaceted and leveraged multiple interventions across numerous parts of the energy and policy system. Specifically, the diverse composition of the group delivered several key benefits:

- *The ability to understand a problem and design a multifaceted, "fit-for-purpose" strategy.* One of the dynamics we've observed in less diverse groups is that any specialized group will define a problem based on their own knowledge. Public-sector participants, for example, tend to view any problem as primarily a legislative or regulatory problem, and conceive of like solutions; corporate leaders often see market dynamics as having primary importance; and communications experts will tend to view problems as communications challenges, and therefore tend to propose communications strategies as the highest-leverage approach. This is true of any group from any field or sector. Only a diverse group drawn from across the whole system can see the system as it truly is, identify the most critical leverage points, and design solutions that fit the specific tactical need.

- *The ability to bring messages to key stakeholders with the right voice.* Each of the diverse leaders in Solar Circle could speak with authority to different constituencies with knowledge and familiarity that few others could match. When the collaboration identified a need to influence policymakers, for example, they drew selectively on researchers and private-sector leaders who could bring the right message in the right voice to those decision makers.

- *The ability to harness diverse types of capabilities and resources.* The resources and capabilities that different participants in Solar Circle brought to the work were unique and incredibly diverse. While some members could produce cogent analyses on the potential economic contribution of the solar sector, others could bring public education and marketing strategies and relationships, while still others could provide detailed technical analysis on the barriers to growing solar production on regional energy grids.

While charitable foundations have embraced collective impact as a systemic change approach in a handful of countries and nongovernmental organization (NGO)–industry collaborations have become more common in recent years, the practice of convening across boundaries is still relegated primarily to development of standards and policy design, and the collaborations are often limited in scope and composition. This may be because of the particular challenges faced when attempting to convene in this deeply collaborative way. These include the lack of a clearly positioned convener, the lack of capacity that organizations allocate to collaboration outside the organization itself, organizational capacity constraints, and lack of seed funding for multistakeholder collaborations that, by their very nature, cannot define their programs or even scopes of work until they have convened and worked together.

It is also the most difficult since, by definition, it requires working across well-established organizational, jurisdictional, cultural, and sectoral boundaries. In most of these collaborations, we are convening people who don't know one another, may not trust one another, and may not even like one another based on past experiences and prejudices. Helping these diverse groups work efficiently and effectively to innovate and scale solutions to complex problems across these many boundaries may be the skill that is most needed in system leadership, but also the one that is most lacking.

Building Empathy

Could a greater miracle take place than for us to look through each other's eyes for an instant?

—Henry David Thoreau

Marina Gallego is the national coordinator of Ruta Pacífica de Las Mujeres (Women's Route to Peace) in Colombia. For the past twenty years, she has led a national movement there to end the decades-long armed conflict between Revolutionary Armed Forces of Colombia (FARC) guerillas and the Colombian government, in part by highlighting the deep and continuing violence against women from the war.

Despite the long and widespread coverage of the fifty-two-year conflict by analysts and media, the specific impacts on women were largely unseen and unacknowledged. As Gallego put it, "Violence against women is a constant and, due to the situation in the country, is often invisible. There are between 3 and 4 femicides per day, which is a pretty high figure. Violence against women in Colombia has connotations of torture to the point of rendering them incapacitated for months, since it is performed with blunt instruments."[4]

When Gallego and her La Ruta colleagues began their work in 1996, women weren't even a recognizable concern in the conversations about the conflict. "There was only talk of the dead, of the men, of the heroes or anti-heroes of the war, of the military, of the whole rise of paramilitarism. No one was talking about women," says Gallego.

That lack of understanding and empathy had a hidden impact: the lack of awareness of the real impacts of the conflict on women meant that their calls to end the conflict went largely unheeded. They weren't included in negotiations and, in a vicious cycle of disenfranchisement, their missing voices meant that the specific impacts of the conflict on women weren't even on the list of issues to be addressed.

To remedy the lack of awareness, Gallego and her colleagues launched a women's "truth commission" in 2008 to document violence against women in Colombia. Over the next five years, the group worked across Colombia's fifteen provinces, interviewing a diverse field of hundreds of women to document the female experience of the armed conflict.

With only volunteer time, no experts, and no academics, by 2013, La Ruta published the results in two six-hundred-page volumes.

The harrowing narrative—from the individual stories to the collective numbers representing years of torture, rape, and abuse stemming from the political conflict—had a powerful impact on political and social leaders. While La Ruta had been calling for negotiations between armed actors long before President Juan Manuel Santos and even former president Andres Pastrana,[5] their calls were now bolstered by the undeniable stories, examples, and numbers of women across the country devastated by the conflict.

The empathy-building approach earned them a long-deserved seat at the table. When the participation and terms of the peace negotiations were being established in 2013, La Ruta and other women's organizations were consulted about, but not initially invited to, the negotiating table. Gallegos recounts, "We told the negotiators in Havana that we did not want peace to be made for us, but to be the peacemakers." After more negotiations and the spread of the stories from the La Ruta publication, a significant shift emerged.

Not only were the women's organizations invited to participate in the negotiations, but President Santos also soon appointed two women to represent the government at a senior level in the talks, an unprecedented move. More delegate spots were assigned to women, and special spaces were created during the talks for women to share their experiences. As United Nations Women noted, "Possibly without precedent in the field of conflict resolution, the women negotiating at the table on both sides met with women affected by conflict. Their testimonies of violations of their rights, including sexual violence and displacement, illustrated the various ways in which the war has affected their lives and those of their communities."[6]

In September 2014, the parties agreed to establish a dedicated subcommittee to ensure a gender perspective and that women's rights are included in all agreements.

Empathy is an elusive experience and difficult for many conventional leaders to embrace in practice, in part because many of us confuse it with sympathy—simply feeling sorry for others who are less well off than us. Others believe that empathy is like sensitivity, a saintly quality that comes naturally to a select few, but that others of us weren't fortunate (or unfortunate) enough to acquire at birth.

Yet empathy is profoundly important for the Systems Leader, as both a skill and a mindset that must be cultivated to effectively lead change in complex challenges.

In our work to address equity and human health issues in global supply chains and communities alike, empathy experiences have often been those moments that pivot leaders from believing that an initiative is a good idea to embracing it as an imperative. It is often the turning point from awareness to meaningful insight and action among leaders. In one community in the United States, one leader's interview with a young child and his unemployed mother about the role of reading in their lives transformed his relationship with the work. He not only realized that the problem was far more complex than he had previously assumed, but he also quickly convened an unprecedented collaboration of leaders across the community to double literacy rates in the county.

Among empathy's many benefits are the following:

- *It galvanizes powerful commitment.* When leaders intimately experience the pain and suffering of others, without judgment or guilt, they are compelled to take action. In our own work, the level of commitment after a meaningful empathy experience has turned corporate leaders from *thinking* about working on an issue to a deep commitment to really *solving the problem.*
- *It releases leaders from their siloed view of the issue.* Empathy is also a powerful way to help leaders develop an "outside-in" view of the problem to be addressed. Leaders who are confused by the complexity of systemic change challenges have often found profound clarity in stepping outside of their organizational or sectoral views and looking back at their work and the rest of the system from the point of view of a real person.
- *It builds the case for collaboration.* One of the common sources of resistance to cross-sector collaboration is the belief that it's simply not necessary because the problem in question can be solved by individual organizations pursuing their own strategies. One of the benefits of leaders seeing a system from the "user" or citizen perspective is that they can clearly see, often for the first time, the need for coordination of services and solutions across organizational, agency, and sectoral boundaries.
- *It points to new solutions.* That "experiential view" on the challenge helps leaders gain leverageable insights into specifically how and where the system needs to change to drive real change for real people. We've found that some of the most innovative strategies in multistakeholder collaborations have come not from deep expert analysis but by seeing the situation from the empathetic, "outside-in" perspectives of real people.

The most powerful system leaders in coming decades will be those who can connect our policies, practices, and behaviors to the real experiences of others, stimulating new levels of commitment and collaboration, and generating new insights that lead to powerful new solution sets.

Despite its power and impact, however, empathy remains elusive in most systems because powerful leaders, especially those who consider themselves "experts" on the system they are trying to change, are loath to spend precious time seeking to understand the real experiences of everyday people. Changing that assumption, and the bias behind it, is one of our biggest challenges on the path to realizing system leadership.

Leading across Competing Values

The dilemmas of the future will be more grating, more gnawing, and more likely to induce feelings of hopelessness. Leaders must be able to flip dilemmas around and find the hidden opportunities. Leaders must avoid oversimplifying or pretending that dilemmas are problems that can be solved. Dilemma flipping is a skill that leaders will need in order to win in a world dominated by problems that nobody can solve.

—Bob Johansen, *Leaders Make the Future: Ten New Leadership Skills for an Uncertain World*

After a string of high-profile crimes in her community of Charleston, South Carolina, in the southern United States, fifth-generation resident Margaret Seidler was fed up. As a frustrated resident and leader of a local resident committee composed of primarily single-family homeowners, she finally visited the municipal police department to demand that they fix the problem.

As the desk officer politely listened to Seidler's demands and her assertion that it was the responsibility of the police department to fix this problem, it suddenly dawned on Seidler that assigning blame was not going to solve the problem or help build a truly safe community. She had to take responsibility, along with her friends and neighbors, to make that happen.

Based on that realization, Seidler took an entirely different approach and invited people to dinner—to eat and talk about their differences.

The group she ultimately convened in her home's dining room one evening included members of her homeowners association, renters from multifamily dwellings in other Charleston neighborhoods, and, not coincidentally, Charleston's new chief of police, whom Seidler had invited on the promise that he could learn more about the community he had just been hired to serve.

As the group talked about their concerns and fears around the recent crimes in their own neighborhoods, Seidler realized something important. "Everyone around the table shared the same greater purpose," she says. "They all wanted a safer community."

With that shared interest serving as the binding purpose of the group, Seidler helped them unpack the tensions that had been at play over years in the community, one of which was the ongoing conflict between single-family homeowners and multifamily apartment residents.

Using an approach developed by Dr. Barry Johnson and the team at Polarity Partnerships, Seidler helped the diverse group map the tensions—which they referred to as "polarities"—underlying this longtime homeowner conflict. "We were able to talk through, in a very systematic way, the many benefits of having single-family homes and multi-family units in a community and the downsides of having one without the other," says Seidler. "That was a real turning point in the conversation. It was clear at that point that this was not just another either-or conversation." By identifying and talking about the deeper conflict within the context of their shared purpose, the group was able to move beyond blaming one another for the problems they faced and lay the foundation for possible collaboration.

Based on the breakthrough conversation that evening and the shared understanding that emerged between those two groups, Greg Mullen, Charleston's new police chief, approached Seidler with a request: "I believe we have these things you call 'polarities' in law enforcement." He asked if she might work with him to map these so that law enforcement could turn the conflicts that it faced into sources of shared understanding with the community.

Over the coming weeks, Seidler and Mullen identified and mapped a handful of critical tensions that had been impacting the community relationship for years, some in profoundly negative ways. Among the tensions they discovered were the following:

- *Quality of policing service and the cost of policing service.* For years, the debate around effective policing in the community had been wrapped around a conflict based on the assumption that the only way to ensure quality of policing was to increase law enforcement budgets. Since additional policy funding seemed increasingly unlikely given economic and funding pressures, it appeared that the city would have to accept lower-quality policing service and accompanying crime. Seidler and Mullen, however, realized that this was a false choice and that the department could clearly pursue robust service delivery at a relatively low cost.

- *The needs of the citizens and the needs of the city.* For years, Charleston's leaders had assumed, as they do in municipalities around the world, that there were inherent and difficult trade-offs to be faced between the interests of citizens and the needs of the local government. In any given situation, one would win and the other would lose. For example, to ensure safety, citizens may have to lose some privacy. By flipping that dilemma, Mullen's approach to community engagement was transformed. Rather than assuming that one party would have to lose, which led to engagements which were primarily driven by the city's need to get citizens to conform to municipal demands, he approached public engagements by hearing the interests of citizens, sharing the needs and interests of the police department, and then turning the engagement into a working session to figure out how to creatively optimize both.

- *Focusing on the department's operational requirements and the department's organizational development needs.* Not all the tensions that Seidler and Mullen discovered lay in the interface between the police department and the community; some were internal to the department but significantly impacted the way officers engaged with the community. With Seidler's help, Mullen realized that the department's mantra of doing things "by the book" had led to a focus on following operational requirements in a way that neglected the real social and psychological needs of both officers and citizens. By pursuing operational and procedural excellence while simultaneously improving human interactions and interpersonal capabilities, Mullen was able to increase both officer morale and community trust of his department.

Seidler's values-based approach turned out to be pivotal in transforming her community's approach to public safety. Indeed, of all the competencies outlined in this chapter, the ability to lead across competing values is arguably the single most transformational skill in today's polarized political and social climate.

It is also increasingly critical. The more grating and gnawing our challenges, and the greater our collective feelings of hopelessness, the more intense our underlying values conflicts will become. Without ways to work across that deepening polarization, our leaders will be ill-equipped to lead the change we need.

Unfortunately, working effectively with values-based conflict may also be the weakest and most elusive skill and mindset among leaders. While the reasons for this may be numerous and diverse, including that leaders are not taught to work directly with people's values or they simply don't have tools for doing so, our own work in collaboration indicates that embracing these tensions proactively and positively is not only helpful to success in complex change, but it is also often the critical factor in success.

Leading through Complexity to Meaningful Action

Any darn fool can make something complex; it takes a genius to make something simple.

—Pete Seeger

Sarah O'Brien is the director of the Clean Electronics Production Network, a multistakeholder collaboration of electronics brands, labor rights NGOs, and workplace safety experts who are working to eliminate worker exposures to hazardous process chemicals used in electronics factories around the world. The network's participants range from leading electronics companies such as Apple, Dell, HP, and Flex to campaign NGOs such as International Campaign for Responsible Technology and Cereal, a worker advocacy group in Mexico.

Their challenge is incredibly complex, partly because the system is large and deep. According to the last estimate published for the International Labour Organization's Better Work Program,[7] over eighteen million people work in the global electronics supply chain, making it likely the largest industrial sector in the world. Those workers produce everything from components for modern "smart" refrigerators to cell phones to the insides of inexpensive electronic toys, with multiple chemicals used at all stages of production. A supply chain for your personal cell phone might be seven or eight layers deep, from extraction of raw materials to materials processing to fabrication of components to the final assembly, and employ over one thousand chemicals.[8]

Even Apple, the world's largest public company by market capitalization, has little direct influence over the entirely of such a vast industry, in which a single supplier can employ over one million employees, so it's important for them to collaborate with other brands, even competitors, to get suppliers to proactively address worker risks.

The group convened in July 2016 and, after introducing themselves, establishing working agreements, and confirming the audacious goal of eliminating worker exposures, began to unpack a map of the current system as it relates to their goal. It took the group over two hours just to understand what was on the map, but by the end of the following day, they had identified the critical intervention points and prototyped four initiatives to develop to achieve their goal. That means that the group had gone from meeting one another for the first time, to unpacking this massively complex system, to building out their first initiatives in twelve hours.

"I think that most of the participants hadn't seen something like this before," says O'Brien. "The movement from establishing the goal to working through the mind-blowing complexity of the global electronics production system to developing a set of four really powerful initiatives in a day and a half was possibly unprecedented, even for an industry that's known for moving fast."

The network launched five initiatives in all: a chemical substitutions group that is piloting programs to replace the most hazardous chemicals with more benign alternatives, a worker empowerment group that is developing standards and practices for workers to raise safety concerns to be resolved quickly and effectively, a team that has designed and is piloting a new process chemical reporting standard, a group that is testing a new quality chemical assessment and intervention approach, and a team developing technology and processes to monitor and reduce exposures within factories.

Changing such a complex system is the type of challenge that the System Leader must be equipped to lead. As the world becomes smaller, as the volume and complexity of information increase, and as we bump up against more competing interests and agendas, we will need, more than ever, to effectively see and understand complex systems together and codesign multifaceted change strategies.

Working effectively with the complexity in these types of systems presents a number of difficult challenges, however:

- *People WANT things to be simple.* Leaders are often overwhelmed by the challenge of seeing a whole system in its raw complexity. They are understandably afraid of getting lost or stuck in what participatory decision-making expert Sam Kaner calls "the Groan Zone," a place in which the complexity of the system is so overwhelming that we risk becoming paralyzed by it. To avoid that uncertainty, especially with the complexity of working in diverse groups, leaders will often present the problem or system as being much simpler than it really is. This in turn leads to poor strategies that fail over time.
- *We tend to talk, analyze, and discuss.* Our common tendency toward talk without action in multistakeholder collaborations is so common that Chris Thompson at Civic Collaboration Consultants has a special term for it: "Coblaboration." "By default, talk is what people do in collaborations—that and commissioning studies," Chris says. "Yes, it's good for learning and even for building the trust that's needed to move forward, but without action, it's meaningless."
- *Leaders often use their power to advance favored solutions.* We have often observed the tendency, especially among more powerful political leaders, to simply decide to ignore the complex and interdependent nature of systems

and instead embrace and advance their own favored—and simple—solutions. As American satirist H. L. Mencken noted, "For every complex problem there is an answer that is clear, simple, and wrong." Not only does this approach fail because the solution isn't adequate to the complexity of the challenge, but the failure of the simple solution and the leader's unilateral approach only increases cynicism and disengagement of the very people needed to solve the issue.

- *We tend to rely on experts, who each see the problem differently.* Working through complexity is also challenging because we each tend to simplify our understanding of the system in our own ways. We each bring our own domain knowledge to bear on understanding and solving a challenge, and this can be the enemy of shared understanding and strategy. If the communications experts keep seeing the challenge as one of communications, policy experts see policy problems and gravitate to policy solutions, and technical experts see the technical dimensions of the problem and filter out the complex human and social dynamics at play, groups quickly get stuck in another kind of polarization—competing over parts of the picture rather than developing a shared analysis of the whole challenge.

To overcome these tendencies, the System Leader must have the mindset, the capabilities, and the tools to help diverse groups working on complex systems change see those systems in all their complexity but move stakeholders to the clear analysis, meaningful strategy, and achievable plans needed to change complex systems.

Some tools from the business world are proving useful in moving from complexity to clear action, including Agile, LEAN, and Design Thinking approaches, and some groups such as CoCreative and ThinkPlace New Zealand have developed training programs to help groups do deep analysis and action planning quickly. However, these and other similar efforts need to be scaled if we are to help more collaborations avoid getting stuck trying to solve the same problem over and over.

Four Elements of a New Leadership Agenda

To help more leaders globally become System Leaders, we must execute a clear leadership agenda across sectors with system leadership at the core. But content alone is not enough; a truly effective global leadership program must itself be systemic. Following are four recommendations for advancing system leadership based on innovations that are already being deployed.

Teach Leadership at All Levels of the System

One of the common refrains we hear from folks working on complex systems change is that leadership needs to be taught earlier in young people's careers than we have been teaching it.

As Jack Zenger argued in a 2012 article in the *Harvard Business Review*,[9] we wait too long to teach leadership and the longer we wait, the more bad habits are ingrained in our leaders. Those habits (which rarely include skills such as building empathy or leading across competing values) then must be untaught or, more often, remain with leaders throughout their careers.

Consider your own early professional leadership experiences. Unless you were a natural leader or born to privilege, it's unlikely that you had a real leadership experience before the age of sixteen, while many didn't experience leadership until later in university education or jobs. And leadership on the job? Any early training was likely too late or inadequate when it comes to the complex change skills described above.

Chris Ernst, author of *Boundary Spanning Leadership*, is leading an organizational leadership transformation initiative at the Gates Foundation. He responded to this leadership challenge by making one critical change in the foundation's leadership development program: whereas before the program was exclusively for senior leaders, it now includes employees across all levels and functions of the foundation.

"This isn't just a case of investing in our future leaders. We realized that leadership is happening constantly at all levels of the Foundation, and that recognition meant that we had to have a program that works across levels," says Ernst. "And building our young leaders earlier means that they can go even further as they mature in their careers. That's the truly exciting part."

Developing system leadership means ensuring that leadership is happening effectively at all levels of a system, yet many organizations continue to reserve leadership development programs for their senior leaders. To equip organizations of all types to engage effectively on systemic problems, we need to leverage the insight, ideas, and resources of all levels of the systems we see to fix.

Teach System Leadership Early

Clearly, the Leader-at-All-Levels strategy helps those early-career employees get a head start on developing their leadership skills, but some leadership development advocates argue that even that is too late, and we must teach systems leadership skills to youth and teens.

Bill Drayton, the dynamic social entrepreneur and founder of Ashoka, has argued, "We have to teach empathy as we do literacy." Peter Senge and his colleagues at Camp Snowball are working with school system leaders around the United States to teach systems thinking to students to equip them to work more effectively with complexity. At the Center for Creative Leadership's Leading Beyond Boundaries (LBB), a small entrepreneurial team advised by a diverse group of Center for Creative Leadership's top leaders, is piloting leadership development programs that can be integrated into curriculum for K–12 education globally.

"We believe that early leadership development is not only critical for our society, but that it can produce real short-term benefits too." Says Lyndon Rego, global director of the LBB initiative. The evidence so far indicates that Rego may be right. In the schools where the LBB's leadership program has been taught, average student test scores have improved 3–5 percent in a single year.

The California Endowment is also testing and advancing approaches to building the capabilities of young people to work across cultural and sectoral boundaries to advance positive community change. Their Building Healthy Communities program includes youth training academies and youth-focused leadership programs to help youth develop skills around building trust with community leaders, shaping effective policy proposals, and building citizen support for those initiatives.

Peter Senge and his colleagues at the Academy for Systems Change offer yet another example of teaching system leadership early through Camp Snowball, an annual summer development program they developed. The program, now in its sixth year, helps teachers and youth integrate collaboration, systems thinking, and other critical systems leadership skills into K–12 educational programs around the United States.

Foster Women in Leadership

According to Dr. Rachel Shafran, women leaders tend to leverage more of the system leadership strategies we describe here.[10] As Shafran notes, "Most change models and strategies are based on a linear understanding of change in which the process is composed of a series of sequential steps; yet most organizational systems are complex, and there is a dynamic network of interactions and relationships."

Women leaders, on the other hand, "often exhibited behaviors that reflected a nonlinear approach to change," she notes, "using systems thinking to lead change, building webs of inclusion and change networks that fostered buy-in, and demonstrating strong interpersonal communication skills like listening and empathy to influence key stakeholders."

Shafran describes strategies such as empathizing with the needs of others, developing ways for those impacted by the change to also participate in decisions, using understanding of cultural differences and diverse viewpoints, and using experiential and experimental learning strategies, to lead change effectively, especially in complex organizations.

Yet, we know that across all sectors, with rare exceptions, women are not reflected proportionally at the most senior levels of leadership. Women account for just over 6 percent of CEOs among Fortune 500 companies, for example,[11] and only fifteen countries are led by women leaders today.[12] Since women exhibit many of the competencies and behaviors we believe are needed for addressing our most complex problems, this gap in itself is a critical problem.

Fund System Leadership

Philanthropic foundations have a unique role to play because many of them are focused on addressing complex problems already. They are positioned to be "solution-agnostic," and have convening power because of their relative independence. Yet, while many funders are realizing the power of collaboration, and even funding elements of System Leadership development among their grantees, it's still considered highly experimental in the funding community at large. The same might be said of many government entities, some of whom have begun funding, if not system leadership programs, at least cross-systems collaborations to address complex challenges.

We believe that a fundamental shift in how we approach social change financing is needed, one that fosters System Leadership and shifts from a "concentrated leadership" approach to a more distributed model. As Ron Dendas of the Rider-Pool Foundation points out, "As funders, we want our grantees to collaborate yet we set them up to compete by the very way we handle funding. That has to change."

We're beginning to see the emergence of a true system leadership approach in the United States, where funders such as the Annie E. Casey Foundation are funding multistakeholder network collaborations in addition to their traditional "responsive philanthropy" programs. Others, such as the California Endowment, have embraced the approach as a core strategy and are creating models for funding not just for individual grantees, but for the collaborations themselves and the capacity-building of Systems Leaders.

We're also seeing more funders addressing the influence of power differentials in the systems they are working to change. These differentials include integrating equity and inclusion considerations into their funding requirements, requiring citizen involvement in systems change initiatives, and building the capabilities of change leaders to work effectively with multistakeholders groups that include participants from across sectors and levels of institutions, especially "citizen leaders," who bring the much-needed voice of experience to the work.

Conclusion

While the systems collaboration approach is far more complex and difficult to lead, the problem is not the complexity of the approach but the complexity of the problems we face. As such, we hope to see a greater focus on equipping leaders across systems to lead collaboratively and systemically rather than (what we fear) a pulling back from the collaborative approach to change. Only by focusing on building true System Leaders can we hope to ultimately solve the truly systemic problems we face today.

Notes

[1] P. Senge, H. Hamilton, and J. Kania, "The Dawn of System Leadership," *Stanford Social Innovation Review* (Winter 2015): 26–33.

[2] *The Future of the Solar Energy: An Interdisciplinary MIT Study*, report (Cambridge, MA: Massachusetts Institute of Technology, 2015).

[3] J. Shankleman and C. Martin, "Solar Could Beat Coal to Become the Cheapest Power on Earth," *Bloomberg*, January 2, 2017. Retrieved July 27, 2017, from https://www.bloomberg.com/news/articles/2017-01-03/for-cheapest-power-on-earth-look-skyward-as-coal-falls-to-solar.

[4] N. Luna, "Entrevista de Nodal a Marina Gallego, coordinadora nacional de Ruta Pacífica de las Mujeres," *Nodal*, March 23, 2017. Retrieved July 27, 2017, from http://www.nodal.am/2017/03/entrevista-nodal-marina-gallego-coordinadora-nacional-ruta-pacifica-las-mujeres-la-violencia-las-mujeres-colombia-connotaciones-tortura-al-punto-pueden/.

[5] http://pacifista.co/un-capitulo-del-nuevo-libro-que-exalta-a-los-pacifistas-de-colombia/.

[6] http://www.unwomen.org/en/news/stories/2015/5/women-build-peace-in-colombia#sthash. CGATbYd2.dpuf.

[7] Better Work, *Electronics Feasibility Study*, Executive Summary, August 2010.

[8] T. Smith and L. A. Byster, "The Electronics Production Lifecycle," in *Challenging the Chip: Labor Rights and Environmental Justice in the Global Electronics Industry*, Ted Smith, David Sonnenfeld, David Naguib Pellow, eds. (Philadelphia: Temple University Press, 2006), 205.

[9] "We Wait Too Long to Train Our Leaders," December 17, 2012.

[10] R. Shafran, "Women Leading Change: A New Model for the Future," April 14, 2017. Retrieved July 28, 2017, from https://www.linkedin.com/pulse/women-leading-change-new-model-future-rachel-shafran-ed-d.

[11] S. Chira, "Why Women Aren't C.E.O.s, According to Women Who Almost Were," *New York Times* Sunday Review, July 21, 2017. Retrieved July 28, 2017, from https://www.nytimes.com/2017/07/21/sunday-review/women-ceos-glass-ceiling.html?_r=0.

[12] A. Geiger, and L. Kent, "Number of Women Leaders around the World Has Grown, but They're Still a Small Group," Pew Research Center, March 8, 2017. Retrieved July 28, 2017, from http://www.pewresearch.org/fact-tank/2017/03/08/women-leaders-around-the-world/.

CHAPTER 14

Crowdsourcing the Feminine Intelligence of the Planet

Jensine Larsen

While there is enormous suppressed human potential existing in individual women and girls today, there is an even greater collective feminine intelligence that will come through massive connected knowledge-sharing among women across cultures. This healing wisdom will be a potent planetary immunological response that does not yet exist on the planet, but it can. It is waiting to be born.

We live at a time when there is no nation where women have an equal voice, in a world where physical violence affects one out of three women globally and spiritual suppression is widespread, all holding humanity back. Feminine leadership principles such as collaboration, nurturing, networked thinking, and long-range priority-setting are increasingly recognized by the global public and world leaders as critical to our future.[1] Can technology unlock unprecedented levels of feminine leadership to bring about a more peaceful, balanced world for all?

My initial quest to unlock women's leadership inspired me to follow my dream and launch a global digital social network in 2007, called *World Pulse*.[2] Today, tens of thousands of women from 190 countries are logging on, telling their stories, and banding together to improve their communities, impacting over three million people. And millions more log on through an ever-growing array of digital platforms connecting us all with each other.

I am riveted by the experiences and energy women are transmitting online, whether it is from the maternity wards of the South Bronx or the schools held under plastic tarp roofs in Karachi. The good news is that from all corners, women and girls are showing us intricate paths forward. I am now convinced that we don't have to wring our hands, burdened with responsibility to figure out how to solve all the world's problems ourselves—local women community leaders hold crucial knowledge and are already taking action. We just have to partner to create spaces and infrastructure to surface this wisdom. They've shown me something that I now believe in every cell in my body: the fastest way we're going to overturn cultures of violence and achieve global sustainability is to use the rapid power of digital communications technology to unleash the collective power of women.

Women's Participatory Use of Technology to Heal the World

Over the past decade of listening to the wisdom of women and girls globally, I have begun to understand the urgent steps we need to take to foster a greater feminine groundswell. In the following chapter, I will speak to the global trends that are pointing us to women and technology as a swift strategy in the face of planetary catastrophe. I will highlight the enormous barriers we face to deploy this strategy, and finally, the top principles for how we—whether you are an individual, impact investor, technology leader, women's rights advocate, or international development agency—can work together with the women of the world to create the right design for a resilient global web that will activate the wave of intelligence and action we need to heal humanity.

Women and Technology Are the Strategic Lever

Both women and technology on their own are proven accelerators for social change—deployed together, they can provide an exponential rocket boost.

Over the last twenty years, we have seen tremendous strides for women, including reduced rates of maternal mortality and increased levels of girls' education. Yet, girls and women remain the majority of the world's unhealthy, unfed, and unpaid.[3] Sadly, despite the hard-fought struggle for gender equality, the violent suppression of women hasn't budged—impeding progress in all areas. The World Health Organization estimates that global rates of gender-based violence are unchanged over the past twenty years, despite billions of public and private investment to combat it, primarily due to the persistence of subconscious beliefs that reinforce power imbalance between men and women.[4]

While I consider the rising leadership of women as one of modern day's unstoppable trends, progress isn't happening fast enough. Projections for full global equality range from one hundred to five hundred years in the future—too late. How can we accelerate this timetable?

More than ever, we must accelerate change when little girls are being shot in the head for wanting to go to school, women are kidnapped into the sex trade, widows are stoned, and rape is used on a mass scale. And we must accelerate change when women face acid burnings, child marriage, domestic violence, street harassment, female genital mutilation, whipping for wearing pants or showing an ankle, and the scourge of honor killings. To this day, the oppression of women is considered by the United Nations to be the most widespread human rights abuse on the planet; physical violence alone affects one billion women and girls, and this doesn't include the spiritual suppression of those who live in fear of it. New research shows that domestic violence against women and children alone is causing an economic cost greater than all wars combined—over eight trillion dollars annually.[5]

Our greatest hope for durable, sustained progress for reducing violence and improving women's leadership is likely to be found in strengthened women's networks and movements. A thirty-year study conducted by Purdue University and New Mexico University spanning seventy countries found that the mobilization of autonomous women's movements is primarily responsible for the most enduring and effective policies reducing violence against women.[6]

The data are definitive: educating and empowering women and girls are the fastest ways to solve all global problems, from climate change to war and hunger.[7] The wisdom and the will to solve these challenges exist in women in every community worldwide. Yet, without the connective tissue of digital communication and engagement to foster stronger women-led networks, this wisdom and will remain largely untapped, underresourced, and too often crushed.

The Unmet Promise of Technology

Technology holds great promise to bring about a quantum leap for society led by women. The rapid spread of communication technology into the hands of previously isolated and unheard women and girls means that they can make world headlines, access information, participate in the global economy, spread inspiration and revolution, and influence culture and policy change. Today, over 50 percent of the global adult population owns a smartphone, which will likely increase to 70–80 percent by 2020, dramatically increasing women's access to the Internet.[8]

It is now possible to hear the voice of a young Iraqi girl in a city under siege through her blog, Baghdad Girl, or see a young Malala from Pakistan rise to win the Nobel Peace prize after she told of her fight for girls' education online before and after she was shot for doing so. Women using cyber activism were at the forefront of the Arab Spring protests in the Middle East, and galvanized mass protests of women into India's streets to protest the horrific rape of a girl on a bus in 2012. US girls used online petitions through Change.org to convince editors of a popular magazine, called *Seventeen*, to cease using airbrushed images of women. In one of the least Internet-connected regions of the world, the Democratic Republic of Congo, women launched their own cyber café and "hero women's movement" to bring peace to Congo. Hollaback, a global movement to end women's street harassment, grows globally with five hundred international chapters. And on January 21, 2017, the US Women's March went global, live streaming simultaneous sister marches all around the world as the largest recorded mass protest in history.

In addition to accelerated waves of social change, new platforms are emerging, such as the Khan Academy and Internet.org, improving women's online access to education and information. The potential of technology for women is so significant that the United Nations' Sustainable Development Goals for the 2030 Agenda specifically highlight the use of enabling technology, in particular information and communication technology, to achieve gender equality and empower all women and girls (Goal 5b).[9]

Since 2005, technology leaders have been extolling the virtues of democratizing participation through the Internet. Techniques such as crowdsourcing, which uses the Internet to broadcast calls to the global public to source new innovations and ideas, ostensibly enable less represented voices to participate in shaping new products, policies, decisions, and solutions. Wikipedia, the seventh most visited website in the world, is one of the largest global experiments in crowdsourcing. Many institutions and companies have now adopted the practice, including global brands and organizations, such as OpenIdeo, which posts online challenges to source solutions to some of the world's most pressing problems, such as water and sanitation and early childhood education.

However, for all the promise of tech for women—it is far from realized.

Baghdad Girl signed off from the web, citing that she no longer believed her voice mattered[10]; and the Arab spring flared up, but was not sustained, with many women's rights having been rolled back. According to women's rights groups in India, not much has changed since the rape protests. Wikipedia, as one of the largest authorities of online knowledge, has acknowledged that approximately 90 percent of their editors are male, and they are struggling to pull in more women.[11] In the technology industry itself, women are represented in only 25 percent or less of all positions.[12]

Overcoming Barriers: No Quick Fixes

There are many reasons why technology alone is no silver bullet. Technology is a tool, one that tends to reinforce and transmit current social values and mindsets. If new values are not embedded into how we use technology, and if women themselves are not making, owning, and shaping the development of this technology, then little will change. Misused technology could have the potential to make things worse. We are in a race to have women claim technology as their own.

The barriers are immense, including the ones discussed next.

The Gendered Digital Divide

Approximately two billion women—one out of two—still do not have access to the Internet. This means that they can't express themselves online, take a course, check the weather, or search for the information they want. This is a significantly higher ratio than seen for men. According to the "Women and the Web" report, in mid- to low-income countries, women access the Internet 25–40 percent less than men.[13]

World Pulse launched a global crowdsourcing campaign to collect homegrown solutions and ideas that spread digital empowerment. Hundreds of submissions poured in from 70+ countries as part of our Women Weave the Web campaign.[14]

Women themselves revealed key challenges—issues of safety, affordability, technological skill, distance to Internet cafés, and gender norms that restrict women's access.

A host of cultural, economic, social, and infrastructural barriers keep women locked out from the empowerment potential of Internet access. Women are often socialized to believe that the Internet is not for them, too dangerous, or of no value. Accessing a device or Wi-Fi can be expensive, power shortages may constrain productivity, and visiting cyber cafés can draw harassment and threats.

Yet, when I ask grassroots women leaders the world over, they say that access to the Internet is not a luxury but a lifeline. Time and time again, women tell me that online access gives them a voice and an outlet to communicate with the rest of the world. They are devising ingenious ways to overcome the access challenge.

I get passionate answers from women like Busayo, a community organizer and health worker from Nigeria who exclaims, "Information is power—it helps us to learn how to change our conditions ourselves!" It has also helped her make change in her community. "In just the two years that I have been online, I have gotten support to start my vision for a women's empowerment center and cybercafé, training over 150 women. We have even stopped cases of child rape. The Internet has opened the sky for us."

Increasing the number of women online is an important step.

The Online Confidence Gap

For those women who are just coming online—they often face additional barriers such as lack of digital skills or confidence to use the full suite of benefits the web offers for their own ends. The "Women and the Web" report cited that there were additional barriers with women not knowing how to use the Internet, becoming overwhelmed, and dropping off. Trainers are often men, and content may not be relevant for them. In the technology industry, they are not accessing enough coding support. It is vital that when women and girls are introduced to the Internet, they have access to skill-building support, relevant content, supportive communities, and motivation from local women who can model the benefits.

The Cyber War Zone

Globally, online harassment has become an epidemic. Women and girls are increasingly targeted for their online participation, causing some to drop off and even more to self-censor and suppress their expression and activity. A recent study in Australia showed that half of women surveyed had been harassed, 76 percent under thirty. The researchers warned that online harassment was at risk of becoming an established norm in society.[15] In Pakistan, a recent study by the Digital Rights Foundation reported that 40 percent of respondents have been harassed or stalked online at some point. However, according to the survey, 70 percent of the women are afraid of putting up their own photos online because they are afraid of them being misused.[16] Fundamentalist online "gangs" of men are literally waging war of terror against women online, from Gamer Gate harassment to Islamic State of Iraq and Syria brutality, complete with rape and death threats—some that have actually been carried out.

Online attacks can be as harmful as offline attacks for women's and girls' sense of safety and self-esteem. Safe, protected online spaces and psychologically supportive communities where women and girls can express themselves, connect, and participate are essential to surface their wisdom.

Disconnected Digital Dots

A plethora of mobile apps, online communities, hackathons, and technology programs have sprouted up globally. However, many of these one-off platforms are not connected or synchronized. They are siloed by sector, geography, or organization, resulting in duplication and more separate pockets of online activity without shared data to benefit women and girls. For example, there have been over eighty mobile health pilots in Uganda, such that the government of Uganda eventually called a moratorium on these mobile pilots.[17]

Recognizing this problem, a set of nine Digital Design Principles were developed through a year-long process to bring together best practices from one hundred organizations in the international development and technology sector.[18] Ultimately, the need was identified for more scalable, cross-sector online platforms to "connect the dots" across ecosystems.

In building a path forward to aggregate women's online contributions, it is critical that existing platforms are strategically linked and that the nine Digital Design Principles are deployed: design with the user, understand the existing ecosystem, build for sustainability, design for scale, be data driven, use open source and open innovation, reuse and improve, address privacy and security, and be collaborative.

The Way Forward: Five Key Design Elements

To ethically and smartly crowdsource feminine intelligence, what matters most is how we design and resource the technology ecosystem and women's networks. The following elements are nonlinear. They are interconnected and must be developed in parallel through feedback loop rhythms with the users of the technology over time. Ultimately, the process of unlocking this wisdom will likely take the shape of a spiral rather than a straight line.

Turn On the Lights

Expand and fortify more online environments that enable voice.

This means strengthening existing safe, accessible online communication platforms and communities to reach as many emerging women leaders as possible who are already online. This will help enable those that are yearning to speak out be heard, and turn on that precious light of belief in the power of her own voice. Quality social interactions and support are critical factors to encourage women and girls to truly express themselves. These enabling spaces will be most useful at large scale if they use the Digital Design Principles and are intersectional: cross-topical, cross-regional, cross-cultural, and multilingual. This includes connecting women from more resource-rich and resource-scarce areas, as there are often shared experiences or a shared desire to support each other and learn from each other. In addition, to reach the most women, mobile-centric design is a must.

Link the Transmitters

Use these online platforms to link and invest in women leaders who are empowering hundreds and thousands in their wider communities to bridge the digital divide.

Since we don't have much time, this strategic focus will strengthen "wired women" leaders who are multipliers. They are motivated to transmit information from the World Wide Web to local women and girls who may be illiterate or off the grid, as well as upload their voices and needs back online—or introduce those who already have access to empowering benefits of the web. This is one of the fastest ways we will create on-ramps to bring more unheard voices online. It is also one of the fastest ways we will facilitate a rich cross-pollination of solutions and support between communities across borders and topics. This exchange across relatively isolated efforts will generate new ideas and ways forward. This will give birth to a new feminine intelligence for solving global challenges that does not yet exist.

Light Up the Grid

Link ecosystems and industries to reduce fragmentation and inefficiencies, grow more women leaders, and enable their networks.

We can "connect the dots" by syncing efforts to grow a digital leadership ladder for women. Currently, many efforts of international development, nongovernmental organizations, philanthropists, and technology and media companies are uncoordinated as they work to bring greater online access to women, provide digital literacy, deliver empowering content and educational materials, provide investments, define data measurements, and implement leadership trainings. We need network leaders and backbone efforts to coordinate the many players who connect and invest in women and create shared measurements. We can connect and elevate so many more women so much faster by syncing a more cohesive ecosystem.

Crowdsource the Code

Surface aggregated solution data defined by women and use it for feedback loops, analysis, and decisions.

As more women participate online, they will be defining on a large scale what matters to them, what impact they would like to create, and what kind of additional support is needed to implement their solutions to community challenges. Women are essentially writing a new code for the system. Additionally, more women exposed to coding and technology opportunities are increasingly designing the technology to capture these data and power society. This "social listening" is a fundamental shift for how development operates today. It is collaborative and networked development, transformed from the ground up versus the top down. It is demand driven, as opposed to supply driven.

Surge the System

Respond to the new intelligence with a massive infusion of resources, funding, education, and support to strengthen the programs, businesses, designs, policies, and vision women are creating.

As an added bonus, there will be tremendous investment between women with captured social capital through networked exchange of resources and knowledge among each other. This social capital is currently "leaking" without mature digital networks for collaboration. This surge of responsive investment will have potential to bring about a giant leap forward to boost women's power to create a more balanced, prosperous, and peaceful world.

A World Wide Web of Women: An Immune System for Earth

This is the moment—when cultures of domination, oppression, and destruction are threatening our existence. This moment is one of the loudest *wake-up calls for women to lead* and keep weaving a web of support and strength, ever wider, online and offline, across the globe. *It is a call for men and allies* to draw upon their own feminine strengths to contribute to and support this growing network. This web will be our most resilient global economic plan and our most secure global security strategy. It will be our immune system for the earth.

As for the technology we hold in the palms of our hands, we hold the power to transform cell phones and social networks from weapons of "mass distraction" to portals of purposeful connection and change. We are moving from the era of information technology into the era of relationship technology, driven by collective, collaborative networks, and women are showing us the way to do this.

I challenge top development experts, technology leaders, innovative visionaries, philanthropists, and policymakers to partner with grassroots women and existing and emerging women's networks the world over and rise to the task. The women I work with every day are ready. With support, these local, women community leaders can lead the charge.

If we do this well, and combine the best of the global technology industry with the ingenuity and resourcefulness of women on the ground, we can unlock a colossal wave of human potential, creativity, and freedom for future generations.

Notes

[1] J. Gerzema, "The Global Feminine Age Is Rising," *US News & World Report*, March 8, 2016. https://www.usnews.com/news/best-countries/articles/2016-03-08/the-global-feminine-age-is-rising; John Gerzema, *The Athena Doctrine, How Women (and Men Who Think Like Them) Will Rule in the Future* (San Faransisco, CA: Jossey-Bass, April 2013).

[2] www.worldpulse.com.

[3] No Ceilings: The Full Participation Project, March 2015. http://www.noceilings.org/report/report.pdf.

[4] World Health Organization as cited in "A New Approach to Gender Lens Grantmaking," *Stanford Social Innovation Review*. https://ssir.org/articles/entry/a_new_approach_to_gender_lens_grantmaking.

[5] "Violence at Home Costs 8 Trillion Per Year," *Reuters*, 2014. http://www.reuters.com/article/us-abuse-costs-idUSKBN0H41AL20140909.

⁶ Mala Htun and S. Laurel Weldon, "The Civic Origins of Progressive Policy Change: Combating Violence against Women in Global Perspective, 1975–2005," *American Political Science Review* 106, no. 3 (2012), available on CJO. doi:10.1017/S0003055412000226.

⁷ World Bank's 2012 *World Development Report: Gender Equality and Development.*

⁸ "10th Annual Cisco Visual Networking Index (VNI) Mobile Forecast Projects 70 Percent of Global Population Will Be Mobile Users," Cisco, https://newsroom.cisco.com/press-release-content?articleId=1741352.

⁹ United Nations, *Transforming Our World: The 2030 Agenda for Sustainable Development,* A/RES/70/1, p. 18.

¹⁰ Baghdad Girl: "The Last Post and Goodbye." http://baghdadgirl.blogspot.com/

¹¹ https://hbr.org/2016/06/why-do-so-few-women-edit-wikipedia.

¹² Women in Tech Facts Report 2016. https://www.ncwit.org/sites/default/files/resources/womenintech_facts_fullreport_05132016.pdf.

¹³ Women and the Web Report. https://www.intel.com/content/www/us/en/technology-in-education/women-in-the-web.html.

¹⁴ https://www.worldpulse.com/en/campaigns/www/welcome.

¹⁵ https://www.theguardian.com/lifeandstyle/2016/mar/08/online-harassment-of-women-at-risk-of-becoming-established-norm-study.

¹⁶ https://www.ifex.org/pakistan/2017/05/31/online-violence-women/.

¹⁷ https://www.devex.com/news/there-are-9-principles-for-digital-development-now-what-87812.

¹⁸ http://digitalprinciples.org/.

PART III

PLANET

CHAPTER 15

Climate Change at Thirty

Eban Goodstein

The first time I heard about global warming was in 1980. I was in university, and there was this thirty-year-old guy with long blond hair and a guitar named Al who, for some reason, would come to our student antinuclear meetings. Al walked in one evening, and his face was ashen. I can still see him, white as a ghost. He said, "The government scientists have proved it. There's this thing called the greenhouse effect and it's heating up the planet, and we're all doomed!"

We looked at each other and shrugged: "Al and his conspiracy theories." In 1980, like 99.99 percent of the world's population, none of us had ever heard of the greenhouse effect or global warming or climate change. We were all climate change skeptics back then. But Al was right. The first US National Academy study confirming a likely global warming of 3°C from business-as-usual CO_2 emissions, the Charney report, had come out a few months earlier.[1]

Eight years later, I was sweating away at my XT desktop in a basement office in Ann Arbor, Michigan, enduring a brutally hot summer, writing a PhD thesis. And NASA's Dr. James Hansen was on the TV, testifying to the US Congress that global warming was here. That year of 1988, more or less, was when climate change was born, bursting into global human consciousness as a full-blown threat to the future of civilization.[2]

The next year, in 1989, Bill McKibben published *The End of Nature*, and in the United States, the message was resonating. A 1990 Gallup poll found—today very hard to believe—that 75 percent of Democrats *and 75 percent of Republicans* agreed that the government was not doing enough to protect the environment.[3] And in 1992, when climate change was just four years old, Republican president George H. W. Bush negotiated and signed the United Nations (UN) Framework Convention on Climate Change (UNFCCC), and the *US Senate voted unanimously* to ratify the treaty.

The days of bipartisan American concern about climate are long gone. And this year, climate change is turning thirty. Long enough for us to take stock of how the phenomenon has affected our physical environment, but also how it has affected our culture. Millennials have no memory of the time before the end of nature, before humans clearly understood that collectively we are heating up the planet. For them, climate change is not controversial.[4] Outside of the millennial demographic, however, in the heavily petro-influenced states of the United States,

Canada, and Australia, political opinion has shifted dramatically. In the United States, for example, the percentage of Republicans who believe that the government is doing too little to protect the environment fell steadily from the previously noted 75 percent in 1990 to only 30 percent today.[5] In these three Western countries, where privately owned fossil-fuel industries are major political players, the entire foundation of science-based policy has come under assault. With this shift in public opinion, and with alternating liberal and conservative governments, each of these countries has experienced dramatic swings in climate policy.

At the same time that a partisan divide over climate change has emerged in some key countries, globally, deep concern over climate change has knit together a surprising international coalition. Dialogue, and eventual agreement, has been reached among indigenous people and multinational corporations, the Global South and the Global North, environmental justice advocates and conservationists, Wall Street bankers and street artists, grassroots activists, and high-level politicians. Ministerial, intergovernmental, and civil society organizations focused on climate have mushroomed, including a truly global grassroots climate organization, 350.org, started by a group of McKibben's former students. And from the seeds of the 1992 UN Framework Convention, after a long hard road, came the 2015 Paris Climate Commitment.

These competing social movements are obviously related. On the one hand, conservative politics in the fossil fuel–producing states has been heavily influenced by oil, gas, and coal money, but also feels genuinely boxed into a corner, where rejecting science is justified to save capitalism from the perceived threat of "eco-socialism." On the other hand, sustainability advocates have organized around a post-socialist, global mission, the urgent decarbonization of the entire world economy. This is our twinned cultural response to climate change at thirty.

In this chapter, I argue that climate change has accelerated and intensified a fossil-led war on environmentalism and science-based policy more broadly, an attack that opened the door to the current ascendancy of a destructive "alternative facts" politics. Concurrently, climate change has also been a sustainability multiplier. Global warming has provided a powerful focus for an emergent global worldview that transcends twentieth-century left/right divisions, focused on the diverse suite of sustainability challenges as represented by the Sustainable Development Goals (SDGs). In this way, climate change has enabled progress on sustainability issues, and perhaps more progress than would otherwise have been the case.

In 2018, a new and major near-term threat to global progress toward sustainable development has emerged: right-wing nationalism. As a political movement—whether in France, the Philippines, Turkey, Egypt, Hungary, or the United States—it is overtly hostile to protection of human rights, an independent press, gender equity, action on climate change, and the environment, and it is also opposed to multilateral international cooperation in principle. But despite this ascendant politics of the moment, the planet continues to heat up. Between 2014 and 2017 alone, the global temperature climbed an astounding quarter of 1°C.[6] As a physical phenomenon that has already begun to reshape human culture, climate change action will provide an increasingly powerful organizing force for an inclusive politics of sustainable development against the xenophobic nationalism that is defining the second half of this decade.

This is not to say, of course, that on balance, climate change is a good thing. We would be much better off with a stable climate and slower progress on the other dimensions of the sustainability agenda. But given the reality of global warming, we need to recognize how the phenomenon itself creates an organizing framework to create a more beautiful, just, and prosperous world for our children and their children.

A World without Climate Change

Consider a thought experiment in which climate change had never been born. A good starting point is the sustainability dialogue as captured in the 1987 UN Brundtland Commission report, *Our Common Future*. Climate change gets a mention, but the focus is on the much broader suite of environment and development questions: poverty, food security, female empowerment, population growth, biodiversity loss and deforestation, health, clean technology transfer, excessive military spending, urbanization, air, water and toxic pollution, and joblessness. This broad agenda has been picked up and carried forward through the UN Millennium Development Goals and SDGs processes. In the SDG version, new concerns have emerged, including failed and failing states (peace, justice, and strong institutions). Not specifically called out, but an urgent issue, is the growing refugee crisis.

The point here is that even in the absence of climate change, meeting the needs of what will soon be ten billion people in a world with limited resources and shaky institutions requires progress on dozens of interrelated fronts. And yet, absent climate change, there is no unifying issue around which a significant political movement for sustainability can be built. This is true, first, because stabilizing the climate, uniquely, requires progress on virtually every one of the other SDGs. For example, climate progress can be substantively advanced through the preservation of standing forests, the empowerment of women in low-income countries, and the creation of millions of new jobs, rewiring the planet. But conversely, protecting forest ecosystems does not (in the medium run) require the rapid global spread of clean energy or greater gender equity. And neither does female empowerment provide a logical priority focus on forest preservation or solar and wind power development. The climate change tent is big and growing because action on climate change yields "cobenefits" for most other SDGs, and conversely, addressing most other SDGs also advances the cause of climate stability.

Climate change also provides a unique focus for a political movement in that global warming poses a serious and increasingly visible and tangible threat to the future of virtually every person's family in every country on the planet. This is only indirectly true of the other broad range of sustainable development challenges. Global warming is now, and will become increasingly, evident as the "asteroid strike" type of event around which common cause can be made. As evidence, consider the two tangible agreements that emerged, post Brundtland, from the Rio Earth Summit: the Biodiversity Agreement and the UNFCCC. The former has led to little progress and notably, even at the high point of US bipartisan concern about environmental issues, was not ratified by the United States.[7] The climate accord, through fits and starts, ultimately delivered a significant global agreement.

Again, this is not to say that assembling a climate change solutions politics that also advances the other SDGs has been, or will be, easy. It was a long and rough twenty-three-year journey from Rio to Paris; Paris itself got us only halfway to the 2°C target, and Trump has already backtracked the United States off of the Paris commitments. However, in many ways, the progress we have made through our imperfect institutions is remarkable. In only thirty years, we have laid the technological, commercial, and political foundations that *could* radically reconfigure the global energy economy. Significant decarbonization by 2050 post Paris is possible, if not probable.[8]

Before exploring the possibilities for progress, however, we need to first consider the political backlash that the fear of a powerful, emergent climate coalition has engendered, in the fossil fuel–producing states in particular. The following section focuses on the US experience, but there are comparable stories in Canada and Australia.

Climate Backlash: The War on Facts

Donald Trump's election in the United States appears to be the ultimate triumph of the fossil fuel–producing state. While Trump's first one hundred days' agenda on most fronts—health care, mass deportation, tax reform—quickly stalled, within weeks, his team dramatically reversed decades of hard-won progress on climate. With the stroke of a pen, the US commitments made in Paris were undone, and along with that, US leadership in the international process. And what a dream team Trump has assembled: the former CEO of ExxonMobil, the former attorney general of Oklahoma, and the former governor of Texas, all parachuting direct from oil country into the heart of the climate policy structure.

This victory was a long time coming. We noted above the remarkable shift in US Republican public opinion on the environment with a high point of bipartisan concern in 1990, and a widening gulf straight through to today. What could have sparked such a dramatic change in thinking? Perhaps increasingly strict environmental regulations have been choking the US economy, causing massive job loss? Well, no. The research is clear that past episodes of major environmental regulation in the United States—which led to dramatic improvements in air and water quality and human health—generated very few plant shutdowns or layoffs.[9] Typically two or three thousand jobs were lost per year over a several-year period, nationwide, when new regulations were implemented. The much-discussed decline in US coal industry jobs has been ongoing for decades, driven primarily by labor-saving technology, and in recent years, cheap natural gas and, to a lesser extent, cheap renewables.[10]

Moreover, outside of the Great Recession, the US economy did well over the 1990–2016 period, including periods of sustained full employment under

Clinton, Bush, and the later Obama years. Of course, trade and technology continued to undermine manufacturing and mining jobs, and have driven a transition throughout the economy to more part-time and transient employment. So life has become harder for many workers without a college education, for whom well-paying service jobs are out of reach. But in terms of raw job creation, the US economy has been second to none. If it was not jobs versus the environment on the ground in Republican suburbs, exurbs, and small towns, then what explains such diverging perspectives?

To understand how climate denialism has now taken over as official US policy, it is necessary to go back to the time before climate change was born, and specifically 1971, the year that the famous "Powell Memo"[11] was drafted. A conservative movement that had been in disarray took Powell's outline and began a disciplined and strategic fight against forty years of liberal ascendancy—against the New Deal, the Civil Rights Movement, the Great Society, and environmental and consumer protection. Attacking perceived excessive regulation and taxation, conservatives had a motivating narrative combining a (fiction) of small government with the protection of "traditional" social values. They also had plenty of billionaires to fund both elections and broader public agenda-shaping through think tanks and media outlets. And they got to work, picking off Republican moderates in the primaries, and reshaping the party around loyalty to a now well-known list of social and economic litmus tests, that have moved further and further to the right.[12]

Given the strong bipartisan political support for environmental protection that had been a hallmark of the 1970s and 1980s, it took a very determined effort to stigmatize "environmentalism." Eventually, the term became caricatured as job-killing, freedom-restricting regulation gone wild, advanced by a cabal of coastal elites, including the "mainstream" media and scientists, the latter group alleged to be in it for the copious grant money provided to further their research. This process of demonization was already underway in the decade before climate change was born, beginning with the Reagan appointments in 1980 of the first anti-environmentalists, James Watt as Secretary of Interior, and Ann Gorsuch (mother of Trump Supreme Court Appointee Neil Gorsuch) to head the Environmental Protection Agency. While neither survived long in government, their ideas were amplified by the rising "movement conservatives." And in 1994, a Republican commitment to rolling back environmental protection became codified permanently as core doctrine in Congressman Newt Gingrich's *Contract with America*.

This was the groundwork laid by a coalition of industry interests, libertarian billionaires, and social conservatives in the United States that, over the ensuing two decades, would lead to the rise and political triumph of climate denialism. In the 1990s, driven by the same concerns of existential threat that had motivated Powell, the fossil-fuel industry turned to the existing anti-environmentalism playbook, and doubled down on one key element: a scientific disinformation campaign. Initially, through a formal industry association, the Global Climate Coalition, and later through "dark money" funding mechanisms, ExxonMobil, the Koch brothers, and others funneled hundreds of millions of dollars to groups casting doubt on the steadily strengthening, and soon overwhelming, scientific consensus that humans were heating up the planet.[13]

To do so, it was no longer sufficient to attack the credibility of individual scientists, as had been done back in the 1960s, for example, with Rachel Carson. Given the weight of evidence, movement conservatives had to wage war on the very legitimacy of peer-reviewed science itself. The "climate skeptics" elevated a postmodern argument, first advanced by leftist intellectuals from the 1960s, that all discourse, including scientific, was fundamentally political and thus suspect. This industry-financed think-tank and public relations work dovetailed with the broader strategy of movement conservatism to tear down the credibility of the "mainstream media" and the university-based scientific establishment. It was enabled, and became self-supporting, by the rise of conservative media through talk radio, cable news, and online media. Climate denialism, pioneered in the 1990s and 2000s, thus paved the way for the far-reaching epistemological assaults of the Trump era. Today, "alternative facts" pronounced by the president achieve validity with a third of the voting population through media echo chambers, while scientifically verifiable facts are dismissed as "fake news."

Despite this effort stretching back to the early 1970s, purging environmental concern from Republican ideology still took time. During the early 2000s, Republican governors in the Northeast and California were still championing climate action. And as late as 2008, the two last men standing in the Republican presidential primary, Mitt Romney and John McCain, had both argued forcefully for a national cap-and-trade system. But following Obama's election, McCain went silent on the issue and Romney changed his position. Climate denialism (or at least agnosticism) became the official party line. In 2016, of the seventeen Republican candidates running for President, only one supported action on climate change.[14] And with this change in ideology and rhetoric, Republican public opinion followed suit. Is there still hope for a conservative renaissance on climate? More on this issue below. Regardless, the rise of a generic "science is politically suspect" perspective among the governing elite of a modern Western political party is remarkable. For today's generation of Republican leaders, climate denialism, or at the least agnosticism, has become a gateway drug they have had to swallow to advance in the party.

Taking the drug was made easier by the fact that, tactically, it supported broader conservative concerns. Beyond the narrow existential interests of the fossil-fuel industry, and in a reprise of the concerns of the 1971 Powell Memo, ideological conservatives were and are also deeply concerned that taking climate change seriously would pose a serious threat to capitalism as a system. Indeed, a number of climate action advocates have argued that if we are really to stabilize the climate at a safe level, then we will need a government-led, "World War II–style mobilization," or that the choice has now become "capitalism versus the climate."[15] This dichotomy poses a difficult challenge for thoughtful conservatives, who argue that, on balance, capitalism has been the greatest engine for reducing human misery and the best guarantor of human liberty ever created. If the choice is really "capitalism or a hotter climate," he or she might take capitalism, thank you. With the stakes perceived to be this high, climate denialism has been adopted by some conservatives more as a convenient tactic to slow climate action, and as a way to avoid a primary challenge from the right, than as a heartfelt commitment.

Regardless, those tactics have had consequences, taking us over the cliff into a world where fact as established by the scientific method is quickly losing authority, and official, easily falsifiable lies gain credence. A war on facts in the fossil fuel–producing states has thus been one key cultural response to climate change. Absent climate change, and given the rise of media bubbles, one would imagine ongoing skirmishes between industry and the academic scientific community around details, as we have seen in the past over tobacco, dioxin, DDT, and genetically modified organisms (GMOs). But it took climate change, both as a specific threat to the fossil-fuel industry and as a perceived generic threat to capitalism as a whole, to generate a politically triumphant attack on the underlying legitimacy of the peer-reviewed scientific process for establishing our basic framework of facts about the natural world.

The Trump ascendancy is likely the ultimate triumph of the fossil-fuel industry in two senses. The first is that oil industry influence has captured the biggest imaginable prize: both the US presidency and Congress, with the potential power to reshape the Supreme Court. But the triumph may also be "ultimate," as in final. In the last few years, the coal industry has collapsed. The oil majors are loaded up with petroleum in the ground that they are not able to drill in the short to medium run with prices low, and will not be able to develop in the long run if we are to preserve a livable planet.[16] As the world continues to heat up, the existential threat that drove the fossil-fuel industry to launch the war on facts twenty-five years ago may indeed materialize. This outcome depends, in part, on the countervailing political power of an international movement for climate action and, indirectly, for the broader sustainability agenda.

Sustainability Politics and Carbon

The war on facts is one side of the cultural climate coin; the reverse is the global climate movement. Given the collapse of US climate policy under Trump, it is a challenging moment for the future of action to slow global warming. So it is worth pausing to evaluate the tremendous momentum that the climate movement has achieved in recent years. Only five years ago, the vision of a decarbonized economy powered by renewable energy and an electric vehicle fleet was just that, a vision. Today, we can actually see the Promised Land. Wind and solar are the fastest-growing energy sources on the planet. On a good day, the biggest industrial power in Europe, Germany, gets 90 percent of its electricity from renewables.

The renewable transition has been dizzying. To lay the foundation to transform a global economy powered by cheap fossil fuels required a tag-team, a forty-five-year push from the United States, Europe, Japan, and most recently, China. Government research and support for nascent industry drove the cost declines that have finally pushed solar and wind, and will soon push electric vehicles and storage, across tipping points into dominant competitive positions in their markets. The revolution will now continue regardless of what the United States does.

Of course, the pace at which it advances, and the places in which it advances most rapidly, will still be affected by regional and national policy. Of great concern is whether US withdrawal from the international climate process, including the climate deal struck in Paris, may cause the whole agreement to unravel. Other nations could walk away from their commitments, and fail to show up in the 2020s with the deeper cuts mandated by Paris. On the other hand, the rest of the world, along with a coalition of US states and cities, may shrug off Trump's disengagement, and continue leading in the policy environment.[17]

In addition, and importantly, even under a president like Hillary Clinton, further US policy pushes on climate were likely to be weak and insufficient. US action beyond Paris will require legislation, and thus a major realignment in support of clean energy and climate policy in American politics. Despite an emerging conservative coalition, including military and business leaders and evangelicals in favor of action on global warming, such a shift in Republican thinking would have been highly unlikely under a polarizing Clinton administration. Trump, by inviting intense backlash, and should his presidency fail, will *perhaps* catalyze a clean energy realignment, bringing some Republicans to support climate action. If so, there is the possibility for an emerging centrist US coalition to support clean energy in the 2020s, in particular, as the pace of warming continues. In sum, despite Trump, it remains too early to declare the Paris targets and the UNFCCC process to be over.

In large part, this is because climate change may have begun life as an environmental concern, but it has grown up to pose a challenge to the stability of human civilization itself. As it has matured, and the threat it imposes has become more apparent, an increasingly diverse group of interests has rallied behind the movement to slow, stop, and eventually reverse global warming. In all cases, the coalition has grown because climate change action also marries well with other central goals of the actors engaged. We can see this by looking at emerging climate leadership from unusual suspects: China, multinational business, and elements of the US Republican coalition.

China

The Copenhagen COP meetings in 2009 marked a critical shift in the Chinese stance in the international negotiating process. Since the signing of the UNFCCC in 1992, China had been a vocal advocate of the G-77 position that climate change action had to be led by the Annex 1 countries. Climate change had been caused by the historical emissions of developed countries, the story went, and low- and middle-income nations could not afford to cut global warming pollution. Of course, the Chinese understood that sea-level rise, loss of freshwater from a disappearing Himalayan snowpack, and projected desertification of much of central China are likely to have devastating impacts on the country, beginning mid-century.[18] But through the 1990s and 2000s, an exclusive focus on growth appeared to tie leadership's hand.

However, in 2009, China joined in the global declaration of a 2°C target, and the country's position began to evolve toward its substantive 2015 Paris commitments: peak coal by 2020 (a goal that has likely already been achieved) and carbon reductions beginning by 2030.[19] And in a move that was unimaginable eight years ago, with the United States now abandoning climate leadership under Trump, China is stepping eagerly into the vacuum with vocal calls for action to slow climate change.

China's evolving climate policy has been widely understood as a response to domestic political pressure arising from the horrendous urban air pollution crisis that the country faces. On the one hand, the Chinese central government has become determined both to pursue clean energy and cut coal use to clean up the air while still expanding electrical generation capacity. So climate action is no longer in conflict with a previous national goal of further electrification and industrial development on the back of coal. With climate commitments no longer perceived as costly, China has been willing to commit to substantive action. On the other hand, by rallying popular support for greenhouse gas reduction, this provides another lever to drive industry to reduce urban air pollution.

Industrial policy options emerging in the mid-2000s and beyond have also been important. China took advantage of Germany's feed-in-tariff policies and Obama's "green stimulus" to ramp up massive exports of solar panels to a booming global industry, soon becoming the number one exporter. More recently, and again, motivated primarily by urban air pollution problems, China has announced its intent to rapidly electrify the domestic vehicle fleet, and in the process, capture global leadership in electrical vehicle technology. Strong international climate action will accelerate the demand for electric vehicles globally, creating another major export market for Chinese industry. These international commercial opportunities have suddenly been made even more attractive as Trump has generously ceded American leadership to China.[20]

The pressing need to cut domestic air pollution; the emergence of renewables as cost-competitive with coal, and electric vehicles as close to cost-competitive with internal combustion engines; and the rise of new clean energy and electric vehicle export markets: all of these factors have moved China from a "climate-is-a-developed-country-problem" position, to embrace a new and surprising role as leader on the international climate stage.

Multinational Business

Climate change has also upended another traditional narrative: "business versus the environment." In the run-up to Trump's Paris decision, the CEOs of more than twenty-five multinational US companies, including General Electric, J. P. Morgan, Apple, Intel, Nike, Disney, Microsoft, PG&E—and even ExxonMobil—publicly called on the president to stay in the international pact.[21] This is quite a shift from the late 1990s, when many big businesses, and not just oil companies, were part of the Global Climate Coalition actively lobbying against climate action.

Given the CEO opposition to Trump's plan, *New York Times* columnist Paul Krugman[22] characterized the Paris pullout as the victory of an extreme anti-regulatory ideology over both economics and common sense. Looked at another way, big business opposition to Trump's actions actually reflects the evolution in the internal ideology of these multinational corporations, and in particular, an at least partial embrace of a sustainable business perspective. This ideological shift stretches back at least to Amory Lovins' 1978 book, *Soft Energy Paths*, in which he argued, pre-climate change, that there was no trade-off between solving energy and environmental problems and earning profits. Rather, both sets of goals could be achieved simultaneously through improved, and often ecologically inspired, design. Lovins, writing with L. Hunter Lovins and Paul Hawken, later expanded these ideas in their 1999 book *Natural Capitalism*.

The work of the two Lovins, Hawken, and others unleashed a quiet revolution in business. The radical redesign which they advocated is now being carried out by an army of professionals, working out of Corporate Sustainability Offices or embedded throughout the functional areas of corporations. The influence of sustainability thinking was showcased by the *Harvard Business Review* (*HBR*) in 2016, when, for the first time, the magazine used "Environmental, Social and Governance" rankings as factors helping determine the leading one hundred CEOs in the world. *HBR* asked the top three CEOs whether Environmental, Social and Governance issues were in fact important to their business strategies. They agreed that, yes, the social and environmental missions of their companies were critical (1) to align their people around common goals, (2) to attract millennial employees, and (3) to engage with their consumers.[23] Of course, some of these pronouncements may be "purpose washing." But significantly, all three CEOs explicitly rejected the official ideology of late-twentieth-century business as established by Milton Friedman,[24] that business should ignore social and environmental issues in order to maximize profits for shareholders. Sustainable business principles argue, by contrast, that firms need to explicitly engage with *material* social and environmental issues precisely to keep earning profits for their shareholders.

Climate change is material to virtually every large corporation. Many CEOs recognize that climate change is a here-and-now risk to global supply chains and retail sales channels, and one that will grow more severe over time. They also face global technology shifts and regulations that are driving a movement toward clean energy that will soon be more affordable and more reliable than fossil fuels. And they know that growing numbers of their customers and employees expect companies to have an authentic commitment to reducing global warming pollution.

This is not to say that most companies are throwing heavy weight behind a climate action agenda. The CEO lobbying of Trump was by far the most visible manifestation to date. The climate action business lobby, BICEP, has only a few large company members, along with a couple of dozen smaller brands. And US industry associations such as the US Chamber of Commerce and the American Legislative Exchange Council remain potent anticlimate lobbying forces.[25] All this said, the ideological shift that has moved thinking beyond "profit versus the environment" to "profit and environment through smart design," combined with the large and growing materiality of climate risk and opportunity, has in turn recruited most international business, in principle at least, to the side of climate action. It seems likely that these companies will continue a shift toward active support of global warming policy, including more defections from the chamber and the American Legislative Exchange Council.

In fossil fuel–dominated political economies where much big business supports climate policy, the remaining opponents of climate action are the fossil-fuel companies supported by anti-regulatory idealogues. These interests are in turn well funded by anti-government billionaires, and their actions are rewarded by polarizing electoral processes that eliminate moderate voices in the primary process. Nevertheless, if changing circumstances have caused China and multinational corporations to flip in support of climate action, are there similar possibilities for elements of the Republican Party in the United States?

Republican Environmentalists

Here, recognize first that Republicans have a long tradition of environmental stewardship that, as we saw, proved quite challenging to dislodge. It seems logical that, for many, those values have gone underground, rather than simply having been eliminated. So the question is, what space will "environmental centrists" occupy in US politics going forward? Centrist leadership is evident in a number of places: among Republican elder statesmen, several of whom recently made a public call for carbon pricing; in the military and intelligence establishments, including US Defense Secretary James Mattis; among red-state politicians who understand the economic development potential of clean energy, and who recently voted to extend US tax credits for renewables; and among some evangelicals motivated by a "creation care" ethic.[26]

The extent to which these voices can coalesce as a centrist political force depends on two things: the degree to which they can self-organize, and the direction the Party takes in response to Trump. In terms of self-organization, this quote taken from the website of RepublicEn, a nonprofit established by former Republican congressman Bob Inglis, himself an evangelical, expresses the opportunity:

> We spoke with thousands of conservatives and free-market advocates . . . and discovered that a robust constituency exists for conservative leadership on clean energy and climate change. We met a lot of conservatives who shared three things in common:
>
> They're energy optimists, confident that market driven innovation can accelerate an energy revolution;
>
> They're climate realists, compelled by the evidence that climate risk requires risk management; and
>
> They are pumped to learn that they are not all alone.[27]

Inglis's group identifies two key elements. First, centrists must claim a narrative that can motivate conservatives: the challenge is not "climate versus capitalism," but rather must be framed as "capitalism solves climate." Second, conservatives have to rebuild institutions in which they can find one another, and where it is once again safe to be a US conservative and support market-based solutions to climate change.

It is important to recognize that while Trump has embraced opposition to climate action, in fact, as we saw above, climate denialism has become the position of the party as a whole. Trump is not the issue here, but it seems likely that a resonant centrist conservative climate position may emerge as part of conservative backlash to Trump's broader political failings. The chief obstacle remains the massive war chest of the Koch brothers' machine that still threatens primary challenges to any conservative who steps out of line. However, there are opportunities at play in the form of an expanded Republican coalition of conservatives in Florida or other climate-impacted southeastern states, plus California and New York; or alternatively, if Trump runs for reelection in 2020, via strategic defection to the Democrats, as in the #NeverTrump movement.[28]

We have looked here at three actors—the leaders of China, of many multinational businesses, and US Republican centrists—all of whom are looking to play a bigger role in a massive and diverse global coalition that has rallied under the banner of climate action. The thesis here is that action on climate change, unique among the seventeen SDGs, has become the *de facto* central organizing principle at the heart of a broader sustainability movement. All climate change action is motivated partially, if not primarily, by the concern of individuals for the welfare of our children and grandchildren. Nevertheless, each group that joins the movement has been able to fold a focus on climate into a narrative that is more immediate—in the cases examined here, attacking urban air pollution, seizing export opportunities, delivering sustainable profits to investors, or reestablishing conservatives' faith in capitalist-driven innovation to solve humanity's environmental challenges. It is this combination of apocalyptic threat plus broad-ranging "cobenefits" that has made climate action the central pole in the big tent of sustainability.

Climate Change at Sixty

In 1988, the same year that climate change was born, my daughter Emma was born as well. They are the same age, and they will grow old together. In 2048, when they both turn sixty, then we will know the future of the earth.

The choices are clear. Post Paris, the world faces three possible climate futures: a heating above preindustrial levels of 2°, 3°, or 4°+. If we can quickly reverse Trump's abandonment of US climate action, and globally recommit to the international community's goal, we get to an increase of just 2°C. If we are able to hang on to Paris but fail to do more, it will be 3°C. And if the international process unravels, we head back to the future anticipating an increase of 4°C or more. By mid-century, we will know down which path we are headed.[29]

Climate policy reversals in the fossil-fuel states have been pushing us toward a more dangerous and unstable world for Emma, her generation, and hundreds of generations to follow. But in 2018, the biggest threat to sustainable development does not lie in the shifting of policy, but rather in the rise of right-wing nationalism and anti-liberal leadership in countries across the globe. This movement appeals to people left behind by globalization, empowered by media echo chambers, and ready to rally behind an ethnic or religious nationalism.

A key pillar of this political movement is an opposition to fact-based policy. And in the fossil fuel–producing states, it was in fact the threat of climate change action that mobilized libertarian billionaires and fossil-fuel interests to fund a movement to discredit the scientific method itself. Twenty-five years of force-feeding fact denialism into political and media institutions in turn set the stage for a political administration in the United States unmoored from basic facts, an administration that has pursued a politics of division unprecedented in living memory.

One half of our cultural response to climate change has been to support a global rise of this kind of authoritarian governance. The other half has been to strengthen a powerful and growing worldwide movement for sustainable development. For the last thirty years, climate change has been at the center of mobilizing that movement, but the goals remain much broader: how to meet the needs of soon-to-be ten billion people in a world where everyone is aspiring to a better quality of life; where we are already fighting over water, and oil, and topsoil, and fish, and forests, and biodiversity; where the oceans are rapidly acidifying; and where it is also getting hotter all the time. Sustainability offers a powerful way to thread the needle, to steer humanity and the creatures of the earth safely through this bottleneck, toward a just and prosperous future.

The rise of a xenophobic nationalism has demonstrated that the ideologies of the twentieth century have run their course. On the one hand, free-market ideology in anything approaching a pure form has also lost whatever mass political appeal it might have had in its Milton Friedman heyday. On the other, the left's utopian vision has also withered. Social democrats and liberals no longer view the state as a savior, but rather as a necessary, imperfect, compromised, and compromising counterbalance against "market failures." For most people, and in spite of the high and rising stakes in all of these areas, politics has become the tedious arena of interest groups. Cynicism and nihilism have replaced idealism among the politically aware, the young in particular.

Conservatives are wrong to level the charge of eco-socialism against sustainability. The way through to a sustainable future will depend largely on the vibrancy of market-driven innovation, guided in key areas by smart policy. But they are right to sense in sustainability a competing and galvanizing political vision, one that has the potential to embrace core tenets of both the socialist left and the libertarian right: communities free of poverty, oppression, and ecological degradation, but also creative communities supportive of entrepreneurship and risk-taking, free of corruption and arbitrary political coercion. The fight to stabilize the climate is central to the growing power of the sustainability narrative.

Humans are hardwired to respond to a narrow tribalistic politics, with insiders pitted against outsiders. The question of the age is if the divisive politics of today will take the world far down a dark and destructive road. The sustainability vision provides a sharp contrast. Sustainability seeks to expand tribal identity, to the whole of humanity alive today and in the future, and to the natural world beyond. Over the next thirty years, our continuing cultural response to climate change will determine which concept of tribe, divisive or inclusive, will define humanity's future.

Notes

[1] National Research Council, *Carbon Dioxide and Climate: A Scientific Assessment Report of an Ad Hoc Study Group on Carbon Dioxide and Climate* (Washington, DC: National Academy of Sciences, 1979).

[2] Of course this is an arbitrary date. In support, Weart sees 1988 as a watershed year. And, for example, the UN's Bruntland Commission Report "Our Common Future," published in 1987 and discussed below, saw climate change as a subset of energy issues, not as a civilizational threat; Spencer Weart, *The Discovery of Global Warming* (Cambridge, MA: Harvard University Press, 2008).

[3] Aaron McCright, C. Xiao, and R. E. Dunlap, "Political Polarization on Support for Environmental Protection in the USA, 1974–2012," *Social Science Research*, 48 (2014): 251–260.

[4] Harvard Institute of Public Opinion, "Millenials on Global Warming," 2015. Accessed June 19, 2017. http://iop.harvard.edu/iop-now/millennials-global-warming.

[5] Justin McCarthy, "About Half in US Say Environmental Protection Falls Short," *Gallup Politics*, April 9, 2015. Accessed July 13, 2017. http://www.gallup.com/poll/182363/half-say-environmental-protection-falls-short.aspx.

[6] NASA GISS, "Global Annual Mean Surface Air Temperature Change (Chart)," 2017. Accessed June 19, 2017. https://data.giss.nasa.gov/gistemp/graphs/.

[7] Eban Goodstein and Stephen Polasky, *Economics and the Environment*, 7th Ed. (New York: John Wiley & Sons).

[8] Frank Jotzo, "Decarbonizing the World Economy," *Solutions* 7, no. 3 (May 2016): 74–83.

[9] Eban Goodstein, *The Trade-off Myth: Fact and Fiction about Jobs and the Environment* (Washington, DC: Island Press, 1999); Hei Sing Chan, Shanjun Li, and Fan Zhang, "Firm Competitiveness and the European Union Emissions Trading Scheme," *Energy Policy* (World Bank, December 2013): 63; Cary Coglianese, Adam Finkel, and Christopher Carrigan (eds.), *Does Regulation Kill Jobs?* (Philadelphia: University of Pennsylvania Press, 2013).

[10] Trevor Houser, Jason Bordoff, and Peter Marsters, *Can Coal Make a Comeback?* (New York: SIPA-Columbia University, 2017).

[11] Lewis Powell, "Confidential Memorandum: Attack on American Free Enterprise System," Washington and Lee University School of Law, 1971, http://law2.wlu.edu/deptimages/Powell%20Archives/PowellMemorandumPrinted.pdf.

[12] This story has been told in many places; see, e.g., Jane Mayer, *Dark Money: The Hidden History of the Billionaires behind the Rise of the Radical Right* (New York: Doubleday, 2016), 72–76.

[13] Ross Gelbspan, *Boiling Point* (New York: Basic Books, 2004); Mayer, *Dark Money*.

[14] The exception was South Carolina senator Lindsey Graham.

[15] Joe Romm, "Democratic Platform Calls for WWII-Scale Mobilization to Solve Climate Crisis," *Think Progress*, July 22, 2016; Naomi Klein, *This Changes Everything: Capitalism Versus the Climate* (New York: Simon & Schuster, 2014).

[16] Tom Sanzillo, *Red Flags on ExxonMobil: Core Financials Show a Company in Decline* (Cleveland: IEEFA, 2016).

[17] Madeline Perkins, "A Group Representing $6.2 Trillion of the US Economy Says They're 'Still in' the Paris Climate Agreement," *Business Insider*, June 5, 2017. Accessed June 23, 2017. http://www.businessinsider.com/we-are-still-in-group-represents-62-trillion-of-the-us-economy-plans-to-stay-in-paris-agreement-2017-6.

[18] Elisa Chih-Yin Lai, *Climate Change Impacts on China's Environment: Biophysical Impacts* (Princeton, NJ: China Environment Forum, Woodrow Wilson Center, 2011).

[19] C2ES, "China's Contribution to the Paris Climate Agreement" (Center for Climate and Energy Solutions, July 2015). Accessed June 19, 2017. https://www.c2es.org/docUploads/chinas-con-tributions-paris-climate-agreement.pdf; Qi Ye, Nicholas Stern, Tong Wu, Jiaqi Lu, and Fergus Green"China's Post-Coal Growth," *Nature Geoscience* 9, no. 8 (July 25, 2016): 564–566.

[20] John Fialka,"Why China Is Dominating the Solar Industry," *Scientific American*, December 19, 2016. Accessed June 23, 2017. https://www.scientificamerican.com/article/why-china-is-dominating-the-solar-industry/.

[21] Jennifer Dlouhy, "Musk Joins CEOs Calling for US to Stay in Paris Climate Deal," *Bloomberg Politics,* May 31, 2017. Accessed June 23, 2017. https://www.bloomberg.com/politics/articles/2017-05-31/musk-leads-ceos-full-court-press-on-paris-as-trump-weighs-exit. ExxonMobil appears to be playing the issue two ways. The company also publicly argues that climate policy will not affect its core business because it is highly unlikely that governments will have the political will to impose significant restraints on fossil fuels; Marianne Levelle, "Exxon Shareholders Approve Climate Resolution," *Inside Climate News*, May 31, 2017. Accessed June 23, 2017. https://insideclimatenews.org/news/31052017/exxon-shareholder-climate-change-disclosure-resolution-approved.

[22] Paul Krugman,"Trump Gratuitously Rejects the Paris Climate Accord," *The New York Times*, June 1, 2017. Accessed June 23, 2017. https://www.nytimes.com/2017/06/01/opinion/trump-gratuitously-rejects-the-paris-climate-accord.html.

[23] HBR, "The Best-Performing CEOs in the World," *Harvard Business Review,* November 2016.

[24] Milton Friedman, "The Social Responsibility of Business Is to Enhance Its Profits," *New York Times* 32, no. 13 (1970): 122–126.

[25] Danny Hakim, "US Chamber Out of Step with Its Board, Report Finds," *New York Times,* June 14, 2016. Accessed on June 23, 2017. https://www.nytimes.com/2016/06/15/business/us-cham-ber-of-commerce-tobacco-climate-change.html.

[26] Fred Rich, *Getting to Green: Saving Nature—A Bipartisan Solution* (New York: W. W. Norton, 2015).

[27] This was the home page text at www.republicen.org in June 2016.

[28] Mark Gunther, "Climate Converts: The Conservatives Who Are Switching Sides on Warming," *Yale Environment 360*, 2017. Accessed June 23, 2017. http://e360.yale.edu/features/climate-converts-the-conservatives-who-are-switching-sides-on-climate-change.

[29] Eban Goodstein and Stephen Polasky, *Economics and the Environment,* 8th Ed. (New York: John Wiley & Sons, 2018), Chapter 22.

CHAPTER 16

Biodiversity-Enhanced Global Agriculture

Harpinder Sandhu, Stephen D. Wratten,
John R. Porter, Robert Costanza, Jules
Pretty, and John P. Reganold

Athough global policies to reduce poverty, ensure food security, and improve environmental protection are in place, a new paradigm shift is required to fast-track sustainable development.[1] This requires a new vision in global efforts and contributions by all sectors of the global economy, including agriculture.[2] The agricultural sector supports 45 percent of the global population as farmers, laborers, and agribusiness organizations and also contributes to the above global goals through the provision of ecosystem goods and ecosystem services (ES) and by improving natural capital.[3] It contributes on average approximately 6 percent to the global gross domestic product (GDP), ranging from only 1 percent in advanced economies to 40 percent in the least developed ones.[4] Agriculture occupies approximately 38 percent of the global land area and houses the largest managed ecosystems on Earth.[5]

One way that agriculture can contribute to the global agenda of sustainable development is mainstreaming ES into current and future farming systems.[6] This will ensure employment for large populations, improve food security, and deliver multifunctional landscapes benefiting not only farm communities, but also society at large. Here, we propose that such a goal comprise sustainable intensification through the development of ES-providing and -enhancing practices as part of modified farming systems.[7] It will require payment mechanisms and market-based instruments to support the adoption of these ES-enhancing protocols.[8] The latter need to be presented to farmers and advisors in a form that facilitates uptake.

Farmland Ecosystem Services and Productivity

ES on farmland need to be enhanced and integrated into global food policy as increasingly dysfunctional biomes and ecosystems appear. Moreover, agriculture, which largely created these problems, has become more intensive in terms of its use of nonrenewable resources, driven by consumption patterns of a world population likely to reach nine billion people by 2050.[9] With growing population demands, biodiversity-enhanced ES in global agriculture is urgent.

In this chapter, we show how simple agroecological approaches can be used to demonstrate that ES can benefit modern farming and be adopted to improve productivity. These involve agroecological experiments to measure ecosystem functions, combined with value transfer techniques to calculate their economic value. These studies demonstrate that some current farming practices have much higher ES values than suggested in previous work.[10] For example, recent data show that the combined value of only two ES—nitrogen mineralization and biological control of a single pest by one guild of invertebrate predators—can have values of $197, $271, and $301 per hectare per year in terms of avoided costs for conventional,[11] organic,[12] and integrated (e.g., combined food and energy [CFE] production) arable farming systems,[13] respectively. Conventional farming systems depend on high rates of synthetic inputs, such as pesticides and fertilizers, to control pests and maintain soil fertility, along with improved seeds, heavy machinery, and irrigation, to produce maximum outputs per hectare.[14] Organic agriculture is a production system that virtually excludes synthetic fertilizers and pesticides. It emphasizes on building up the soil with composts and green manures, and managing pests using natural pest control and crop rotations.[15] The CFE system is a production system which is a net energy producer and is managed organically.[16] It produces more energy in the form of renewable biomass than consumed in the planting, growing, and harvesting of food and fodder. The bioenergy component is represented by belts of fast-growing trees (willows, alder, and hazel) that are planted orthogonally to fields that contain cereal and pasture crops. The total value of these two ES to global agriculture, if used on only 10 percent of total area, exceeds the combined cost of pesticides and fertilizers.[17] The above values comprise reduced variable costs (labor, fuel, and pesticides) and lower external costs to human health and the environment. Although paying for these variable costs does contribute to GDP, it is a poor indicator of sustainability and of human well-being.[18] Instead, the expenditure on cleaning up those externalities should be subtracted from the GDP.

We think that a better understanding of ecological processes and their economic contribution in agroecosystems can help develop protocols that do not require major farming system changes but enhance ES by returning selective functional agricultural biodiversity to agriculture.[19] Functional agricultural biodiversity is defined as the biodiversity in and around agricultural landscapes that enhances ES and thereby benefits food production. In addition, it can facilitate sustainable intensification and have positive spinoffs for the society.[20] For example, nutrient cycling, including the role of leguminous crops in nitrogen fixation, is a well-known enhancement of farmland ES and can have a value of $1,200 per hectare per year.[21] More recent ES improvements are illustrated by agroecological research on biological control of insect pests. In New Zealand and Australia, strips of flowering buckwheat *Fagopyrum esculentum* (Moench) between vine rows provide nectar and other nutrients in an otherwise virtual monoculture, and thereby improve the ecological fitness and efficacy of parasitoid wasps that attack grape-feeding caterpillars (see textbox 16.1). This in turn leads to the pest population being brought below the economic threshold. An investment of $3 per hectare per year in buckwheat seed and minimal sowing costs have been shown to lead to savings in variable costs of $200 per hectare per year and fewer pesticide residues[22] and can aid the conservation of endemic butterfly species.[23] Such protocols have

Box 16.1 Vineyards and Flowering Buckwheat

Vineyard management practices, such as growing strips of flowering buckwheat between vine rows, decrease the mean number of leafroller (*Epiphyas postvittana*) caterpillars in grape bunches in New Zealand. These practices help to keep the caterpillars below the economic threshold for managing them with pesticides. The strips of flowering buckwheat provide nectar for parasitoid wasps that attack grape-feeding caterpillars, which in turn leads to the pest population being brought below the economic threshold. A service-providing unit (SPU; see text) has been developed for easy uptake of this protocol.

been taken up by grape growers in New Zealand, as in the above case.[24] However, for rapid adoption and uptake, further research is required to understand the full costs and benefits of such protocols for different farming systems.[25]

There are other examples of protocols not requiring a major farming system change. With biological control of weeds in Australia, returns on investment of up to 300:1 have been achieved following the introduction of appropriately selective biodiversity in the form of insects for weed biological control.[26] In Africa, the development of "push-pull" ecotechnologies, whereby plant and insect chemistry is used to deter pests ("push") and attract pests' natural enemies ("pull"), has improved yields to such an extent that milk production has increased and benefits have been community-wide.[27] Fungicide use in vines can also be avoided if such ecotechnologies are deployed. The life cycle of botrytis (*Botrytis cinerea*) disease on grapes can be disrupted by the appropriate use of mulches below vines. The resulting enhanced ES in this case can save $570 per hectare per year in fungicide and associated costs.[28]

Scalability of Future Farming

Although the ecotechnologies now exist to improve farming sustainability when the negative consequences of a continued reliance of oil-based inputs are well recognized,[29] farmers are commonly risk-averse.[30] In industrialized countries, they have tended to reject the notion that noncrop biodiversity on their land can improve production and/or minimize costs. However, farmers in many developing countries tend to agree and utilize this farm biodiversity.[31] The challenge now for agroecologists and policymakers is to use a range of market-based instruments or incentives, government interventions, and enhanced social learning among growers to accelerate the deployment of sound, biodiversity-based ES enhancement protocols for farmers.[32] These protocols need to be framed in the form of service-providing units,[33] which precisely explain the necessary ES enhancement procedures and should ideally include cost–benefit analyses. Such a requirement invites the design of new systems of primary production that are species-diverse, have low inputs, and provide a diverse suite of ES, including a positive net carbon sequestration.

A comparison of the economic values of ES associated with farming in organic, conventional, and a CFE system indicate that well-designed agricultural systems have the potential to produce multiple ES in addition to food and fodder (see figure 16.1).[34] Any potential loss in farm income under these systems can be compensated with sound market mechanisms, such as payment for ecosystem services (PES) schemes and tax deductions.[35] In this approach, those who benefit from the provision of ES make payments to those who supply them, thereby maintaining ES. Examples of informal functioning PES schemes in different areas of the world are summarized in table 16.1.

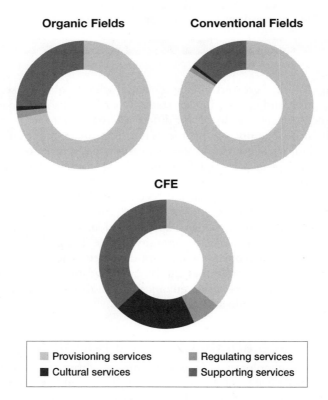

Figure 16.1   Combined Food and Energy (CFE) Systems

Note: Proportion of four different categories of ecosystem services provided by organic fields, conventional fields, and combined food and energy (CFE) systems. Food and fodder production is included in provisioning services. Organic and conventional fields produce comparable provisioning services at the expense of regulating services and cultural services. However, CFE systems are able to balance food production and bioenergy production with minimizing impacts on regulating services and cultural services. Supporting services, such as nutrient cycling, pollination, and biological control of insect pests, which are necessary for the production of provisioning services, are also higher in CFE systems.

Source: H. S. Sandhu, S. D. Wratten, R. Cullen, and B. Case, "The Future of Farming: The Value of Ecosystem Services in Conventional and Organic Arable Land. An Experimental Approach," *Ecological Economics* 64 (2008): 835–848; J. Porter, R. Costanza, H. Sandhu, L. Sigsgaard, and S. Wratten, "The Value of Producing Food, Energy and Ecosystem Services within an Agro-Ecosystem," *Ambio* 38 (2009): 186–193.

TABLE 16.1 Summary of Key "Payment for Ecosystem Services" (PES) Schemes Associated with Agroecosystems

PES Scheme	Location	Ecosystem Services Provided
National PES Program[a]	Costa Rica	Functioning watersheds, carbon sequestration, aesthetics in the form of landscape attractiveness
Rewarding the Upland Poor for the Environmental Services (RUPES)[b]	The Philippines, Indonesia, and Nepal	Functioning watersheds
The Chinese Sloping Lands Conversion Program (SLCP)[c]	Yangtze and Yellow Rivers regions, China	Reduced flood risk
Madhya Pradesh Lake Conservation Authority[d]	India	Water quality improvement, organic agriculture support
Pro-Poor Rewards for Environmental Services in Africa (PRESA)[e]	Kenya and Tanzania	Watershed function, carbon capture, water quality improvement
Agri-Environmental Measures[f]	European Union	Environmentally favorable extensions of farming, management of low-intensity pasture systems, integrated farm management and organic agriculture, preservation of landscape and historical features, conservation of high-value habitats and their associated biodiversity, beetle banks
The US Conservation Reserve Program[g]	USA	Soil erosion reduction, water quality improvement, and wildlife habitat enhancement
CFEES (see note 16)	Denmark	Biological control of pests, nitrogen regulation, soil formation, carbon accumulation, hydrological flow, pollination, aesthetics

[a] Costa Rica–National Payment for Environmental Services (PES) programme. International Institute for Environment and Development [online] (2012). http://www.watershedmarkets.org/casestudies/Costa_Rica_National_PES_eng.html.
[b] Rewarding poor rural people for nurturing the land. Rural Poverty Portal, International Fund for Agricultural Development [online] (2012). http://www.ruralpovertyportal.org/country/voice/tags/china/rupes.
[c] China–Sloping Lands Conversion Programme (SLCP). International Institute for Environment and Development [online] (2012). http://www.watershedmarkets.org/casestudies/China_SLCP_eng.html.
[d] Environmental Planning and Coordination Organization (EPCO) [online] http://www.epco.in/.
[e] Pro-poor Rewards for Environmental Services in Africa 2008–2011. PRESA [online] (2011). http://www.fidafrique.net/IMG/pdf/PRESA_2011.pdf.
[f] Agri-environment measures. European Commission [online] (2015). http://ec.europa.eu/agriculture/envir/measures/index_en.htm.
[g] Conservation Reserve Program. United States Department of Agriculture Farm Service Agency [online] (2016). https://www.fsa.usda.gov/programs-and-services/conservation-programs/index.

In these schemes, those who benefit from the provision of ES, such as consumers, make payments to those who supply the services, such as farmers, to improve the environment and human well-being. Such PES schemes not only help in doing so but also ensure food security and long-term farm sustainability.

The current focus of these schemes is on water, carbon, and biodiversity in addressing environmental problems through positive incentives to land managers.[36] Such schemes not only help to improve the environment and human well-being but also ensure food security and long-term farm sustainability.[37] For example, beetle banks on arable land in the European Union deliver vertebrate conservation ES, which builds on the original pest-management intention of these banks.[38]

The Way Forward

The extensive Millennium Ecosystem Assessment of global ecosystems provided a framework for analyzing socioecological processes and suggested that agriculture may be the "largest threat to biodiversity and ecosystem function of any single human activity."[39] The Millennium Ecosystem Assessment raised awareness of ecosystems and their services, but the global environment continues to degrade because of a lack of any coherent plan of action. Recently, the United Nations (UN) established the Intergovernmental Science-Policy Platform on Biodiversity and Ecosystem Services to translate ecosystem science into action and to track the drivers and consequences of ecosystem change worldwide.[40] This action plan is focused on strengthening assessment, relevant policy, and associated science at spatial and temporal scales.

Furthermore, the UN Sustainable Development Goals (SDGs) aim to increase food production and to achieve food security and poverty alleviation by 2030, among other development goals.[41] However, growing sufficient and nutritious food for nine billion plus people worldwide by 2050 will need greater coherence in global efforts, partnerships with developed and developing countries, and careful planning and implementation of the required programs with science and policy collaboration. It also requires assessment and valuation of ES in agriculture to understand interdependencies and trade-offs between production and the environment, as advocated by the Economics of Ecosystems and Biodiversity for Agriculture and Food, a project of the UN Environment Program.[42]

Achievement of human well-being as agreed by the SDGs is not possible without clear pathways for the design of future agroecosystems and new agricultural policies. Efforts to intensify agriculture since the 1960s partly succeeded due to technology transfer to farmers and support of and financial investments in agricultural research, extension networks, and governments at regional and national levels.

Here, we provide some recommendations to the agricultural science, farming, and policy communities that might be useful in shaping global agricultural goals by utilizing biodiversity and ES to increase productivity, protect the environment, and contribute to human well-being:

- Global agriculture needs to embrace and implement the value of biodiversity and ES into farming. This requires designing farming systems that can use ES through sustainable intensification, reduce or eliminate fossil fuel–based inputs to increase productivity, and enhance efficiencies of other inputs, such as water and nutrients. Agroecology has the potential to enhance productivity and farm sustainability through the adoption of ES.
- Agricultural research should focus more on developing and refining agroecological techniques to enhance farmland ES, such as natural pest control, managing habitat for wild pollinators, increasing soil organic matter, and improving nutrient cycling, so that they can be integrated into the current farming systems. These techniques can also help improve vital natural capital in agriculture.
- Social capital in agriculture that includes contributions from farmers and farming families should be acknowledged and rewarded by recognizing their value in achieving the SDGs. This can help future-proof farming and the livelihoods of millions of farmers.
- The livelihood of farming communities should be protected by agricultural policy while developing long-term strategies for sustainable intensification.
- Country-level and global studies are required to estimate the value of all environmental benefits and costs of current and alternative agricultural systems. This economic valuation will provide policymakers with a tool that can guide policy development to incentivize ES-enhancing agricultural practices and to penalize detrimental practices.

Current agricultural systems can be diverted toward sustainable intensification by governments developing and adopting appropriate policy responses at regional and national levels, matched by financial investments. Various UN efforts to tackle climate change and protect biodiversity and ES should focus on the agriculture sector for positive spin-offs for the environment, economy, and society.[43]

Notes

[1] This chapter is based on an article, "Mainstreaming Ecosystem Services into Future Farming," by Harpinder Sandhu, Stephen D. Wratten, John R. Porter, Robert Costanza, Jules Pretty, and John P. Reganold, *Solutions Journal* 7, no. 2 (March 2016): 40–47.United Nations, The Future We Want. United Nations Conference on Sustainable Development [online] (2012). http://www.un.org/en/sustainablefuture/.

[2] O. D. Schutter, *Right to Food*. Report submitted by the special rapporteur, United Nations, New York [online] (2010). http://www2.ohchr.org/english/issues/food/docs/A-HRC-16-49.pdf.

[3] S. Wratten, H. Sandhu, R. Cullen, and R. Costanza (eds.), *Ecosystem Services in Agricultural and Urban Landscapes* (Oxford: Wiley-Blackwell, 2013); E. P. Fenichel et al., "Measuring the Value of Groundwater and Other Forms of Natural Capital," *Proceedings of the National Academy of Sciences* 113 (2016): 2382–2387.

[4] World Bank, "Agriculture, value added (% of GDP)" [online] (2015). http://data.worldbank.org.

[5] Food and Agriculture Organization of the United Nations, FAOSTAT online database [online] (2016). http://faostat.fao.org/site/377/default.aspx#ancor.

[6] H. S. Sandhu, S. D. Wratten, R. Cullen, and B. Case. "The Future of Farming: The Value of Ecosystem Services in Conventional and Organic Arable Land. An Experimental Approach," *Ecological Economics* 64 (2008): 835–848; H. Sandhu et al., "Significance and Value of Non-Traded Ecosystem Services on Farmland," *PeerJ* 3 (2015): e762.

7 J. Pretty, C. Toulmin, and S. Williams, "Sustainable Intensification in African Agriculture," *International Journal of Agricultural Sustainability* 9 (2011): 5–24; J. Pretty and Z. P. Bharucha, "Sustainable Intensification in Agricultural Systems," *Annals of Botany* 114 (2014): 1571–1596.

8 G. W. Luck, G. C. Daily, and P. R. Ehrlich, "Population Diversity and Ecosystem Services," *Trends in Ecology and Evolution* 18 (2003): 331.

9 J. A. Foley et al., "Global Consequences of Land Use," *Science* 309 (2005): 570–574.

10 R. Costanza et al., "The Value of the World's Ecosystem Services and Natural Capital," *Nature* 387 (1997): 253–260.

11 Sandhu et al., "The Future of Farming," 835–848.

12 N. Lampkin, *Organic Farming* (Ipswich, UK: Farming Press, 1991).

13 J. Porter, R. Costanza, H. Sandhu, L. Sigsgaard, and S. Wratten, "The Value of Producing Food, Energy and Ecosystem Services within an Agro-Ecosystem," *Ambio* 38 (2009): 186–193.

14 Sandhu et al., "Non-Traded Ecosystem Services," e762.

15 Ibid.

16 Porter et al., "The Value of Producing Food," 186–193.

17 Sandhu et al., "Non-Traded Ecosystem Services," e762.

18 I. Kubiszewski et al., "Beyond GDP: Measuring and Achieving Global Genuine Progress," *Ecological Economics* 93 (2013): 57–68.

19 G. M. Gurr, S. D. Wratten, and M. A. Altieri (eds.), *Ecological Engineering for Pest Management: Habitat Manipulation for Arthropods* (Australia: CSIRO, 2004).

20 Pretty, Toulmin, and Williams, "Sustainable Intensification," 5–24; Pretty and Bharucha, "Sustainable Intensification," 1571–1596.

21 H. Sandhu, V. V. S. R. Gupta, and S. Wratten, Ch. 11 in *Soil Microbiology & Sustainable Crop Production*, G. R. Dixon and E. Tilston, eds. (Dordrecht: Springer, 2010); D. F. Herridge, M. B. Peoples, and R. M. Boddey, "Global Inputs of Biological Nitrogen Fixation in Agricultural Systems," *Plant Soil* 311 (2008): 1–18.

22 The Bio-Protection Research Centre, Sustainable bioprotection [online] (2009). www.bioprotection.org.nz.

23 M. Gillespie, S. D. Wratten, R. Cruickshank, B. H. Wiseman, and G. W. Gibbs, "Incongruence between Morphological and Molecular Markers in the Butterfly Genus Zizina (Lepidoptera: Lycaenidae) in New Zealand," *Systematic Entomology* 38 (2013): 151–163.

24 The Bio-Protection Research Centre, Sustainable bioprotection [online] (2009). www.bioprotection.org.nz.

25 Sandhu et al., "Non-Traded Ecosystem Services," e762; Pretty, Toulmin, and Williams, "Sustainable Intensification," 5–24; Pretty and Bharucha, "Sustainable Intensification," 1571–1596.

26 Economic impact assessment of Australian weed biological control [online] (2009). http://www.weeds.crc.org.au/index_noflash.html.

27 International Association for the Plant Protection Sciences, "ICIPE Develops Safe New Methods for Controlling Stem Borers, Termites and Striga," *Crop Protection* 20 (2001): 269–272.

28 M. A. Jacometti, S. D. Wratten, and M. Walter, "Understorey Management Increases Grape Quality, Yield and Resistance to *Botrytis cinerea*," *Agriculture Ecosystems & Environment* 122 (2007): 349–356.

29 Gurr, Wratten, and Altieri (eds.), *Habitat Manipulation for Arthropods*; Food and Agriculture Organization, *The State of Food and Agriculture: Paying Farmers for Environmental Services* (Rome: FAO, 2007).

30 K. D. Warner, "Extending Agroecology: Grower Participation in Partnerships Is Key to Social Learning," *Renewable Agriculture and Food Systems* 21 (2006): 84–94.

31 Pretty, Toulmin, and Williams, "Sustainable Intensification," 5–24.

32 Warner, "Extending Agroecology," 84–94.

33 Luck, Daily, and Ehrlich, "Population Diversity and Ecosystem," 331.

34 Sandhu et al., "The Future of Farming," 835–848; Porter et al., "The Value of Producing Food," 186–193.

35 International Association for the Plant Protection Sciences, "ICIPE develops safe new methods for controlling stem borers, termites and striga," *Crop Protection* 20 (2001): 269–72.

36 Food and Agriculture Organization, *The State of Food and Agriculture*.

[37] Schutter, *Right to Food*.

[38] A. MacLeod, S. D. Wratten, N. W. Sotherton, and M. B. Thomas, "'Beetle Banks' as Refuges for Beneficial Arthropods in Farmland: Long-Term Changes in Predator Communities and Habitat" *Agricultural and Forest Entomology* 6 (2004): 147–154.

[39] Millennium Ecosystem Assessment, *Millennium Ecosystem Assessment Synthesis Report* (Washington, DC: Island Press, 2005).

[40] Intergovernmental Platform for Biodiversity and Ecosystem Services (IPBES), United Nations [online] (2010). http://www.ipbes.net/.

[41] Sustainable Development Goals, United Nations [online] (2015). https://sustainabledevelopment.un.org.

[42] *TEEB for Agriculture & Food: An Interim Report*, United Nations Environment Programme [online] (2015). www.teebweb.org/agriculture-and-food/interim-report/.

[43] UN Framework on Climate Change (UNFCCC), Conference of the Parties 21, Paris [online] (2015). http://www.cop21paris.org/.

CHAPTER 17

Cities and the New Global Agenda
Implementation Strategies and Priorities
Michael A. Cohen and Lena Simet

The Global Context

In the almost two years since the approval of the Sustainable Development Goals (SDGs) by the United Nations (UN) General Assembly in September 2015, and almost a year since the signing of the New Urban Agenda (NUA) at the Habitat III Conference in Quito in October 2016, there has been little public discussion, much less debate, about the complex relationships between the individual SDGs and their achievement. While more than two million people participated in discussions leading to the approval of the SDGs, it is clear that the vast majority of discussion focused on the "what" and relatively little attention addressed the "how."

Addressing the "how" first requires an understanding of the new global context, not only its changed political settings, ecological transformations, and new climate patterns, but also its demographic and cultural shifts. This new context comes with a set of opportunities, but also many challenges. Economic downturns, extreme weather events and a changing climate, old and new wars, a refugee crisis, expressions of political polarization and populism, and even new waves of xenophobia and nationalism are just some of these challenges.

This chapter focuses on the role of cities in implementing and monitoring the "New Global Agenda." Cities, now the dominant form of human settlement, exemplify and display many of the fundamental concerns and challenges of our times. Focusing on cities in the implementation of the global agenda is therefore necessary for multiple reasons. First, the last two centuries have been marked by a move to urban areas, where now more than half of the world's population lives. UN-Habitat in 2009 and the International Organization for Migration in 2015 estimate that around three million people are joining the global urban population every week, that is, more than four hundred thousand people by the day.[1] To accommodate for this rapid urban growth, each year, the equivalent of two cities the size of Tokyo are built.[2] Second, cities are the drivers of national economic growth. In the Organisation for Economic Co-operation and Development (OECD) countries,[3] cities have contributed 60 percent of total employment creation in the past fifteen years.[4] However, this growth is often not distributed in an equitable fashion, leading to intra-urban inequality and social exclusion. Using the words of Mike Davis, we are moving toward a "planet of slums," where slums are becoming the blueprint of urban development.[5] Rapid urbanization is leading to infrastructure stresses, and the construction of new cities has a huge impact on our ecological footprint, making it hard to believe that we won't pass the 2°C target in global warming.[6]

Local authorities have an important role to play in tackling these challenges and can serve as the engines of inclusive and sustainable growth. In OECD countries, 40 percent of total public spending, and 60 percent of total public investment, is carried out by local governments.[7] More broadly, the 2030 Agenda has a substantial and important urban dimension, where twelve of the seventeen SDGs require involvement of local urban stakeholders to ensure their achievement.

Habitat III was perceived as the first implementation conference of the 2030 Agenda, with the NUA envisioned to represent a global plan of action, comparable to a toolbox of activities, policies, and practices guiding local, national, and subnational governments on responding to question of the "how": how to translate the 2030 Agenda into actions on the ground, tackling the new global context and its challenges.

Unfortunately, the NUA that was signed in 2016 could hardly be seen as an action plan. Its lack of metrics, priorities, and an institutionalized review system feel more like a déjà vu of the "old" Habitat Agenda of 1996 and its shortcomings with respect to monitoring and reporting.

Interestingly, the first of this new set of Global Agendas, the 2015 COP21 Paris Agreement, tackled the "how" since its inception. It did so by integrating milestones, targets, and thresholds, and by providing concrete implementation advice. The concreteness of the Paris Agreement is important for two reasons: (1) it allows for proper monitoring of the achievements, which creates accountability, and (2) it created peer pressure among global governments to meet targets, which contributed to public shaming of the US administration at the July 2017 G20 meetings in Hamburg for being the only nation to not comply with the Paris Accord.

Recent debates about how to monitor progress toward the achievement of the SDGs have not opened up the Pandora's box of questions about how individual goals are related to each other or, given their interdependence, what might be the most effective implementation strategies for countries, cities, and neighborhoods. Acknowledging this complexity might not be comfortable or politically correct, but it is nonetheless an essential part of the process of implementation. Simply put, if we do not know how complicated it is to achieve our goals, it is unlikely that we will succeed.

This chapter addresses the issue of the complexity of cities and examines the origins of inequality and social exclusion as a first step toward more deeply understanding how intra-urban inequality might be reduced within the framework of the emerging global agenda. We start from the notion that urban areas have grown not just through economies of scale and what are called "economies of agglomeration," but also through the generation of differences in economic activities, cultures, neighborhoods, architectures, and ecologies. As noted in a sixteenth-century German saying, "urban air makes man free,"[8] free from feudal structures, free to produce new goods and services, free to express nonconformist ideas and political perspectives, sing new songs, and wear new and different clothing.

Such emerging differences are at the core of creating new markets and social contracts, with new forms of supply and demand as well as providers and consumers. The economic surplus required to be different does not just come from urban areas themselves but also through their relationships with the rural countryside and their broader regional contexts. Rural production allows rural consumption of urban goods and services, which in turn permits urban consumption of rural products and commodities. The rural and the urban depend upon one another.

Over time, these different economic activities started generating varying levels of remuneration and income, affecting the stratification of the population by income that also allows the purchase and consumption of urban assets such as housing and land. The productive side of the city determines who earns how much and, over time, the level of income differences within a particular urban area.[9] Cash income becomes an essential determinant of the education and health status of urban residents. These determinants are also expressed in the accumulation of private wealth and, as well illustrated in the work of Thomas Piketty, a tendency for wealth inequality to increase.[10] Growing differences in private wealth are increasingly reflected in the choices of the rich for private schools, health care, security, transport, and many other "nonpublic" solutions.

Other factors such as gender, race, class, religion, caste, and culture also contribute to the well-being or poverty of urban residents, frequently in determining ways. These factors affect not only income but also wealth and access to the services mentioned above. Economic and social factors work together to harden the differences found in urban areas.

If the city was initially a space of opportunity, it soon also became the locus of growing poverty and inequality. This paradox is in part a result of rapid urban demographic growth and rural–urban migration, but it also is a consequence of myriad individual and group preferences, the economic structure of production, and lacking social protection and redistributive mechanisms that result in entrenched differences over time. If some urban residents are able to generate considerable income and wealth—and thus access to key services such as education and health—others have very little, generating patterns of difference and, ultimately, diverse forms of social exclusion.

Social patterns materialize in space and location. If the rich are able to exercise influence in local systems of governance, they are able to obtain needed infrastructure investments, security, social services, and other conditions of quality of life with connectivity to the wider urban area and to the world itself.

Communities lacking infrastructure suffer cumulative disadvantages, including the social stigmas of "being poor" and living in "bad neighborhoods." This suggests that individual's opportunities and freedom to choose are significantly conditioned by social class, and not by one's understanding of creativity and mental framework, as writers such as Richard Florida suggest.[11]

This narrative is not definitive in any sense, but it does suggest historical and contemporary processes that give rise to differences of many kinds and to cumulative disadvantages affecting various categories of urban residents. It also raises the question of what are the most effective entry points if one's objective is to reduce intra-urban inequality? The SDGs imply that everything—improving maternal and child health, education, water supply, sanitation, housing, access to employment, environmental quality, cultural freedom, and much more—has to be addressed and significantly improved by 2030. If the objectives are all worthy, how can they be achieved?

From Differences to Asymmetries and Linkages

The strong emergence of the framework of human rights, particularly economic and social rights, has asserted the importance of individuals in the context of the SDGs.[12] Individuals have "rights" to services such as health, education, and water supply. Deprivation is largely understood as individual deprivation, although there is a parallel discourse about "underserved communities." Reducing intra-urban inequality in the SDG framework thus becomes reducing differences between individuals and households, and less about differences between neighborhoods or communities.

This approach, however, ignores recent findings by Milanovic and others that, since the early 2000s, global inequality (differences between individuals and households) has started to decline, while intranational, and also intra-urban, inequalities have become the drivers of inequality.[13] It also ignores the contexts of inequality, contexts in which communities exist and, notably, their linkages to wider urban economies, ecologies, cultures, and systems of governance. And finally, it ignores the collective foundation of the city. Instead of debating and acting upon the complexities of urban life in a concerted, collective way, we often go back to singular technical solutions, deferring the consequences of comprehensive politics. As evidenced in the contextualization of today's challenges, individual and singular works are not enough, and collective engagement is becoming more important than ever.

At the city scale, there are asymmetric ways in which individual communities relate to these wider systems. For example, a slum might be located in the center of the city and its location reflects the preferences of its residents to be close to employment, transport, and education for their children. Another slum might be on the periphery of the city, far from all of those opportunities desired by its residents who cannot afford the costs of urban transport. A similarly distant location might be the site of a middle- and urban-class neighborhood, but its residents can afford transport to allow access to these opportunities. The poor cannot. People's relationships to the opportunities of the city are asymmetrical. They are also reified by binary categories such as formal/ informal, legal/illegal, or inside/outside the jurisdiction, and often appear in public policy debates and research reports. These asymmetries are integrated into our language of description and understanding.

This suggests that inequality may not just be about differences in the components of real income and capital, but also asymmetries in a wider contextual and social sense, such as in the differential access to spaces, opportunities, resources, and information.[14] These asymmetries can also take specific material forms such as in the linkages between a community and the city as a whole, for example, in whether a bus line services the community. These linkages are inherently integrative in the sense that they help to integrate communities, households, and individuals to wider contexts, thereby overcoming social exclusion. An example at the regional level might be the existence of transport infrastructure required to connect a poor and underdeveloped region, such as the state of Bihar in northern India, to the Indian economy and thus allow the sale of agricultural goods produced in the state.[15]

An implication of these observations is that interventions in one space, without linkages to the wider economic, social, cultural, and ecological context, can be another example of urban practice that results in social exclusion. The decision, for example, not to build a primary school in a slum in order to ensure that children go to another neighborhood each day is a way to encourage integration and overcome social exclusion.

Toward a Strategy of Implementation

The above suggests that a strategy to achieve the SDGs that acknowledges these asymmetries would be one that did not focus exclusively on one service, say health, but also linked health with water and sanitation; or that education should be linked to transport. SDG Goal 10 on "reducing inequalities" illustrates this interdependence particularly well. Inequalities cannot be reduced by simply providing a school in a low-income neighborhood, but requires careful linking with all other goals to achieve long-term change. The defining characteristic of this approach would be linkage and integration rather than individual service delivery. In the words of Jaime Lerner, former Mayor of Curitiba in Brazil, "[W]e do not have time for one solution at a time."

This proposed approach might be regarded as impractical and too complicated in operational terms. Yet when we consider the results of "single-sector" interventions, we can see that the framing of solutions has often been too narrow. For example, low-cost sanitation solutions were proposed during the UN Drinking Water and Sanitation Decade of the 1990s, but these approaches failed to take into account the likelihood that they would result in polluted aquifers. Housing solutions far from employment and other essential services have been abandoned in many countries such as Mexico, where there are five million empty housing units, or in China, where there are sixty-two million empty apartments.[16] People have voted with their feet when they are faced with impractical solutions and when these solutions prove to be unaffordable; witness the distant location of housing estates in South Africa, where the poor are expected to travel two hours each way to work. The objective is not to produce "more," the objective should be to produce "better," more integrated, and sustainable solutions.

This suggests that multisector, integrated interventions are necessary to generate better quality-of-life outcomes for people. This approach requires a bundling of improvements and sector coordination across both public and private institutions. No participatory process ever concluded that the people wanted water and nothing else. This requires more professional communication and collaboration across sectors, institutions, and professions. In cities, it requires new ways of working, and a "new urban practice."

When speaking about "urban practice," we refer to policies, programs, and projects, both public and private, that have individual and collective consequences, for example, the organization of institutional structures, characteristics of officials and staff in urban institutions, availability and asymmetry of information, the formal–informal/planned–unplanned continuum, or types of knowledge that are included in or excluded from complex decision-making processes. Assuming that cities have a great stake in the implementation of the New Global Agenda, current urban practices will require extensive review, research, and revision in order to function in a more inclusive and collective fashion.

An example of urban practice that exacerbated social and productive exclusion is the geographic distribution of public investments in Buenos Aires, Argentina. A study by Cohen and Debowicz finds that individuals living in wealthier parts of the city enjoy a much greater quality of life than those living in low-income neighborhoods.[17] "These golden 11.5% of the population received 68% of public investment in infrastructure . . . In contrast, the bottom 67% of the population in the Far West and the South-Belt received 25.3% of the public investment in infrastructure . . . ."[18]

Two important conclusions can be drawn from this study. First, place, at the most local level, matters, determining social mobility to a great extent. Second, welfare and quality of life depend not only on macroeconomic factors and demand for labor but also on local policy choices and public urban investment. As the latter point reinforces the former, physical manifestations of these policies and investments shape a landscape of inequality that affects the mobility of future generations, which in turn is likely to negatively affect national economic growth.

Recent changes in income inequality in Latin America also suggest that we need to understand more about the effects of urban practice. Starting in the early 2000s, national-level inequality started to decline in the majority of the countries in the region.[19] However, during the same time, about a third of the region's cities experienced rising intra-urban inequality despite declining inequality at the national level. What is particularly striking is that within the same country, under the same macroeconomic and social policies, some cities are becoming more equal, and others more unequal. This suggests that certain city characteristics and urban practices affect intra-urban inequality. Taking the example of Argentina, the city Neuquén experienced significant increases in the Gini coefficient (a statistical measure of income inequality) between 1990 and 2010, rising from 0.54 Gini points in 1994 to 0.61 in 2010.[20] In the city Resistencia on the contrary, inequality declined from 0.52 Gini points in 1994 to 0.45 in 2010. How can this disparity be explained without considering city characteristics and urban practices?

The Need for a New System to Monitor and Evaluate Progress

One implication of this changed global dynamic and the acknowledgment of the importance of the local is that a new system to monitor and evaluate progress toward the achievement of the SDGs is needed—not only at the national level, but also at the local level. This will be very difficult to design and implement, because national and local statistical offices are very protective of their data systems and definitions of each kind of data. Yet seeking more integrated outcomes will necessarily require more integrated monitoring instruments as well.

Strong follow-up and review processes are essential to maintain commitment and engagement over time, thus contributing to the implementation of an agenda. By identifying implementation successes and challenges, follow-up and review facilitate policy learning and provide evidence base for implementation activities, and strengthen inclusiveness and accountability. The lack of a proper review system, as we experienced in Habitat II, had three important consequences: (1) no accountability of commitments, (2) generality trumped specificity and context appropriateness, and (3) the repetition of past mistakes. The absence of comprehensive review and evaluation tools to follow-up on the eighty-two commitments that were made in the 1996 Habitat Agenda created an accountability void, where country reports, the only official reporting mechanism for Habitat III, often painted a rosy picture, neglecting to review the social and economic struggles in cities.[21]

Activist groups and nongovernmental organizations, for example, the Habitat International Coalition, responded to this accountability void by drafting shadow reports for countries and regions, reflecting on the past twenty years through the eyes of the public. In an effort to complement such punctuated attempts and to generate a broader understanding of urban development since 1996, the Global Urban Futures Project at The New School designed the *Habitat Commitment Index* (HCI), a quantitative tool to assess country effort in meeting commitments made in the 1996 Habitat Agenda.

A unique feature of the HCI is its methodology, which is based on the rationale that when looking at the performance of countries and cities, capacity has to be taken into consideration. This suggests that it makes little sense to compare Togo and Sweden in their achievement in improved urban sanitation, because Sweden comes with vastly superior economic resources. The HCI therefore assesses performance as a function of available resources.

The HCI study has three important takeaways. First, *economic growth does not guarantee improved urban performance*. India and China serve as examples—both countries with strong economic growth over the past two decades, but very little translation of these resources in improved urban conditions. This is particularly worrisome because both countries have the largest and fastest-growing urban population.

Second, another important conclusion is that many *social indicators show very little correlation with economic growth and economic resources*. For example, inequality, measured by the Gini coefficient, had no correlation with gross domestic product (GDP) per capita at the global level. The same holds true for indicators measuring gender equality. Only three of the forty-two gender-related indicators that were analyzed in the HCI indicated a statistical relationship with a country's GDP level.[22]

Regarding country performance since 1996, we found that about *42 percent of the 169 countries included in the study had no significant change in the HCI score* between 1996 and 2016. This suggests that many countries could have performed significantly better, and that Habitat II did not have a significant impact on urban policy.

Finally, the study points to a *severe lack of disaggregated urban data*, especially in socioeconomic, social, and cultural dimensions. While the HCI's contribution to measuring past performance was applauded by many, our focus should now be on what lies ahead of us. How can we use this experience to inform the monitoring and review of the NUA and the SDGs? More specifically, how can it help us to monitor different kinds of inequalities?

The locational dimension of inequality points to the need for more disaggregated monitoring efforts. While ranking and assessing country performance is thought provoking and stimulating, it does not reveal the disparities that exist within countries. These disparities exist in all countries, regardless of income status, and have particularly increased in higher-income countries over the past decade. Ranking the United States ninth in meeting the SDGs does not help local authorities and civil society identify policies and practices that could help improve the living conditions in their respective city. Assuming that priorities in New York City are quite different from those in Baltimore, it is crucial to establish a monitoring system that tracks and evaluates performance at the city or metropolitan scale.

A Global Urban Performance Tool

Implementing the New Global Agenda therefore requires a *Global Urban Performance Tool* to assess performance but also to identify priorities. Creating such a tool is a highly ambitious endeavor, not only because of the complexities of cities and the interdependence of SDG dimensions and variables, but also because of the scarcity of disaggregated data.

We propose a two-pillared approach for a new system to monitor and evaluate progress at the city level (see figure 17.1). The first pillar of such a tool could be *collectivity*, with an emphasis on collective design and data collection,

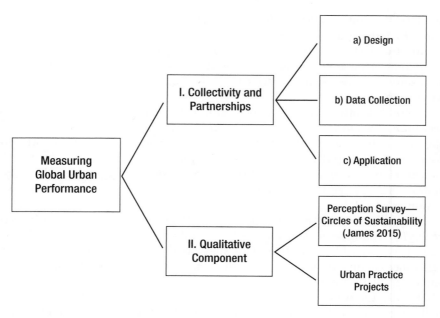

Figure 17.1   City-Level Two-Pillared Monitor and Evaluation Tool

as well as its application. The second pillar would constitute a *qualitative* component that validates and complements quantitative data findings. Such qualitative assessments help identify positive and negative cases of urban practice, which can be shared on a global knowledge platform.

Collectivity

Why collective design and what does that mean? Designing a tool to measure global urban performance should incorporate government representatives, the private sector, and also civil society (including academia, nongovernmental organizations, and communities). Only by involving all layers of society can we measure whether a city works for everyone. Doing so, we also ensure that everyone is part of the analysis, including those working and living in the informal sector. This is particularly pertinent for cities where a majority of the population is, to some degree, "informal." How valuable is it, for example, to rank Kisumu's or Cebu's performance, cities where more than 60 percent of the population lives or works outside the formal sector, without considering the informal? A tool to measure urban performance has to encompass everyone.

Effective monitoring therefore requires the use of multiple sources of data. Informal settlements are often ignored by local governments and excluded from basic services, but also from official statistics. Community-based data can fill this gap. It can also serve as an advocacy tool for the urban poor to negotiate with local governments, providing a baseline against which progress can be measured. Such a stakeholder ownership should be considered when capitalizing on potential synergies with existing processes.

The global campaign "Know Your City" by Shack/Slum Dwellers International offers an excellent example of how the collection and consolidation of community-collected citywide data on informal settlements can help form a dialogue and partnership between local governments and the urban poor.[23] It also helps minimize additional and excessive burdens, particularly for cities and member states with limited means. Monitoring mechanisms that aggregate existing sources of data improve the inclusiveness of the monitoring mechanism, but also help minimize costs and additional monitoring burdens for local governments. In addition, such monitoring can go beyond administrative city boundaries, and capture the totality of the city. Data sources should therefore include community-based data and information, private-sector data, data from city networks, spatial data, and open-source data.

A quantitative tool also requires careful reflection on the relationship between variables. Thinking back to the example of addressing inequality by sending children from lower-income neighborhoods to school in wealthier parts of the city exemplifies such a complexity. In this case, we can examine what independent variables (e.g., a neighborhood) are affected by what kind of intervening variables (linking or not linking) that generate connected or unconnected spaces, which could then be expressed in formal and even perhaps mathematical terms to be tested.

Finally, we oppose the idea to create proprietary monitoring tools and therefore stress the need for open use and sourcing. Assessing and monitoring performance requires financial and human resources, and also time—things that many local authorities face great scarcities of, especially intermediary and smaller cities, which often lack such financial and human resources. However, intermediary cities are the fastest-growing urban settlements and thus are increasingly relevant. It won't be sufficient to track the performance of capital cities and large metropolitan areas. We therefore call for a tool that can be used and adjusted by civil society groups, academia, foundations, or, of course, local authorities.

A Qualitative Component

Quantitative data will not be sufficient to assess urban performance in the New Global Agenda for three main reasons: quantitative data gaps, the inability of quantitative data to capture improvements in all urban conditions and the lack of contextualization, and the inability to draw conclusions about the effects of urban practice.

While quantitative data gaps may be supplemented by community-gathered data, as suggested above, an improved score in urban infrastructure and housing does not necessarily tell us whether the improved score relates to improved conditions for all households, or whether the score improved due to waves of gentrification based on displacement and evictions. The same holds true for data on slums. An improvement in the slum indicator does not tell us whether the number of households in informal settlements decreased due to successful slum upgrading, or due to the bulldozer method. The missing contextualization of quantitative findings therefore needs to be validated by qualitative studies.

To understand the drivers of improved or deteriorated scores, we also need to study urban practices. What policies, programs, public or private interventions had a positive or negative effect? Why was Santa Fe in Argentina so successful in increasing urban resilience and reducing the risk of flooding? Sharing such qualitative findings on a platform that all actors and stakeholders have access to could be very enriching and would go beyond the case studies that became most famous in the world of urban policies, such as a Medellin or a Curitiba. Such qualitative components could take the form of the *Circles of Sustainability* approach by James, or a case study approach of urban practices.[24]

As suggested by Halle and Wolfe, a multitude of data sources and the mix of qualitative and quantitative data require us to identify the appropriate balance between flexibility and comparability[25]—flexible in a sense that the global goals fit the local context and support local interests and priorities, and comparability to ensure that cities and countries can learn from each other and also to ensure compliance with commitments.

Conclusion

A successful implementation of the New Global Agenda requires a multivariate monitoring and review mechanism and a focus on cities. Cities are now the dominant form of human settlement, the drivers of economic activities, the places of pluralist ideas and opportunities; but they are also places of increasing inequality and exclusion. Cities within the very same country are very different from one another in terms of urban form, economic composition, demographics, public services, and also deficiencies. Everyone would agree that the needs and priorities are quite different in New York City and Baltimore in the United States, or Santander and São Paulo in Brazil. For this reason, it is essential to localize the new global agenda, and identify local priorities and action plans.

The design of such an action plan requires an in-depth understanding and analysis of local conditions and needs, which in turn presupposes the availability of disaggregated data and local knowledge. In addition, to ensure that an action plan will survive election cycles and political changes, monitoring and review systems will have to be installed to ensure political accountability for broken and unfulfilled promises. It is unlikely that official data will be sufficient to fulfill these two conditions for assessment and monitoring. We therefore made the case for the need of a new tool to monitor and assess global urban performance. Such a tool would need to have two main components: (1) a collective component, referring to the inclusion of community-driven data and an open-source character, and (2) a qualitative component to study urban practices that lead to more or less social inclusion in cities.

At the Habitat II Conference, Dr. Wally N'Dow, Assistant Secretary-General of the UN and Executive Director of UN-Habitat, declared that the value of Habitat II will not be known in 1996, but in the aftermath following the conference. While this statement certainly has a lot of value, it is not clear how he envisioned to make a normative judgment without a proper assessment tool or monitoring system in place. Only thanks to critical analyses by civil society and the HCI, we now know that the value of Habitat II was limited. If we want to ensure that the SDGs and the New Global Agenda have a greater value than Habitat II did, research and a review and monitoring system will be necessary to identify solutions and priorities—to respond to the *how* that current discussions remain so silent about—and to raise accountability and political attention. It won't be sufficient to tackle the seventeen SDGs one after another or with cylindrical thinking. Instead, we need to understand their interdependence, connectivity, and linkages across goals and targets, as well as their asymmetrical character.

Notes

[1] See https://www.iom.int/world-migration-report-2015.

[2] Paul James, *Circles of Sustainability* (London: Routledge, 2015).

[3] For a list of OECD countries, see http://www.oecd.org/about/membersandpartners/list-oecd-member-countries.htm.

[4] Justine Boulant, Monica Brezzi, and Paolo Veneri, "Income Levels and Inequality in Metropolitan Areas: A Comparative Approach in OECD Countries," *OECD Regional Development Working Papers, No. 2016/06* (Paris: Organisation for Economic Co-operation and Development, 2016).

[5] Mike Davis, "Planet of Slums," *New Perspectives Quarterly* 23, no. 2 (2006): 6–11.

[6] The 2°C target has been adopted by the countries within the United Nations Framework Convention on Climate Change. For the significance of a 2°C increase in global warming, see Intergovernmental Panel on Climate Change, http://www.ipcc.ch/.

[7] Boulant, Brezzi, and Veneri, *Income Levels and Inequality*.

[8] Translated from "Stadtluft macht frei." This German saying describes a principle of law in the Middle Ages, wherein serfs fled to cities to free themselves from their lords. It became customary law that a serf living in a city for a year and a day could no longer be claimed back from his lord. Hence, serfs would flee feudal lands to gain freedom in cities.

[9] Cimoli et al., *Institutions and Policies Shaping Industrial Development: An Introductory Note*, 2006.

[10] Thomas Piketty, *Capital in the 21st Century*, (Cambridge, MA: Harvard University Press, 2014).

[11] Richard Florida, *Cities and the Creative Class* (London: Routledge, 2005), 5.

[12] See publication by Sakiko Fukuda-Parr, Terra Lawson-Remer, and Susan Randolph, *Fulfilling Economic and Social Rights* (Oxford: Oxford University Press, 2014).

[13] Branko Milanovic and John E. Roemer, "Interaction of Global and National Income Inequalities," *Journal of Globalization and Development* 7, no. 1 (2016): 109–115.

[14] Joseph E. Stiglitz, "Information and the Change in the Paradigm in Economics," *The American Economic Review* 92, no. 3 (2002): 460–501.

[15] Gunnar Myrdal, "The Soft State in Underdeveloped Countries," *UCLA Law Review* 15 (1967): 1118.

[16] See Eduardo López Moreno, and Zeltia González Blanco, "Ghost Cities and Empty Houses: Wasted Prosperity," *International American Journal of Social Science* 3, no. 2 (2014): 207–216; Michael Cohen, Margarita Gutman, and Maria Carrizosa, "Habitat en Deuda," *Cafe de ciudades* (2016): 23–101.

[17] Michael Cohen and Darío Debowicz, "The Five Cities of Buenos Aires: Poverty and Inequality in Urban Argentina," *Human Settlement Development* IV (2009): 280.

[18] Ibid, p. 12.

[19] Giovanni Andrea Cornia, *Falling Inequality in Latin America: Policy Changes and Lessons* (Oxford: Oxford University Press, 2014).

[20] UN-Habitat, *Construction of More Equitable Cities* (Nairobi: UN-Habitat, CAF, Avina, 2014).

21 The US country report, e.g., referred only marginally to issues of income and racial inequality, highlighting many of the projects and programs that have positively affected urban development since 1996. Ironically, the US report was released shortly before the Baltimore riots, which pointed to a very different picture in many US cities.

22 The three indicators that showed a correlation with GDP per capita are female tertiary enrollment, maternal mortality, and female employment in the nonagricultural sector.

23 See http://www.sdinetherlands.org/contact/42.html.

24 James, *Circles of Sustainability*.

25 Mark Halle and Robert Wolfe, *Follow-Up and Review for the 2030 Agenda: Bringing Coherence to the Work of the HLPF* (International Institute for Sustainable Development, 2016).

CHAPTER 18

The United Nations, New Wars, and the Challenge of Peace Operations

Alynna J. Lyon

Today, peace support operations are conducted where there may be no peace to keep, or where the fragile peace constantly teeters on the edge of violence. We need to understand conflict better. We need to look at the root cause of conflict, and think of innovative ways to move forward.

—*Canadian Defense Minister Harjit Sajjan*[1]

Global Conflict: Transnationalism and Twenty-First-Century Threats to Peace

The Preamble to the United Nations (UN) Charter pledges "to save succeeding generations from the scourge of war." Yet, over the past seventy years, the nature of war and human-created violence has changed. Perhaps the most significant development is a sharp decrease in interstate war. Since 1945, there have been no wars between major powers and a rapid decline in other state-to-state conflicts, motivating one scholar to write that "war has almost ceased to exist."[2] At the same time, intrastate (internal) armed conflicts are increasing, and from 2007 to 2014, researchers note a tripling of civil wars.[3] In addition, many conflicts are scrambling our categories; to adjust for these developments, in 2016, the Heidelberg Institute for International Conflict Research's annual "conflict barometer" added a new category of "transstate" to include hybrid conflicts that involve state and non-state actors.[4] Unfortunately, hybrid and intrastate conflicts produce great human suffering, with an unprecedented refugee crisis, as almost sixty-five million left their homes to escape the bloodshed in 2017. One report finds that "the number of people killed in conflict in 2014 and 2015 is higher than any other time in the post-Cold War period."[5] Although these numbers decreased a bit in 2016 (from 167,000 in 2015 to 157,000 in 2016), with thirty-eight countries listed on the Fragile State Index on "alert" or higher (up from twenty-eight, ten years ago), the need for some stabilization mechanism is high.[6] Given the changing nature of violence, the UN is changing its approach to the mitigation of violence, going beyond traditional peacekeeping, with the authorization of four "peace operations," which include peace-building as well as peace enforcement operations.[7]

This chapter reviews the evolving approaches of UN peace operations, with a focus on the transnational elements of violence that are unique to the twenty-first century. The analysis explores what makes these new UN peace operations distinct and surveys whether the UN is equipped to address these changing demands. Through this discussion, we find several paradoxes and pathologies associated with peace operations—particularly those labeled "complex multidimensional peacekeeping." The UN is a Westphalian or state-centered organization that is operating in non-Westphalian environments, as many conflicts are neither state based nor operating within the confines of a single country. There are also inherent pathologies in the creation and implementation of multidimensional operations, given the political nature of their authorization. As Syria (2011–) brutally underlines, the process of selecting which people are saved from the "scourge of war" is political, and not based on the extent of human suffering. Moreover, from an administrative perspective, these new peace operations continue and even magnify enduring pathologies of UN peacekeeping, with gaps between mandates and capacities, as peace operations are chronically underfunded, undertrained, and understaffed.

"New Wars" and the Changing Nature of Global Conflict

The last decade witnessed what one scholar describes as "new wars," with an increase in both the numbers of civil wars and the human costs of those wars. New wars are categorized as "internal armed conflicts waged primarily by non-state actors who subsist on illicit and parasitic economic behavior, use small arms and other low-technology hardware, and prey upon civilians, including aid workers and journalists."[8] These conflicts require new approaches to reducing violence, as traditional peacekeeping, or what one scholar calls the "UN's flagship activity," is increasingly ineffective.[9]

The UN is challenged by the fact that these conflicts do not correspond with state borders, there is an increased presence of non-state actors (both benign and violent), many new wars are illegal financed, and civilians are the primary victims of these conflicts. Further complicating the situation, many recent civil wars have become internationalized with intervention by other states in support of either the government or opposition groups. Syria (2011–), Libya (2011), Yemen (2015–), and the Democratic Republic of the Congo (DRC; 2008–) all illustrate the volatility of cross-border diffusion of armed conflict. Religious violence and sectarianism are also part of the driving forces behind recent trends.[10] The number of jihadist groups increased by 60 percent, and the number of fighters associated with these group doubled, and are now committing triple the number of attacks.[11] Specific examples include the Islamic State of Iraq and the Levant and the al-Nusra Front; both groups pose significant threats to peace and security and often directly target civilians and UN personnel. The fact that these groups do not conform to state borders also threatens regional stability and the capacity of the UN to de-escalate violence. These trends are exacerbated by a growing connection to transnational criminal activities. From a regional perspective, the Middle East and portions of Africa are witnessing the largest increases in violence. In 2017, *Foreign Policy Magazine* indicated that the most violent places on the planet were Syria, Iraq, Turkey, Yemen, the DRC, South Sudan, Afghanistan, Myanmar, Mexico, and Ukraine.[12] Furthermore, these conflicts produce crises that go beyond the need for violence reduction, as they often trigger refugee crises, humanitarian emergencies, the looting of resources, famine, internal displacement, failing states, the spread of disease, child soldiers, and increases in sexual abuse and exploitation. More and more, the UN is called on to intervene, stop the violence, rebuild society, repatriate citizens, and promote human rights.

The Evolution of UN Peacekeeping

The UN Charter never mentions peacekeeping—it is an innovation established incrementally, based on need and changing capacities. Yet, the UN's founding document does outline several methods to promote peace. Chapter VI outlines a non-forceful approach for the settlement of disputes which may include mediation, reporting, and observation. UN personnel (donated by UN member states) would don blue helmets, obtain the consent of parties, maintain strict neutrality, and assist combatants in their efforts to end the conflict (usually armed only with walkie-talkies and binoculars). The first peacekeeping operation was the 1948 United Nations Truce Supervision Organization, which authorized a small group of military observers to oversee the implementation of a cease-fire agreement in Palestine. Here, the foundation of peacekeeping was built on a commitment to limit the use of force. Prior to 1989, most peacekeeping operations were created after a cessation of hostilities agreement between warring parties. Yet, the UN Charter acknowledges that force may be necessary in some cases, and thus, Chapter VII allows for more potent approaches, including requesting member states to contribute military forces. Beginning in the 1990s, we find a rapid expansion of UN peacekeeping operations with some Chapter VII authorization and enhanced engagement. These operations are often referred to as "peacemaking," as UN personnel were used to compel warring factions to end their hostilities. At the time, many were hopeful that the UN would be effective in putting out fires and de-escalating violence. However, the civil war in Somalia (1991–1992), genocide in Rwanda (1994), and ethnic cleansing in Bosnia and Kosovo dampened this optimism.[13] The UN did not prevent the deaths of over eight hundred thousand lives in Rwanda. While the UN's mandate expanded in Bosnia, its capacities to protect civilians did not. Lack of resources, lack of political will from the international community, and a restrictive UN institutional mandate undermined peacekeeping effectiveness. The attacks on seven thousand civilians in Srebrenica in July 1995, with UN peacekeepers acting as *de facto* witnesses, highlight this disparity. The Bosnian case revealed the paradoxes the UN must contend with, as its mandate required its personnel in the field to remain a "neutral" party. Over time, peacekeeping expanded to include providing humanitarian assistance, creating a political infrastructure, and even acting as the temporary government in places such as East Timor (1999) and Kosovo (1999). With its operations in Kosovo (UN Interim Administration Mission in Kosovo [UNAMIK]), the UN took on unprecedented and ambitious efforts in its attempt to construct a viable government. In both cases, the UN served as an interim government as it assumed all government powers from administration of the judiciary to trash collection.

In considering the evolution of peace operations, there is a collective view that "there must be a better way to assist and protect people."[14] These failures and others forced the UN community to realize that good intentions did not always yield good outcomes.

As figure 18.1 illustrates, of the more than sixty operations created since 1948, the majority were initiated in the 1990s, with fifteen new operations since the turn of the century. The spike in UN peace operations in the post–Cold War era was accompanied by changes in the nature of many conflicts. Growing instances of transnational violent conflicts with failing governments sparked the need for what are now labeled as *multidimensional peacekeeping operations*. Each of the four most recent peace operations are authorized under a Chapter VII mandate and permit UN personnel to use force. These trends are echoed in the number of peacekeeping personnel (illustrated in figure 18.2). From December 2004 to December 2016, the number of uniformed person increased from 64,701 to 100,376—a 55 percent increase.

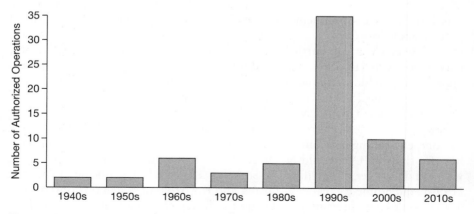

Figure 18.1   UN Peacekeeping Operations (Created by Decade)

Source: http://www.un.org/en/peacekeeping/operations/current.shtml.

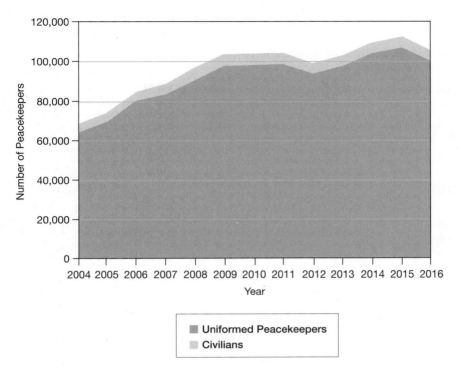

Figure 18.2 UN Peacekeeping Personnel 2004–2016: Civilian versus Uniformed
Source: http://www.un.org/en/peacekeeping/operations/current.shtml.

Expansion of Operations: Vertical (Mandates) and Horizontal (Actors)

While the number of new operations declined after the 1990s, the breadth and depth of those new authorized operations expanded substantially. The UN is increasingly being asked to create conditions on the ground to bring conflicting parties to a cease-fire, protect civilian populations, mitigate humanitarian crises, and assist in laying the foundations for durable governments. As outlined on the UN Department of Peacekeeping Operations' website,

> Today's multidimensional peacekeeping operations are called upon not only to maintain peace and security, but also to facilitate the political process, protect civilians, assist in the disarmament, demobilization and reintegration of former combatants; support the organization of elections, protect and promote human rights and assist in restoring the rule of law.[15]

Blurring lines between Chapter VI and Chapter VII of the UN Charter, most new peace operations are "stabilization efforts" and include elements of counterinsurgency and counterterrorism (e.g., Mali, DRC, Central African Republic [CAR], and South Sudan). Table 18.1 lists the four most recently authorized peace operations and the ambitious agendas the UN is pursuing. These four

TABLE 18.1 Recent Multidimensional UN Peacekeeping Operations 2010–2017

Country	UN Organization Stabilization Mission in the Democratic Republic of the Congo	Multidimensional Integrated Stabilization Mission in Mali	United Nations Mission in the Republic of South Sudan	Multidimensional Integrated Stabilization Mission in the Central African Republic
Mission	MONUSCO	MINUSMA	UNMISS	MINUSCA
Dates	2010–	2013–	2011–	2014–
Refugees	452,000	130,000	1,867,870	467,800
Internally displaced persons	2,200,000	36,000	2,400,000	384,300
Specified UN targeted actor	Democratic Forces for the Liberation of Rwanda, Allied Democratic Forces, Lord's Resistance Army, National Liberation Forces	Ansar Eddine, Movement for Unity and Jihad in West Africa, the Organization of al-Qaeda in the Islamic Maghreb	Sudan People's Liberation Movement	Lord's Resistance Army
Peacekeeping casualties	107	116	48	34
Troops (maximum strength)	16,743	10,797	11,512	10,091
Police	1,360	1,731	1,625	1,731
Chapter VII authority military tasks	Peace enforcement, disarmament	Monitor cease-fire, disarmament	Monitor cease-fire	Monitor cease-fire, peace enforcement, disarmament
Refugee and humanitarian aid tasks	Refugee return, assist civilians, protect international workers	Refugee return, assist civilians, protect international workers	Refugee return, assist civilians, protect international workers	Refugee return, assist civilians, protect international workers
Civil/political tasks	Police retraining, electoral assistance, constitution/judicial reform	Police retraining, electoral assistance		Police retraining, electoral assistance, constitution/judicial reform, monitor elections

Sources: https://www.un.org/en/peacekeeping/resources/statistics/factsheet.shtml#MONUSC; https://www.hrw.org/world-report/2017; https://www.un.org/press/en/; and https://www.un.org/press/en/2017/sc12772.doc.htm.

operations combined account for 60.1 percent of all current active UN peace-keepers. While these missions average over twelve thousand military troops, all other operations average three thousand military personnel. It appears that as the UN is increasingly asked to "mend broken states and societies," more and more, it is pursuing these goals with military tools.[16]

These increasingly complex operations are raising concerns about the line between peacekeeping and peace enforcement. These operations (based on Article 42 of Chapter VII) allow the UN to "take such action by air, sea, or land forces as may be necessary to maintain or restore international peace and security." In the DRC, the Council committed three infantry battalions under the UN Organization Stabilization Mission in the Democratic Republic of the Congo (MONUSCO), who were authorized to

> carry out targeted offensive operations . . . prevent the expansion of all armed groups, neutralize these groups, and disarm them in order to contribute to the objective of reducing the threat posed by armed groups to state authority and civilian security in eastern DRC and to make space for stabilization activities.[17]

In March 2013, the Council authorized a Force Intervention Brigade of troops and unmanned drones for reconnaissance on militia activity within the DRC (Resolution 2098).[18] One month later, this robust mandate was followed by another in Mali, with Resolution 2100 authorizing "all necessary measures to stabilize population areas and to take active steps to prevent the return of armed elements to those areas." Overall, the UN appears to be moving away from impartial operations with limited use of force and is now focused on "disarming" and "neutralizing" specified groups, and in doing so, it specifies an enemy. These new mandates and the issues surrounding the use of force led one researcher to describe "the UN at war."[19] This expanded role can be described as a vertical extension, where directives are increasingly ambitious. As illustrated in table 18.1, the spectrum of tasks is tremendous—ranging from repatriation of almost two million refugees in South Sudan to demobilizing three insurgent groups in both the DRC and Mali.

At the same time, the presence of other states' operations and actors represents a horizontal broadening of directives. As regional organizations have come online, new partnerships develop with UN peace operations. In Mali, the Council mandate created a UN mission combining the African Union, Economic Community of West African States (ECOWAS), Malian, and French Special Forces to effectively conduct offensive operations against al-Qaeda in the Maghreb and combat organized crime (Resolution 2100). In the CAR, Council authorization meant UN peace operations would take over responsibility from other groups, including operations by the African Union, ECOWAS, the Portuguese, the French, and the European Union forces stabilizing the country and obstructing ethnic cleansing (Resolution 2149).

Within this dynamic, who becomes a peacekeeper has also changed, as traditional peacekeeping usually included two dozen or so contributing countries. Today, peacekeeping is more inclusive, with over 125 countries—mostly from the Global South—contributing peacekeeping personnel in 2017. Figure 18.3

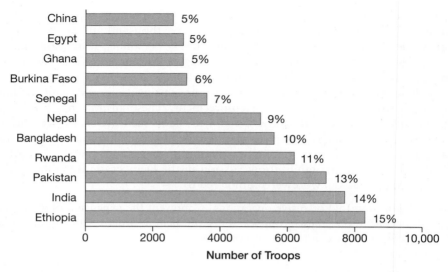

Figure 18.3   Top Eleven Peacekeeping Troop Contributors (Number of Troops, Percentage of Top Eleven)

Source: http://www.un.org/en/peacekeeping/contributors/2016/dec16_1.pdf. Numbers are those reported in December 2016.

underscores this trend as it lists the top troop-contributing states; it is notable that all of the top ten are Global South countries.

Furthermore, as operations expand and the number of personnel on the ground increases, the risk and the probability of misconduct also rise.

The next section turns to a discussion of how the vertical and horizontal expansion of mandates, combined with the endemic challenges of peacekeeping operations, may be undermining the potential for peace in war-torn societies. We review the different challenges of different stakeholders, the member states of the UN (often labeled "the First UN"), the UN bureaucracy (the "Second UN"), and the "peacekept" or governments and civilians on the ground.

The Paradoxes and Pathologies of Peacekeeping

The First UN: Member States' Responses to the Challenge of Multidimensional Peacekeeping

The pathologies of peace operations begin with their origins as UN peace operations face structural challenges that impede success. In addition, the recent "robust" operations undermine the very logic and normative pillars that peacekeeping is built upon. Peace operations are established at the whims of powerful countries, particularly the members of the Security Council. This is often a highly political process based on strategic interest and power structures rather than need. In addition, as the Permanent Five (P5) members of the Security Council hold veto capacity, any one of the five can block an initiative. The obstruction-ism of one country regarding the conflict in Syria (2011–) demonstrates the bias in authorization and the politicization of selectivity. Since the start of the con-flict, the Syrian government has faced allegations of war crimes, the use of chem-ical weapons, and ethnic cleansing. Yet, despite significant evidence, Russia has vetoed six resolutions to mitigate violence in Syria—China joined the veto in all but one October 2016 vote. Effectively, great power consensus is essential for authorization. This failure to act presents a crisis of legitimacy to the UN. It no longer protects all people from "the scourge of war" and even appears to shelter certain perpetrators of mass violence from accountability.

The UN also faces challenges with finding the capacity and resources to do the work it is called upon to do. The organization relies on member states' financial contributions to fund its work. In many regards, peace operations are perpetually underfunded mandates. Research indicates that adequate funding and capacity are essential elements to successful peacekeeping operations.[20] Yet, in mid-2015, together, five peace operations faced operating budget deficits of close to $90 million and troop-contributing countries were owed $63 million in payments.[21] In 2016, then US president Barack Obama assembled a "peacekeeping summit" aimed at securing commitments from member states to support the more robust mandates. Many describe peace operations as fraught with lack of training, staffing, and equipment. Figure 18.4 illustrates the ongo-ing crevasse between what the UN needs for peace operations and what the UN actually receives. The trend points to some optimism, as the average percentage of outstanding contributions declined from around 44 percent (2004–2009) to 25 percent (2010–2015).

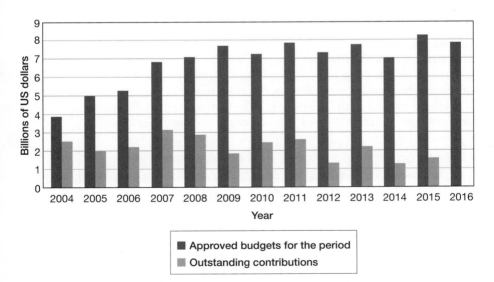

Figure 18.4 UN Peacekeeping Approved Budget and Outstanding Contributions

Source: http://www.un.org/en/peacekeeping/resources/statistics/factsheet_archive.shtml.

It is notable that while some countries are reluctant to support UN peace operations, others are finding new levels of commitment. Both China and Canada recently increased their level of engagement to embrace a more activist role. In 2015, China committed the most troops of any P5 state, making it one of the top eleven contributors (see figure 18.3); donated $100 million to an African Union rapid reaction force; and pledged $1 billion to create a UN Peace and Development Trust Fund.[22] Regardless of payments, there are many observers who lament what they see as a growing discrepancy between what the UN is called upon to do and the tools that it is given to carry out these new mandates.

The UN is quite aware of the tensions and paradoxes within which it is asked to operate. After the failure of the 1990s, the UN commissioned the Report of the Panel on United Nations Peace Operations (2000), also known as the Brahimi Report, which reiterated the need for resources and highlighted the issue with UN peace operations trying to "create" post-conflict situations. To revisit these issues and those associated with the vertical and horizontal expansion of mandates, then secretary-general Ban Ki-moon organized a High-Level Independent Panel on Peace Operations (HIPPO), chaired by Jose Ramos-Horta of East Timor, in late October 2014. The outcome document notes "a widening gap between what is being asked of UN peace operations today and what they are able to deliver."[23] HIPPO reports that the UN peace operations are adapting, yet also notes a "reversal" as "changes in conflict" are "outpacing" the capacities of the UN to mitigate such conflicts. The following section explores the challenges that more "robust" operations pose to the foundational ideas of peacekeeping.

Erosion of the Foundations of Peacekeeping: Consent, Impartiality, and Minimal Use of Force

Beyond the challenges that member states impose on peace operations, there are also structural problems with Chapter VII peace operations. The essential elements of peacekeeping are consent of the parties, impartiality, and limited use of force. These pillars are failing in the most recent peace operations and in the UN efforts to deal with "new wars." The bedrocks of traditional peacekeeping are no longer functional—and in some cases, no longer feasible.

Use of Force: Blue Helmets and Green Berets

The idea of Chapter VII–based operations has always entailed an inherent paradox: the idea that deploying military force will end violence.[24] This tension increases as the UN is called on to attend to military goals as well as societal goals. A lack of clarity about the rules of engagement and the "greening" or militarization of the UN are also problematic as blue helmets, known as symbols of peace, are replaced with green berets, symbolic of war. The operations in the CAR (MINUSCA), the DRC, and Mali (MINUSMA) reflect a serious move away from the foundations of UN operations. These operations are more apt to use force and provide "stabilization" services and even counterterrorism maneuvers. The use of robust mandates holds significant implications for how UN operations are perceived and for troop-contributing countries. As the UN's experience in Somalia in 1993 demonstrated, the targeting of an enemy is particularly problematic if the UN wishes to maintain its impartiality. The UN cannot be effective if it becomes a party to a conflict.[25] The authorization to use force, for purposes other than to protect civilians, looks more like war-making than peacekeeping and jeopardizes the safety of the UN peacekeepers, as well as civilian and humanitarian workers. Karlsrud goes as far as to write, "The UN, representing all the states of the world, uses peacekeeping operations to wage war, it violates the core principles of peacekeeping."[26] This issue is further complicated by lack of general consensus surrounding the desirability of these operations and increasing wariness among troop-contributing countries. Robust operations compromise the traditional role of the UN as a neutral arbitrator.

Two UN reports echo the use of force contradiction. Within the 2000 Brahimi Report, there are contradictions where "[r]ules of engagement should not limit contingents to stroke-for-stroke responses but should allow ripostes sufficient to silence a source of deadly fire that is directed at United Nations troops or at the people they are charged to protect."[27] The HIPPO report acknowledges the "conflict management role" and recommends that the guiding priorities in these cases be clarity of mandate, the use of entry and exit strategies, and the protection of civilians. The expanding mandates also raise alarm within the P5 states, as China and Russia in particular express repeated concerns about the threat to the safety of peacekeeping personnel and threats to the impartiality doctrine. Russia articulated concern that with the militarization of peacekeeping "what was once the exception now threatens to become unacknowledged standard practice."[28] The HIPPO report emphasizes that peace operations are not "designed or equipped to impose political solutions through sustained use of force" and "are not the appropriate tool for military counterterrorism operations." Yet, as demonstrated in table 18.1, military personnel completely shadow nonmilitary personnel in each of the four cases listed. The staffing levels clearly reflect the priorities and strategies of these new operations.

Consent and Local Community Priorities

Coordination with local government officials and communities is key to success; a lack of authentic country consent brings immediate logistical challenges and can create a hostile relationship between the host government and the UN. In the most difficult cases, the target state may be controlled by the perpetrators of the violence, and thus, obtaining "consent" is impossible. In these situations, the UN may be called upon to infringe upon a state's sovereignty, particularly in light of an evolving normative context that establishes an obligation to protect human rights. The state system and legal parameters of sovereignty collide with the parallel developments of UN commitments to human rights, human security, and emerging norms of the Responsibility to Protect (R2P). Partial consent leaves UN personnel (both troops and civilians) uninvited and potential targets of violence. The Brahimi Report acknowledges these tensions and notes,

"[I]n the context of intra-state/transnational conflicts, consent may be manipulated in many ways."[29] As recent peace operations have been deployed prior to combatants' commitment to stop fighting, the UN faces significant challenges in terms of creating the foundation for political solutions. Even in situations where the government is supportive of the UN's presence, command and control issues are still problematic, as local leaders may be prone to compete with or dispute UN mandates. One field observer points out, "Contingents often follow national directives rather than orders from force commanders."[30] While the UN takes into account these discrepancies, recent peace operations may lose sight of political priorities as military tactics tend to dominate (as evidenced by the proportion of military personnel highlighted in figure 18.2).

Impartiality

Impartiality, or lack of bias, in peace operations is another essential element that was part of the original idea of peacekeeping but is again challenged with more robust operations. In terms of domestic constituencies, lack of impartiality undermines the ability to engage in confidence-building measures. The idea of impartiality is essential in supporting a political process. However, peacekeepers cannot be neutral (i.e., passive or noninterfering), particularly regarding violations of peace agreements and attacks on civilians.[31] The lessons of the 1990s point out the perils of neutrality (or passivity) regarding the protection of civilians. Once again, the Brahimi Report discusses the issue: "Impartiality is not the same as neutrality or equal treatment of all parties." Protection of civilians is also highlighted as a priority throughout the HIPPO report. To complicate the impartiality issue, in both Mali and the CAR, authorization was given for pursuit of a specified group. If the UN personnel on the ground are perceived as advocating for one side or the other, they risk becoming parties to the conflict rather than the panacea. In essence, the UN loses its umpire role.[32]

The matter of impartiality raises another key question: "Whom does the peacekeeper serve?" There are at least three distinct constituencies that peace operations are serving: the member states of the UN (particular Security Council members), the host state, and then the civilians. These actors may not always share the same goals. With impartiality, there are three layers, yet the first (member state) is almost impossible. In addition, while protection of civilians provides a moral priority, in cases with limited consent, and limited mandates, there is little the UN can do to save civilians from the scourge of violence, particularly if the government is backing those who target noncombatants. The question remains, how do we get all of these constituencies to come together in a peace operation in order for it to be effective?

The Second UN: Institutional Response to Transnational Conflict and Challenges in the Field

Outside of issues created by countries and their commitment to upholding sovereignty and strategic self-interest, the UN as a bureaucracy and instrument of implementation faces many challenges in carrying out these ambitious mandates. Each of the most recent peace operations involves cross-border issues, which include arms transfers, refugees, and non-state actors. In this regard, the objects or targets of services are not well-defined. The country-based approach that the UN operates within is not consistent with the transnational environments which are pervasive in these conflicts. Indeed, there is inconsistent jurisdiction—the UN is operating within one state and insurgents are operating within several. This disconnect provides insurgents access to safe havens in bordering states.[33] As one scholar explains, "the international community's peacebuilding toolkit is not well equipped" and the UN is "particularly hamstrung by its focus on domestic conflict drivers, host-state capacity-building and national boundaries."[34]

Along these lines, peace operations are under increasing pressure, training and managing over one hundred thousand personnel in the field. Underresourced often means underprepared and undertrained. In Liberia, UN personnel were surprised to find an estimated twenty distinct factions engaged in a civil war. The local conditions, preferences, and voices are often tertiary to operational structures and mandates. In fact, one of the most problematic components of peace operations is that some peacekeepers are themselves perpetrators of violence. The recent operations are particularly troubled with allegations of sexual abuse. The majority of the accusations of sexual abuse by peacekeeping personnel in 2015 were from the CAR. In an attempt to be responsive, the Security Council passed Resolution 2272 in March 2016 calling for an increase in vetting, reporting, awareness training, and troop-contributing country accountability mechanisms.

Mali exemplifies the increasingly complex operational environment where UN peacekeepers are called upon to engage in enforcement operations and coordination with regional organizations. In 1960, the former French colony gained independence, and since that time, the country has witnessed repeated conflicts as the Tuaregs, an ethnic group from the northern region, waged several campaigns seeking self-determination. Many Tuaregs immigrated into Libya and worked in the oil industry under the government of Qaddafi. With a large influx of weapons into Libya in 2011, some returned to their native Mali and began a rebellion in 2012. Their insurgent group, the National Movement for the Liberation of Azawad, joined forces with an al-Qaeda–linked Islamist insurgent group. In April 2013, the UN Security Council responded to growing attacks on civilians, child soldiers, disappearances, rape, and forced marriages after half a million people were forced to flee their homes.

With the lessons of the peacekeeping failures in the 1990s in mind, under Chapter VII, the Multidimensional Integrated Stabilization Mission in Mali (MINUSMA) was given a mandate that allowed for self-defense and the use of "all necessary means" to protect civilians and UN personnel under imminent threat of physical violence. However, it was not given the authorization to initiate offensive operations against the al-Qaeda–linked group behind the violence. Richard Gowan from New York University described MINUSMA as "a potentially flawed peace operation" and accused the Security Council of creating a peacekeeping operation with no peace to keep.[35] UN officials acknowledge that this model was not ideal for addressing the threats posed by asymmetrical conflict consistent with terrorism. In addition, coordinating 11,500 UN peacekeepers with AFISMA and 3,000 French troops on the ground was also a challenge. The operation also comes at a high cost to the UN. Since April 2013, over 120 peacekeepers have been killed. Targeted attacks on UN personnel raised concerns that troop-contributing countries would reduce the number of peacekeepers they contribute. In similar fashion to the DRC, the conflict evolved into a regional situation, with many groups streaming into Mali with different agendas and tactics. The UN, while recognizing the regional nature of the violence, faces significant challenges in developing and coordinating regional responses. In Mali, the UN has found regional rivalries, lack of national and regional consensus, and lack of resources particularly challenging. The Mali case opened discussions about the need to protect UN staff—this conversation includes whether employing private security contractors or creating a UN guard force is feasible and/or desirable.

Challenges in New York

The UN acknowledges many of the challenges of peace operations and has attempted to be reflective and anticipatory. The Brahimi Report remarks, "There are many tasks which United Nations peacekeeping forces should not be asked to undertake and many places they should not go." The UN itself is not blameless in this dysfunctional dynamic. Many point out that the UN is compromised by the desire to appease member states and its reluctance to air systemic issues. Despite efforts at reform and adaptation, "[t]he organisation's response to its mistakes can be as damaging as the errors."[36] Together, these issues diminish the legitimacy and stature of the UN. In fact, there are growing accusations that the UN is plagued with "a culture of denial."[37]

All of these issues raise several fundamental questions. Should the UN be allowed to reject an assignment? Should the UN be allowed to withdraw from situations it deems intractable? Are there places in which there is no peace to gain, given the parameters that the UN must operate within? In some regards, the deployment of peacekeepers acts as a "Band-Aid" that allows the international community to move on without addressing the foundational elements of the violence. Furthermore, in considering a global agenda for people, how can UN operations best protect human life? There are several lessons in taking the peacekeeping/peace operation agenda forward. The UN must move beyond the shackles of the state-based approach to address conflicts that do not correspond to state borders. It must work to move beyond organizational boundaries. Furthermore, addressing systemic causes of violence at the community level is essential and operations must reject short-term approaches that tackle symptoms, not causes. The tasks in reduction of violence must be more inclusive in terms of engagement of stakeholders, but also in leading troubled communities through the complexities of restoration.

In mapping how to restore societies to peace and revive the UN's credibility and capacity to operate, there are a number of suggestions to consider.

One scholar identifies several key components for effective operations—these include (1) the parties in conflict are cooperating with the operation, (2) the operation provides adequate security, (3) the operation is addressing root causes of the conflict, (4) outside actors and parties are cooperating with the operation, (5) the operation is installed at the right time, and (6) the command personnel and leadership are competent.[38] Of the six listed, two refer directly to the principle of consent. It is abundantly clear that the UN cannot be the only actor on the ground making efforts to transition a country from war to peace.

Peace cannot be an edict from New York or found at the end of the barrel of a gun. An approach needs to move beyond using force to counter force. Twenty-first-century peace operations should begin at the very local level and build trust between and within communities to work toward robust agreements. In this case, peace operations must integrate a more holistic approach, with a focus on equality, sustainable development, and decreasing the probability of renewed conflict. Early identification and prevention is essential, and toward that effort, a rapid reaction force is an important tool to expeditiously address situations on the ground before they escalate. This approach was proposed over twenty-five years ago by former UN secretary-general Boutros Boutros-Ghali.[39] More recently, in 2008, the UN introduced Mediation Standby Teams to serve as rapid deployment advisors to help with preventive diplomacy, establish ceasefires, and devise power-sharing agreements. Yet, none of these mechanisms was able to assist the people of Syria.

Thus, the creation of peace operations themselves must be depoliticized and based on a needs assessment, not strategic interest or politics in the Security Council. Particularly in cases of mass atrocities, the politics must be removed from the UN's ability to respond. Peace operations must also be more inclusive to be effective. Creating inclusive societies may help preclude conflict in general and rebuff militarized solutions to political conflicts. In 2000, the Security Council passed Resolution 1325 calling for more gender parity in peacekeeping, which includes more recruitment of women in peace operations and leadership positions. Then, in 2015, the Security Council passed Resolution 2242 calling for women protection advisers. Preliminary research indicates that when female peacekeepers are included in an operation, their presence can help build trust relations with local communities and decrease sexual misconduct.[40]

Violence has a long shadow and can damage communities for multiple generations. To address the global agenda of peace in the twenty-first century, the UN (as well as the international community) needs to move away from power politics in responding to "new wars," emphasize inclusivity, create more adept and nimble mechanisms to prevent violence, and move societies away from cycles of destruction. In 2017, the newly appointed UN Secretary-General Antonio Guterres echoed these concerns:

> Too often, U.N. peacekeepers face an impossible task in countries that are still at war and where there is no real peace to keep. Greater conceptual clarity and a shared understanding of the scope of peacekeeping must pave the way for

urgent reforms that create a continuum from conflict prevention and resolution to peacekeeping, peacebuilding and development.[41]

Conclusion

For the United Nations, peacekeeping is one of its highest achievements, central to its purpose and core identity. As one UN report explains, "[P]eace operations are not simply something the United Nations does but what the United Nations is."[42] Overall, most scholars find that, indeed, peacekeeping works. It reduces uncertainty, reigns in spoilers, and prevents the contagion of conflict across borders.[43] There is also research that finds that rates of attacks on civilians sharply decline if UN peace operations are well staffed.[44]

The tradition of peacekeeping, shaped by Lester B. Pearson, is one that finds a path out of conflict with limited resources and support. Carroll, explaining the leap of faith that the peacekeeping endeavor rests upon, writes, "[T]hey would stand between combatants and, somehow, by their presence, keep the peace," at the same time, "seldom did commentators reach behind the stalwart image . . . because to do so would have revealed how very shaky the peacekeeping enterprise really was."[45] In part, this dilemma concerns the fact that the UN is a Westphalian-based organization bound by the parameters of sovereignty. Its capacities to authorize operations and fund and staff operations are dependent on states. This also presents an administrative dilemma in that peace operations must work with state governments in which they are operating, which can mean that the perpetrators of violence are partners with UN operations.

In what may be deemed good news, UN peace operations clearly demonstrate an evolutionary process. The UN was responsive after Rwanda and Srebrenica and implemented much of what was directed in the Brahimi Report. The HIPPO report presents a road map to reform some of the most blatant pathologies. The decrease in trends of underfunding provides another limited silver lining. There is also optimism in terms of a decline in peacekeeping fatalities.[46] However, the UN remains reactive rather than proactive, and the assumptions of peacekeeping have been stretched too thin. Trying to contort to the original parameters established decades ago presents a chasm that is too vast and threatens to undermine the credibility of the UN itself. The UN now faces an increasing degree of difficulty in task, of growing ambitions, of human need, and of less capacity to meet those demands.

Notes

[1] Lee Berthiaume, "Peacekeeping Canada: Feds to Make Hundreds of Troops Available for Future Missions," *HuffPost*, August 26, 2016.

[2] John Mueller, "War Has Almost Ceased to Exist: An Assessment," *Political Science Quarterly* 124, no. 2 (2009): 297–321.

[3] Human Security Report Project, *Human Security Report 2013: The Decline in Global Violence: Evidence, Explanation, and Contestation* (Vancouver: Human Security Press, 2013); Joshua S. Goldstein, ed., *Winning the War on War: The Decline of Armed Conflict Worldwide* (New York: Dutton, 2011).

4 "The Conflict Barometer 2016," The Heidelberg Institute for International Conflict Research, 2017, 2.

5 Kendra Dupuy et al., "Trends in Armed Conflict, 1945–2015," in *Conflict Trends Project* (Peace Research Institute Oslo, 2016).

6 Mats Berdal, "Whither UN Peacekeeping?" in *Armed Conflict Survey 2017* (International Institute for Strategic Studies, 2017).

7 The UN's review by the High-Level Independent Panel on Peace Operations encourages the use of this term to capture the broad spectrum of UN operations and mandates. Alex J. Bellamy and Charles T. Hunt, "Twenty-First Century UN Peace Operations: Protection, Force and the Changing Security Environment," *International Affairs* 91, no. 6 (2015): 1277–1298.

8 Thomas G. Weiss, *Humanitarian Intervention* (Cambridge, UK: Polity, 2007), 72.

9 Berdal, "Whither UN Peacekeeping?"

10 Institute for Economics and Peace, "Global Terrorism Index 2014: Measuring and Understanding the Impact of Terrorism," (2014).

11 David Rothkopf, "We Are Losing the War on Terror," *Foreign Policy* (2014).

12 Jean-Marie Guehenno, "10 Conflicts to Watch in 2017," *Foreign Policy*, no. 2 (2017).

13 Alynna J. Lyon, "Beyond Rwanda and Kosovo: The Interactive Dynamics of International Peacekeeping and Ethnic Mobilization," *Global Society* 19, no. 3 (2005): 267–288.

14 Weiss, *Humanitarian Intervention*, 77.

15 United Nations Department of Peacekeeping, "List of Peacekeeping Operations," (2017).

16 Bellamy and Hunt, "Twenty-First Century UN Peace Operations: Protection, Force and the Changing Security Environment."

17 United Nations Security Council, Resolution 2147 (2014).

18 Foreign militias operating within DRC include the Democratic Forces for the Liberation of Rwanda (FDLR), the Allied Democratic Forces (ADF) from Uganda, Lord's Resistance Army (LRA) from Uganda, and the National Liberation Forces (FNL) from Burundi.

19 John Karlsrud, "The UN at War: Examining the Consequences of Peace-Enforcement Mandates for the UN Peacekeeping Operations in the CAR, the DRC, and Mali," *Third World Quarterly* 36, no. 1 (2015): 40–54.

20 Micheal W. Doyle and Nicholas Sambanis, "The UN Record on Peacekeeping Operations," *International Journal* 62, no. 3 (2007): 495–518; Lisa Hultman, Jacob Kathman, and Megan Shannon, "United Nations Peacekeeping and Civilian Protection in Civil War," *American Journal of Political Science* 57, no. 4 (2013): 875–891.

21 "Delegates Examine 2016/17 Peacekeeping Budget, Concerns over Payment Arrears, Borrowing between Missions, as Fifth Committee Begins Resumed Session," (General Assembly, 2016).

22 Michael Martina and David Brunnstrom, "China's Xi Says to Commit 8,000 Troops for U.N. Peacekeeping Force," *Reuters*, September 28, 2015.

23 "Uniting Our Strengths for Peace: Politics, Partnership and People," in *Report of the UN High-level Independent Panel on UN Peace Operations* (New York: United Nations, 2015).

24 Brian L. Zimbler, "Peacekeeping without the UN: The Multinational Force in Lebanon and International Law," *Yale Journal of International Law* 10, no. 1 (1984).

25 Patrick Cammaert, "The UN Intervention Brigade in the Democratic Republic of the Congo," *International Peace Institute* (July 2013).

26 Karlsrud, "The UN at War," 41.

27 Lakhdar Brahimi, *Report of the Panel on the United Nations Peace Operations* (United Nations, 2000), 9.

28 "Peacekeeping," *Security Council Report* (June 2014).

29 Brahimi, *Report of the Panel*, 9.

30 Fred Strasser, *Africa Peacekeeping: Lessons from a Ghanaian Commander* (United States Institute of Peace, 2016).

31 Doyle and Sambanis, "UN Record on Peacekeeping Operations."

32 John Gerard Ruggie, "The United Nations: Stuck in a Fog between Peacekeeping and Enforcement," *McNair Papers*, (1993): 24–25.

33 Damien Deltenre and Michel Liégeois, "Filling a Leaking Bathtub? Peacekeeping in Africa and the Challenge of Transnational Armed Rebellions," *African Security* 9, no. 1 (2016): 1–20.

[34] Erwin van Veen, "Upgrading Peacekeeping to Counter Transnational Conflict Drivers," in *Policy Brief* no. 1 (Netherlands Institute of International Relations, 2014).

[35] Richard Gowan, "Diplomatic Fallout: A Summer of Political Storms Looms for U.N.," *World Politics Review* (2013).

[36] "View on UN Peacekeeping: Admirable Aims but a Troubled Record," *The Guardian*, August 21, 2016.

[37] "A Tale of Horror at the United Nations," *The New York Times*, February 17, 2016.

[38] Jair van der Lijn, "Success and Failure of UN Peacekeeping Operations: UNMIS in Sudan," *Journal of International Peacekeeping* 14, no. 1–2 (2010): 27–59.

[39] Boutros Boutros-Ghali, *An Agenda for Peace: Preventative Diplomacy, Peacemaking, and Peace-Keeping* (New York: United Nations, 1992).

[40] Sahana Dharmapuri, "Not Just a Numbers Game: Increasing Women's Participation in UN Peacekeeping. Providing for Peacekeeping," *Providing for Peacekeeping No. 4* (New York: International Peace Institute, July 2013).

[41] António Guterres, "U.N. Secretary-General António Guterres: My Vision for Revitalizing the United Nations," *Newsweek* (2017).

[42] "Politics, Partnership and People," 6.

[43] Doyle and Sambanis, "UN Record on Peacekeeping Operations"; Virginia Page Fortna, *Does Peacekeeping Work? Shaping Belligerents' Choices after Civil War* (Princeton, NJ: Princeton University Press, 2008); Kyle Beardsley, "Peacekeeping and the Contagion of Armed Conflict," *Journal of Politics* 73, no. 4 (2011): 1051–1064.

[44] Hultman, Kathman, and Shannon, "United Nations Peacekeeping."

[45] Michael K. Carroll, *Pearson's Peacekeepers: Canada and the United Nations Emergency Force, 1956–67* (Vancouver, Canada: UBC Press, 2009), xi.

[46] Marina E. Henke, "Has UN Peacekeeping Become More Deadly? Analyzing Trends in UN Fatalities," (New York: International Peace Institute, December 2016).

CHAPTER 19

Nuclear Weapons and the Rules-Based Global Multilateral Order

Ramesh Thakur

We may be at a nuclear inflection point in a world in disarray. One of many strong headwinds buffeting world affairs is intensifying and multiplying nuclear threats. Boundaries are being steadily eroded between nuclear and conventional munitions; regional, global, tactical, and strategic warheads; and nuclear, cyber, and space domains. Geopolitical tensions have risen in Europe, the Middle East, South Asia, and East Asia. Little wonder that former US defense secretary William Perry warns that "the danger of a nuclear catastrophe today is greater than during the Cold War."[1]

Two contradictory trends were in evidence in 2017 with regard to subjecting weapons of mass destruction (WMD) to the discipline of a rules-based, global multilateral order. On April 4, 2017, a chemical weapon incident occurred in Khan Sheikhun in Syria. Washington blamed the Syrian air force for the attack, and two days later, President Donald Trump ordered the Syrian air base from which the attack was launched to be bombed by fifty-nine Tomahawk cruise missiles. Meanwhile in New York, a United Nations (UN)–mandated conference to negotiate a legally binding instrument to prohibit nuclear weapons held two sessions on March 27–31 and June 15–July 7. On July 7, the conference adopted the Nuclear Weapon Prohibition Treaty (NWPT),[2] which prohibits the acquisition, development, production, manufacture, possession, transfer, receipt, testing, extraterritorial stationing, use, and threat of use of nuclear weapons. Scheduled to be opened for signature during the UN General Assembly (GA) on September 20, 2017, it will come into force after fifty states have ratified it.

Previously, on September 27, 2013, the UN Security Council (UNSC) unanimously adopted Resolution 2118, requiring the destruction of Syria's chemical weapon stockpiles in line with the 1997 Chemical Weapons Convention under UN supervision and International Atomic Energy Agency (IAEA) verification. On April 2, 2013, the GA adopted the Arms Trade Treaty to regulate the estimated $70 billion global arms commerce, and on September 26, 2013, the UNSC adopted a first-ever resolution on small arms and light weapons (S/RES/2117).

On July 14, 2015, Iran signed the Joint Comprehensive Plan of Action (JCPOA), through which its nuclear weapon program was effectively shrink-wrapped under IAEA oversight in return for sanctions relief. Multilateralism helped to get the Iran deal; permanent obligations on Iran under the 1968 Nuclear Non-Proliferation Treaty (NPT) not to acquire nuclear weapons will remain after the JCPOA has run its course; and the multilateral nature of JCPOA acts as an external discipline on the erratic instincts of the Trump administration to abrogate the deal. Between them, all these developments in 2013–2015 reaffirmed the value, utility, and continuing relevance of multilateral arms control regimes and enforcement measures by the UNSC to ensure compliance. In the case of the NPT, however, in 2017, the five Permanent Members (P5) of the Security Council boycotted the UN ban conference, thereby risking a split in the multilateral nuclear arms control regime.

In this chapter, I will first describe the importance of the UN-centered multilateral nuclear order, followed by brief descriptions of the key treaty-based nuclear arms control regimes. Next, I will describe the stress experienced by the NPT recently, before examining the NWPT. The chapter concludes by looking ahead to the UN high-level disarmament conference scheduled for 2018.

UN-Centered Multilateral Nuclear Arms Control

The core of the mandated multilateral order is the UN. Normatively, the essence of multilateralism is a rules-based global order. In an interdependent, globalizing world, multilateralism will continue to be a key aspect of international relations. Even the most powerful states cannot achieve security, environmental safety, and economic prosperity as effectively in isolation or unilaterally, and so the international system rests upon a network of regimes, treaties, international organizations, and shared practices that embody common expectations, diffuse reciprocity, and equivalence of benefits. However, while the UN system plays an essential role in setting international standards and global norms, it is far from effective in policing and enforcing these laws, norms, and standards.

During the UN's existence, the use of force by states has been brought under the legal discipline of the UN Charter,[3] including normative and legal prohibitions on the types of armaments permissible for use. The pursuit of multilateral arms control is based on a careful judgment that such regimes contribute to the national security of states party to agreements. In signing international arms control treaties, states accept binding legal obligations. But because multilateral agreements are negotiated outcomes, they are typically imperfect bargains, reflecting the compromises that all sides had to make in the interests of getting an agreement that meets the minimum concerns of all parties while falling short of their maximum aspirations.

The UN has historically served as a funnel, forum, and font for processing arms control and disarmament proposals,[4] and this role continues today. The very first GA resolution on January 24, 1946, called for the newly established UN Atomic Energy Commission to make proposals for the elimination of atomic weapons and other WMD. The UN has unmatched convening and mobilizing power rooted in its unique legitimacy as the only authenticated voice of the international community. The GA is the world's normative center of gravity where contested norms can be debated and reconciled. It can adopt resolutions that initiate new negotiations on arms control and disarmament, and also adopt treaties negotiated in the Geneva-based Conference on Disarmament (CD), as with the Comprehensive Nuclear-Test-Ban Treaty (CTBT). It has often been the forum for negotiating new international instruments and the depositary organization for many treaties negotiated outside the UN framework.

The GA First Committee is charged with considering disarmament and international security. Many resolutions are mere repeats of previous years' resolutions, but new resolutions are introduced every year and serve as a litmus test of progress or lack of it, and weathervanes of current international thinking on disarmament and international security. Voting is by a simple majority. After the committee has completed its consideration of items and submitted draft resolutions, all issues are voted on through resolutions passed in GA plenary meetings, usually toward the end of the regular session.

The CD is not a true UN body and does not follow formal UN rules and procedures. For example, there is no voting procedure, and it operates by consensus. The consensus rule, originally designed to help states find agreement, is now providing a convenient cover for countries that want to block progress. Former Secretary-General Kofi Annan acknowledged frankly that the CD faced "a crisis of relevance resulting in part from dysfunctional decision-making procedures and the paralysis that accompanies them."[5]

With 168 member states and a secretariat of 2,500 professional and support staff,[6] the IAEA is the world's nuclear watchdog. Although autonomous, it is a member of the UN system and reports annually to the GA on its work. If the IAEA finds a State Party not to be in compliance with the NPT, enforcement action is the responsibility of the Security Council. There are also several other international bodies set within the UN framework as part of the implementation mechanism for disarmament: for example, the IAEA (Vienna), the Organisation for the Prohibition of Chemical Weapons (The Hague), and the Comprehensive Nuclear Test Ban Treaty Organization (CTBTO) (Vienna).

Multilateral treaties do not have to be negotiated within standing international machinery. Even if negotiated outside UN fora, treaties are often submitted to the UN machinery for formal endorsement that has no bearing on the legal standing of the treaty but does substantially enhance its moral weight. This has been true, for example, of the various regional nuclear weapon–free zones (NWFZ). The ideas behind many of the existing regimes were often first funneled through the UN system, including an end to nuclear testing proposed by India at the GA in December 1954.[7] Similarly, the idea of negotiating a South Pacific NWFZ was submitted to the GA for endorsement in 1975, and the 1985 treaty links the regional verification system for the South Pacific to the global IAEA inspections regime within the UN system.[8] Even though the NPT was negotiated outside the UN framework, its conceptual origin lies in GA resolutions from the late 1950s onward. On June 12, 1968, the GA commended the draft text of the NPT (Resolution 2373) before the NPT was opened for signature on July 1, 1968, in London, Moscow, and Washington (capitals of the three designated depositary countries) and entered into force on March 5, 1970.

Treaty-Based Arms Control Regimes

The NPT is the mother lode of all nuclear treaty–based regimes (table 19.1), embraced by virtually the entire family of nations. It has kept the nuclear nightmare at bay for five decades while underpinning and facilitating the global trade in nuclear material for peaceful purposes. At the heart of the NPT lie three bargains involving nuclear energy, nonproliferation, and disarmament:

1. The nonnuclear weapon states (non-NWS) established a bargain among themselves never to acquire nuclear weapons. The number of countries with nuclear weapons is still in single figures.
2. They entered into a deal with the NWS whereby, in return for intrusive end-use control over nuclear and nuclear-related technology and material, they were granted access to nuclear technology, components, and material for peaceful purposes.
3. They struck a second deal with the NWS that, in return for the non-NWS forever forswearing the bomb, the NWS would pursue good-faith negotiations for complete nuclear disarmament. Article VI of the NPT is the only explicit multilateral disarmament commitment undertaken by all the NWS.

A NWFZ deepens and extends the scope of the NPT and embeds the nonnuclear weapon status of NPT States Parties in additional treaty-based arrangements.[9] A NWFZ is characterized by five "No"s: no testing, possession, hosting, deployment, or use of nuclear weapons. The first NWFZ was established in uninhabited Antarctica in 1959. Since then, five more have been established in Latin America and the Caribbean, the South Pacific, Southeast Asia, Africa, and Central Asia, with a combined total of around one hundred States Parties or more than half the UN membership. The most substantial gap in relation to existing NWFZs is the failure of the relevant NWS to accede to all the various protocols. Additionally, there is the question of proposed new zones for regions such as Northeast Asia and the Middle East.

The CTBT, signed by 183 countries and ratified by 166, is a key barrier to both vertical and horizontal proliferation. This still leaves eight out of forty-four Annex 2 countries[10] whose ratifications are needed to bring it into force (China, Egypt, India, Israel, Iran, North Korea, Pakistan, and the United States). Uniquely among arms control agreements, the CTBT is in the paradoxical position of not having entered into force, yet it is fully operational with a network of monitoring stations that span the world and a fully staffed implementing agency based in Vienna.

There are three main global treaties underpinning nuclear security. The 1980 Convention on the Physical Protection of Nuclear Materials and Facilities, along with a major Amendment adopted in 2005 that entered into force in 2016, establishes measures related to the physical protection of nuclear material

TABLE 19.1   **Status of Key Multilateral Nuclear Treaties**

	Date adopted	Entry into Force	States Parties	Signed but Not Parties
NPT	June 12, 1968	March 5, 1970	188[a]	
NWPT	July 7, 2017			
CTBT	September 10, 1996		166	17[b]
CNS[c]	June 17, 1994	October 24, 1996	78	17
CPPNM[d]	October 26, 1979	February 8, 1987	155	1 (Haiti, 1980)
CPPNM Amendment[e]	July 8, 2005	May 8, 2016	109	N/A [155 – 108 = 47]
ICSANT[f]	April 13, 2005	July 7, 2007	109	6

Sources: http://www.iaea.org/Publications/Documents/Conventions/cppnm_status.pdf; http://www.iaea.org/Publications/Documents/Conventions/cppnm_amend_status.pdf; and https://treaties.un.org/Pages/ViewDetailsIII.aspx?src=TREATY&mtdsg_no=XVIII-15&chapter=18&Temp=mtdsg3&lang=en. All accessed June 12, 2017.

Note: NPT = Non-Proliferation Treaty; NWPT = Nuclear Weapon Prohibition Treaty; CTBT = Comprehensive Nuclear Test Ban Treaty; CNS = Convention on Nuclear Safety; CPPNM = Convention on the Physical Protection of Nuclear Material; ICSANT = International Convention for the Suppression of Acts of Nuclear Terrorism.

[a] The Holy See and the State of Palestine are also NPT parties. Only five UN member states are not party to the NPT: India, Israel, North Korea, Pakistan, and South Sudan.
[b] Of the forty-four CTBT Annex 2 states whose ratification is required to bring it into force, five have signed but not yet ratified (China, Egypt, Israel, Iran, and the United States), while another three have yet to sign (India, North Korea, and Pakistan).
[c] As on December 31, 2016
[d] As on December 6, 2017
[e] As on May 4, 2017
[f] As on June 11, 2017

during domestic use and storage, and domestic and international transport. It also provides a general framework for cooperation among states in the protection, recovery, and return of stolen nuclear material.

The International Convention for the Suppression of Acts of Nuclear Terrorism was adopted unanimously by the GA in 2005. Its focus is on individual criminal responsibility of persons for specific acts of a terrorist nature. It seeks to do three things: protect against attacks on a broad range of potential targets, including nuclear power plants and reactors; punish the perpetrators through domestic criminalization of acts of nuclear terrorism; and promote international cooperation in the prevention and investigation of acts of nuclear terrorism and the prosecution or extradition of the alleged terrorists. Gaps in the existing national and multilateral machinery of nuclear security include lack of universality, binding standards, transparency and accountability mechanisms, compulsory IAEA oversight, and insufficient attention to nuclear weapons.[11]

The most important of the global nuclear safety treaties is the 1994 Convention on Nuclear Safety, which commits states to ensuring nuclear safety and provides for regular reviews of their nuclear safety arrangements. However, it does not require mandatory compliance with IAEA safety standards as best practice.

Nuclear Non-Proliferation Treaty under Stress

Over the years, despite being the most successful arms control agreement in history and the normative sheet anchor of nuclear orders from peaceful uses to safety, security, and non-proliferation, the NPT has built up an accumulating series of anomalies, shortcomings, flaws, and gaps between promise and performance. With a global retreat from nuclear power since the Fukushima accident in 2011, the lead on nuclear security being taken over by the four Nuclear Security Summits 2010–2016, the universalization of nonproliferation obligations to all countries that do not possess nuclear weapons, and the complete stall of disarmament efforts, by 2017, it was difficult to contest the claim that the NPT's normative potential was exhausted.

Problems inherent in the NPT became clearer with time. Within the constraints of the NPT, a nonnuclear weapon industrialized country such as Japan can build the necessary infrastructure and acquire fissile materials to provide it with the "surge" capacity to upgrade quickly to nuclear weapons. By relying on the promise of signatories to use nuclear materials, facilities, and technology for peaceful purposes only, it empowered them to operate dangerously close to a nuclear-weapon capability, as with Iran. It proscribed non-NWS from acquiring nuclear weapons, but failed to design a strategy for dealing with nonsignatory countries. It is impossible to deal with non-NPT nuclear-armed states from within the treaty. The odd result is that the five NPT-licit NWS are legally obligated to eliminate their nuclear weapons, but India, Israel, and Pakistan have no such obligation. It also means that the non-NPT nuclear-armed states cannot be asked to join the NWFZ protocols, even if they are regionally relevant. The treaty's withdrawal clause is far too lax, enabling North Korea's exit in 2003.

The NPT may be creaking even with respect to its nuclear energy bargain as the nexus of security, economic, energy, and environmental imperatives can no longer be adequately nested within the regime. As more countries bump against the nuclear weapons ceiling, there is interest in creating a new international market under the auspices of multilateral nuclear arrangements.[12] Internationalizing the nuclear fuel cycle and entrusting supply to a body like the IAEA would simultaneously ensure security of supply divorced from political hostilities and eliminate the need for enrichment and reprocessing plants in countries interested in acquiring nuclear power for civilian use.[13]

Most importantly, with the refusal of the NWS to accept and implement the International Court of Justice Advisory Opinion in 1996 that Article VI obliges them to engage in and bring to a conclusion good-faith negotiations to eliminate their nuclear arsenals,[14] the NPT was subverted from a prohibition into a nonproliferation regime. There is a marked imbalance of obligations between the different bargains. The nonnuclear weapon status was immediate, legally binding, and internationally verifiable and enforceable. But there were no intrusive safeguards for the NWS in their roles as suppliers of critical technology and components. More importantly, their commitment to disarm was neither timetabled nor precise nor binding.[15] This has ensured that the NPT is not the primary normative framework for reducing nuclear warheads and delegitimizing the possession and deployment of nuclear weapons. Global numbers of nuclear warheads have fallen dramatically from over seventy thousand in the 1980s to fifteen thousand in 2017, but this has occurred chiefly as a result of bilateral measures between Moscow and Washington. All nine nuclear-armed states pay lip-service to the ultimate elimination of nuclear weapons. But their actions with respect to weapons arsenals, fissile material stocks, force modernization plans, declared doctrines, and observable deployment practices demonstrate the intent to retain nuclear weapons indefinitely.

In 2018, the NPT will mark fifty years since its adoption. During that period, not a single nuclear warhead has been eliminated through a multilateral agreement. In addition, the bilateral US–Russian process had also stalled and was in serious risk of being reversed. In December 2016, the Defense Science Board urged president-elect Donald Trump to consider acquiring a greater number of lower-yield weapons that could provide a "tailored nuclear option for limited use."[16] In a tweet on December 22, Trump himself promised to "greatly strengthen and expand [US] nuclear capability."[17] In February 2017, President Trump insisted that the United States would stay at the "top of the [nuclear] pack."[18] In addition, increasing attention is being paid to the possibility of nuclear weaponization by Japan and South Korea in the Pacific,[19] and to an independent European nuclear deterrent in the Atlantic.[20] A review commissioned by the German Parliament concluded that Germany can legally finance British or French nuclear weapon programs in return for their protection.[21] All such worrying developments imply a rejection of the NPT as the globally legitimate framework for regulating nuclear policy. A lack of progress on disarmament makes it more challenging to hold the line on nonproliferation, while any additional or suspected instance of proliferation makes progress on disarmament more difficult.

The Nuclear Weapon Prohibition Treaty

In retrospect, the present global divide has its roots in the decision taken unanimously at the NPT Review and Extension Conference in 1995 to extend the treaty indefinitely. As the conference began, there was strong but by no means unanimous support for making it permanent. The price of gaining unanimous support for the indefinite extension was a four-part package. According to NPT Review and Extension Conference president Jayantha Dhanapala, "without this political foundation—which at the last minute of the conference was extended to include the Middle East resolution—the States Parties would never have been able to agree to the indefinite extension without a vote."[22]

First, the "Principles and Objectives for Nuclear Non-Proliferation and Disarmament" outlined the goal of two further key multilateral agreements: the negotiation of a CTBT and the negotiation of a complementary treaty banning the production of fissile materials. As already noted, the CTBT is yet to enter into force and negotiations for a fissile material cutoff treaty have not even begun.[23] Second, the strengthened review process with more substantive agendas for the NPT Preparatory Committee meetings that would feed into the five-yearly Review Conference has not quite worked out as envisaged.[24] Third, the 1995 "Resolution on the Middle East" and the 2010 Review Conference called for a conference to be convened in 2012 on a Middle East WMD-Free Zone. This too did not take place. Thus, not one of the three other elements of the package has been realized and some states have undoubtedly experienced buyer's remorse at having surrendered the only leverage they had over the nuclear policies of the NWS.

The combination of growing awareness of nuclear threats and rising impatience and frustration with the perceived obstructionism of the nuclear-armed states generated a powerful alliance of civil society activists and like-minded states rooted in humanitarian principles. At the conclusion of the final humanitarian imperative conference in Vienna on December 9, 2014, 127 countries signed a humanitarian pledge "to stigmatize, prohibit and eliminate nuclear weapons."[25] The GA set up an Open Ended Working Group in December 2015 (A/RES/70/48) and, based on its recommendation, in December 2016, it mandated a conference in 2017 to negotiate a legally binding prohibition treaty that would lead to the eventual elimination of nuclear weapons (A/RES/71/258). In sharp contrast to the stalemated CD, the 2016 Open Ended Working Group made decisions by voting according to GA rules instead of the veto-inviting consensus rule by which the CD operates. Similarly, the 2017 ban conference also operated under GA rules that permit decisions by vote.

To advocates, the UN ban talks were the first serious effort to fill a critical legal void in the normative architecture of nuclear weapons. In contrast, the NWS and their allies argued that the talks posed a fundamental threat to the existing NPT regime that has served the international community extraordinarily well for more than half a century. None of the nine nuclear-armed countries, and almost none of the NATO and Pacific allies who shelter under the US nuclear umbrella, attended the UN conference, describing it as impractical, ineffective, and likely to damage the NPT. Conversely, their boycott of the conference was an open act of defiance and disrespect of a multilaterally mandated disarmament process involving two-thirds of the NPT membership. *Prima facie*, nonparticipation also put them in noncompliance with the Article VI obligation of *all* 188 NPT States Parties, not just the NWS, to pursue and conclude disarmament negotiations.

In most respects, and with the caveat of qualifications noted below, the draft NWPT text is significantly stronger than the NPT. Five prohibitions listed in Article 1 are especially noteworthy. First, it prohibits the possession of nuclear weapons for *all* signatories. Second, it bans the use of nuclear weapons. Third, it proscribes the threat of use of nuclear weapons, thereby delegitimizing the doctrine and practice of nuclear deterrence. Fourth, it prohibits nuclear testing and is thus more closely aligned to the CTBT. And fifth, it bans the stationing of nuclear weapons, so signatories would be legally required to ask for the withdrawal of all warheads stationed on their territory. This would affect NATO allies such as Germany and Turkey, but not any of the three Pacific allies, although it would preclude the reintroduction of US tactical weapons into South Korea.

The NWPT also improves on the NPT in three other respects. It requires assistance to the victims of the use or testing of nuclear weapons and for environmental remediation of areas contaminated by the use or testing of nuclear weapons (Article 6). The NWPT also offsets some of the NPT's institutional deficits by scheduling biennial assemblies of States Parties, with the first to be convened by the UN Secretary-General within one year of the treaty's entry into force. In addition, extraordinary meetings can be convened as necessary (Article 8). Moreover, as the NPT regime is treaty based, its legal obligations do not extend to nonsignatories. The NWPT has been crafted to bring all nine states under one common normative framework with the simple expediency of referring to any state "that after 7 July 2017 owned, possessed or controlled nuclear weapons or other nuclear explosive devices" (Article 4.1).

The NWPT provides pathways for possessor states to eliminate nuclear arsenals and programs, and then join the treaty (Article 4.1); or to join the treaty first and commit to a time-bound, verifiable, and irreversible elimination (Article 4.2). In both cases, independent confirmation and verification would be required. Those that host nuclear weapons controlled by possessor states can also join on condition of verifiably removing them promptly (Article 4.4). Although the treaty is of indefinite duration and not subject to any reservations, a State Party may withdraw from it on twelve months' notice if "extraordinary events . . . have jeopardized [its] supreme interests" (Article 17).

Areas that will need clarifications and improvements in order to align the final agreed NWPT with the NPT include: safeguards, testing, stationing, the meaning and scope of assistance and encouragement to other states engaged in activities prohibited under the NWPT (e.g., support for nuclear deterrence postures), institutional arrangements for review and amendments, and linkage with the non-NPT nuclear-armed states. The two sets of obligations can coexist, as do the differing commitments of the NPT and CTBT—but it will require management.

The NWPT represents the most significant multilateral development on nuclear arms control since the indefinite extension of the NPT in 1995 and the adoption of the CTBT in 1996. From one point of view, the UN-mandated conference is clearly a vote of no confidence in the NPT that—potentially, although not necessarily—poses an existential threat to the NPT. The primary drivers of the ban negotiations were twofold: (1) deepening concern at the risks and threats posed by the existence and deployment of nuclear weapons and doctrines and (2) mounting frustrations at the failure to eliminate them under existing frameworks and processes. Thus, the exasperation extended both to the process and forum—the consensus-based and veto-paralyzing stalemate of the CD, and to the substance—the nearly complete lack of progress.

The nuclear policy goals can be summarized as: delegitimize, prohibit, cap, reduce, and eliminate. In this five-part agenda, only those possessing nuclear weapons can undertake the last three tasks. But the non-NWS, who constitute the overwhelming bulk of the international community, can pursue the first (delegitimization) and second (prohibition) goals on their own, both as an affirmation of global norms (standards as distinct from prevailing patterns of behavior) and as one of the very few means available to them of exerting pressure on the possessor states to pursue the other three goals.

The nuclear weapon ban treaty will draw on the UN's long-recognized unique role as the sole custodian and dispenser of collective international legitimacy. By changing the prevailing normative structure, it will shift the balance of costs and benefits of possession, deterrence doctrines, and deployment practices, and create a deepening crisis of legitimacy for all possessor states. In addition, it will harden the normative boundaries between conventional and nuclear, regional and global, and tactical and strategic weapons that are being blurred by technological developments. The NWPT will also reaffirm the global nuclear norms of nonproliferation, disarmament, security, and nonuse and thereby devalue the currency of nuclear weapons.

Forty-nine years after its adoption, the NPT has yet to produce a nuclear disarmament treaty. By contrast, the UN conference succeeded in negotiating a prohibition treaty within four weeks. The successful ban conference under direct UN auspices could shatter irretrievably the NPT and the CD as the sole normative framework and multilateral forum, respectively, for nuclear nonproliferation and disarmament. But it will do so by revitalizing the multilateral machinery for the task. The immediate policy challenge is how to ensure that the two separate streams of the ban conference and NPT Preparatory Committee processes are brought together in a smooth confluence. If the NWS wish to rescue the NPT as the preferred framework and process, it is for them to demonstrate practical outcomes, through deeds not words, by bringing the step-by-step approach to some productive conclusions.

The NPT regime therefore is at a crossroads. If the NWS continue to disrespect the mandated multilateral process and negotiated treaty, the divide between the two camps could harden. It is hard to see how such a destabilizing outcome would be in anyone's interest. The polarization and divisions have resulted from the decision of the nuclear-armed states and their allies to part company with the dominant sentiment and policy preferences of the international community. It is time for them to rejoin the global mainstream on nuclear policy.

The UN High-Level Conference on Nuclear Disarmament (2018)

The NWPT should also provide an impetus for efforts to achieve a Nuclear Weapons Convention that is universal, nondiscriminatory, verifiable, and enforceable. Actual elimination could be spread out over more than a decade to ensure that decommissioning, dismantlement, and destruction of weapons and weapon-producing materials and infrastructure are carried out safely, securely, verifiably, and irreversibly. One structured opportunity to reconcile the different streams of nuclear policy activities and dialogues will come at the UN High-Level Conference on Nuclear Disarmament in 2018, as called for by the GA (Resolution A/68/32, December 5, 2013).[26] "Convinced that nuclear disarmament and the total elimination of nuclear weapons are the only absolute guarantee against the use or threat of use of nuclear weapons" and recalling NPT Article VI, the resolution decided to convene the high-level conference "no later than 2018" to review the progress made on nuclear disarmament. Like other high-level UN conferences, this will elevate the issue of nuclear disarmament in national policy priorities and in the global agenda, garner widespread media attention, and mobilize civil society.

China and France acceded to the NPT in 1992, the last of the NWS to do so.

Notes

[1] Quoted in Doyle McManus, "The new nuclear arms race," *Los Angeles Times*, 3 April 2016. http://www.latimes.com/opinion/op-ed/la-oe-0403-mcmanus-nuclear-danger-20160403-column.html.

[2] A/CONF.229/2017/CRP.1; http://www.icanw.org/wp-content/uploads/2017/05/DraftTreaty.pdf.

[3] See Marc Weller, ed., *The Oxford Handbook of the Use of Force in International Law* (Oxford: Oxford University Press, 2015).

[4] Patricia Lewis and Ramesh Thakur, "Arms Control, Disarmament and the United Nations," *Disarmament Forum*, no. 1 (2004): 17–28.

[5] Kofi A. Annan, *In Larger Freedom: Towards Development, Security and Human Rights for All.* Report of the Secretary-General (New York: UN, document A/59/2005, March 21, 2005), para. 97.

[6] "IAEA by Numbers," https://www.iaea.org/about/by-the-numbers.

[7] Savita Pande, *India and the Nuclear Test Ban* (New Delhi: Institute for Defence Studies and Analyses, 1996), 25.

[8] Ramesh Thakur, "The Treaty of Rarotonga: The South Pacific Nuclear-Free Zone," in D. Pitt and G. Thompson, eds. *Nuclear-Free Zones* (London: Croom Helm, 1987), 23–45.

[9] See Ramesh Thakur, ed., *Nuclear Weapons-Free Zones* (New York: St. Martin's Press, 1998).

[10] Annex 2 states are the forty-four states that formally participated in the 1996 session of the Conference on Disarmament and possessed nuclear power or research reactors at the time, *all of whom* must ratify the Treaty for it to enter into force (http://www.ctbto.org).

[11] See Ramesh Thakur, "The Global Governance Architecture of Nuclear Security," *Policy Analysis Brief* (Muscatine, IA: Stanley Foundation, March 2013).

[12] Downstream agenda would have to include also the conversion of existing national facilities to international control while ensuring that new facilities being constructed are multinational from the start.

[13] See John Carlson, "An Asia–Pacific Nuclear Energy Community," APLN/CNND *Policy Brief* No. 4 (Canberra: Asia Pacific Leadership Network and Centre for Nuclear Non-Proliferation and Disarmament, June 2013); John Thomson and Geoffrey Forden, "Multilateralism as a Dual-Use Technique: Encouraging Nuclear Energy and Avoiding Proliferation," *Policy Analysis Brief* (Muscatine, Iowa: Stanley Foundation, March 2008).

[14] International Court of Justice, "Legality of the Threat or Use of Nuclear Weapons: Advisory Opinion," http://www.icj-cij.org/docket/files/95/7495.pdf. The normative status of the Court's Advisory Opinion is strengthened by the frequency of its recitation in GA resolutions.

[15] For a contrary interpretation, that the vague and weak disarmament obligations confirm that the treaty's real purpose was nonproliferation, see especially Christopher A. Ford, "Debating

Disarmament: Interpreting Article VI of the Treaty on the Non-Proliferation of Nuclear Weapons," *Nonproliferation Review* 14, no. 3 (2007): 401–428. In 2017, Ford was appointed to a senior position in the Trump administration.

16 Charles J. Carrigan, "Board Backs Off Lower-yield Nukes," Arms Control Association, April 2017. https://www.armscontrol.org/act/2017-04/news/board-backs-off-lower-yield-nukes.

17 https://twitter.com/realDonaldTrump/status/811977223326625792.

18 In a Reuters interview: Steve Holland, "Trump Wants to Make Sure U.S. Nuclear Arsenal at 'Top of Pack,'" *Reuters*, February 24, 2017. http://www.reuters.com/article/us-usa-trump-exclusive-idUSKBN1622IF.

19 "Abe Cabinet says Article 9 does not ban possessing, using N-weapons," *Asahi Shimbun*, April 2, 2016. http://www.asahi.com/ajw/articles/AJ201604020026.html; Peter Hayes and Chung-in Moon, "Should South Korea Go Nuclear?" *EAF Policy Debates* No. 7, July 28, 2014; Henry Sokolski, "Japan and South Korea May Soon Go Nuclear," *Wall Street Journal*, May 8, 2016. http://www.wsj.com/articles/japan-and-south-korea-may-soon-go-nuclear-1462738914.

20 Max Fisher, "Fearing U.S. Withdrawal, Europe Considers Its Own Nuclear Deterrent," *The New York Times*, March 6, 2017. https://www.nytimes.com/2017/03/06/world/europe/european-union-nuclear-weapons.html.

21 Max Fisher, "European Nuclear Weapons Program Would Be Legal, German Review Finds," *New York Times*, July 5, 2017. https://www.nytimes.com/2017/07/05/world/europe/germany-nuclear-weapons.html?.

22 Jayantha Dhanapala and Randy Rydell, *Multilateral Diplomacy and the NPT: An Insider's Account* (Geneva: UN Institute for Disarmament Research, UNIDIR/2005/3, 2005), 50.

23 Nor have the thirteen "practical steps" from the 2000 and the twenty-two "action items" from the 2010 review conferences produced greater results and transparency. For an assessment of the 2010 action plans, see Gareth Evans, Tanya Ogilvie-White, and Ramesh Thakur, *Nuclear Weapons: The State of Play 2015* (Canberra: Centre for Nuclear Non-Proliferation and Disarmament, 2015). https://cnnd.crawford.anu.edu.au/publication/cnnd/5328/nuclear-weapons-state-play-2015.

24 See Tariq Rauf, *Preparing for the 2017 NPT Preparatory Committee Session: The Enhanced Strengthened Review Process* (Stockholm: SIPRI Brief, February 25, 2017). http://www.non-proliferation.org/wp-content/uploads/2017/04/NPT2017_25FEB_RAUF_PrepCom.pdf.

25 "Humanitarian Pledge," http://www.icanw.org/wp-content/uploads/2015/03/HINW14vienna_Pledge_Document.pdf.

26 http://www.un.org/en/events/nuclearweaponelimination/pdf/4-International-Day-for-the-Total-Elimination-of-Nuclear-Weapons-Resolution-A-68-32.pdf.

CHAPTER 20

The Geopolitical Convolutions of Fighting the Global War on Terrorism

Hall Gardner

In the aftermath of the September 11, 2001, attacks on the World Trade Center and Pentagon, the George W. Bush administration was able to mobilize the support of the United Nations (UN) Security Council, NATO, the European Union (EU), and much of the world, for the global war on terrorism (GWOT). At that time, GWOT was largely perceived as a war against the "anti-state terrorist" organization al-Qaeda and its affiliates, and against those states that appeared to provide protection or support for al-Qaeda, primarily the Taliban leadership of Afghanistan. Yet, as time progressed, GWOT has morphed into a truly global war against a number of different "anti-state terrorist" groups as well as so-called rogue states that support different forms of "terrorist" actions. President Donald Trump has now hoped to forge a US-led coalition of sixty-eight countries against al-Qaeda and the Islamic State (IS). Yet without a truly engaged international diplomatic peace offensive, there will be no end in sight to the ongoing GWOT, despite the apparent defeat of IS in Iraq and Syria.

The September 11, 2001, attacks on the World Trade Center and Pentagon killed as many as three thousand people of differing social, economic, and religious backgrounds and may have cost at least $1–2 trillion in damages (including estimated stock losses), of which roughly $40 billion was actually insured and lost by insurance companies.[1] Nevertheless, the GWOT has been disproportionate and not entirely, nor exclusively aimed at al-Qaeda and those individuals actually responsible for committing the September 11, 2001, atrocity. Both the human and political-economic costs of the US retaliation far exceed the actual damage caused by those attacks.

Since 2001, approximately 370,000 people have been killed by violence in Iraq, Afghanistan, and Pakistan. At least 200,000 civilians have died in this fighting. Moreover, at least 10.1 million Afghans, Pakistanis, and Iraqis have been surviving as war refugees in other countries, or been forcibly displaced from their homes. The United States alone has spent or committed $4.8 trillion dollars on the wars in Afghanistan, Pakistan, and Iraq. These current wars have been paid for almost entirely by borrowing. Depending on the costs of the ongoing wars against the IS, future interest payments could total over $7.9 trillion by 2053.[2] And it is only in early 2017 that the US Congress began to consider revoking the 2001 Authorization for Use of Military Force after sixteen years.[3]

These costs are, to a large extent, due to the new form of post–Cold War "short war illusion," and in part due to the geopolitical complications of fighting wars against both states that support "terrorist" movements (i.e., Afghanistan under the Taliban, Iraq under Saddam Hussein, and Syria under al-Assad) and anti-state "terrorist" movements (such as al-Qaeda and its affiliates, the IS, and the Taliban). The situation has been made even more complex in that Washington, while fighting states that support terrorism in American eyes, has aligned itself with states that have been accused of supporting differing terrorist movements, such as Saudi Arabia, Pakistan, Qatar, and Turkey, and which do not necessarily support the same groups that Washington supports. For example, Washington has backed differing partisan groups, such as the Kurdish People's Protection Units (YPG), which represents the armed wing of the Democratic Union Party (PYD), but which both Syria and NATO ally Turkey consider to be a "terrorist" organization.

In terms of the "short war illusion," the actual military interventions in Afghanistan in 2001 and Iraq in 2003, and elsewhere, such as Libya in 2011, have generally been short. There has been a minimum of American (and European) deaths in accord with the "zero death syndrome," at least in the initial offensives of these conflicts. But in the aftermath, "peacekeeping," "peacemaking," and "nation building" have proven to be very long, costly (both in terms of resources and in terms of personnel, with considerable numbers of US soldiers severely wounded[4]), and not very coordinated or effective. For example, US efforts at rebuilding Afghanistan (and engaging in "peacemaking") have cost more in comparative terms than the US Marshall Plan did in rebuilding Europe after World War II. The United States and other international donors have continued to fund more than 60 percent of the Afghan national budget, as well as numerous reconstruction programs and projects that currently operate off budget. It consequently appears that the Afghan government is not self-sustainable just at a time when the United States and NATO have considered pulling out most of their forces.[5] This does not even take into account the potential costs of rebuilding Iraq and Syria, among other countries.

These considerations raise questions as to whether or not the GWOT, with its focus on both states that support terrorism and anti-state terrorist groups, has generally caused more harm than good. US-led military interventions were not initially wars of existential necessity or wars of strategic imperative from the standpoint of American national interests—but purely discretionary and noncompulsory conflicts.[6] Arguably, the Bush administration's efforts to counter the perceived loss of US hegemony over the Arab/Islamic world by means of massive military interventions in Afghanistan and Iraq (in effect falling into the trap set by Osama bin Laden) has actually worked to accelerate the loss of American authority and legitimacy, and possibly helped fuel the spread of differing terrorist movements. Moreover, the ongoing state and anti-state resistance to GWOT—has continued to draw the United States deeper into the quicksand of wider wars.[7]

The question remains as to whether President Trump's approach to GWOT—including his efforts to forge a US-led coalition of sixty-eight countries against the IS[8]—may trigger the spread of militant Islamist movements even further throughout the wider Middle East, Europe, and into other regions as well. The issue is further complicated by the fact that different states, including US allies, appear to be backing different partisan or "terrorist" organizations, whether by funding through government or private sources or through Islamist charities. Trump's apparent tilt in support of Saudi interests since his May 2017 trip to Saudi Arabia risks exacerbating the ongoing proxy war in which both Saudi Arabia and Iran back rival Sunni and Shi'ite "terrorist" organizations or authoritarian state leaderships throughout the "wider Middle East." This ongoing Sunni–Shi'a rivalry is further embroiled by conflict among Sunni states and different anti-state "terrorist" factions. The Trump administration's tilt toward Saudi Arabia, coupled with a number of US attacks on Russian-backed Syrian or Iranian forces—including the Tomahawk cruise missile strikes on a Syrian airbase in response to reports of a Syrian chemical attack on its own population—now risks the possibilities of major power war.[9]

To address these questions and consider strategies to reduce or put an end to acts of terrorism, this chapter explores multiple dimensions of terrorism, analyzes the US-led GWOT, examines potential ramifications of the Trump administration, and finally concludes with the geopolitical complications and implications of GWOT in Syria as an emerging threat to global security, while pointing to the need for engaged international diplomacy to bring GWOT to an end.

The Question of State-Supported versus Anti-State Terrorism

In order to move beyond stereotyped, one-dimensional conceptions, it is important to develop a clearer understanding of the multiple dimensions of "terrorism"—as it takes both state-supported and anti-state forms. To try to provide a simple definition (there are more than one hundred definitions), "terrorism" can be defined as a sociopsychological concept that describes any act that intends to bring fear into the mind of others. Any person threatening significant harm to another person for any reason can be considered as engaging in an act of "terror." Yet, when one is speaking of an act of "terrorism," then this generally implies a socially or politically organized act of violence against others, or even an act of an individual (or "lone wolf") that is staged against a sector of society or members of a government. Social and political acts of "terrorism" take essentially two conflicting, yet often interacting and intercommunicative, forms: state-sponsored and anti-state terrorism.[10]

State-Sponsored Terrorism

The first form of terrorism—which is actually more prevalent—is "state-supported" or "state-sponsored" terrorism, in which the state leadership, regardless of its political orientation (whether democratic, socialist, communist, fascist, theocratic, monarchist, authoritarian, etc.), threatens some form of violence against a rival state's political leadership, its military, and/or its population in an effort to provoke fear and terror. The threat and use of force is part of the panoply of tools that states can use against each other in order for one state leadership to attempt to press the rival state (and its population) to behave in the manner demanded. The greater the threat to use force, and the greater the force is actually used, the greater the sociopsychological impact of the use of terror on the general population and state elites—particularly if the attacks hit members of the civil society and are not merely aimed at a state's official military or police forces, which are generally the target of terrorist groups with more traditional or realistic goals.

State leadership can also threaten its own citizens if it is judged to be in the so-called national interests of the leadership—however those interests are determined. Even democratic states—although to a lesser extent than authoritarian and totalitarian regimes, which are not constrained by rules of law—can "terrorize" their own citizens or those of other countries who are believed to be subverting the established order. In democratic societies, acts of state-supported "terrorism" (including acts of torture or the euphemistic "enhanced interrogation techniques") against presumed "terrorists" or other designated individuals can be rationalized and legally justified under official declarations of a national "state of emergency."[11] These actions are often carried out covertly, by intelligence agencies that may or may not be under the full control of the legislative, judicial, or executive branches. The CIA's drone operations in countries such as Pakistan, Yemen, Somalia, and Libya, for example, may not be under full US governmental control and possess questionably legal validation.

Whether a state is democratic or not, fears of anti-state terrorism can undermine legal safeguards against the abuse of state power. This can result in infringements of civil rights and counteractions ranging from invasion of privacy to curfews, state repression, torture, internment camps, extrajudicial execution, democide, and even genocide. The response of states to both nonviolent and violent actions may result in acts justified as "counterterrorism" or "terrorizing the terrorists"—in the effort to obtain and sustain both allegiance and obedience, and to repress dissent and opposition. This can result in state counteractions that are disproportionate to the crimes committed, because the anti-state terrorists are seen as directly challenging the legitimacy of leaders to rule. To underscore the point, even though traffic accidents generally cause more deaths per year in most countries than do acts of anti-state terrorism, leaders do not necessarily react to even major traffic accidents—unless these daily travesties are somehow seen as challenging their political legitimacy.

Anti-State Terrorism

The second and opposing form of terrorism is "anti-state terrorism." Anti-state terrorism seeks to challenge the hegemony of the state often in response to acts of state-supported terrorism—although it is generally debated as to which side committed the first and most severe acts of violence against the other. The basic motivation for an anti-state and/or anti-society attack is often based on differing ideological rationale, which may or may not be logically consistent or based on verifiable facts.

There are several types of anti-state "terrorist" movements with differing goals and objectives. First, there are anti-state secessionist movements that seek to achieve political independence from governments generally described as oppressive so as to gain social, political, economic, and cultural control over those territories once separated. These movements often claim to represent a specific ethnic identity, regional group, or other groups with common beliefs and ideologies. Second, there are political succession movements which seek to change governments by force through revolution or some form of *coup d'etat*, but which generally hope to control the same boundaries of the former state. Third, there are transnational pan-movements which seek to link differing leaderships across state boundaries.

In the case of al-Qaeda and the IS, transnational propaganda seeks to reach and recruit populations spanning the breadth of the Sunni Islamic world before the collapse of the Ottoman Empire. These groups critique, often in apocalyptic terms, what they see as the general oppression of Sunni Muslims caused by the territorial division of the Ottoman Empire at the hands of the rival European powers, Russia, and China—due to the latter's control over Muslim Uighurs in the energy- and mineral-rich Xinjiang province (former eastern Turkestan). As takfiri jihadists, with Wahhabist-Salafist ideological roots, al-Qaeda and the IS not only oppose Zionism and Shi'a Iran, but they also likewise seek to overthrow the Arab Gulf monarchies, whose leaderships are perceived to be corrupt and only superficially Islamic. More specifically, in the case of the IS, the goal has been to forge a unity of Sunni Muslims in both Iraq and Syria—to the exclusion of other ethnic and religious communities. This goal may soon begin to morph as IS members join Islamist struggles in other countries. Already, in India, Pakistan, Afghanistan, and Bangladesh, the IS has attempted to link its version of Wahhabist-Salafist ideology with a Deobandi version of Islamic theosophy, but has thus far been opposed by the Taliban.[12] It is not always clear who is actually in charge of anti-state terrorist or partisan groups. Some anti-state groups may represent indigenous partisans who oppose a specific state or states for somewhat similar reasons and who hope to obtain support from other partisans either inside or outside that particular state and society. The dilemma is that such groups can eventually become supported or financed by states that possess sympathy with their cause or that believe they can manipulate that cause to their advantage—usually with covert aid and assistance. Anti-state groups that cannot find domestic sources of funding, or that cannot engage in self-sustaining black and/or gray market activities (such as drug trafficking), may accordingly fall under the sway of wealthier states or organizations. In such a way, one cannot be certain if anti-state groups necessarily possess their own self-realized goals and agenda as they claim. It is possible that these groups may be operating as surrogates in the interests of another state or organization. The latter states or organizations may want to support acts of "terrorism" through surrogates precisely because they do not want to exhibit their influence and activities openly.

Comparative Analysis of Terrorism Forms

There is a key difference between state-supported and anti-state terrorism. States are generally seen as possessing *legitimate* means to threaten compliance to the government as perceived by both the domestic society and international governments—assuming that the state is recognized by those governments. State-supported "terrorism" generally possesses the social, political, and international legitimacy that the state can then abuse if it decides to engage in violence—even state leaderships can step beyond the boundaries of domestic and/or international laws governing human rights and the laws of war.

Unlike states, anti-state movements possess no real legitimacy to use violence—and must build their legitimacy over time. That legitimacy is often—and ironically—achieved by the use of violence, so that leaders described as "terrorists" can become "freedom fighters," and even win the Nobel Peace prize, such as Menachem Begin, Yasser Arafat, and Nelson Mandela. But there is no way to know whether anti-state "terrorist" or partisan groups will rule fairly and justly—once, and if, they obtain power. Both Nelson Mandela and Robert Mugabe, for example, were considered "terrorists" at early stages of their career, prior to seizing power. Yet Mandela voluntarily stepped down from the presidency of South Africa, while Mugabe has tightened his dictatorship in Zimbabwe.[13]

Both state-supported and anti-state "terrorism" possess a whole range of possible threat options and tools that are intended to induce fear or terror in others and achieve domestic and/or international ends, depending upon their capabilities, intentions, and will to power. Both state-supported and anti-state "terrorism" are in a dialectical battle to claim legitimacy for their various causes, and often by using violence to achieve those causes and in accusing their rivals of acts of "terrorism."

In contrast to already established states, including countries with highly repressive governments, anti-state movements generally possess little legitimacy unless they have built up a substantial popular following. They rely primarily on "moral" claims against state injustice and corruption, which they denounce and critique by means of counter-ideology. For example, anti-state movements can propagandize about high levels of unemployment and underemployment in an effort to attract followers. These groups can blame state leadership for corruption and police repression or for mismanagement of the economy and for the "terror"—often attributed to globalization—that can result from the loss of one's livelihood.

At the same time, however, once anti-state groups go underground, they often oppose even legitimate state reforms in the fear that such reforms will eventually gain popular support and thereby strengthen the power and authority of those state authorities whom they oppose. Such groups then demand "revolution" on their terms, and do not advocate mere reforms of the leadership in power.

Hard-line opposition to government policies does not, however, mean that it is absolutely impossible to make some form of political trade-offs with such terrorist groups depending on the situation. Differing political accords can be reached with some groups, such as Sinn Fein and the Irish Republican Army (IRA) in Northern Ireland, Nelson Mandela's African National Congress, and the Revolutionary Armed Forces of Columbia (FARC), among others. These organizations had been denounced as anti-state "terrorist" groups in the past, but were eventually willing to accept power-sharing accords.[14] Even Hizb'allah, denounced by the United States as a terrorist organization, has engaged in political compromises and power sharing in the Lebanese cabinet and parliament. The political problem is that once an organization is labeled a "terrorist" organization, this makes it extremely difficult to engage in diplomacy with such organization as both government officials and private individuals (including nongovernmental organizations) may be banned from making any form of contact. Often, negotiations need to take place through third parties, which recognize both sides to a dispute.

Anti-state terrorism usually adopts a critical ideology in an effort to undermine the legitimacy of the states and societies that the group is struggling against—often in the proclaimed hope that the sociopolitical movement can achieve a new form of governance. Effective marketing of an anti-state group's counter-ideology is crucial. Acts of terror become a trademark for some anti-state organizations for media and promotional purposes. Some acts of terror and suicide missions are staged to show the world that the group is still alive and that the cause is not lost. Contrary to realism and rational actor models, suicide for a cause greater than oneself is seen as a means to attract new followers. Moreover, the asymmetrical nature of new forms of "hybrid warfare" (involving cyber sabotage, use of drones, suicide bombings, passenger planes, or vans, among other techniques to kill and provoke terror) can provide some tactical advantages to lesser anti-state actors—including "lone wolves"—relative to states, which generally possess superior force capabilities.[15]

Anti-state groups accordingly need a powerful system of beliefs and interpretation of social, political, and religious "reality" to attract followers and to critique and undermine state legitimacy. Concurrently, such groups need to build up their own legitimacy over time against the beliefs, ideology, and religion of their "oppressors," "enemies," or "infidels." The more the state represses, it is hoped, the greater the social resistance will grow. The IS, for example, possesses strong propaganda capabilities given its use of social media, a radio station, magazines, videos, photos, and propaganda distribution in many languages.[16] Attacks against cultural and religious symbols (such as the IS's demolition of two mausoleums in Palmyra, the Taliban's destruction of the Buddhas of Bamiyan, and Ansar Dine's destruction of nine mausoleums and the door of the Sidi Yahia mosque in Timbuktu) are not only crucial for destroying the "oppressor's" identity, but also in helping to build a counter-ideology.

The US-Led GWOT

To understand how the US-led GWOT impacts the future of global security, this section reviews how the crisis came about. Just after the al-Qaeda attacks on the World Trade Center and Pentagon, the two major symbols of American financial and military power, respectively, the Bush administration declared a "global war on terrorism" (GWOT) on "every terrorist group of global reach." This declaration then led to major US-led military interventions into both Afghanistan in 2001 and Iraq in 2003—even though those countries, particularly Iraq, were only tangentially related to the al-Qaeda attacks on the United States.

The direct military intervention phase of the Bush administration's GWOT in Afghanistan (Operation Enduring Freedom, OEF) was initiated on October 7, 2001, under a general UN mandate—which the Bush administration largely used as a blank check for a more extensive war against both "rogue states" that support "terrorist" organizations and anti-state "terrorist" organizations. The peacekeeping, peacemaking, and "nation-building" phase of that war began in December 2001 after the International Conference on Afghanistan held in Bonn, Germany, which had established a provisional government under the leadership of Hamid Karzai, which was protected by the NATO-led International Security Assistance Force, but which largely excluded the majority Pashtun tribal population, even if the latter did not all back the Taliban.

OEF was officially ended by the Obama administration on December 31, 2014, but this operation has been succeeded by Operation Freedom's Sentinel. In the meantime, GWOT has spread to the largely uncontrolled tribal Pashtun regions of northern Pakistan, which have thus far served as a safety zone for anti-NATO Afghan militias. Osama bin Laden was able to escape to Pakistan after the battle of Tora Bora in December 2001—in part because the Pentagon relied on Afghan militias and did not deploy sufficient US forces, and in part because the Pakistani Inter-Services Intelligence purportedly wanted to keep bin Laden alive in order to provide support for differing Islamist factions in Afghanistan, Kashmir, and elsewhere, after the September 11, 2001, attacks. Even after bin Laden's assassination in Pakistani territory by US Navy SEALs under President Obama's command in 2011, Islamabad, as a major non-NATO ally, continued to support a number of Islamist groups in Afghanistan and in India-controlled Azad Kashmir and Gilgit-Baltistan—in a hope to gain what it has called "strategic depth" versus India.

In addition to the Afghanistan/Pakistan dimension of OEF, other regional dimensions of OEF included the battle against differing Islamist movements in the Philippines, around the Horn of Africa, in the Trans-Sahara, and in the Caribbean and Central America. The OEF forces also possessed basing rights until 2014 in Manas, Kyrgyzstan, which helped to supply US and NATO forces in Afghanistan. (The US military presence in Kyrgyzstan was protested by both Russia and China.) The OEF force was concurrently involved in fighting Islamist groups in the Georgian Pankisi Gorge valley near the Chechen border. Both Boris Yeltsin and Vladimir Putin had intervened against Islamist secessionist movements in the first (December 1994 to August 1996) and second (August 1999 to April 2009) Chechen wars—in which the Chechen groups involved were seen by Moscow as backed at least in part by Saudi Arabia. (Pankisi Gorge has a Chechen/Ingush Muslim population of roughly ten thousand.) Here, for example, Northern Caucasian suicide bombers, often called "Black Widows" because they may have lost close relatives in the brutal Russian-Chechen wars since 1994, or in more recent clashes with Russian-backed forces, have engaged in a number of "terrorist" attacks throughout Russia.[17]

In 2003, GWOT entered into yet another phase with the US-led military intervention against the Iraqi regime of Saddam Hussein, this time without a UN Security Council mandate. Operation Iraqi Freedom largely diverted resources, manpower, and intelligence away from the initial focus on al-Qaeda, the Taliban, and ineffective "nation building" in Afghanistan. As was the case in Afghanistan, the actual military intervention phase of that war was brief (from March 20 to May 1, 2003), but the peacekeeping and peacemaking phase still has not come to a full end despite President Obama's promises to pull US forces out in 2014.

The US-led military intervention was not only intended to eliminate weapons of mass "terror" (which were not found) and Saddam Hussein's leadership, but was at least initially intended to bring peace, if not "democracy," to the entire region. In order to help justify the United Kingdom's participation in the Iraqi war effort, UK prime minister Tony Blair in particular argued that the US-led intervention in Iraq would be followed by international efforts to achieve peace between Israel and the Palestinians—efforts led by the Quartet Group of the UN, the EU, the United States, and Russia. Those efforts largely fizzled out by 2015, when Blair stepped down as Middle East peace envoy. But similar peace talks need to be revived in a new format and under new leadership—just as protest has begun to erupt over new Israeli security measures at the al-Aqsa Mosque in July 2017. As to be argued, more extensive international diplomatic efforts will be needed if a modicum of peace can be established throughout the wider Middle East.

Following the forced regime change and total collapse of the Iraqi state in 2003, largely due to the Bush administration decision to eliminate the Ba'ath Socialist Party altogether (which had controlled the entire government, military, and educational system), the country became a highly unstable and conflictual "democratic federation" of essentially Shi'ite, Kurd, and Sunni regions. In effect, the US intervention in Iraq in 2003 eventually served the interests of al-Qaeda, IS, and Iran—particularly given Iranian infiltration of the collapsed Iraqi state in an effort to support the Iraqi Shi'a population after that war and to gain an ally.[18] Burgeoning Iranian influence inside oil-rich Iraq has consequently helped to generate a regional proxy war between Saudi Arabia and Iran—given Saudi fears that Iran and Iraq together could eventually dominate oil export markets.

The ongoing conflict between Sunnis (which fell from being the ruling elite under Saddam Hussein to become a minority population in relatively poorer regions of Iraq) and the Shi'a majority led to the eventual rise of the IS. This took place after Abu Musab al-Zarqawi pledged allegiance to Osama bin Laden and formed al-Qaeda in Iraq in 2004 to fight against the predominantly Shi'a Iraqi federal government. By 2006, al-Qaeda in Iraq created an umbrella organization, Islamic State in Iraq (ISI); the latter was countered by the US troop surge and by the Sahwa (Awakening) councils, which had been created by Sunni Arab tribesmen with US assistance to fight al-Qaeda affiliates.

Abu Bakr al-Baghdadi, who had created Jamaat Jaysh Ahl al-Sunnah wa-l-Jamaah, the Army of the Sunni People Group, then became leader of ISI in 2010 and began rebuilding ISI's capabilities to fight the Iraqi government. By 2013, al-Baghdadi joined the ongoing post–Arab Spring rebellion against President Bashar al-Assad in Syria. Al-Baghdadi then helped set up the al-Nusra Front before merging his forces in Iraq and Syria in the creation of "Islamic State in Iraq and the Levant" (ISIL). The leaders of al-Nusra and al-Qaeda were opposed to this decision, and separated from ISIL. At the end of December 2013, ISIL shifted its focus back to the Iraqi struggle and took control of Fallujah.

By June 2014, ISIL was able to overrun Mosul; it then advanced south toward Baghdad. ISIL declared the creation of a caliphate and changed its name to "Islamic State" (IS). Although Allied forces have attempted to combat IS in Mosul, Iraq and Raqqa, Syria from 2016 to June 2017 with heavy civilian casualties, IS members have nevertheless been able to create a network of affiliates in Afghanistan, Egypt, Pakistan, Jordan, Indonesia, Lebanon, Palestine, the Philippines, and Libya.[19] Singapore, Malaysia, and Indonesia, and possibly Thailand, are also on the IS hit list. By 2016, Moscow began to warn that the Pankisi Gorge region has been attracting IS militants, just as the region once attracted al-Qaeda.[20]

IS has also been gaining entry into Afghanistan, and it took Tora Bora away from the Taliban after the US military bombed the former position of IS with the largest nonnuclear bomb in the US arsenal, the MOAB, as a means to "terrorize the terrorists."[21] After al-Qaeda sought to support the Islamist struggle against India in Kashmir, thus aligning with Pakistan, it has been reported that IS has begun to enter the Kashmir region as well. This dispute needs UN and Contact Group diplomatic attention before it once again heats up into violent conflict.[22]

The Trump Administration

Unlike his predecessor, President Obama, who tried to remove "terror" and "Islam" from the focus of GWOT and implement instead the "Struggle against Violent Extremism (SAVE)," President Donald Trump has gone in the opposite direction. Trump's anti-Islamic propaganda and rhetoric go far beyond any previous US administration. In his February 2017 address to Congress, Trump vowed to "eradicate 'radical Islamic terrorism' from the face of the Earth." Trump thus became the first American president to use the term "radical Islamic terrorism."[23] Neither the administration of George W. Bush nor Barack Obama had officially referred to "Islamic terrorism" because it conflates Islam as a religion with "terrorist" organizations that seek to manipulate Islamic beliefs for their own political purposes.[24]

Moreover, Trump's own anti-terrorist propaganda has appeared to provide ideological cover to the Sunni Wahhabist claims of Saudi Arabia against Iranian-backed Shi'a claims—even if Saudi Arabia and Iran have both been accused of supporting acts of "terrorism" over the years, and even if Saudi Arabia possesses major political disputes with other Sunni states, such as Turkey and Qatar. On the one hand, during his presidential election campaign in 2016, Donald Trump himself accused Saudi Arabia of secretly supporting the al-Qaeda September 11, 2001, attacks; other American political leaders have accused Riyadh of having prior knowledge of the attacks.[25] Saudi Arabia has likewise been accused of being a major financier of both the Afghan government and the Taliban through private and government channels.[26] For its part, Iran has also been accused of complicity with the September 11 attacks by granting al-Qaeda members responsible for the attacks passage through Iranian territory[27]—in accord with the dictum "the enemy of my enemy can become one's friend (at least on occasion)." On the other hand, by June 2017, President Trump appeared to be giving full support to the Saudi Arabia against Iran.[28]

Obama's approach had sought to counterbalance Saudi and Iranian interests, in the hope of achieving an eventual Saudi-Iranian *rapprochement*. By contrast, the Trump administration has strongly denounced Obama's efforts to forge a *rapprochement* with Iran. This was after the Obama administration, in working with the UN Security Council, plus Germany and the EU, had signed the Iranian nuclear framework accord (or Joint Comprehensive Plan of Action) in 2015. Washington then opened up the possibility of trade accords with Iran for the sale of Boeing commercial aircraft, for example, in rivalry with Europe's Airbus.[29] While Obama had initiated a major $110 billion arms sale to Saudi Arabia that Trump himself has appropriated (but in which not all contracts have been signed),[30] it was nonetheless the Obama administration's intent to prevent a regional arms race of nuclear "terror." Nevertheless, it appears highly unlikely that Trump will tear up the nuclear deal with Iran despite his accusation that it represents the "worst deal ever."[31]

In addition to engaging both overtly and covertly in conflicts in Afghanistan/northern Pakistan, Somalia, the Philippines, the Trans-Sahara, Libya, Iraq, and Syria, the United States since Obama has also provided arms for Saudi Arabia's battle against Iranian-backed Houthis—ostensibly in order to prevent Iran from obtaining a foothold in the Red Sea, while concurrently fighting al-Qaeda affiliates and IS in Yemen.[32] GWOT has consequently spread over an even wider area from Libya to Syria to Yemen as well as to sub-Saharan Africa—largely in the aftermath of the so-called 2011 Arab Spring movements.

Geopolitical Complications and Implications of GWOT in Syria

While the initial focus of GWOT was on al-Qaeda and the Taliban in Afghanistan, its scope has expanded dramatically. Although President Trump has reluctantly started to build up forces in Afghanistan (justified in part for the United States to obtain Afghanistan's mineral wealth), GWOT's major focus now appears to be shifting toward the complex struggles taking place in Syria and Iraq. In September 2015, Moscow intervened in the Syrian conflict in order to quell the civil war that had largely been initiated during the Arab Spring in 2011. Contrary to US and European strategy, Moscow has generally opposed all groups that are unwilling to work with the essentially Iranian-backed Alawite regime of Bashar al-Assad. For their part, the United States and Europeans have focused on destroying the IS. The differing groups that oppose al-Assad are essentially Sunni Muslim, Christians, Yazidis, or secular Kurds. Sunni groups have been seen by the al-Assad regime as backed by Saudi Arabia, Turkey, and Qatar, while the United States and France, among other countries, have generally claimed to be backing the Kurds or so-called moderate Islamist forces—even if these latter groups must sometimes align with the battle-hardened al-Nusra Front (an affiliate of al-Qaeda). In late January 2017, the al-Nusra Front merged with four other groups to become Tahrir al-Sham.

The conflict between the Syrian al-Assad regime, seen as a state supporter of terrorism, and anti-state "terrorist" factions epitomizes the convoluted geopolitical struggle between state and anti-state forces. While President Obama had opted not to strike Syria after the al-Assad regime was accused of using Sarin poison gas in 2013 (without absolute proof) against its own people, the Trump administration ordered a strike of fifty-nine cruise missiles against a Syrian airbase after the regime was once again accused (again without absolute proof) of using poison gas in April 2017.[33] While Trump's cruise missile attack may have been intended to send a signal for Syria not to use chemical weaponry, this has evidently not prevented the Syrian regime from refraining from the use of conventional bombs, cluster bombs, phosphorus weapons, or "barrel bombs" (which can contain toxic materials and chlorine gas)—which evidently also kill innocent populations. Nor does it stop the extreme torture of the Syrian regime's opponents.

The US Tomahawk attack represented a new phase in GWOT—in that the Pentagon was not attacking an anti-state "terrorist" movement but the interests of a "rogue" state, which is nonetheless backed by both Russia and Iran. Then, in June 2017, Moscow put Washington on warning after a US F/A-18 Super Hornet shot down a Syrian SU-22 which had been dropping bombs near pro-US Syrian Democratic Forces. Washington has dubbed the latter group as "moderate," but this group is nevertheless seen by the al-Assad regime as a "terrorist" organization that has been seeking to undermine Assad's rule. Washington, along with Israel, may have also struck Iranian-backed militias, including the Lebanese group Hizb'allah, which has also moved into the oil-rich region where the United States shot down the Syrian jet.[34]

Further geopolitical convolutions in GWOT involving state-supported and anti-state "terrorism" are shown in Turkey–US relations with respect to the Kurds. US support for secular Kurdish factions in Syria to fight against IS angers Turkey, which sees Kurdish groups as anti-state "terrorist" factions. Ankara believes that Kurdish political parties and militias in Syria, such as the PYD, are linked to the radical Kurdistan Workers' Party (PKK) in Turkey. These

Kurdish groups have been seen by Turkey as demanding independence and not "autonomy" as they claim.[35] Ironically, it is the Kurdistan Regional Government leadership which previously opposed independence, but which has begun to demand independence against the interests of the Turkish PKK and against the advice of the US government.[36] This would open a new can of worms if the Iraqi Kurds begin to fight the Iraqi government.

Other geopolitical complications arise from the dispute between Saudi Arabia and Qatar (both are Wahhabist states) over the latter's support for the Muslim Brotherhood and its efforts to forge a more balanced approach toward Iranian interests in the region. Saudi Arabia, the United Arab Emirates (UAE), Egypt, and Bahrain have all accused Qatar of supporting al-Qaeda affiliates, among other terrorist groups; they have also demanded that Doha close down its TV station Al Jazeera.[37] Concurrently, Hamas was enraged when Saudi Arabia demanded that Qatar put an end to its support for the Muslim Brotherhood and for Hamas as well. For its part, Turkey, which is aligned with the Muslim Brotherhood, has strongly backed Qatar, stating that the latter does not support "terrorist" movements.[38] In essence, Saudi Arabia opposes Qatar's close ties to Iran (due to their shared gas field), while the UAE and Egypt have strongly opposed Qatar's support for the Muslim Brotherhood, ironically, as the UAE has close trade ties with Iran. Saudi Arabia's thirteen demands placed on Qatar in June 2017 to stop backing "terrorism"—with Turkey backing up Qatar to deter the tacit threat of Saudi invasion—nevertheless appear eerily reminiscent of Austro-Hungarian demands on Serbia not to support terrorist groups such as the Black Hand, which had assassinated the Archduke Ferdinand.[39]

Qatar claims that it does not back "terrorism." Doha argues that its real "crime" is to demand that all Arab countries permit greater freedom of debate through its TV station Al Jazeera—which has been seen as a major ideological force behind the Arab Spring protests—in that Al Jazeera journalists have been regarded as supporting both Islamist and democratic movements against authoritarian regimes and against US and European interests. A further irony is that Qatar hosts the Al Udeid Air Base from which the United States has operated many of its "counterterrorist" military operations in Syria, Iraq, Afghanistan, and elsewhere.

The problem of who is supporting whom is further complicated by the fact that the IS, to some extent, may have been initially enabled by Washington itself. Former US director of defense intelligence Michael Flynn asserted that the creation of a "Salafist principality" (which could include IS or other groups) in eastern Syria was a "willful act" by Washington. IS was then purportedly supported by the United States; Europeans; Saudi Arabia, Qatar, and other Arab Gulf states; and Turkey—in order to combat Syrian leader al-Assad.[40] In any case, whether or not the United States and Sunni Gulf states were directly or indirectly involved in the founding of the IS, the genie is out of the bottle and the states that may have initially been involved in the creation of IS have all accused each other of continuing to support IS—or else not doing enough to cut off its finances or destroy it. In any case, the Trump administration has reportedly ended funding for a number of anti-Assad groups secretly supported by the CIA. This should somewhat strengthen the position of Syria, Russia, and Iran in the struggle for control over Syria and could possibly open the door to a confederal solution between the Assad government and those few partisan groups willing to work with the Assad regime. But this assumes that the United States, Europeans, and Saudi Arabia can eventually reach a common accord with Russia and Iran.

One way or another, the complex conflict between Iran and Saudi Arabia impacts all the above actors. On the one hand, Iran sees itself engaged in a war of counter-encirclement against pan-Sunni movements that could destabilize the northern Caucasus, Central Asia, Iraq, and other areas in the wider Middle East. Tehran also opposes the essentially American-backed regimes of Saudi Arabia, plus the other Arab Gulf states—in addition to clashing with Israel, which has threatened to preempt Iran's proclaimed "peaceful" nuclear energy program if Iran does attempt to develop nuclear weapons. On the other hand, Saudi Arabia fears Iranian efforts to augment its political-economic influence in Lebanon, Iraq, Syria, Bahrain, Yemen, and along the Red Sea, plus closer economic and energy ties to Qatar.

Increasingly backed by the Trump administration, Riyadh has supported differing Sunni rebel groups which have been struggling against the al-Assad regime, while also fighting a disastrous and expensive war (at $7 billion a month) against the Houthis in Yemen—who are seen as Iranian proxies. The United States has been assisting Saudi Arabia in the war with military supports and arms sales, but has been focusing primarily its air strikes on al-Qaeda affiliates and IS in Yemen. Ironically, Saudi Arabia's efforts to blockade Qatar as an indirect means to contain Iran may actually strengthen Iranian influence by bringing Iran and Turkey, plus Russia, closer together.[41]

Given these kind of complex, convoluted, and often contradictory approaches of major and regional powers toward differing partisan or "terrorist" movements—in which so-called anti-state terrorist organizations appear to be increasingly backed by states—the Trump administration will find it very difficult, if not next to impossible, to establish an effective sixty-eight-member coalition of military forces, involving the United States, NATO, the Europeans, Turkey, the Kurds, Saudi Arabia, Qatar, and other Arab Gulf states, in the struggle against the IS. And if the latter does spread into new regions, it will prove very difficult to smother.

A separate, but related, issue is that President Trump's intent to slash the State Department budget by as much as 28 percent could undercut the long-term prospects for peace—as it would mean less resources for postconflict peacekeeping, for diplomatic solutions, and for social and political development in many of the areas where they are most needed. The defeat of IS alone will not put an end to the ongoing conflict between state-supported and anti-state "terrorist" or partisan factions. And despite the general failure of nation building in Afghanistan, different forms of international assistance, coupled with UN-mandated peacekeeping to provide stability, will be needed to help foster the development of the populations living in Afghanistan, northern Pakistan, Iraq, and Syria, among others that have been ravaged by GWOT—if a general peace can eventually be implemented.

GWOT will not come to an end unless the Trump administration—or its successor—eventually finds a way to reach a *rapprochement* between Israel, Iran, Turkey, Qatar, and Saudi Arabia by way of settling the horrific conflict in Syria. Washington—in working in multilateral Contact Groups with Russia and other major and regional powers—also needs to engage in sincere diplomatic efforts to reconcile Israel and the Palestinians in a variant of the "two-state" solution. It will also prove necessary to reconcile Turkey, Syria, Iraq, and the Kurds, as well as India and Pakistan over Afghanistan and Kashmir—among many other disputes impacting the "wider Middle East." This means reaching power-sharing accords, high degrees of autonomy in certain regions, coupled with arrangements involving confederal governance—if partitions are to be avoided.

Despite the accusations against Qatar for its support for "terrorism"—of which many states are guilty, including the United States—one of Doha's strengths has been its diplomatic and financial role in engaging in *conflict mediation* in Lebanon, in Yemen, and throughout the region, including the 2011 Darfur Peace Agreement, with efforts also undertaken in Palestine (given Qatar's ties with both Israel and Hamas) and in the border conflict between Djibouti and Eritrea. Qatar is one of the few Sunni Arab countries that can negotiate with Iran. Doha has also sought to achieve positive ties with Israel—despite their disputes over the role of Hamas.

Doha had permitted the Afghan Taliban to open a political office in Qatar in 2013, which was abruptly closed, but has nevertheless helped to sponsor a number of international peace conferences, such as the Track II Doha Dialogue on "Peace and Security in Afghanistan" organized by the Pugwash Conferences on Science and World Affairs in 2016.[42] This conference took place when the official Quadrilateral Coordination Group on Afghan Peace and Reconciliation was at a standstill due to lack of Taliban participation. In April 2017, Moscow likewise organized a conference with Taliban participation, but in which the United States refused to participate. One option being considered is that of regional power-sharing arrangements between the Taliban and the Afghan government.

The point is that many of Qatar's efforts in *conflict mediation*—even if not all were successful—need to be supported by the United States, Russia, and the UN Security Council, through initiatives such as the Quartet Group of the UN, the EU, the United States, and Russia, among other possible Contact Groups involving regional powers. By drawing Qatar, Turkey, Saudi Arabia, and Iran, as well as Israel, among other states, into wider international discussions, there will be a better chance to achieve *conflict resolution* throughout the "wider Middle East," as these states—and many (but not all) of the "terrorist" factions that they overtly or covertly support—will be pressed to make concessions and compromises. Without geopolitical settlements over the aforementioned regions, there is a real possibility that the GWOT will soon transmogrify into the next Major Power War.[43]

Notes

1. "How much did the September 11 terrorist attack cost America?" http://www.iags.org/costof911.html. The attackers themselves probably spent around $500,000 in the effort to organize the attacks from Afghanistan, Hamburg, Germany, and the United Arab Emirates (UAE), and from US territory as well.
2. http://watson.brown.edu/costsofwar/costs/economic.
3. http://thehill.com/policy/defense/340330-possible-war-authorization-repeal-reflects-growing-shift-in-gop.
4. http://watson.brown.edu/costsofwar/costs/human/military/wounded.
5. Special Inspector General for Afghanistan Reconstruction (SIGAR) (July 30, 2014). https://www.sigar.mil/pdf/quarterlyreports/2014-07-30qr.pdf.
6. Chester Crocker, "The Place of Grand Strategy, Statecraft and Power in Conflict Management," in *Leasing Dogs of War*, Chester A. Crocker, Fen Osler Hampson, and Pamela R. Aall, eds. (Washington, DC: United States Institute for Peace Press, 2007).
7. It was the Carter administration which had initially encouraged the rise of Islamist movements in the effort to make it more likely that Moscow would intervene militarily in Afghanistan in December 1979. See Hall Gardner, *American Global Strategy and the "War on Terrorism"* (Farnham, UK: Ashgate, 2007).
8. http://www.newsweek.com/us-allies-middle-east-nations-isis-trump-fight-571876.
9. See Hall Gardner, *World War Trump: The Risks of America's New Nationalism* (Prometheus Books: 2018, forthcoming).
10. See my concept of "four forms of terrorism," Gardner, *American Global Strategy*.
11. "The Committee finds, based on a review of CIA interrogation records, that the use of the CIA's enhanced interrogation techniques was not an effective means of obtaining accurate information or gaining detainee cooperation. Senate Select Committee on Intelligence (Declassification Revisions December 3, 2014). http://gia.guim.co.uk/2014/12/torture-report-doc/torture_report.pdf.
12. Deobandi is a movement within Sunni (primarily Hanafi) Islam that is centered in India, Pakistan, Afghanistan, and Bangladesh but generally opposes the Wahhabist-Salafist theosophy of both al-Qaeda and the Islamic State. http://thediplomat.com/2015/02/islamic-state-goes-official-in-south-asia/.
13. Leon Hartwell, "The Democrat and the Dictator: Comparing Nelson Mandela and Robert Mugabe," *Southern African Peace and Security Studies* 4, no. 1(2015): 19–40 http://www.saccps.org/pdf/4-1/4-1_Hartwell_2.pdf.
14. See discussion in Gardner, *American Global Strategy*.
15. Hall Gardner, "Hybrid Warfare: Iranian and Russian Versions of 'Little Green Men' and Contemporary Conflict" (Rome: NATO Defense College, 2015). http://www.ndc.nato.int/news/news.php?icode=885.
16. https://www.theguardian.com/world/2014/oct/07/isis-media-machine-propaganda-war.
17. http://www.telegraph.co.uk/news/worldnews/europe/russia/8279043/Moscow-airport-attack-timeline-of-attacks-in-Russia.html.
18. Hall Gardner, "Hybrid Warfare", 2015. http://www.ndc.nato.int/news/news.php?icode=885.
19. Rod Nordland and Fahim Abed, "ISIS Takes Tora Bora, Once bin Laden's Afghan Fortress," *New York Times* (June 14, 2017). See also http://nymag.com/daily/intelligencer/2014/11/isis-now-has-military-allies-in-11-countries.html.
20. http://www.bbc.com/news/world-europe-36035312; https://www.rt.com/news/330234-georgia-pankisi-isis-lavrov/.
21. http://www.reuters.com/article/us-afghanistan-islamic-state-idUSKCN0P91EN20150629.
22. http://thediplomat.com/2016/04/why-violence-in-kashmir-is-getting-worse/.
23. http://nypost.com/2017/02/25/mcmaster-reportedly-splits-with-trump-on-radical-islamic-terror/. Trump overruled his newly appointed national security advisor, Lt. Gen. H. R. McMaster, who had argued that these groups are really "un-Islamic" even if they claim to represent Islamist beliefs.
24. Former CIA agent Robert Baer put the issue this way: "I think it's a mistake in US foreign policy, first of all, to paint Islam as an enemy, because you get dragged into a cultural war which

we can't win." The goal was "to isolate the people who really do sponsor mass murder or kidnappings or individual murders of people . . . Those are isolated individuals which don't have anything to do with Islam in general. Same way in Hezbollah. It's a small group of people kidnapping, murdering. But Hezbollah itself is not a terrorist organization." Robert Baer, *Frontline* interview with Neil Docherty, "Terror and Iran" (March 22, 2002). http://www.pbs.org/wgbh/pages/frontline/shows/tehran/interviews/baer.html.

25 https://theintercept.com/2017/05/18/donald-trump-said-saudi-arabia-was-behind-911-now-hes-going-there-on-his-first-foreign-trip/. A lawsuit claims that the September 11, 2001, al-Qaeda hijackers received assistance and financial support from individuals connected to the Saudi Arabian government, implicating intelligence officers, embassy staff, and members of the country's royal family. http://www.independent.co.uk/news/world/americas/saudi-arabia-911-victims-lawsuit-prior-knowledge-world-trade-center-terror-attack-twin-towers-a7644016.html.

26 https://www.nytimes.com/2016/12/06/world/asia/saudi-arabia-afghanistan.html?_r=0.

27 In *Havlish et al. v. bin Laden et al.*, Judge Daniels held that the Islamic Republic of Iran, its Supreme Leader Ayatollah Ali Hosseini Khamenei, former Iranian president Ali Akbar Hashemi Rafsanjani, and Iran's agencies and instrumentalities, including, among others, the Iranian Revolutionary Guard Corps (IRGC), the Iranian Ministry of Intelligence and Security (MOIS), and Iran's terrorist proxy Hezbollah, all materially aided and supported al-Qaeda before and after 9/11. http://www.iran911case.com/. Former CIA agent Robert Baer reported that Iran may have discussed a strategic partnership with al-Qaeda in July 1996, but what happened after is not certain. Interview: Robert Baer, http://www.pbs.org/wgbh/pages/frontline/shows/tehran/interviews/baer.html.

28 http://edition.cnn.com/2017/05/21/politics/trump-saudi-speech-transcript/index.html. Trump's speech on Saudi Arabia: "From Lebanon to Iraq to Yemen, Iran funds, arms, and trains terrorists, militias, and other extremist groups that spread destruction and chaos across the region. For decades, Iran has fuelled the fires of sectarian conflict and terror. It is a government that speaks openly of mass murder, vowing the destruction of Israel, death to America, and ruin for many leaders and nations in this room. Among Iran's most tragic and destabilizing interventions have been in Syria. Bolstered by Iran, Assad has committed unspeakable crimes, and the United States has taken firm action in response to the use of banned chemical weapons by the Assad Regime—launching 59 tomahawk missiles at the Syrian air base from where that murderous attack originated."

29 https://www.bloomberg.com/news/articles/2017-04-04/boeing-reaches-3-billion-deal-to-sell-jets-to-iranian-airline.

30 http://www.aljazeera.com/news/2017/05/saudi-arabia-sign-arms-deals-worth-110bn-170520141943494.html. By contrast, the United States also sold Qatar $12 billion worth of arms. https://www.wsj.com/articles/u-s-qatar-move-toward-arms-deal-estimated-at-12-billion-1497484240.

31 http://www.bbc.com/news/world-us-canada-39950827.

32 http://www.latimes.com/world/middleeast/la-fg-yemen-us-arms-2017-story.html.

33 Daniel Lazare, "Luring Trump into Mideast Wars," *Consortium News* (April 8, 2017). https://consortiumnews.com/2017/04/08/luring-trump-into-mideast-wars/; Seymour Hersh argues that "poison gas" was caused by secondary explosions and not by the chemical weaponry; see "Trump's Red Line," De Welt, https://www.welt.de/politik/ausland/article165905578/Trump-s-Red-Line.html; https://www.theatlantic.com/politics/archive/2017/04/trumps-attack-on-syria-has-already-been-forgotten/524454/. Other analysts argue "Assad's forces' military activities along critical choke points, such as Khan Shaykun, indicate that recent CW use was not an exception. Furthermore, given the complexities of the battlefield in Idlib, coupled with this province's military importance regarding Hama, a key hub linking the capital to Aleppo in the north and the Mediterranean gateway to the west, the regime probably saw many practical benefits in CW use." https://www.frstrategie.org/publications/recherches-documents/web/documents/2017/201703.pdf.

34 https://www.nytimes.com/2017/06/18/world/middleeast/iran-syria-missile-launch-islamic-state.html.

35 For an outline of Kurdish parties in the region: http://www.rubincenter.org/2013/08/the-main-kurdish-political-parties-in-iran-iraq-syria-and-turkey-a-research-guide/.

[36] http://www.reuters.com/article/us-iraq-kurds-idUSKCN0VB2EY; https://www.dailysabah.com/politics/2017/06/22/pkk-leader-slams-krgs-referendum-says-kurds-dont-need-a-state. Masoud Barzani, the president of the Kurdish Regional Government, has threatened to hold a referendum in September 2017 to break away from Iraq—a position which is actually opposed by the Turkish PKK and its imprisoned founder Abdullah Öcalan, who has argued that "it is possible to build confederate structures across all parts of Kurdistan without the need to question the existing borders." This approach represents a compromise between demands for total independence and those for total assimilation. See my argument in *American Global Strategy and the "War on Terrorism"* and my interviews in Iraqi Kurdish: Hall Gardner, *Digital Gulan* (December 2007); Hall Gardner, interview with Ferhad Mohammed, "Questions on the Philosophy of Revolution," *Digital Gulan* (September 2011): "I do not believe in the formula that an independent nation-state and national identity automatically means Liberty . . . The problem then is how to establish democratic forms of governance within the same ethnic community or identity group while also engaging in power sharing arrangements with other minority groups and with neighboring countries. Rather than seeking national independence, a loose confederation of autonomous regions can be the goal" (from my original text).

[37] https://www.alaraby.co.uk/english/news/2017/6/9/qatar-blasts-baseless-saudi-allies-terrorism-list.

[38] https://www.alaraby.co.uk/english/news/2017/6/10/turkeys-president-erdogan-backs-qatar-in-gulf-terrorism-row?utm_campaign=magnet&utm_source=article_page&utm_medium=recommended_articles;https://www.alaraby.co.uk/english/News/2017/6/10/Qatar-says-al-Jazeera-foreign-policy-are-sovereign-non-negotiable-matters.

[39] https://www.theguardian.com/world/2017/jun/25/erdogan-rejects-saudi-demand-to-pull-turkish-troops-out-of-qatar. For a comparison of causes of World War I with today, see Hall Gardner, *The Failure to Prevent World War I: The Unexpected Armageddon* (Farnham, UK: Ashgate, 2015); Hall Gardner, *Crimea, Global Rivalry and the Vengeance of History* (Basingstoke, UK: Palgrave-Macmillan, 2017).

[40] https://levantreport.com/tag/judicial-watch-dia-foia-release/.

[41] http://www.al-monitor.com/pulse/originals/2017/06/saudi-qatar-blockade-iran-turkey-convergence-crisis.html.

[42] http://www.cittadellascienza.it/centrostudi/2016/01/meeting-on-peace-and-security-in-afghanistan/.

[43] See Gardner, *World War Trump*.

CHAPTER 21

US-UN Relations and the Global Agenda
Rejecting One's Protégé?
Alynna J. Lyon

The global agenda is full and the list is long. As former UN Secretary-General Kofi Annan wrote in 2009, the world is challenged by many "problems without passports."[1] From terrorism, environmental devastation, an unprecedented refugee crises, lethal pandemics, and transnational criminal networks to the proliferation of weapons systems that can kill millions—the world needs strong global governance. The United Nations (UN), despite its organizational faults, provides the only global organization that brings together almost every country in the world (as well as civil society and the private sector). Indeed, the UN is the only organization granted legitimate authority to preserve international peace.

Historically, the United States has been one of the most vocal supporters of promoting global cooperation and multilateralism. In 1945, the United States was a leading architect in creating the UN and pursuing a global agenda to prevent war. In addition, it has repeatedly provided the UN with the capacity to enforce international law and breaches of peace (e.g., Korea 1950 and Iraq 1991). Together, the United States and the UN were tasked with maintaining a partnership to preserve global stability. Over time, the US-UN relationship has been rocky, with peaks and valleys; the overall trend is one of a growing divide.[2] While the United States advocates working with others, promoting nonviolent conflict resolution, social and economic development, and the establishment of human rights, it also frequently rejects the parameters of international law and works outside the frameworks of international institutions. The sentiment of 1945 when the United States championed the creation of the UN is fading. In fact, many in the Trump administration—including the president—convey that the UN is weak, irrelevant, and antiquated. While the signals coming out of Washington demonstrate little taste for global diplomacy, this posture did not begin with President Trump.

In 2014, under President Obama, the United States launched both a bombing campaign and a humanitarian operation in Northern Iraq. Although the Obama administration did mention the importance of partners and coordinated

275

with several countries in the Middle East, the administration did not engage the UN. Before the Obama administration, the United States rejected the Kyoto Protocol (a treaty reducing greenhouse gas emissions), the creation of the International Criminal Court, the UN Arms Trade Treaty, and the UN Convention on the Rights of Persons with Disabilities. The Iraq War in 2003 marks a clear low point in relations, as the Bush administration could not convince members of the UN Security Council that Iraq possessed a weapons program that posed a threat to international peace. The result was a barrage of attacks on the UN from the White House and members of Congress. In addition, the United States went to war with few allies and significant opposition from the international community.[3] Prior to that, in 1999, the Senate rejected the ratification of the Comprehensive Test Ban Treaty in a 48–51 vote—we saw "the first time since the Treaty of Versailles that the Senate has defeated a major international security agreement."[4] For these issues, as well as many others, the UN is not on the American agenda. As a result of this dynamic, many scholars note a "crisis of multilateralism" as the United States increasingly rejects cooperative global policy initiatives.[5] According to one scholar, "American idealism created the UN and American skepticism is killing it."[6] Thus, at the same time that there are extensive demands for global cooperation, the United States appears to be avoiding—and in some cases even undermining—the very institutional framework it helped create to manage these demands.

US Funding of the UN

As primary architect and financier, the United States is key to UN viability. Figure 21.1 shows US funding from 1999 to 2018. Currently, the United States funds 22 percent of the UN's regular operating budget and almost 29 percent of the UN peacekeeping budget. (These numbers are based on a formula about capacity to pay, so numerically, the United States pays its "fair share.") When the United States withdrew from the United Nations Educational Scientific and Cultural Organization (UNESCO) in 2011, it also took with it 22 percent of UNESCO's funding. The impacts of the US actions were described as "crippling" for the organization.[7] Beyond payment of dues, US relations with the UN impacts the creation and support of peacekeeping initiatives, the capacity for controlling nuclear weapons, and the promotion of human rights.

As funding UN peacekeeping costs the US taxpayer around $2 billion a year, the question often arises about why the United States would spend money on UN military operations rather than supporting its own troops. There are three responses to that question: first, UN peacekeeping is cheap compared to US operations; second, UN peacekeeping is generally more effective than US operations; and finally, UN operations carry much less risk to the United States and its people. In terms of cost-effectiveness, in one comparison, the US Government Accountability Office speculated that the cost of a US mission in Haiti would have been around $876 million, whereas the actual cost of the UN mission in Haiti was $116 million.[8] It is much cheaper to pay the salaries of Rwandans and Ethiopians than Americans. In another example, the cost of supporting US troops for one year in Iraq in 2004 was $4.5 billion, in stark contrast to the just under $4 billion the UN spent in all seventeen missions combined that same year.[9] Furthermore, as one scholar points out, this meant that "there were at least seventeen other places where Washington did not face calls to intervene because the UN was already doing the job."[10] Recent UN peace operations, like the one in Mali, where the UN is fighting an al-Qaeda–linked group, also assist with the US agenda to address global terrorism. Overall, the UN fosters burden sharing and provides a low-cost approach to global security, and despite several failures and areas of essential reform, it does this fairly well. Most studies finds that UN peacekeeping is effective and reduces violence, particularly over the long term.[11]

The UN is a source of power and influence for the United States as well. Prickly relations with the UN limit the US ability to rally allies to share the responsibility and cost of promoting international peace and security. The UN assists with containing international "spoilers," be they countries or terrorist organizations, which threaten stability and the status quo (a system in which the United States is quite privileged). When the United States operates without the UN, it loses UN resources (additional personnel, financing, and knowledge base) and its shield as a legitimate defender of global security. Furthermore, reluctance to work within the Security Council in situations of use of force carries costs to America's legitimacy and international standing. Without the UN, the United States loses soft power. This was revealed by a delegate from China criticizing the US rejection of China's veto of a 2012 UN Security Council resolution on Syria. The Chinese official, opposing US legitimacy and credibility, declared, "What moral basis does it have for this patronizing and egotistical super-arrogance and self-confidence?"[12]

Working with and Against the UN

While the United States assists and funds the work of the UN, it can also be obstructionist. In this regard, the United States often approaches the UN as an owner, not as a member. There are times when the United States has a tendency to show up, make demands, and disregard the voices of 192 other countries. In fact, in 2001, the United States lost its seat on the Human Rights Commission, in part due to obstructionist votes on several human rights standards, its opposition to a treaty banning landmines, and to making AIDS medications universally available. In another example, despite repeated calls for reform of the Human Rights Commission, much to the dismay of 175 other countries, the United States voted against the creation of the Human Rights Council (although it later joined in 2009). The Israeli-Palestinian conflict is another sticking point, as the United States has vetoed over thirty Security Council resolutions regarding Israel. Yet another area of friction comes with periodic attempts to impede the work of the United Nations Population Fund. In part, these dynamics are the result of US domestic politics. For instance, in December 2016, when the Security Council passed as resolution condemning Israel's settlements (as the Obama administration chose to abstain), many in the US Congress, including

Senator Lindsey Graham (R-SC), called for withholding all US funding of the UN.[13] In spring 2017, the new presidential administration offered a preliminary UN budget that followed recommendations from longtime UN critic Ileana Ros-Lehtinen (R-FL), of the House Foreign Affairs Committee, and threatened to cut up to 50 percent of both the Contributions to International Organizations and the Contributions to International Peacekeeping Activities.

Despite the negative press about the UN and its relationship with the United States, there are also places of cooperation and success. In September 2013, after allegations of the use of chemical weapons in Syria, the UN-affiliated Organisation for the Prohibition of Chemical Weapons sent a team into Syria to begin removing the chemical agents. The effort was part of a multinational operation organized by the United States and its allies through the UN. In a rare moment of cooperation, Russia provided armor, Italy contributed a port, and the United States supplied containers and technology.[14] International efforts to address the Iranian nuclear weapons program represent another example of successful US cooperation within other countries through the UN. In November 2013, the group known as the P5 + 1 (the United States, Britain, France, Russia, China, and Germany) created the "First Step Agreement" that convinced Iran to begin converting nuclear materials into nonweapon form and allow UN inspectors access to nuclear sites. In January 2014, negotiations successfully established a six-month Joint Plan of Action cutting Iran's production of nuclear materials, with oversight from the International Atomic Energy Agency (IAEA). Then, intense multilateral negotiations produced an agreement in July of 2015 that was unanimously supported by the Security Council and set provisions for a verification process by the IAEA.

The UN, like most bureaucracies, is prone to inefficiency, bloat, and corruption. There is consensus that the UN needs reforming and updating, and US presidents and members of Congress join current Secretary-General Antonio Guterres and many scholars who find the organization failing to meets it goals.[15] Toward this effort, the US payment of dues often comes with strings, as the Congress regularly makes the payments contingent upon UN implementation of congressionally mandated reforms. Although many of the reforms may be relevant and indeed necessary, when the United States unilaterally imposes provisions, it creates resentment within the UN system and from the other 192 countries that are members of the organization. At the same time, the UN uses calls for reforms to leverage US funding. In one instance in the spring of 2017, a spokesperson for the newly minted UN Secretary-General argued that US funding cuts would undermine long-term UN reform efforts.[16] Observers claim that rather than making US–UN relations stronger, a fickle US funding process creates financial insecurity at the UN and rarely results in authentic reforms.

The UN is often called upon to assist with the most difficult situations. Yet, the UN has a publicity problem, as the work that it does well (aid after natural disasters, disease prevention, food and medical assistance) seldom makes headlines. It is now tasked with the return of over sixty million refugees and displaced persons, preventing the outbreak of multiple infectious diseases, assisting countries in climate adaptation, fighting terrorism in several African states, and ensuring access to education and water for millions. At the same time, the UN frequently gets blamed for the ills of a globalized world. The world expects the UN to be there, but also finds it a convenient scapegoat. The organization is an easy target for those who are skeptical of globalization, as the UN gives shape and even an address to fear about intrusions on sovereignty and suspicions of foreign agendas. Yet operations such as Korea (1950), Iraq (1991), and Somalia (1993) illustrate that when the United States works with the UN, it does not lose control of the policy, and as a country with veto power, the United States can block any UN peace and security initiatives that it doesn't support.

American power and capacities are not what they used to be. The ability of the US military to determine events on the ground in places such as Iraq, Afghanistan, and Syria demonstrate that the hard power approaches are costly and often not effective. Furthermore, even superpowers are not immune to global pandemics, climate change, unstable financial markets, and threats from nuclear proliferation. Despite its flaws, the UN remains essential. As Walter Russell Mead points out, "If the U.N. disappeared today, we'd have to try to reinvent it tomorrow. But the day after that, we'd be disappointed in it again."[17] The fate of the UN is intimately tied to the United States; when the UN looks good, the United States looks good.[18] When the UN is weak and under international pressure, the United States is usually in a weakened position as well. Cumulatively, perpetual lack of funding and blocking of international initiatives—specifically multilateral treaties—has a toll on both US-UN relations and US relations with the international community. For most countries, UN resolutions are viewed as the general will of the international community and hold global legitimacy. Most Americans support US engagement with the UN. In public opinion polls over the past fifteen years, 60–70 percent of Americans surveyed indicate the UN should take a "leading" or "major" role in world affairs (see figure 21.2) and about 40 percent of Americans find the UN doing a "good job" in facing the problems it is tasked with (up from a low of 26 percent in 2009).[19] If the United States rejects the UN, it is not only a rejection of the international organization, but also a rejection of allies.

This dysfunctional dynamic raises several questions. Is the United States turning inward? Often the reality of level of engagement is not reflected in the rhetoric.[20] What does it mean for the United States to disengage? Does it undermine UN capacities and even viability? If the withdrawal of US leadership creates a vacuum, will other countries fill that space (e.g., Russia and China)? And, if so, will those countries try to shape the political content as well as normative approach at the UN? For instance, if China (which has recently become one of the top troop-contributing countries to UN peacekeeping missions) emerges as the new leader within the UN, will this undermine the organization's capacity to "reaffirm faith in fundamental human rights"?

As UN membership has grown, it has become less and less a Western/American-dominated institution. The sheer numbers, regardless of agenda or orientation, make cooperation and coordination more difficult; the United States comes to the UN as a minority, and working through venues such as the General Assembly places it in a compromised position. In 1958, Scott and

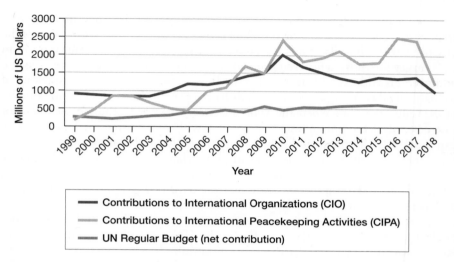

Figure 21.1 US Funding of International Organizations, Peacekeeping, and the UN Regular Budget, 1999–2018

Note: CIO includes US dues payments to forty UN and non-UN international organizations, including NATO, the World Health Organization, and the International Atomic Energy Agency. Years 2017 and 2018 proposed budgets.

Source: FY 1999–2016, http://www.un.org/en/ga/contributions/budget.shtml; FY 2017–2018, https://betterworldcampaign.org/us-un-partnership/fy17-funding-request/.

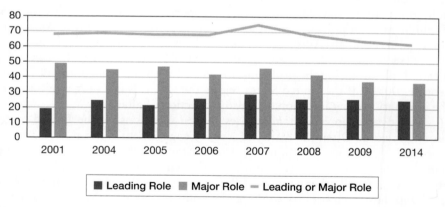

Figure 21.2 US Survey: Should the UN Play a Leading, Major, or Minor Role? Specific wording: "Now thinking more specifically, which of the following roles would you like to see the United Nations play in world affairs today—should it play—[a leading role, where all countries are required to follow UN policies; a major role, where the UN establishes policies, but where individual countries still act separately when they disagree with the UN; or a minor role, with the UN serving mostly as a forum for communication between nations, but with no policymaking role]?"

Source: Gallup Poll Social Series (2017). Available at http://www.gallup.com/poll/116347/united-nations.aspx.

Withey wrote, "The United Nations cannot succeed, not even survive in anything like its present form—without the participation of the United States."[21] Beyond financing, the United States serves as a pivotal leader, bringing relevant stakeholders to the table, committing resources and credibility to international initiatives. Perhaps, without the shadow of the US Permanent Mission looming over the UN, there could be new opportunities? Yet, at this point, it is difficult to see who would take up the mantle of global leadership and promote a secure, sustainable, and just planet.

Notes

[1] Kofi Annan, "Problems without Passports," *Foreign Policy* (2009).

[2] Alynna J. Lyon, *US Politics and the United Nations: A Tale of Dysfunctional Dynamics* (Boulder, CO: Lynne Rienner, 2016).

[3] "'Million' March against Iraq War," *BBC News*, February 16, 2003.

[4] Christopher Jones and Steve Hook, eds., *Handbook of American Foreign Policy* (London: Routledge Press, 2011), 144.

[5] James P. Muldoon et al., eds., *Multilateral Diplomacy and the United Nations Today*, 2nd Ed. (Cambridge: Westview Press, 2005); Stewart Patrick, "Multilateralism À La Carte: The New World of Global Governance" *Valdai Papers* 22 (2015).

[6] Edward C. Luck, *Mixed Messages: American Politics and International Organization, 1919–1999* (Washington, DC: Brookings Institution Press, 1999), 4.

[7] John Irish, "UNESCO Chief Says U.S. Funding Cuts 'Crippling' Organization," *Reuters*, October 11, 2012.

[8] Ramesh Thakur, *The United Nations, Peace and Security*, 2nd Ed. (Cambridge: Cambridge University Press, 2017), 71.

[9] Ibid., 70.

[10] Ibid., 71.

[11] Micheal W. Doyle and Nicholas Sambanis, "The UN Record on Peacekeeping Operations," *International Journal* 62, no. 3 (2007); Virginia Page Fortna, *Does Peacekeeping Work? Shaping Belligerents' Choices after Civil War* (Princeton, NJ: Princeton University Press, 2008); Kyle Beardsley, "Peacekeeping and the Contagion of Armed Conflict," *Journal of Politics* 73, no. 4 (2011).

[12] "China Calls US Critique on Syria 'Super Arrogant,'" *BBC News China*, February 27, 2012.

[13] Josh Rogin, "Inside the Coming War between the United States and the United Nations," *The Washington Post*, December 28, 2016.

[14] Charbel Raji, "100% of Declared Chemical Weapons Materials Destroyed or Removed from Syria," *OPCW-UN Joint Mission in the Syrian Republic*, June 23, 2014.

[15] Donald Puchala, "Reforming the United Nations or Going Beyond," in *U.S. Foreign Policy and the United Nations System*, Charles William Maynes and Richard S. Williamson, eds. (New York: W. W. Norton, 1996); Committee on International Relations, *United Nations Rhetoric or Reform* (Washington, DC: United States Government Printing Office, 2005); Ruth Wedgwood, "100 Days to a Better United Nations," *Los Angeles Times*, October 20, 2006; Bardo Fassbender, "UN Reform and Collective Security, the Report of the UN High-Level Panel on Threats, Challenges and Change of December 2004 and the Recommendations of the UN Secretary-General from March 2005," in *Global Issues Papers* (Institute for International and European Law at the Humboldt University, 2005); G. John Ikenberry, "America and the Reform of Global Institutions," in *Can the World Be Governed? Possibilities for Effective Multilateralism*, Alan S Alexandroff ed. (Waterloo: Wilfrid Laurier University Press, 2008); Bob Deans, "The United Nations: Underachiever Due for Overhaul," *The Atlanta Journal – Constitution*, September 11, 2005; Thomas G. Weiss, *What's Wrong with the United Nations and How to Fix It*, 2nd Ed. (Cambridge, UK: Polity Press, 2012); Annan, "Problems without Passports."

16 Lyndal Rowlands, "UN Facing Famines, Conflicts and Now U.S. Funding Cuts," *Inter Press Agency*, March 30, 2017.

17 Deans, "Underachiever Due for Overhaul."

18 John Ikenberry, *After Victory: Institutions, Strategic Restraint and the Rebuilding of Order after Major Wars* (Princeton, NJ: Princeton University Press, 2000).

19 Thakur, *Peace and Security*.

20 Lyon, *Tale of Dysfunctional Dynamics*.

21 William A. Scott and Stephen B. Withey, *The United States and the United Nations: The Public View 1945–1955* (New York: Manhattan, 1958), 2.

Epilogue

Do not be arrogant; do not think that you alone can finish the job. Trust in your children and generations yet unborn to take up the task. Know that you are part of the living chain of people who have dreamed, worked for a better world . . .

—Attributed to Rav Tarfon, *Pirkei Avot*, 2:21

EPILOGUE

Index

About the Editor and Contributors

Editor

Diana Ayton-Shenker is Global Catalyst Senior Fellow at The New School and founding CEO of Global Momenta, a philanthropic strategy and social innovation firm. As Fast Forward Fund founder, she was honored by President Bill Clinton and selected as a Social Venture Network (SVN) Social Innovation Award finalist. She was the Inaugural Nazarian Social Innovator in Residence at Wharton, senior fellow in venture philanthropy at Bard College, and mentor to Clinton Global Initiative University, Global Engagement Summit, and the Unreasonable Institute. Named one of "25 Leading Women Changing the World" by *Good Business NY*, Diana has been featured in *Knowledge at Wharton* and World Economic Forum's Global Agenda and showcased among Inspiring Women in Nonprofit Management (University of North Carolina). She is the author of *A Global Agenda: Current Issues before the U.N.* (2002–2003 and 2001–2002 editions), *Tumbalalaika: A Collection of Poems* (2007), and the influential UN publication *The Challenge of Universal Human Rights and Cultural Diversity*. She holds an LLM in International Human Rights Law (University of Essex) and an honors BA in International Relations (University of Pennsylvania).

Contributors

T. Alexander Aleinikoff is a university professor at The New School and has served as director of the Zolberg Institute on Migration and Mobility since January 2017. He received a JD from the Yale Law School and a BA from Swarthmore College. Professor Aleinikoff has written widely in the areas of immigration and refugee law and policy, transnational law, citizenship, race, and constitutional law. Before coming to The New School, he served as United Nations Deputy High Commissioner for Refugees (2010–2015) and was a professor at Georgetown University Law Center, where he also served as dean, and executive vice president of Georgetown University. He was cochair of the Immigration Task Force for President Barack Obama's transition team in 2008. From 1994 to 1997, he served as the general counsel, and then executive associate commissioner for programs, at the Immigration and Naturalization Service (INS). Professor Aleinikoff was inducted into the American Academy of Arts of Sciences in 2014.

Laurie Adams is the CEO of Women for Women International (WfWI), a leading global organization dedicated to working with women survivors of war. With more than twenty-five years of experience working in international development and human rights, Ms. Adams is an innovative leader, strategist, and gender rights advocate. As the chair of the founding board for the Other Foundation in South Africa, Ms. Adams launched a community foundation model to catalyze local philanthropy after securing matching funds from the Atlantic Philanthropies.

In addition, she served as a director on the boards of the Forum for the Empowerment of Women in South Africa and ActionAid Brazil.

Karen J. Alter is professor of political science and law at Northwestern University; a permanent visiting professor at the iCourts Center for Excellence, Faculty of Law, University of Copenhagen; and the codirector of the Global Capitalism & Law Research Group at the Buffett Institute at Northwestern University. Alter is author of the award-winning book *The New Terrain of International Law: Courts, Politics, Rights* (2014), and also *International Legal Transplants: Law and Politics of the Andean Tribunal of Justice* (2017, with Laurence Helfer), *The European Court's Political Power* (2009), *Establishing the Supremacy of European Law* (2001), and more than fifty articles and book chapters on the politics of international law, comparative international courts, and international regime complexity. She is also coeditor of the *Oxford Handbook on International Adjudication* (2014) and *International Court Authority* (2018).

Gina Bria Anthropologist and author Gina Bria collects stories and strategies from around the globe on where to find water. Gina researches, consults, and speaks on topics related to integrative nutrition and hydration strategies. She founded the Hydration Foundation and created the first hydration program for brain function and behavior at the Ideal School, a New York City independent school advancing autism spectrum–inclusive education. Trained at Columbia University, Gina was named Real World Scholar with World Evolved Lecture Series, a Berlin Fellow with the Social Science Research Council, a Harvard summer fellow, and National Endowment for the Humanities finalist. Her first book, *The Art of Family: Rituals, Imagination, and Everyday Spirituality*, was a Starbucks selection. She is author of *QUENCH: A Five-Day Plan for Optimal Hydration*, with Dr. Dana Cohen, MD, and *How to Grow Water: It's Not Only Blue, It's Green*, exploring water inside plants. She serves as founding member on the board of the Worldwide Water and Health Association and senior advisor for the TEDxNewYorkSalon.

Gillian Christie is a doctoral candidate at the Harvard T. H. Chan School of Public Health. Gillian has served as Health Innovation Manager at the Vitality Group, worked at Grand Challenges Canada and at the Sandra Rotman Centre. She is a regular speaker at noteworthy events, including those convened by the World Economic Forum, the Organisation for Economic Co-operation and Development (OECD), and the National Academies of Sciences, Engineering, and Medicine. She is a fellow of the Salzburg Global Seminar and a contributing author to *The Lancet* and Rockefeller Foundation's Commission on Planetary Health (July 2015). Gillian completed a master's (MPhil) degree at the University of Cambridge in Innovation, Strategy and Organization and holds an MA (Hons) in Management from the University of St Andrews in Scotland. Gillian was born and raised in Toronto, Canada.

Michael A. Cohen is professor of international affairs and founding director of the Julien Studley Graduate Program in International Affairs at The New School university in New York, where he also directs the Global Urban Futures Project and the Observatory on Latin America. He worked at the World Bank from 1972 to 1999, served as chief of the Urban Development Division for many years, as well as senior advisor for Environmentally Sustainable Development, and worked in fifty-five countries. He is the author of many books and articles on urban issues and development and has advised UN Habitat, the World Bank, the Corporacion Andina de Fomento, the Inter-American Development Bank, UN agencies, and many other foundations.

Peter Dietrich works with regulatory and industry compliance, helping companies comply with state, federal, and international laws. A graduate of The New School's Environmental Policy and Sustainability Management program, Pete served as senior assistant editor and project coordinator to support and supervise the New Global Agenda Fellows team.

Hall Gardner is professor and cochair of the International and Comparative Politics Department of the American University of Paris. He is the author of over a dozen books on contemporary international affairs and global security issues, including his forthcoming *World War Trump: The Risks of America's New Nationalism* (March 2018), and an original collection of poetry, *Wake Up Blast*. He received his PhD and MA from the Johns Hopkins Paul H. Nitze School of Advanced International Studies (SAIS) and has served on the advisory boards of the Cicero Foundation, New Policy Forum (Gorbachev Foundation), and *Geostrategique*, the French journal of international politics.

Russ Gaskin is managing director of CoCreative, a consulting firm that designs collective impact networks to solve complex social problems. Prior to launching CoCreative, Russ served as the chief business officer of Green America; managing director of US SIF, the Forum for Sustainable and Responsible Investment; and founder of the Green Business Network, the country's first network of triple-bottom-line businesses. He serves as a senior fellow for the Green America Center for Sustainability Solutions and on the Expert Panel on Social Innovation & Design at the UN Development Program. He has also served on the leadership board of the National Education Association, the Green Good Housekeeping Seal advisory board, and the eBay World of Good advisory board.

Pape Amadou Gaye president and CEO of IntraHealth International, draws on three decades of leadership in international health and development as he oversees work in forty countries to strengthen their health workforces and systems. A native of Senegal, Gaye began his career as a trainer of Peace Corps volunteers in Senegal and Benin and has worked for the US Centers for Disease Control and Prevention and the 1984 LA Olympics Committee. Gaye serves on the advisory boards of Duke University's Global Health Institute, Speak Up Africa and Triangle Global Health Consortium. He holds an MBA from the University of California at Los Angeles.

Eban Goodstein is director of the Center for Environmental Policy and Bard MBA in Sustainability. In recent years, Goodstein has coordinated a series of national educational initiatives on climate change involving over 2,500 colleges, universities, high schools, and community organizations. He is the author of *Economics and the Environment*, 8th edition (2017); *Fighting for Love in the Century of Extinction: How Passion and Politics Can Stop Global Warming* (2007); and *The Trade-off Myth: Fact and Fiction about Jobs and the Environment* (1999). His work has been featured in the *New York Times*, *Scientific American*, *Time*, *Chemical and Engineering News*, the *Economist*, *USA Today*, the *Chronicle of Higher Education*, the *Journal of Environmental Economics and Management*, *Land Economics*, *Ecological Economics*, and *Environmental Management*. He serves on the editorial board of *Sustainability: The Journal of Record* and on the board of directors of the Follett Corporation.

Jensine Larsen is the founder of *World Pulse*, a digital communication network connecting women worldwide and bringing them a global voice. She is a frequent speaker on how social media and technological innovation are powerful accelerators for women's global empowerment, appearing in media and on stages from National Public Radio and the Clinton Global Initiative to TED. She is also the recipient of multiple awards and recognitions including the Rockefeller 100 Game Changers and the Tribeca Innovative Disruptor fellowship. In 2015, Jensine became a fellow of the Academy for Systemic Change, a ten-year fellowship training the planet's next generation of system change leaders.

L. Hunter Lovins is founding president of Natural Capitalism Solutions and founding partner of Change Finance, an impact investing firm. She is professor at Bard MBA in Sustainability and a fellow of the Fowler Center for Business as an Agent of World Benefit at Case Western University. She was named a Master at the Chinese De Tao Academy, where she helped launch the Institute for Green Investment in Shanghai. Hunter has coauthored sixteen books and hundreds of articles and was featured in the award-winning film *Lovins on the Soft Path*. Her best-known book, *Natural Capitalism*, won the Shingo Prize and has been translated into more than three dozen languages; its sequel, *The Way Out: Kickstarting Capitalism to Save Our Economic Ass*, won the Atlas Award. Her latest book, *Creating a Lean and Green Business System*, also won the

Shingo Prize. She serves on the Executive Committee of the Club of Rome, steering committee of the Alliance for Sustainability and Prosperity, and advisory board of the Capital Institute and was founding mentor of the Unreasonable Institute. She has won dozens of awards, including the European Sustainability Pioneer Award, Rachel Carson Award, and Right Livelihood Award; *Time* magazine recognized her as a "Millennium Hero for the Planet," and *Newsweek* called her the "Green Business Icon."

Alynna Lyon is an associate professor of political science at the University of New Hampshire. Her expertise lies in conflict mobilization, peacekeeping, and American foreign policy. She has published several book chapters and articles on these topics, including her most recent book publications, *US Politics and the United Nations: A Tale of Dysfunctional Dynamics* and the fifth edition of *The United Nations in the 21st Century*. Alynna Lyon is the faculty advisor of the UNH Model United Nations and serves as the chair of the Ethnicity, Nationalism, and Migration section of the International Studies Association.

Lars Fogh Mortensen heads the European Environment Agency (EEA) Group on Network Coordination and International Cooperation, where, for many years, he led EEA's work on sustainable consumption and production and waste management. A trained economist from the University of Copenhagen, he was Sustainability Director for the Copenhagen Institute on Risk and Sustainability (CopenhagenIRIS) and worked previously at the OECD and the UN Rio Secretariat. He has written numerous reports, articles, and book chapters on sustainability policy, metrics, and systems of sustainable consumption and production.

Alex Neve is secretary general of Amnesty International Canada. He has participated in human rights missions to dozens of countries, represented Amnesty International at international meetings such as the Summit of the Americas and the G8 Summit, and appeared before numerous Canadian parliamentary committees, the UN, and Inter-American human rights bodies. Mr. Neve is chair of the Canadian Centre for International Justice and serves on the board of directors of Partnership Africa Canada and of the Centre for Law and Democracy; he served as a Trudeau Foundation Mentor. Mr. Neve holds an LLB (Dalhousie University), an LLM in International Human Rights Law (University of Essex), and a honorary Doctorate of Laws received from the University of New Brunswick. He was named an Officer of the Order of Canada in 2007.

Karen Lund Petersen is associate professor at the University of Copenhagen and director of the Centre for Advanced Security Theory. As member of the so-called Copenhagen School within security studies, she has contributed to the debate on securitization and a widened concept of security. Among her most recent publications are "Intelligence Expertise in the Age of Information Sharing: Public–Private 'Collection' and Its Challenges to Democratic Control and Accountability" (*Intelligence and National Security*, 2017) and "Risk: A Field within Security Studies?" (*European Journal of International Relations*, 2012).

Courtney C. Radsch PhD, is advocacy director at the Committee to Protect Journalists (CPJ) and author of *Cyberactivism and Citizen Journalism in Egypt: Digital Dissidence and Political Change.* Prior to joining CPJ, Radsch worked for UNESCO, edited *World Trends in Freedom of Expression and Media Development*, and managed the Global Freedom of Expression Campaign at Freedom House. She has worked as a journalist with *Al-Arabiya*, the *Daily Star,* and the *New York Times*. Radsch holds a PhD in international relations from American University.

Harpinder Sandhu is author of *Ecosystem Functions & Management* (2017); is senior research fellow at Flinders University, Australia; and serves as an expert and lead author of a global assessment for the United Nations Intergovernmental Platform on Biodiversity and Ecosystem Services. He is also a contributing lead author at the Economics of Ecosystems and Biodiversity for Agriculture and Food (TEEBAgriFood), a United Nations Environment Programme–hosted project. Harpinder heads the Global Sectoral Group on Agricultural Production Systems and Thematic Group on Poverty Alleviation at the Ecosystem Services Partnership (ES-Partnership), coordinated by the Environmental Systems Analysis Group, Wageningen University, the Netherlands, and serves on the advisory panel of the Multi-Stakeholder Consultation on Agroecology for Asia and the Pacific at the Food and Agriculture Organization (FAO). He holds a PhD in Agroecology (Lincoln University, New Zealand).

Lena Simet is the coordinator of the Global Urban Futures (GUF) Project at The New School, where she codesigned the "Habitat Commitment Index," a quantitative tool to assess country performance in fulfilling urban-related goals. She is a teaching fellow at The New School and adjunct professor at the City University of New York. She has worked for UN-Habitat, GIZ, and CAF and is a doctoral candidate in Public and Urban Policy at The New School.

Joel Simon is executive director of the Committee to Protect Journalists (CPJ) and author of *The New Censorship: Inside the Global Battle for Media Freedom* (2015) and *Endangered Mexico: An Environment on the Edge* (1997). Simon has written widely on press freedom for publications including *Slate*, the *New York Review of Books*, the *New York Times*, *World Policy Journal*, *Asahi Shimbun*, and the *Times of India*; he is a regular columnist for *Columbia Journalism Review*. Prior to CPJ, Simon worked as a freelance journalist in Latin America. He holds an MA from Stanford University and a BA from Amherst College.

Ramesh Thakur is director of the Centre for Nuclear Non-Proliferation and Disarmament (CNND) at the Crawford School, Australian National University, and coconvenor of the Asia-Pacific Leadership Network for Nuclear Non-Proliferation and Disarmament (APLN). He was senior vice rector of the United Nations University and Assistant Secretary-General of the United Nations from 1998–2007. Educated in India and Canada, he has been a professor at the University of Otago, New Zealand; professor and head of the Peace Research Centre at the Australian National University; professor at the University of Waterloo; distinguished fellow of the Centre for International Governance Innovation; and foundation director of the Balsillie School of International Affairs. Prof. Thakur is editor-in-chief of *Global Governance* and author or editor of fifty books on the UN, global governance, and international security issues.

Gracey Vaughn is the special projects advisor for the president's office at IntraHealth International. Prior to IntraHealth, Gracey worked with the USAID Africa Bureau and served as a Peace Corps volunteer in Mozambique. She holds an MPH with a concentration in Maternal and Child Health from the University of North Carolina (UNC) Gillings School of Global Public Health and a BA degree in International Studies and Spanish from UNC-Chapel Hill.

Mary R. Watson is executive dean at The New School, a progressive university in New York City committed to creating a more just and better-designed world. As executive dean, Watson leads a portfolio of applied graduate schools and programs in international affairs, media, writing, management, environment, and public policy, as well as the university's undergraduate program for adults. Watson is a recognized leader in global networks advancing change in higher education worldwide, and her scholarship considers the redesign of industries toward more sustainable practices globally. Watson holds a PhD in Organization Studies from Vanderbilt University and is the recipient of The New School's Distinguished University Teaching Award.

Derek Yach is founder and president of the Foundation for Smoke-Free World. He is the former chief health officer (CHO) of Vitality and founder of the Vitality Institute. Previously, Dr. Yach was senior vice president of Global Health and Agriculture Policy at PepsiCo; director of global health at the Rockefeller Foundation; a professor of global health at Yale University; executive director for Noncommunicable Diseases and Mental Health Cluster of the World Health Organization (WHO); and established the Centre for Epidemiological Research at the South African Medical Research Council. Dr. Yach has authored or coauthored over two hundred articles covering the breadth of global health. He has served on several boards of directors and advisory boards including those of the Clinton Global Initiative, World Economic Forum, Cornerstone Capital, and the NIH's Fogarty International Centre; he is chair of the World Economic Forum Global Agenda Council on Ageing.

Andrew Zolli works at the intersection of global innovation, foresight, social change, and resilience. The author of *Resilience: Why Things Bounce Back*, Zolli is the vice president of Global Impact Initiatives for Planet, Inc., a breakthrough global sensing company that is deploying the largest constellation of earth-observing satellites in human history. He is a fellow of the National Geographic Society and former curator and executive director of PopTech, and he has served on the boards of Garrison Institute, DataKind, Brooklyn Academy of Music, Blurb, Cure Violence, and One Concern.

Notes on the Artwork by William T. Ayton

I approach my artwork as a meditation upon the meaning of humanity in our world—its dreams, hopes, failings, and fears. Illustrating this book, *A New Global Agenda*, was an opportunity to revisit some familiar themes and interpret them in different ways.

Book Cover

It's a Small World (acrylic on hand-made rag paper from India, 2017)

For the cover, I created a painting of a colorful, yet vulnerable, planet. I wanted the image to be bright and appealing, yet convey a sense of urgency and perhaps danger. The rays of hope still shine through . . .

Part I: People

Humanity and the Fragile Earth (brush and ink on paper, 2017)

A multitude of faceless figures strive for survival in a ragged world—are they tearing it apart or building it up? Or both at the same time? Despite the fragility of their environment, the vulnerable people stare outward hopefully. Their human rights, their freedoms, and their very existence are in peril. What will the future hold for them?

Part II: Society

Toward a New Society (brush and ink on paper, 2017)

The drawing shows an imagined urban scene. In the foreground, tiny figures make their way across a bridge from the past to the future. Above them, the looming buildings offer stepped structures, signifying a pathway to freedom, while menacing dark windows imply authoritarianism and the occasional emptiness of modern life. Above all, there is a stylized representation of the Tower of Babel, a timeless archetype and symbol of the modern interconnected world and its overarching media saturation.

Part III: Planet

The World and Its Pearl (brush and ink on paper, 2017)

In this drawing, a mountainous landscape dominates the image, with gathering clouds above. In the plains below, there is a small facsimile of the world itself, like a pearl, seed, or beacon of light. The pyramidally structured mountains above protect this proto-world from the looming storm clouds. Who knows what life may come from this tiny world?

William T. Ayton
www.ayton.net

307